ADDITIONAL PRAISE FOR *SPINNING THE LAW*

"I have read and savored every page of this book. It is truly a fresh, original, and fun piece of work."
—Hugo Black Jr., courtroom attorney for sixty years

"For more than a decade, Kendall has been my go-to guy for all quick, concise, and accurate legal analysis. His breadth of legal knowledge and acumen has been a valuable resource for many of us in network news. It stands to reason that he would write the definitive guide to navigate us through the legal spin zone!"
—Ashleigh Banfield, ABC News and formerly Court TV

"Kendall Coffey has given us a sweeping historical survey of the treacherous ground where the news media and the legal system meet, do business, and, often enough, do battle. He's a deft writer and a savvy lawyer, the veteran of a sizable number of legal brawls of his own, and his book is both wise and smart—provocative and knowledgeable, a pleasure to read and a must to keep on your book shelf to double check facts and settle arguments."
—Edward Wasserman, Knight Professor of Journalism Ethics, Washington and Lee University

"Kendall Coffey has written the book that every attorney in America needs to read.

We are living in a time when a lawyer is frequently called upon to make his case before the media as well as the jury. Public opinion has a longer shelf life than a verdict.... Publicists, press reps, media consultants, and 'spin doctors' will also find the book to be extremely useful in the public presentation of their clients.

Spinning the Law is a must read for everyone who watches the news, follows cases unfold daily, and wishes to gain greater insight into the synergistic relationship between the law, the press, and themselves."
—Elliot Mintz, media consultant

"Kendall Coffey has walked the walk, so when he starts to talk the talk in his new book, it is well worth reading. His profound insights into some of the key cases of our time, together with tidbits from cases of the past, make this the perfect book to read. *Spinning the Law* provides more than just an account of key, recent trials; it serves as a handbook on the lessons of the 'trials of the centuries.'"
—Laurie L. Levenson, professor of law, David W. Burcham Chair of Ethical Advocacy, Loyola Law School

SPINNING THE LAW

KENDALL COFFEY

SPINNING

TRYING CASES IN THE COURT OF PUBLIC OPINION

THE LAW

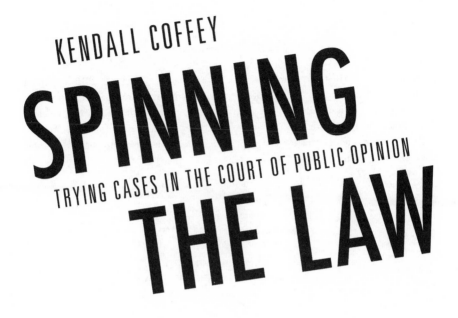

FOREWORD BY
ALAN M. DERSHOWITZ

 Prometheus Books

59 John Glenn Drive
Amherst, New York 14228–2119

Published 2010 by Prometheus Books

Inquiries should be addressed to
Prometheus Books
59 John Glenn Drive
Amherst, New York 14228–2119
VOICE: 716–691–0133
FAX: 716–691–0137
WWW.PROMETHEUSBOOKS.COM

14 13 12 11 10   5 4 3 2 1

Library of Congress Cataloging-in-Publication Data

Coffey, Kendall, 1952–
    Spinning the law : trying cases in the court of public opinion / Kendall Coffey.
        p. cm.
    Includes bibliographical references and index.
    ISBN 978–1–61614–210–0 (cloth : alk. paper)
    1. Pulic relations and law—United States. 2. Mass media and public opinion—United States. 3. Free press and fair trial—United States. I. Title.

KF390.5.P8C64 2010
347.73'5—dc22

2010020538

Printed in the United States of America on acid-free paper

Cover design by Nicole Sommer-Lecht
Images © 2010 Media Bakery

CONTENTS

FOREWORD

When it comes to the practice of law, Kendall Coffey is truly "a man for all seasons." He combines the talents necessary to defend his clients in an age when it is not enough to be a great trial lawyer in the courtroom—where he excels not only as an eloquent presenter of the facts but also as a creative master of the law. This is a rare combination in a world of specialization, where so many "jury-fact" lawyers are incapable of presenting coherent legal arguments and so many "judge-law" practitioners are incapable of communicating effectively with juries. Coffey does both with exceptional skill. He never talks down to juries and never shows off for judges. Juries love his warm, direct approach to the facts; and judges admire and respect his mastery of the law and his extraordinary commitment to preparation and research. But as this wonderful book demonstrates, in today's world of multimedia, twenty-four-hour news cycles, the role of the lawyer does not stop at the courtroom door, or even at the courthouse steps.

Clients, whether civil or criminal, are increasingly brought to trial not only before a judge in robes and a jury of peers but also in the court of public opinion, where every citizen gets to "cast a vote" on the legal and moral aspects of the case. For some clients in the public eye—political figures, entertainers, business moguls, even ordinary citizens—the "verdict" rendered by the court of public opinion may be as important as the verdict of the jury or court.

But being aware of the importance of winning in the media is not enough. A good lawyer must be prepared to face the media, where the usual rules of evidence do not prevail. A good "all-purpose" lawyer must learn the very different rules of the court of public opinion and must develop the skills with which to win in that important forum as well.

There is no better lawyer to teach those skills than Kendall Coffey, and there is no better book from which to learn these skills than this one. Coffey has done it all, and from every vantage point—prosecutor, defense attorney, talking head, teacher, and writer. His cases are legendary, and his success rate is the envy of the bar. Every lawyer, young or old, novice or old-timer, can learn from Coffey's vast and diverse experience and from his unique ability to extract lessons from his exposure to every manner of legal encounter. I know that I learned so much from reading about cases that I thought I knew well.

But this is not a book for only lawyers. All concerned citizens—all who compose the court of public opinion—not only will benefit from reading this book but also will enjoy the war stories, the good yarns, and the inside accounts of cases both famous and obscure. Coffey brings the cases alive with his engaging style and his elegant yet straightforward writing. This is more than a page-turner. It is a memorable book that will change the way we look at law.

In a democracy, where the people ultimately rule, this exciting book is an indispensible guide for all who care about justice.

Alan M. Dershowitz
Professor of law, Harvard Law School, and
author of *Trials of Zion*

INTRODUCTION

When attorneys spin, it's about trying to win. And yet there's much more to it. While lawyers represent clients, we also represent their reputations. Deflecting collateral damage to a client's good name is something they don't teach in law school. That curriculum is created by experience. The often hard lessons learned about trying cases in the court of public opinion are examined in the chapters that follow.

THE ROTHSTEIN PONZI SCHEME

Getting in Front of the Bad News Means Getting There Fast

When the lead partner of Florida's flashiest new law firm flees to Morocco, it makes for an interesting Saturday night's work. I arrived at the Fort Lauderdale offices of Rothstein Rosenfeldt Adler early in the evening of October 31, 2009. It was Halloween, an appropriate occasion for the nightmare weekend that was engulfing Stu Rosenfeldt, Russell Adler, and a host of other top-echelon attorneys. Scott Rothstein, the first named partner of Rothstein Rosenfeldt Adler, was a friend and confidant to Florida's luminaries. The firm's *RRA* logo was emblazoned throughout the region's civic and charitable programs. There would be no more photo ops with politicians, though, now that Rothstein had fled the country after allegedly stealing hundreds of millions of dollars in a Ponzi scheme.

Rosenfeldt and Adler and another half dozen of the firm's attorneys assembled that weekend in a state of shock. In little more than seven years, the firm had skyrocketed from a few attorneys to more than seventy—a dazzling collection of the best and brightest legal talent—thanks to Rothstein's charismatic leadership and political connections. Along the way, there had been a few whispers about how so much success could come so fast. But South Florida is a well-traveled launching pad for meteoric success stories. And yet it had also featured soaring rockets that fizzled. It now seemed that Rothstein belonged to the rogue's gallery of high-flying crooks who had made Florida their home since the days of Al Capone.

Throughout that Saturday, Rosenfeldt and his colleagues were moving fast, getting up to speed about the many missing millions from law-firm trust accounts.

As our discussions progressed to the next afternoon on Sunday, it became apparent that Rothstein had been enticing investors to pay huge sums to acquire the rights to various settlements of employment and whistleblower claims. By paying the purported victim a discounted sum up front before the supposed defendant was due to pay, the investor would, over time, supposedly reap the entire amount of the settlement. The problem was that the settlement agreements were fakes. Meanwhile, Rothstein allegedly either kept the investors' money to fund his own lavish lifestyle or used portions to make distributions to placate earlier Ponzi victims. Information from Rothstein's attorney indicated early on Sunday that investor losses ranged from $410 to $440 million—although later estimates would peg it at more than $1 billion.

My inquiries on that Sunday indicated that only Rothstein and three of his most trusted nonattorney assistants had electronic access to the trust accounts that had funds missing. It was also evident, though, that many in the legal and business community might be reluctant to accept the simple truth that the other attorneys and the entire staff were not aware of his gigantic scam.

Getting out in front of a problem is the stock advice for crisis management. With a megaton disaster due to ignite by Monday, getting to the front instantly was imperative. For the attorneys and the staff of RRA, it meant separating themselves from Rothstein, the dominant figure of the law firm and a major player in legal and political circles.

We also had urgent legal issues to address. Because Rothstein had inter-mingled client funds with law-firm accounts, we needed a legal frame-work for dealing with the dizzying difficulties in the firm's finances. But Rothstein owned 50 percent of the firm and was unwilling to let others take control. As a result, we prepared a lawsuit overnight and proceeded to court first thing the next morning, arguing that the law firm's other attorneys and staff were also victims betrayed by Scott Rothstein. The focus was to seek immediate judicial assistance to get to the bottom of a convoluted pile of finances, records, transactions, and still-undiagnosed problems. In addition to explaining our legal issues, we expressed our own shock upon learning what appeared to be the truth about Rothstein:

> *It is with surprise and sorrow that the attorneys of Rothstein Rosenfeldt Adler, PA have learned that Scott W. Rothstein, the managing partner and CEO of the firm, has, according to the assertions of certain investors, allegedly orchestrated a substantial misappropriation of funds from investor trust accounts that made use of the law firm's name.*[1]

Also on Monday, but without fanfare, we contacted the US Attorney's Office and the Florida Bar to inform them of the weekend's develop-ments and to pledge our cooperation in untangling the bizarre web of missing funds. We took the prudent step of engaging a professional communications expert, Charles Jones, to assist with media inquiry and strategies. The next afternoon, the trial judge agreed with our request to appoint a receiver for the firm's financial matters while allowing Rosenfeldt to serve as CEO for its ongoing legal work. The distinction between the financial side formerly handled by Rothstein and the legal side headed by Rosenfeldt was critical for us. The court-ordered sepa-ration of financial and legal dealings not only furthered the proper functioning of the firm but also enabled the public to see the distinc-tion between the two parts of the organization. The finances were a mess, but the legal work was highly professional and the clients' rights were still being diligently protected.

For the first few days, the reaction was positive, even sympathetic. But as time goes by in high-profile cases, the media's questioning gets deeper and tougher. By Thursday morning, the press was sending mixed signals concerning whether key lawyers in the firm had knowledge of Rothstein's scams. Fort Lauderdale's *Sun Sentinel* led with an excerpt from one of Rothstein's text messages that said, "Sorry I let you all down," and added, "I am a fool. I thought I could fix it."[2] On the not-so-good-news side, a respected columnist for another South Florida paper, the *Miami Herald*, highlighted his skepticism toward the firm attorneys with a headline, "Surprise from Rothstein's Scheme Unlikely." The author's doubts permeated the column: "Rothstein's crew had to know the scheme was crazy."[3]

As the media questioned more that morning, I realized that we had gone as far as we could with court pleadings or even hearings. A more dramatic strategy was needed. One of the best ways to gain insight about message strategies for newsrooms and even courtrooms is listening closely to what reporters have to say. One reporter expressed fascination concerning rumors that Rothstein had installed surveillance cameras and listening devices throughout the law firm. Meanwhile, a media-savvy attorney kept mentioning Rothstein's palatial inner sanctum.

Quickly convening a conference call with several law-firm leaders as well as PR consultant Jones, I reviewed the firm's physical layout, focusing on its custom features for concealment and surveillance. My suggestion for a media walk-through to depict the realities of Rothstein's secretive operations was immediately supported by Jones, who had been thinking along similar lines. Within a few hours, and with amazing speed, Jones organized a succession of tours. The media walk-throughs were conceived to explain to reporters—and to allow videographers and photographers to capture—the extraordinary characteristics of the law firm, creating not only a great visual for television but also an opportunity to dispel the pounding waves of doubt about all the other lawyers and staff.

As we walked reporters and cameras through the office, skepticism shifted toward fascination. We noted for the media the many hidden cameras and microphones as well as the soundproof bunker Rothstein had created inside his own law firm. An intercom outside Rothstein's inner sanctum was needed in order to gain admittance, even for the firm's leading lawyers. There was a private elevator for Rothstein leading to a cordoned-off section of the garage, to allow him to come and go without being seen by the rest of the law firm. We escorted the media inside Rothstein's opulent office, replete with photographs that showed Rothstein in the warm embrace of any number of leading state and national politicians. After all, big-time fund-raising secures prime-time photo ops, and the media did not ignore the array. Reporters relished pictures like the one of Rothstein and one very prominent politician leaning over to blow out birthday candles together. Other firm members were conspicuously absent from Rothstein's display.

Struck by the dramatic secretiveness of Rothstein's inner sanctum, the television coverage that evening was "phenomenal," according to legal observers. The next day's newsprint response was equally encouraging. As we had explained to each of the three groups of journalists who toured the office, this was an "extraordinary" secretiveness "not seen in any law firm."[4] At the same time, we focused on Rothstein's "very flashy lifestyle," a contrast with the hard-working professionals outside the sanctum.[5] The *Sun Sentinel*, the hometown newspaper for the careers and reputations of the RRA attorneys, featured a picture of Rothstein's luxury office with a front-page banner, "Life in the Fast and Secret Lane," along with the subhead, "Hidden Microphones, Surveillance Cameras, Private Elevator."[6] The other local newspapers adopted themes similar to the headline proclaiming, "Inner Sanctum a Display of Power, Secrecy."[7]

It now became apparent how Rothstein, inside his walled-off security bunker, could have concealed his wrongdoing from others. The growing skepticism toward Rothstein's colleagues and staff was met with an explanation that reporters—and the public—could see with their own eyes.

Many difficult miles would lie ahead for the attorneys and staff whose professional world had been shattered by one of the biggest explosions in Florida's legal history. The law firm itself was doomed from the moment that nightmare weekend started, but the vast majority of people in the firm had good names and future livelihoods to protect. To be sure, there would be more bad news and potentially more indictments, especially for the highest-paid lawyers and for Rothstein's inner circle of staff members.[8] When there are months of unrelenting media coverage, winning the battle in one news cycle does not always win the war to protect reputations. Even so, for weeks to come, articles would flash back to descriptions of Rothstein's "inner sanctum, complete with video cameras, a second entrance, and [a] hidden private elevator."[9] The efforts to put a case forward proactively—immediately bringing the lawsuit to get judicial guidance, fully cooperating with authorities, and focusing on the needs of the firm's clients—brought a few spoonfuls of antidote to the toxins of Florida's worst legal scandal.

CHAPTER 1

DEAD MAN VOTING
AND THE ABC'S OF LAW SPIN

Election defeats are never an enhancer of friendships. In Miami, where no one has lineage or history, the obliteration that comes with losing is stunning and complete. Yet, while losing imposes an instant blackout on public support, even upon friendships, almost all perceptions have fleeting lives. And so I urged my friend, the just-defeated mayor, to remain mindful that Miami always offers fertile ground for comebacks, mapping for him several pathways that could return him to city hall in a few years. His wounded eyes and slow words, however, said that he was finished.

The runoff defeat of Joe Carollo, the incumbent mayor who led the field of candidates after the first election, astonished the Anglos in the community. After all, he earned solid marks for his work in heading the city's efforts to overcome a shattering financial crisis that he inherited from past administrations. The *Miami Herald* supported him, as did the downtown business establishments and many community leaders.[1]

Moreover, in the nine days between the first round of balloting on November 4, 1997, and the election runoff on November 13, a torrent of voter fraud allegations detonated across Miami's political landscape and in the media. One allegation concerned a veritable cottage industry of absentee-ballot brokers. During the runoff campaign, workers for the mayor's principal opponent, Xavier Suarez, were arrested for election crimes. In view of Carollo's accomplishments, his support, and his first-place finish in the first round of voting, the barrage of evidence concerning election fraud by those accepted in the opposing camp would surely have guaranteed a landslide margin in any major metropolitan area. In any city, that is, except Miami.

THE RADIO REVOLT

The day before that grim election night, I received a call from Joe's wife, Mari Carollo, who was privately sensing defeat. Like her husband, Mari was a Cuban American who knew more about Miami than the English-language television stations and newspapers. Mari listened to local Spanish-language radio and was deeply concerned about what she heard in the final days before the runoff. Cuban American radio commentators and their call-in listeners were reacting angrily to the charges of voter fraud. Instead of blaming Carollo's enemies, they were castigating Carollo for presenting the charges through venues such as the civil lawsuit that I had filed.

Radio listeners were sympathetic to the people who were arrested, one of whom was in his nineties. Hauling an aging vote broker off to jail amid the glare of television cameras would not be a pleasant picture anywhere. But in this town, the backlash was devastating. The elderly, the very young, and those who fight Castro are cherished in Hispanic Miami. The arrest of an elderly campaign worker was not seen as an attempt to stop vote stealing but rather as an outrageous mistreatment of an *anciano* that was supposedly orchestrated by Carollo and his Anglo police department. Outraged, radio barrages dominated the airwaves with accusations that Carollo was maligning Cuban Americans and collaborating with the liberal *Miami Herald*, a longtime target of Spanish-language talk show hosts and their listeners.

While Mari Carollo feared these radio talk shows, few Anglos in the city had any idea of their influence. While English-language talk shows in the region concentrate on sports and reserve their anger for struggling quarterbacks and poor free-throw shooting, the Spanish-language stations focus almost exclusively on politics. The impact can be dramatic. After a new topic greets the morning's listeners, the message resonates wildly throughout the community by early afternoon. And because listeners who call in usually speak anonymously, they feel free to make extreme allegations that range from aligning local political figures with mistresses (bad), with the *Miami Herald* (really bad), or even with Fidel Castro (time to leave town). Local gossip travels fast in any city, depending on its sensationalism, but even when accelerated by e-mail and chat rooms, it cannot strike the public with Delta Force unless it is validated by mainstream news reporting. In Miami, once embraced by the radio shows, raw accusations move at warp speed to elderly listeners who thereupon spread gossip to the younger generations of their close-knit families—adult children, grandchildren, nieces, and nephews. With radio stations blasting Carollo for instigating prosecutions against Hispanics, all as part of a *Miami Herald* conspiracy, Carollo's lead from nine days earlier suddenly evaporated. It was a defeat that startled only the many who did not understand a chronically polarized community in which everyone is part of some minority.

The mayor's wife knew what we did not know. While we understood the importance of the court of public opinion, we failed to recognize that there can be more than one such court in session at the same time—including one in which legal action against voter fraud can backfire badly. I should have known better. Miami is not a melting pot. It is a stir-fry of languages and people spiced with their own unique histories. The pieces often sizzle, but many do not blend. Some ask whether it is a Spanish-speaking community where English is spoken, or a US city going through its foreign-language phase. Meanwhile, there are billboards beckoning in Portuguese, while radio announcements are heard in Creole. The premise that Miami lacks tradition because its people all come from somewhere else ignores its most obvious tradition—a legacy of newcomers that is continually replenished.

One of the few constants is the *Miami Herald.* Although proud of its distinguished history and many Pulitzer Prizes, the newspaper, like many Anglo institutions, has struggled to find its place among the fast-moving pieces that continually revise Miami's political and cultural landscape. The paper was a staunch supporter of Mayor Carollo during his efforts to salvage the city from financial crisis. Supporting Carollo, who was dubbed "Crazy Joe" by the unkind,[2] was not always easy. While he was respected for his honesty, he was a polarizing political figure. For many, his uncompromising positions, while based on high standards of personal integrity, were better suited for a police chief than for a big-city mayor surrounded by more flexible politicians.

Personally and politically conservative, Carollo had a relentless style that made him the right leader to turn around the financial crisis he inherited when he arrived at city hall the previous year. New York bankers holding the city's bonds found him credible, a welcome change from the politics-as-usual that had brought Miami to near insolvency.

After the mayor helped stabilize the city, though, he collided increasingly with business interests that were used to a more compliant city hall. For the *Miami Herald*, Carollo's attempts to honor its anticorruption traditions as well as to build support in the Cuban American community made him a very acceptable leader. That reform-minded leader, though, lost his city-paid driver and left his lawyer with a quixotic legal challenge.

CHALLENGING THE ELECTION

On November 4, following wild swings in the opinion polls, Carollo received 49.6 percent of the voters, Suarez received 46.8 percent, and a handful of votes went to minor candidates. Although barely missing the majority needed to win outright in the first round, Carollo won by a decisive margin, 51 to 45 percent in the precinct polling places of Miami. With absentee ballots, on the other hand, Suarez achieved a striking advantage of 61 to 35 percent.[3]

Potential explanations for the troubling discrepancy abounded. In those years, absentee voters were citizens who could not go to the polls on Election Day due to out-of-town travel, physical disability, or insurmountable work obligations. Through requests to the elections department, such voters secured by mail or by personal delivery ballots that they completed at home and returned in time for the election.

Since absentee ballots were not completed in the private sanctity of a voting booth, Florida courts considered them to be susceptible to third-party manipulation, even fraud, calling them a "fruitful means of corrupting the ballot if not carefully safeguarded."[4] In extreme instances, absentee ballots could be intercepted from the mail and fraudulently completed by vote thieves. Unless a trained handwriting expert reviewed the voter's signature appearing on the outside of the ballot envelope and compared it with the signature on file at the elections department, fraud was virtually undetectable. No supervisor of elections has the resources to employ handwriting experts to review the thousands, sometimes tens of thousands, of absentee ballots that have to be counted within the brief period before and during the day of the election. Since signature comparison, invariably a quick glance from untrained eyes, constituted the only official means for verification, the process was notoriously unreliable. With little protection against forgeries, rumors long circulated in Miami about brokers collecting absentee ballots and delivering them to campaigns. For operatives with access to the elderly, the absentee ballots of shut-ins and even nursing-home patients could be collected in bundles and delivered to the broker's candidate. At times, some collectors might "assist" the voter in completing the ballot, actually punching through the candidate's number in the days of punch-card ballots—ballot brokers did not leave hanging chads, as I kept hearing from local politicos. Some agents received a fixed price per ballot (ten dollars each was commonly quoted) while others wanted the present and future gratitude of the soon-to-be officeholder. Such bundles could deliver what no amount of television advertising could guarantee—a fistful of votes that were already "in the can," as the Miami-Dade Democratic Chair Joe Geller would explain.

Street talk was alive with reports of unusually aggressive absentee-ballot collecting by Carollo's adversaries. Although his opponent was Suarez, Joe Carollo's nemesis was Miami City Commissioner Humberto Hernandez, who was purportedly politically armed and dangerous with a massive absentee-ballot operation. An avowed enemy of Carollo, Hernandez would be considered a nonfactor in most communities due to a distinction recently awarded by a federal grand jury: he was an indicted defendant awaiting trial for millions of dollars in mortgage fraud. In Miami's unique political environment, Hernandez swept to reelection on the Miami Commission, the city's governing body, by portraying himself as a victim of an anti-Hispanic establishment. Along the way, he amassed an army of hundreds of followers, some of whom may have made careers out of collecting questionable absentee ballots. As we calculated Hernandez's ballot machinery into the curious disparity between absentee ballots and polling-place votes, our suspicion turned to investigation.

The following morning, we reviewed the thousands of absentee envelopes that accounted for Carollo's failure to win an outright majority on November 4.

In Florida, as in other states, the election workers separate the ballot envelope signed by the voter from the unidentifiable ballot itself so that the voter's name cannot be matched to the selections made on the punch-card ballot. While visual inspection of ballot envelopes could not identify the candidate selected by that voter, the absentee ballot envelope still contained two critical pieces of information: the signature of the voter and the signatures of his or her witnesses. Fortunately for our investigation, ballot brokers almost always signed the ballot envelope as witnesses for the absentee voters they enlisted. As a result, by totaling the number of times the same name kept appearing as a witness, we quickly identified the leading vote collectors as well as the votes they collected.

One of the largest collections belonged to Alberto Russi. As we analyzed the Russi votes, discrepancies materialized. Suspiciously similar voter signatures appeared from supposedly different voters. And very large families were registered as living in small dwellings, some of which were unoccupied. Meanwhile, anecdotal reports about apparent fraud continued to flood our offices. As we moved quickly toward filing a lawsuit challenging the absentee balloting, we remained optimistic that with or without it, Joe would likely win the runoff. And by taking public action against the voter fraud being perpetrated by his adversaries, an anticorruption lawsuit would assuredly resonate positively among the voters.

With the runoff election just days away, velocity was as crucial as accuracy. By late Friday night, I had prepared a lawsuit and made arrangements with the Miami-Dade Circuit Court to file it on Saturday morning as an emergency action.

THE LAWSUIT PRESS RELEASE

In some ways, drafting a lawsuit is much easier than lawyers want the public to believe. We might encourage the world—and especially well-paying clients—to believe that only attorneys know the incantations required for legal papers, as we stand behind the wizard's curtain with a vast repertoire of legalese. Most lawsuits are actually simple creatures. They include summaries of the key facts, usually in chronological order, followed by a few sections that use boilerplate language to establish each legal claim or count. For example, a three-count lawsuit (like a three-count criminal indictment) is essentially a written chronology of a controversy's basic facts, followed by three different itemizations of the elements for the three legal theories.

The rules for preparing lawsuits in state as well as federal courts require a "short and plain" statement of the claims. Underscoring this entreaty for simplicity, the courts have created forms for lawsuits as models for lawyers to follow, forms that are remarkably bland and brief. In the court of public opinion, though, there is nothing short and plain about the way high-profile lawsuits are presented. Many such court papers bear a striking resemblance to press releases. And, in political cases, comparisons can be made to a Fourth of July stump speech.

While there was much about election challenges that I was learning for the first time, I was already experienced in drafting lawsuits reviewed by reporters. A decade earlier, a developer client with a giant project in the Florida Keys was abruptly cut off from tens of millions of dollars in funding by his lender, Continental Illinois National Bank. After the lender dropped its bombshell on a Friday, we worked through the weekend to prepare not only a lawsuit focused on financial recovery for the massive damages but also a message aimed at the business community.

When I read the news reports the day after the lawsuit was filed, I was struck by how extensively the reporters had relied on verbatim quotes lifted directly from the pleadings. Fortunately, we had included plenty of hard-hitting phrases laced with adjectives not found in most legal dictionaries. That lawsuit was eventually transferred to a different state, and while I did not participate in the $110-million verdict that went to the plaintiff years later, I received a crash course on the media and court papers.

That coursework taught me why reporters like to quote court papers. With a word-for-word account of the litigant's own claims, journalists cannot be accused of misquotes or distortions. More significant, papers filed in court are immunized from defamation suits, no matter how extreme the allegations may be. At times, this immunity from defamation can become a license for lawyers to take extreme liberties with the truth. In recent years, the media's immunity has created an opportunity for press-savvy lawyers to draft papers that are designed to be quotable.

Good reporters exercise caution before repeating obvious non-sense, but trash-talking lawyers can sometimes exploit reporters to publicize vilification that would otherwise allow the victim to counter with massive claims for defamation. While courts can enter orders striking out outrageous allegations, such rulings would occur, if at all, in a court hearing well after the fact.

In matters like our election challenge, immunity was the least of our concerns; we already had a credible case. Since the investigation was only days old and much digging remained to be done by authorities, we needed wording for our pleading that would be general but also press provoking. We relied on words like *abuse* and *irregular*, as well as their more sinister-sounding cousin, *illicit*. We used *multiple* as the quantifier and crafted language to suggest the prospect of serious problems without overstating the evidence actually available at the time. Later, our adversaries asked the court to delete such words, complaining that they were too vaguely ominous and that words like *multiple* could mean "few" or "many." But we won the word-splitting skirmishes with language that was literally accurate yet vague and troubling.

LEGAL ACTION BACKFIRES

We filed the lawsuit on the Saturday after the first election. Viewed initially as a few doses of legal substance sprinkled over a large helping of publicity for the runoff, our papers generated some positive attention because they featured the role of ballot brokers. In particular, the lawsuit zeroed in on Alberto Russi, who appeared to be the most flagrant and active among them. With an intensifying interest in voter fraud, agents of the Florida Department of Law Enforcement went to Russi's house the following week, found plenty of blank ballots on his table, and arrested him the day before the runoff election. Unfortunately for

Carollo, Russi was ninety-two years old. The television image of a Cuban American *anciano* being arrested by two burly state agents was a political disaster. None of us asked for Russi's arrest, but the radio stations were flooded with calls blaming Carollo.

During the twenty-four hours before the runoff, Commissioner Hernandez seized upon Russi's value as a victim of complicity with the Anglo establishment and took him to key polling places throughout Election Day to mobilize opposition to Carollo. Later, on the evening of November 13, as the returns confirmed Carollo's runoff defeat, Russi was loudly applauded as the hero of the hour at Suarez's victory party. The next morning, I arrived at my office to hear a chorus of demands that Carollo should concede and abandon the litigation challenging the first election. Even my law partner, Manny Diaz, came to my office that day bluntly declaring to me, "It's over."

Diaz had supported Carollo during the election despite having a number of longtime friends in the Suarez camp. Like many involved in politics, though, he had strong feelings about respecting the wishes of the voters and a philosophical opposition to trying to reverse their decisions through legal maneuvering. Four years later, Diaz became mayor of Miami, and he won based on the combination of fund-raising, television ads, and politics that he and most politicians believe are the only forces that should decide elections. With such feelings shared almost universally throughout Miami, Joe had only closet support during the rest of November. It was understandable because no one believed we had any chance of success in proving massive voter fraud.

Invalidating a modern mayoral election in a major US city through court proceedings was virtually unprecedented. By virtue of the principle of separation of powers between the courts and the other branches of government, most judges are reluctant to interfere with the outcome of even bad elections.

THE NEW ELECTION QUANDARY

Our challenge was that even if we could convince a court to order a new election, that outcome could well be more fool's gold than golden.

By the time a new election could be held, the mayor's opponents would be sufficiently entrenched through numerous appointments and reshufflings of city agencies to assure that a revote would simply mean a reelection of the mayor's opponent. In fact, some years earlier, in the mayoral election for Hialeah, another city in Dade County, a court case established sufficient proof of voter fraud to secure a new election for the mayor's office. When the votes came back in the new Hialeah election, however, the winner of the earlier illegal election won again—this time by an even bigger margin.[5]

For these reasons, we made a high-risk strategic decision early on— we did not ask for a new election in our court papers. Instead, we requested that if voter fraud could be sufficiently proven, Mayor Carollo would be returned to office by order of the court without a revote. Although that legal strategy seemed brazenly antidemocratic—asking the courts to install an elected official whom the voters seemingly chose not to elect—it was, in practical terms, our only hope, given the inevitable defeat that a new election would offer. In legal terms, our goals were not so far-fetched. The strategy was based on a series of Florida court decisions that did indeed support our position. According to those rulings, if the absentee ballots were sufficiently tainted by fraud, a judge should discard them and base the results solely upon the Election Day votes at the polling places, where Carollo won soundly, if not quite decisively. We requested that this majority be the final result if the absentee ballots were knocked out.

Predictably, the view of our case from others was unsympathetic, even hostile. Business leaders who admired Carollo's service as a mayor thought little of his chances as a litigant. The overwhelming view throughout Miami was that we had a slim chance of winning in the courts and no chance of winning a revote with Miami's voters. As to the legal theory of having Mayor Carollo returned to the office by court order—rather than through a new election—the legal, business, and political communities all agreed that no such seemingly undemocratic position could possibly prevail.

LONG LIVE THE DEAD VOTER

None of the skeptics had ever met Manuel Yip. In fact, nobody would ever again have the chance to meet him, even though his vote was registered in the Miami mayor's election. Mr. Yip represented that ineffable component that can take a cause from obscurity to celebrity through a single snapshot of memorable sensationalism. Just as football games have game-changing plays, courtroom battles can turn upon a single case-changing event. Manuel Yip sparked that transformation because he was that most unforgettable of all figures in election challenges: the dead voter. And, in election cases, it only takes one dead voter to overcome a hundred thousand skeptics.

Yip represented more than a rallying cry for our challenge to rampant voter fraud. He would also be the catalyst for an unspoken cooperation between our legal team and the newspaper that provided the only hope of reshaping the harsh landscape we were confronting. Indeed, a reporter's phone call crystallized the moment at which I began to believe that the seemingly futile representation accepted out of friendship could evolve into historic election litigation.

Within days after the defeat, *Miami Herald* reporter Joe Tanfani called with some general questions about our litigation plans. At the end of the conversation, he suggested that the recent articles highlighting gross disparities between the absentee ballots favoring Suarez and the polling-place votes favoring Carollo could give traction to our lawsuit.

For me, his observation prompted some critical realizations. Nothing flattens an uphill legal battle better than strong media support. While media coverage rarely takes a case beyond the legal limits, it can surely drive you as far as the law allows. And several Florida court precedents provided us with a legal framework for winning.[6] From that point forward, we saw the *Miami Herald* and its team of investigative journalists as the key to building a public awareness that might make an unwinnable case winnable.

When Stephanie Lydecker and Kelly Mallette, two of Carollo's assistants, discovered Manuel Yip, we immediately contacted Tanfani. As he promptly confirmed our information about the dead voter, the *Miami Herald* had a story and would soon have a cause. Though his political friends stopped returning his phone calls, Joe Carollo won a critical ally.

With his election lawsuit pending and several *Miami Herald* articles detailing possible irregularities, Joe met with Tony Ridder, the chairman of Knight-Ridder, the parent company of the *Miami Herald.* Joe and Tony knew each other from the drive to build a new arena to keep Miami's NBA team, the Miami Heat, from leaving the city. Impressed by the information developed so far, Ridder committed major resources to cover the investigation of voter fraud. Ridder would later relocate the corporate headquarters of Knight-Ridder to his hometown of San Diego, prompting some to say he was never truly comfortable in Miami. His commitment to fighting corruption, however, was unmistakable and proved critical for Carollo.

By early December, the *Miami Herald* was intensely engaged. After the headline "Dozens of Votes Questionable in City Election" appeared above the fold on page one, a few closed minds began to open.[7] Most important, volunteers, including leading attorneys, joined the ranks of an operation that began with one ousted mayor and one attorney. Ben Kuehne, one of the community's top criminal defense lawyers, and Joe Geller, a leading election lawyer, became contributors to the daily flow of court papers, witness depositions, and trial preparation. We even secured expert witnesses willing to serve on a *pro bono* basis. Hugh Cochran, a former FBI agent, led our investigation, finding that scores of Suarez supporters had falsely registered to vote in the city of Miami, even though they lived outside its limits. Professors Chris Warren and Kevin Hill of Florida International University also joined without charging for their services and provided expert testimony that overwhelmed any thesis that illegal voting was either isolated or tolerable. And, while we would have to pay for the services of our handwriting expert, whose work was critical in establishing a myriad of bogus voter signatures, the funding suddenly arrived. It came from a donor who remained anonymous, fearful of retaliation from Carollo's enemies.

While we knew the battle for public opinion was important, it never erased the need to have a compelling case in the courtroom if we were to vaporize a major election. Florida law allowed two different but extremely difficult avenues for that challenge. We could win by jettisoning at least one hundred sixty absentee ballots, enough to give us a 50-percent-plus-one majority of the November 4 voting. But that process required ballot-by-ballot challenges with individualized evidence of illegality, and, in effect, one hundred sixty different court decisions canceling each such vote. Or we could prove that a systematic fraud was perpetrated on a scale so egregious and pervasive that it had destroyed the integrity of the election. The vast majority of our time was dedicated to the daily search for evidence needed to climb one of these mountains.

As more hard-hitting headlines appeared ("Cashing in on Helping the Elderly"[8] and "Dubious Tactics Secured Votes for Suarez, Hernandez"),[9] we pushed for a trial date as quickly as possible. The public's attention span can be short, and favorable press reports can quickly fade away—each day brings fresh news of all kinds. Timing, therefore, was everything. In election cases, courts are supposed to move at lightning speed because the need to resolve which person is entitled to hold public office is necessarily a matter of great public importance. And with each passing day—if the challenge is valid—the person holding office is exercising power illegally, to the detriment of the public as well as the challenger.

THREE MONTHS LATER, A LANDMARK CASE BEGINS

On February 9, 1998, some three months after the election, Judge Thomas Wilson convened a trial that the media now described as a landmark case rather than a loser's long shot. We were armed with eyewitness accounts, at least five different expert evaluations, and mountains of paper indicating a widespread pattern of illegality and irregularity. And, of course, we had Manuel Yip. As the trial commenced, a *New York Times* article headlined "Dead Voters" accorded multiple identities to the late Mr. Yip.

While the two dozen individuals who testified were crucial, so too were twenty-one witnesses who declined to say a word in court, invoking their Fifth Amendment rights—a silence that proved devastating for our opponents. In a criminal trial, the constitutional protections embodied in the Fifth Amendment demand that no inference of guilt be allowed in respect to the defendant or witness. If a prosecutor even suggests to a jury that the defendant's failure to testify suggests guilt, a new trial would be granted. In civil court, however, the opposite prevails. Civil courts affirmatively adopt the inference that a witness who invokes Fifth Amendment rights is doing so because that testimony would be harmful. And it can be a disaster in the court of public opinion.

In one headline, the *Miami Herald* reported, "Sergeant, Wife Refused to Testify in Vote Case. Pair Tells Lawyer: We'll Take the Fifth."[10] When more than a score of election participants took the Fifth, media reports were blistering. While we will never know what impact such refusals had on Judge Wilson's decision making, he commented pointedly about "common sense" concerning witnesses who withheld testimony. As dramatic developments hammered open the ugly side of Miami politics, vocal attacks against the *Miami Herald* and Carollo were made on Spanish-language radio and television, aimed at Miami voters who would decide a new election.

As the trial progressed, the *Miami Herald*'s investigation continued. Midway through the court proceedings, headlines proclaimed "It's a Crime, but Felons Vote, Too"[11] and "One Hundred Convicted Felons in Miami Election."[12] Another headline exclaimed, "Coach, 34, Charged in Vote Scheme."[13] The headlines showed that motivated reporters can usually uncover more facts than a private party's own investigation. Less obvious is the truism that media investigators can race ahead of law enforcement agencies, too. In fact, federal investigators often get the critical information that leads to a major corruption prosecution by reading it for the first time in a newspaper.

Furthermore, some people are more willing to talk to reporters than to FBI agents for several reasons. Many witnesses seek the spotlight that only reporters can provide, and the press corps is trained to engage subjects without intimidating them. On the other hand, for witnesses who want to provide information anonymously, reporters are better equipped at keeping the identities of their sources confidential, which police often cannot guarantee. Many times the first chapters of corruption scandals appear in newspapers and are followed by sequels authored by the federal and state authorities as they launch their probes.

As matters developed in this case, state agents arrested dozens of operatives in the months following the election trial. Interestingly, one such defendant, Angel Gonzalez, was later elected to the Miami commission.

WINNING THE BATTLE, BUT WHAT ABOUT THE WAR?

As the two-week trial proceeded, skeptics started to believe. Some "Suaristas" grew concerned enough to attempt an unusual form of intervention against our legal challenge. Sitting outside the courtroom, some practitioners of Santeria—a Cuban folk religion combining voodoo with saints—whispered chants against Carollo and his lawyers. The turnaround in our fortunes was also reflected by headlines such as, "Mayor's Attorney Faces Daunting Task as Case Resumes Today."[14] With momentum building in our favor, the question of the final decision deeply worried us. As one *Miami Herald* account described the issue, "Would the judge award Carollo the office he sought? Or would he order a new election?"[15] The perception that a new election was the only result we could realistically pursue was so strong that would-be candidates, including Suarez, began planning their campaigns. One aspirant was not. Joe Carollo knew that a new election was hopeless for him and would unleash yet more hostility.

Our closing argument emphasized repeatedly the Florida law that specified that the absentee ballots in the first election should be completely nullified and that Joe's 51 percent majority in the polling-place tallies should be upheld. We urged that while the past election was the problem, a new election was not the solution.

Meanwhile, during the week we waited for Judge Wilson's decision, another front-page story appeared above the fold, "Suarez Aide Probed in Vote Buying." Excitement swept across town on March 4, following a notice that the judge was ready to release his decision. Dozens of reporters and more than twenty television cameras were waiting on the steps of the Miami-Dade County courthouse. Judge Wilson found massive and systematic fraud, holding that ballot brokers "literally and figuratively stole the ballot from the hands of every honest voter in Miami."[16] We were struck by the court's eloquence and effectiveness in capturing the key elements of the evidence to find that "the integrity of the election was adversely affected."[17]

As our eyes sped to the final paragraphs of the order, however, we saw a prescription for winning the courtroom battle but losing the political war. The court had ordered a new election within sixty days, rather than reinstalling Joe Carollo as mayor.[18]

Although a significant disappointment, it was still a remarkable victory. As Joe faced the television cameras, he declared it a "great day for democracy" and sounded every bit the victor. When we convened privately minutes later, however, a different mood engulfed the winner. Away from the camera's glare, his face grimly betrayed deep concerns about the new election. As Joe described the many advantages Suarez would enjoy as the incumbent who would hold the mayor's powers during the court-ordered campaign, gloom filled the room. After an extraordinary four-month ordeal that began with a despondent isolation and took us to the edge of an impossible victory, we seemed more distant than ever from redemption.

Then, as I started to reread the order, I was struck by a remarkable omission: it said nothing about who would serve as mayor of Miami now that the Suarez election was invalidated. As I started to describe the different legal explanations that could be made, George DePontis brought those legal musings to an abrupt halt. DePontis, the one political veteran who had remained close to Carollo throughout the litigation, had spent decades in political trench warfare in Florida, in other states, and even in other countries. Sensing an opportunity, he declared to us, "If the order is silent, then no one is mayor."

As we absorbed George's thesis, its legal viability seemed clear and its potential impact spectacular. Since Judge Wilson's order declared the Suarez election invalid, the process of replacing Carollo was incomplete. Under Florida law, Joe, as the original mayor, was the lawfully elected officeholder. Therefore, we argued that he should remain in the mayor's office until a successor was validly named. Denying Suarez the advantage of incumbency was important enough, but even more sensational was the image of an empty mayor's office, with its potential for political chaos—perhaps a warrant, even an invitation, for extraordinary judicial intervention.

This ammunition required rapid-fire delivery. The press and the public were already assuming that Suarez would continue as mayor until the new election. Armed with a legal argument and fueled by urgency, part of our team stormed back to the courthouse, tracking down any reporters we could find, while others phoned those who had already left. Our message was simple but stunning: the court's order left vacant the office of the mayor of Miami. Initial skepticism quickly melted as we explained in detail why erasing Suarez's election could only mean erasing his tenancy at city hall.

On the following day, the result of the verdict in this landmark litigation was accorded second-class status with a small-print headline, "Citing Massive Fraud, Judge Voids Vote, Orders New City Election in Sixty Days."[19] In bold letters, the main headline demanded to know, "Who's the Mayor of Miami?"[20] Other newspapers trumpeted the same theme, spotlighting Miami's chaos. The headline in the *Tallahassee Democrat* declared "Miami Mayor Is Anybody's Guess."[21]

APPEALING A PYRRHIC VICTORY

As the dysfunctional image of an empty mayor's chair resounded throughout the media, we prepared papers for an appeal. Working all night, we drafted an emergency appeal to persuade the Third District Court of Appeal to reverse the order for a new election and reinstate Carollo. We had legal support and the spectacle of a bewildered city government that cried out for help from the courts. Yet as we scrambled to finalize our appellate papers, Suarez supporters launched their own counterattack. To overcome the swelling anxieties about a leaderless city, the commission, led by its indicted but powerful chairman, scheduled an emergency meeting to select an interim mayor. That interim mayor would assuredly be Suarez.

As we fretted over the apparent change of fortune, hours before the five-member commission was to meet, I received a call from Arthur Teele, the only black member of the commission. At the time, he had a decent relationship with Carollo and a decidedly unsympathetic view of the Suarez/Hernandez alliance. Teele was extremely bright, a lawyer as well as a politician, and he offered a cryptic but critical suggestion. Without explanation, he told me immediately to send a letter to the commission. I followed his advice and demanded that the body take no action because of the trial court's order. I argued that the office belonged to Carollo and informed the members that our emergency appeal would likely yield a quick result from the appeals court. The letter worked. Armed with my demand and his own considerable skills of advocacy, Teele persuaded the city commission to take no action in selecting an interim mayor and, instead, to await the emergency appeal. Sadly, eight years later, Commissioner Arthur Teele would shoot himself in the lobby of the *Miami Herald* amid corruption allegations and a downward spiral of personal circumstances.

Two days after the decision, we requested the fastest possible action by the appeals court. Although we hoped that the specter of a mayoral vacancy might prompt judicial concerns, once again, a *Miami Herald* headline sounded the alarm more loudly than anything in our legal briefs. Three days before the appeals court was to hear the case on March 11, the newspaper dramatized the crisis at city hall with headlines saying, "Investors Skittish on Miami,"[22] and "City's Political Crisis Could Upset Economy."[23]

Ironically, the weekend before the appeals court argument, the *Miami Herald* itself weighed in against our request for judicial intervention with an editorial that commended Judge Wilson's decision to order a new election and opposed installing Carollo by appellate decree.

March 11 was a Monday, and the courtroom was packed that morning. After the argument before the appeals court, I reported to Joe that things went well, but I could not make any predictions. Until a jury has spoken or the ink dries on a judge's signature, attorneys know better than to predict positive outcomes for clients. Optimism, though, was palpable. Later that morning I received a call from David Lyons, who covered the case extensively for the *Miami Herald*. An outstanding reporter who knew more about courtroom realities than most lawyers, he told me that the word among the media was that our argument went well and that the appeals court might actually be thinking the unthinkable.

Although I expected an expedited ruling from the appeals court, I was astonished to get a call that very afternoon. As I raced through traffic to the courthouse ten miles away for the decision's 4:30 p.m. release, I told Joe that a ruling was imminent and prepared him for a spectrum of possibilities. Upon my arrival, the written order was already being read. Reporters told me about the ruling even as co-counsel handed me a copy. We had won. The Third District Court of Appeal returned Joe Carollo to the office of mayor.

Immediately calling Joe with the news, I read him the key paragraphs of the decision. There was a long silence on the other end of the line. He then asked me several times to confirm that what I had just told him really happened. He was stunned and deeply moved. It was a remarkable vindication after four months of political quarantine and virtual seclusion for the man who had been Miami's mayor and would now be its mayor once more.

The next day, the headline on the front-page section was "Carollo Back as Miami Mayor."[24] The top of the local section described the reaction of an amazed community saying, "Carollo's Return as Mayor Stuns Miami."[25] As I read those articles, I reflected on the incredible roller-coaster ride of the last four months. It began as a nearly impossible long shot. But a passionate legal challenge combined with outstanding newspaper reporting achieved a legal miracle. After the exhausting intensity of our four-month ordeal, there was no such celebration for Mayor Joe Carollo. And even if we had had one, we could not have invited the man who perhaps should have been the guest of honor—Miami's most famous dead voter, Manuel Yip.

The *Miami Herald* went on to win a well-deserved Pulitzer Prize for its coverage of the voter fraud scandal that repeatedly mentioned its discovery of Yip. Kelly Mallette (now a prominent lobbyist) and Stephanie Lydecker (now a producer for *American Idol*), the Carollo team members who uncovered Yip's posthumous contribution to democracy, received no recognition for their discovery. But they, too, learned several valuable lessons about high-profile litigation: these cases must be won in the court of public opinion as well as in a court of law, and it takes only one dead voter to rewrite a city's history.

CHAPTER 2

SPINNING CASES THROUGH THE AGES

When Adam was hauled into court for eating the apple, he blamed Eve. Eve blamed the snake. The snake refused to testify. We have been arguing about the case ever since. The court of public opinion is always in session. Endlessly fascinated by our fellow humans, we know that human affairs are always about the narrative, and whoever spins the narrative controls the story—and often its consequences. Sometimes the story is no bigger than two people. And sometimes it is very, very big.

An idea is not responsible for the people who believe in it.

—Don Marquis

SOCRATES

In 399 BCE the Athenian poet Meletus made a citizen's arrest. In front of witnesses, he accused the philosopher Socrates of "refusing to do reverence to the gods recognized by the city and [of] introducing other new divinities,"[1] and also of "corrupting the youth."[2] This set in motion one of history's most famous trials and executions.

Why then? Socrates, the self-styled "gadfly" of Athens, was seventy years old. He had been annoying the Athenians for decades. Smug, condescending, and relentless in his philosophical inquisitions, he had been known to provoke men to the point of their pummeling him or tearing his hair out. He was often the butt of jokes, and he was mocked mercilessly by the playwright Aristophanes in the comedy *The Clouds*.[3]

Then, after a lifetime of teaching as he pleased, the situation changed. How did this happen in the birthplace of democracy, where free speech was a national sport, parties were judged by the liveliness of their debates, and orators were the celebrities of their day? Politics.

Democracy had flourished in Athens since 590 BCE. But twice in the final fifteen years of Socrates' life, former students briefly overthrew the city's democratic government, imposing dictatorships in its place. First, in 411 BCE, an oligarchy supported by the renegade general Alcibides took temporary control. Then, in 404 BCE, another Socratic disciple, Critias, imposed a brutal regime. During an eight-month reign of terror, Critias and his cohorts, known as the Thirty Tyrants, slaughtered fifteen hundred Athenians—mostly leaders and proponents of democracy—and banished five thousand. Soon Athenians had had enough. The exiled General Thrasybulus deposed the Thirty Tyrants and restored democracy.[4]

This is the background against which Meletus and two other accusers brought charges against Socrates. Although the court system in Athens had no judges, defense attorneys, prosecutors, or rules of evidence, it had a fairly sophisticated jury system. Athenians were fond of suing each other. Juries consisted of five hundred to fifteen hundred citizens (on the theory that there was no slush fund large enough to bribe so many). Trials lasted one day, and jurors were paid three obols for their trouble (by our current monetary standards, this was probably close to the going rate of fifteen to fifty dollars, depending on the state).[5]

In addition to Meletus, an undistinguished poet and possibly a stooge, Socrates' accusers were Lycon, an orator, and—the one who mattered—the powerful businessman and democrat Anytus. Meletus's sworn affidavit functioned as an oral summons. Once the local magistrate reviewed the charges and questioned both sides, he made the determination that a full trial was warranted. Plaintiffs and defendants each had three hours to present their case, measured by a water clock.

In the event of a guilty verdict, each side proposed a possible punishment. The jury was free to choose between the two. Socrates' accusers demanded death, while the old philosopher suggested free meals in the center of the city for life, an honor reserved for civic benefactors and winning Olympic athletes. Many scholars consider this joking suggestion an example of the "suicide defense," a signal Socrates had no intention of defending himself against what he viewed as unjust prosecution.[6] A recent example of a suicide defense is al Qaeda terrorist Zacarias Moussaoui, who pled guilty to various crimes, including conspiracy, in connection with the 9/11 atrocities. He proclaimed that he welcomed the death penalty. The jury did not oblige him, though, and he was sentenced to life in prison.

> ### HISTORY LESSON
> Suicide defenses are not recommended.

Although the vote for conviction was close, two hundred eighty discs in the "guilty" urn, and two hundred twenty in the one marked "innocent," the vote for death in the penalty stage of the trial was three hundred sixty to one hundred forty.[7] Socrates, whatever he may have said in his defense—and some scholars think he may have stood silently before his accusers—was not a crowd pleaser.

Some revisionist scholars assert that Socrates was actually tried and condemned for being an enemy to democracy. Journalist-scholar I. F. Stone argues this perspective forcefully in his 1989 revisionist history, *The Trial of Socrates*.[8] But as he's most often portrayed, Socrates stands in the tradition of great spiritual teachers, holding that a human being's fundamental obligation is to find out what is moral and true and to behave accordingly, regardless of the nature of government.[9]

Indeed, the trial of Socrates and the life of free inquiry that preceded it is one of the touchstones of Western civilization, the founding myth of what scholar Karen Armstrong calls "the Western rationalist tradition." Nothing enhances a tradition so much as a founder willing to suffer martyrdom for his beliefs and principles. Socrates' antagonism toward democracy is conveniently left out of this version of the story.

If Socrates ever wrote anything, it is yet to be discovered. But he has the advantage of being represented in history by two of his accomplished students, Xenophon and Plato, and Plato was the only one actually present at the trial. While Plato's *Apologia Socratous* (*Defense of Socrates*) is entirely partisan, its beauty and power cannot help but incite feelings of sympathy for the noble Socrates it portrays. Stone says that the reader "comes away with the impression that this wonderful old philosopher had been condemned simply because he had spent his life exhorting his fellow citizens to be virtuous."[10]

Plato, however, was an aristocrat, a poet, and a cousin of the bloody tyrant Critias, and he was devoted to Socrates. He hated democracy, deriding it as "mobacracy." As Stone says in an interview with the *New York Times Magazine*,[11] to depend on Plato and Xenophon for our knowledge of the trial of Socrates is "like trying to cover a trial when one is barred from the courtroom except to hear the defendant's summation to the jury."[12] No transcript exists, nor do accounts from the prosecution's point of view. Seeking to put their beloved teacher in the best possible light, neither Xenophon nor Plato makes mention of any political reason for Socrates' trial and execution—nothing about the antidemocratic philosophic teachings the Athenians may have viewed as subversive and treasonous. Indeed, a democrat like Anytus may have considered Socrates culpable for the crimes of Critias.

Seen in this light, the enduring image of Socrates as a great moral teacher stands as one of history's great masterpieces of spin.

HISTORY LESSON

Whether it's Plato or cable news, the push to get the lead correspondents on your side is important no matter what side you're on.

JOAN OF ARC

> Since God had commanded it, it was necessary that I do it. Since God commanded it, even if I had a hundred fathers and mothers, even if I had been a King's daughter, I would have gone nevertheless.
>
> —Joan of Arc

It was the trial of the fifteenth century. Full of political tricks, twists, and manipulations, it was spun in every direction—but the real incarnation of propaganda was Joan of Arc, manipulated for political purposes by competing sides in the Hundred Years' War between France and England. To paraphrase Voltaire, if she had not existed, it would have been necessary to invent her.

The Hundred Years' War actually lasted more than a century (1337–1453), as the French and English fought over succession to the French throne. Although there were periods of relative peace during the long conflict, France by 1429 was demoralized and close to defeat. The English and their allies in Burgundy occupied much of the country, including Paris. The French population, suffering not only from foreign occupation but also a ruined economy, famines, and plague, had declined by two-thirds.[13] Fourteen years earlier, Henry V had scored a brilliant military and propaganda coup in the battle at Agincourt, where he defeated a much larger French force. The French king Charles VI was schizophrenic, and his wife, Isabel of Bavaria, signed away the succession in the Treaty of Troyes in return for what was, essentially, a little peace and quiet. Their son, the dauphin Charles VII, was determined to regain the crown, but he was weak and also indecisive. After the deaths of Charles VI and Henry V, the royal English baby Henry VI technically became ruler of two realms, Britain and France.[14]

For centuries the French kings had been crowned at Rheims, but the cathedral town was now under the control of the Burgundians, while the English laid siege to Orleans. Strategically sited on the Loire River, Orleans was the last northern city to remain loyal to France. If it fell, the English would sweep into the heartland and take the rest of the country.[15] Vague prophecies of a maid from Lorraine who would arise to rescue France had circulated for years. When Joan, sixteen, claimed to have visions in which God commanded her to liberate France from English domination, many were primed to believe. She gained a private interview with Charles VII, who was impressed by her intelligence, confidence, and manner. But in a world dependent, like our own, on public opinion, he first had to verify her religious orthodoxy.[16] Joan was packed off to Poitiers for a theological examination. In April 1429, the commission of inquiry "declared her to be of irreproachable life, a good Christian, possessed of the virtues of humility, honesty and simplicity."[17]

HISTORY LESSON

Always vet the candidate's lowlights as well as highlights before turning on the spotlights.

After the initial vetting, Joan was ordered to Orleans. Defying the cautious French military leadership, she led a series of aggressive actions that broke the English siege in only nine days. "She turned what had been a dry dynastic squabble that left the common people unmoved except for their own suffering into a passionately popular war of national liberation."[18]

Charles agreed to make Joan co-commander of the French army with Duke John II of Alençon. Instead of retaking Paris, Joan embarked on a bold campaign to capture Rheims, twice as far away, but she proved her courage and military acumen at each battle. She took an arrow to the neck at Orleans, yet led the final charge on English lines. A cannonball struck her helmet at Beaugency, but she survived to direct French forces to victory. By the time she reached Rheims, English resistance had been routed and she entered the city without a fight.

The coronation of Charles VII took place in Rheims on July 17, 1429. Joan and her family were in attendance, after which she returned to battle. On May 30 of the following year, she was captured by the Burgundians outside the walls of Compiègne. Although it was customary for prisoners of war to be ransomed by their families, Joan's family had no money. Inexplicably, Charles VII refused to pay for release of the woman whose valor, military leadership, and sense of purpose had secured his throne. The Duke of Burgundy then sold Joan to the English for ten thousand livres and an annuity.[19]

> ### HISTORY LESSON
>
> Charles VII was not the first leader to throw overboard someone who had made him what he was. But he is one of history's most spectacular examples.

In its medieval way, Joan's trial was all spin. The English regent, the Duke of Bedford, still hoped to regain the French throne for his nephew, Henry VI. Discrediting Joan as a heretic was a critical step in undermining the legitimacy of Charles's coronation. As a result, the Inquisitorial trial, held at Rouen, the English capital of occupation, was so rife with irregularities that some court officers had to be compelled by threat of death to participate, including the Inquisitor, Jean Lemaître.[20] The presiding officer, Pierre Cauchon, the bishop of Beauvais, was an English partisan with no legitimate jurisdiction.[21] And the prosecution's evidence was thin. An investigator sent to Joan's village of Domremy returned without any testimony against her, leaving the court no grounds to initiate action against Joan. The English proceeded anyway.[22]

In addition to sorcery, witchcraft, and heresy, Joan was charged with the crime of wearing men's clothing. An examination overseen by the Duchess of Bedford confirmed Joan's virginity, forcing the court to drop the charge of witchcraft on the grounds that a witch could not also be a virgin. The court violated ecclesiastical law by denying Joan a legal advisor as well as by holding her in a secular jail under guard of English soldiers instead of in a church prison guarded by nuns.

Some modern commentators, seeking to explain Joan's vision by way of medicine or psychiatry, have diagnosed various mental or physical diseases, including epilepsy, tuberculosis, and schizophrenia. None of these is persuasive, given the written historical record. Joan is among the most thoroughly documented figures of the Middle Ages, with transcripts of both her trial and the later rehabilitation trial fully extant, as well as copious eyewitness accounts of her actions and exploits.[23] The rigors of Joan's military career prove sufficient evidence against physical debility, and her performance during the trial suggests both a keen intelligence and a level head. She frequently confounded clerical interrogators with the subtly of her answers.

Most famously, Joan was asked if she knew she was in God's grace. This was a trick question. No one, according to Catholic doctrine, could be certain whether or not he or she was in God's grace. Had Joan replied *yes*, she would expose herself as a heretic; answering *no* would be the same as admitting guilt. Instead, Joan replied, "If I am not, may God put me there; and if I am, may God so keep me." One eyewitness later testified, "Those who were interrogating her were stupefied."[24]

HISTORY LESSON

Throughout the millennium, inquisitors have asked questions like "have you stopped beating your spouse?" and the best course is to object or deflect.

Nonetheless, the English would settle for nothing less than Joan's conviction and death. Under threat of immediate execution, Joan, who was illiterate, signed an abjuration confessing to bearing arms, cutting her hair, and wearing men's clothes. But since she had confessed, she could not be put to death. Only a lapsed heretic could be burned. Two days later, after being sexually assaulted by prison guards, she again donned men's clothing, either as a protection against further molestation or because her dress had been stolen and she had nothing else to wear. She was handed over to the English, who burned her at the stake on May 30, 1431.[25]

If Joan's original trial was the product of spin, so, at least in part, was the posthumous rehabilitation trial. In 1455 and 1456, a panel of theologians from throughout Europe analyzed testimony from one hundred fifteen witnesses. Pierre Cauchon, dead by then, was declared a heretic for convicting an innocent woman. Among the findings, Joan's wearing of men's clothing was determined to be justified and legal. She had dressed as a page during travels through enemy territory, she had worn armor during battle, and she had dressed as a man in prison to preserve chastity—all accepted doctrinal exceptions to biblical strictures on women's dress.[26]

Joan was pronounced innocent on July 7, 1456. This verdict came as a relief to Charles VII, now reigning over a unified France, for it no longer meant he owed his crown to an executed heretic.

Centuries later, Joan remains a remarkable figure, one whose curious life and achievements cannot be easily explained. At the time of her death, she was nineteen. Her example inspired French nationalism, her tactics reinvigorated French military leaders. Barely two decades after her execution, the English were routed.[27]

Since then, Joan has proven a convenient symbol for all sides of almost any French ideological debate. Napoleon claimed her. So did monarchists, liberals, and conservatives. In World War II, the Vichy Regime played up her antagonism to the English, while the French Resistance emphasized her principled struggle against foreign occupation. The Catholic faithful revere her as a saint, and feminists lay claim to her as a role model for female strength in a male-dominated society.

Joan was canonized by Pope Benedict XV on May 16, 1920. A yearly national festival is held in her honor.

HISTORY LESSON

One of history's worst examples of prosecutorial vendetta, the trial of Joan of Arc, led to one of history's greatest post-trial rehabilitations.

AMERICA'S FIRST DREAM TEAM, AND THE TRIAL OF LEVI WEEKS

America's first celebrated murder trial seems oddly familiar. It had a dream team of defense lawyers. It had an attractive young woman allegedly murdered by her lover. It had an angry public infuriated at the verdict.

Gulielma "Elma" Sands lived in a boarding house in Greenwich Village that was owned by a cousin, Catherine Ring, and her husband, Elias, who were considered "a respectable Quaker family."[28] On December 22, 1799, Elma told Catherine that she was to be secretly married that night to fellow boarder Levi Weeks. She left the house around 8:00 p.m. and was not seen again until January 2, when her body was found at the bottom of Manhattan Well, a newly dug reservoir on marshland between Greenwich Village and New York City, which at the time had not expanded beyond what is now lower Manhattan.[29] "There were marks indicating that the unfortunate girl might have received rough treatment, but the tears in the dress and the bruises and abrasions were not conclusive."[30]

Elma's body was carried the half mile to the boarding house on a shutter and trailed by a mob. The murder shocked New York, then a fast-growing metropolis of sixty thousand, generating such sympathy for the victim that "her body was laid out in the street in front of the boarding house so the hordes of mourners could pay their respects."[31]

Public opinion and the press quickly settled on Weeks as the villain. A carpenter living in modest circumstances, Weeks was the brother of a wealthy builder, Ezra, who had political connections. As the case ballooned into what we would now consider a celebrity trial, few prominent lawyers wanted to be left out of the action.[32]

Cadwallader David Colden, New York State assistant attorney general and future mayor of New York City, prosecuted the case. With the team of Henry Brockholst Livingston (soon to be a Supreme Court justice), Alexander Hamilton, and Aaron Burr (yes, those two together), Weeks had possibly the most distinguished defense counsel in US history.[33] Despite the lack of any direct evidence, the circumstantial evidence was powerful. A number of witnesses confirmed the attachment between the murdered young woman and the defendant. Catherine Ring and her sister Hope testified that Elma left the house in good spirits, presumably to meet Weeks. He returned alone at 10:00 p.m., "looking pale and agitated."[34] The following day he denied knowing anything about her whereabouts. Witnesses testified that Weeks had used his brother's sleigh that night, while others told of hearing cries of "Murder!" in a female voice near the well. Doctors testified the marks on Elma's body might have been the product of violence.[35]

The defense offered in turn several witnesses attesting to Weeks's good character. Chief Judge John Lansing upheld defense motions and objections, enabling a novel strategy by Weeks's attorneys, who attacked Elma's reputation. They implied that she was promiscuous, that she was pregnant, and that she had declared more than once an intention to kill herself.[36]

The defense's strongest point, however, came in the testimony of Ezra Weeks, who provided his brother an alibi for the entire evening in question. Levi, he said, had come to his house for a visit sometime between 5:00 p.m. and 6:00 p.m. Except for a period of fifteen or twenty minutes, he remained there, talking of the next day's business, until 10:00 p.m. The brief period he left the house, at about 8:00 p.m., was not sufficient to allow him to go to the Ring house, lure Elma to the well, murder her, throw the body into the water, and then return to his brother's home.[37] This element, much discussed during the trial, is a particularly close parallel to the O.J. Simpson murder trial, with its conflicting version of how long it would take to drive from O.J.'s mansion to Nicole Brown Simpson's townhouse and back.

Lansing's charge to the jury heavily favored the defense. The evidence, he said, was not sufficient to warrant a guilty verdict. The jury required only five minutes of deliberation to agree.[38]

The public was not amused. Two pamphlets about the case appeared the very day of the verdict, with many more to follow. Elma's murder and Weeks's acquittal remained a source of public fascination as late as 1833, when Theodore Fay used it as the basis for his novel, *Norman Leslie.* Crowds shouting "Murderer!" hounded Levi Weeks in the streets. Eventually he gave up and left town, moving to Natchez, Mississippi, where he became a prosperous architect, married, had four children, and died at the age of forty-three.[39] According to one legend, Catherine Ring pointed at the defense attorneys upon hearing the verdict and said, "If thee dies a natural death, I shall think there is no justice in heaven!"[40]

THE BURR TREASON TRIAL

The law is whatever is boldly asserted and plausibly maintained.

—Aaron Burr

Four years later, on July 11, 1804, Aaron Burr killed his co-counsel, Alexander Hamilton, in a duel. Burr was vice president at the time, having narrowly lost the election of the presidency to Thomas Jefferson in 1800. Later, Burr ran unsuccessfully for governor of New York, a loss he blamed on Hamilton as the architect of a prolonged smear campaign, mounted by way of political persuasion and low-rent pamphleteers. Burr challenged, Hamilton accepted. It was pistols at dawn in a New Jersey meadow.[41]

While dueling was legal in the Garden State, Burr was indicted for murder, though never brought to trial. His political life was at an end, however, and his career as New York's leading lawyer was in little better shape. Penniless, he cast around for a reversal of fortune.

After serving out the last months of his single term as vice president, Burr set out on a grand and eventually disastrous adventure in the West, where, unlike in the East, his popularity was still high. Exactly what he was up to remains a mystery, but it involved carving a considerable swath of land from either the western territories of the United States or the Mexican holdings of Spain. The first would be treason, the second a violation of the Neutrality Act of 1794. Left with nothing but debt, ego, and ambition, Burr had the vision to plan big. "At its core, however, the Burr conspiracy clearly was about conquest and adventure."[42] In 1805, war with Spain over western boundary disputes seemed inevitable. Following the Louisiana Purchase, Mexican troops were stationed along the Sabine River to prevent American settlers from entering Texas. Americans west of the Alleghenies believed the United States should take Texas and Florida by force. The Jefferson administration, however, sought to maintain neutrality.[43]

If Burr was conspiring to dismember the United States, his actions were an open secret. His efforts to enlist allies, gather arms and material, and recruit an army in Ohio, Kentucky, Texas, and Louisiana attracted attention, fueling rumors in newspapers and alerting British, French, and Spanish agents. Complicating Burr's grand plan, he enlisted the aid of an actual traitor, General James Wilkinson, chief of the US Army at New Orleans and governor of the recently acquired Louisiana Territory, who was secretly in the employ of Spain.[44] When Burr failed to raise significant funding, Wilkinson decided the plan had no chance of success and portrayed Burr in the worst possible light to President Jefferson.[45] Forwarding a copy of a letter he attributed to Burr, Wilkinson claimed the ex–vice president, with an army of seven thousand, was bent on seizing unnamed western territories. In fact, Burr never had more than sixty or so lightly armed men.[46]

HISTORY LESSON

Even in the beginning, US history has been filled with accomplices who "turn state's evidence" and cooperate with the authorities to save their own hides.

Jefferson issued a proclamation of conspiracy and dispatched a federal agent to arrest Burr. Meanwhile, the president declared to Congress in January 1807 that Burr was guilty of treason "beyond question." Former president John Adams, a political adversary to Jefferson, remarked, "If his guilt is as clear as the noonday sun, the first magistrate of the nation ought not to have pronounced it so before a jury had tried him."[47] Despite a society based on travel by foot, horse, and boat, news spread quickly. The press lined up along party lines. Virginians, naturally, were strongly Republican, and since the legal proceedings all took place before the United States Circuit Court at Richmond, most of the spectators and newspaper coverage took Jefferson at his word.

Eager to exploit the strong public interest, newspapers covered the trial in depth, hiring reporters to take notes during proceedings and later publishing them in book form. Standing in the way of Jefferson's judicial freight train, however, was a worthy adversary: John Marshall, Chief Justice of the Supreme Court.

At the preliminary hearing, Marshall found probable cause to commit Burr, but only for the misdemeanor of planning an attack on

Spanish territory in violation of the neutrality act. He set bail at ten thousand dollars and directed Burr to appear before the grand jury on May 22 at the US Circuit Court.[48]

Jefferson was not pleased. He was already at odds with Marshall over the *Marbury v. Madison* decision of 1803, which ruled an act of Congress unconstitutional, thereby establishing the right of judicial review and greatly enhancing the power of the Supreme Court. Although US Attorney George Hay was technically in charge of the Burr prosecution, the president maintained tight control. Jefferson took it as a personal mission to secure Burr's conviction.[49] The Republican majority in Virginia complicated jury selection. Burr combatively challenged prospective grand jurors and succeeded in removing two prominent Jefferson supporters by alleging personal bias. When the prosecution complained that such generalized questioning might impede jury selection, Marshall countered with a reminder that both the Constitution and common law guaranteed the right to an impartial jury.

Jefferson's intrusiveness in the case opened him up to allegations of a personal vendetta, and the defense made the most of them. During the argument over serving the president with a subpoena to produce papers, which was demanded by the defense, Burr's second-in-command, the brilliant Luther Martin, rose to the occasion. "It is a sacred principle, that in all such cases, the accused has the right to all the evidence which is necessary for his case."[50]

ALTHOUGH DEFENSE CLAIMS OF VENDETTA USUALLY SEEM LIKE SMOKE, SOMETIMES THERE'S A REAL FIRE

Marshall's decision was historic. "The propriety of introducing any paper into a case as testimony must depend on the character of the paper, not the character of the person who holds it."[51] Not even the president was above the law. Marshall also gave a nod to executive privilege by admitting the legitimacy of presidential discretion—there could be sound reasons why the president might need to keep certain documents secret. But the court was the final arbiter.

> **HISTORY LESSON**
>
> The best way to settle turf wars is by marking the boundaries.

Marshall also affirmed Burr's right to subpoena Jefferson to appear in person as a witness, although no such subpoena was issued. "The rights of the accused are sacred," Marshall wrote, quoting the Eighth Amendment to the Constitution, which provides "a right to a speedy and public trial and to compulsory process for obtaining witnesses in his favor."[52]

When Wilkinson finally showed up at the grand jury on June 15, his testimony was just persuasive enough to allow Hay's resubmitted treason charge to prevail. The grand jury indicted Burr for treason along with a charge of high misdemeanor. Aaron Burr pleaded not guilty, and a trial date was set for August 3, 1807.[53]

To accommodate the mass of spectators, the trial was relocated from the circuit court to the hall of the Virginia House of Delegates, itself barely adequate. Most had come to see the traitor burn, but the government did not have much of a case. After dozens of witnesses and a great deal of rhetoric, Hay could only hope for a conviction if Marshall's interpretation of the law was broad enough to encompass someone who had masterminded a plot but was not physically present to carry it out.

Marshall, in his ruling on the constitutional question, defined treason in the narrowest possible way. Burr's role as an accessory in so serious a crime was not enough. The Constitution required, Marshall said, "an overt act." The jury had no choice but to acquit.[54]

The Republican press savaged Marshall. The *Virginia Argus* complained, "The extraordinary proceedings in the case of Aaron Burr... clearly show that an independent judiciary (that is to say, a judiciary not controlled by the laws and above the fear of violating them) is a very pernicious thing."[55]

HISTORY LESSON

The independence of the federal judiciary has long been an annoying obstacle to those who pursue political agendas in the courtroom.

The court of public opinion concurred, and both Marshall and Burr were burned in effigy.[56] Still, Marshall's reputation not only recovered but also flourished—he dominated the Supreme Court for three decades, strengthening the independent judiciary in a series of decisions, while also establishing federal supremacy over the states. To escape his debts, Burr decamped for Europe, where he became a close friend of the English philosopher Jeremy Bentham and spent time in Scotland, Denmark, Sweden, Germany, and France while trying unsuccessfully to raise money for another Mexican land grab. He returned to New York under an alias to elude his creditors, eventually returning to private law practice. At the age of eighty, he died of a stroke on Staten Island in 1836, his great intellect and talent largely wasted.[57]

Those dismayed by the extreme partisanship and rancor of modern politics, law, and the media, might take solace in the knowledge that such unpleasantries are nothing new.

THE TRIALS OF OSCAR WILDE

> **I am one of those who are made for exceptions, not for laws.**
>
> —Oscar Wilde

Victorian standards of decorum took a toll on more than corset-crushed ribcages. In the 1895 prosecution of Oscar Wilde, public opinion put on trial the countercultural movements of aestheticism, decadence, and homosexuality. Already known as a wit and a poet, Wilde enjoyed a growing fame in the early 1890s with the publication of his only novel, *The Picture of Dorian Gray*, as well as the production of several of his plays. Never one to make little of his talents, he would write near the end of his life, "I awoke the imagination of my century so that it created myth and legend around me."[58] In 1891, Wilde made the acquaintance of a promising poet sixteen years his junior, Lord Alfred Douglas (now often known by Wilde's nickname for him, "Bosie").[59] This bond was more than a friendship. Bosie's father, John Sholto Douglas, the Marquess of Queensberry, was less than pleased with the implications of his son's new relationship. A sportsman—the Marquess of Queensberry Rules of Boxing are named for him—Queensberry exalted manliness and was particularly sensitive to the subject of homosexuality. Another of his sons, Francis Douglas, had been suspected of having an affair with Prime Minister Archibald Philip Primrose, the Earl of Rosebery, and had mysteriously died in a hunting accident, today believed to have been suicide.[60] A furious Queensberry excoriated Bosie in letters and threatened to cut him off financially, to which the latter heedlessly responded, "What a funny little man you are."[61] Spoiled and selfish, Bosie frequently quarreled with Wilde, too, not least for his extravagant spending. Yet the smitten Wilde could never bring himself to end the relationship. Curiously, Bosie began to leave love letters and other tokens of affection in conspicuous places. (Wilde would later reflect that rather than being an ally, his companion "scented the chance of a public scandal and flew to it.")[62] In the meantime, Queensberry made good on his threat to expose the affair to the public. After confronting Wilde at his home and following him "from restaurant to restaurant," the angry father planned to storm the stage at the opening of Wilde's *The Importance of Being Earnest* in February 1895 and proclaim to the audience the immoralities entailed in the playwright's decadent lifestyle.[63] Though this effort failed—Queensberry was barred from entering the theater—Wilde felt that, under public scrutiny, he was left with no choice but to strike back: "If I retaliated I would be ruined, and if I did not retaliate I would be ruined also."[64]

HISTORY LESSON

Stay far away from others' family feuds.

Wilde sued Queensberry for libel, and the ensuing trial was character-ized by Wilde's chronic and witty banter. Upon cross-examination by Queensberry attorney Edward Carson—an old rival from their Oxford days—about a teenage male acquaintance, Wilde answered that he had never kissed the boy in question, because, after all, "he was a peculiarly plain boy. He was, unfortunately, extremely ugly. I pitied him for it." Seizing upon the carelessness of the answer, Carson pressed, "Was that the reason why you did not kiss him?" Wilde dismissingly replied, "Oh, Mr. Carson, you are pertinently insolent."[65] Though Wilde's answers were amusing and memorable, they often contradicted one another (he even lied about his age) and negated any persuasive power of his wit and charm. Wilde admitted over the course of the interrogation that "at times one says things flippantly when one ought to speak more seri-ously." In the 1891 essay "The Decay of Lying," he scorns truth telling and consistency as dull and lacking in artistic value. At stake in this instance, however, was not a question of aesthetics but Wilde's public reputation and legal standing. When Douglas's defense team threatened to bring male prostitutes to testify, Wilde dropped the case on the advice of his counsel.

> **HISTORY LESSON**
>
> Credible is better than clever.

Wilde knew he was in trouble, but before he could muster the humility and resolve to flee the country, he was arrested and charged with twenty-five counts of gross indecencies and conspiracy to commit gross indecencies.[66] This trial had none of Wilde's famous aphorisms or sar-donic rejoinders, but his eloquence, now sincere, gave the trial its most memorable moment, the famous "love that dare not speak its name" speech. Shedding his previous arrogance, Wilde spoke of "a great affec-tion" between an older man and a younger, citing David and Jonathan from the Bible and writings by Plato, Michelangelo, and Shakespeare. It is, Wilde said, "beautiful, it is fine, it is the noblest form of affection. There is nothing unnatural about it. That it would be so, the world does not understand. The world mocks it and sometimes puts one in the pillory for it." This brave speech, discarding Wilde's customary arrogance, met with applause and earned Wilde three weeks of freedom on bail, as the jury could not reach a decision on all but one charge (of which he was acquitted).[67] Even former adversary Edward Carson believed the government should "let up" on Wilde at this point, and public opinion seemed to in part swing back in Wilde's favor.[68] The prosecution, however, only intensified its case. Some evidence suggests an angry Queensberry may have blackmailed Prime Minister Primrose, threatening to release information of his relationship with Francis if Wilde were not prosecuted and punished to the full extent of the law.[69] Wilde was acutely aware that his public image was irretrievably tarred. "People say, 'Ah! he first tried to get the kind father put into prison and failed: now he turns around and blames the innocent son for his failure. How right we were to despise him! How worthy of contempt he is!'"[70] Wilde's celebrity was of no help, and he was ultimately convicted on all but one count. The judge, sparing not a breath of mercy, concluded, "It is the worst case I have ever tried."[71] Wilde served the maximum sentence: two years of imprisonment at hard labor.

HISTORY LESSON

Tragically, it can be too late for humility.

From prison, Wilde lamented his public and personal downfall: "I thought life was going to be a brilliant comedy. . . . I found it to be a revolting and repelling tragedy." Never fully regaining his personal or creative vitality, Oscar Wilde died in 1900 at the age of forty-six, only three years after the completion of his prison term. The disgrace of this once-respected writer did not generate sympathy toward "the noblest form of affection." On the contrary, public opinion hardened against homosexuality for the next sixty years, until the gay liberation movement of the 1970s. Wilde's literary reputation has soared in the intervening decades, while Queensberry is now vilified.

> ### HISTORY LESSON
>
> Celebrity defendants sometimes play too much to the court of public opinion and forget that the bad press follows along in a court of law.

THE LINDBERGH KIDNAPPING

They think when I die, the case will die. They think it will be like a book I close. But the book, it will never close.

—Bruno Richard Hauptmann

A "trial of the century" has certain obvious requirements: intense national and international public interest, continuous media coverage and speculation, interesting questions of law or advances in forensic techniques, and an ensuing cottage industry based on the crime—books, plays, documentaries, and films—that ensure a long afterlife of interest. The Lindbergh trial had all that and more. Of the thirty-three "trials of the century," the Lindbergh case had by far the best claim for the title, at least until O. J. Simpson came along.

On March 1, 1932, Charles Lindbergh Jr., twenty months old, disappeared from his second-floor nursery at the Lindbergh house in East Amwell, New Jersey. At 10:00 p.m., the family nursemaid, Betty Gow, discovered the empty crib and went downstairs to see if the baby was with his parents. His father, the aviator-hero Charles Lindbergh, found a ransom note on the windowsill. Police arrived within thirty minutes, and close behind, a pack of reporters. On the ground below the window, police found marks of a ladder and footprints. About seventy-five feet away, they discovered a ladder in three sections.[72] Footprints leading away from the house caused police to conclude at least two people had participated in the crime.[73]

News of the kidnapping brought an overwhelming response. Not only did local and state police show up at the Lindbergh home within thirty minutes, so did Colonel Herbert Norman Schwarzkopf, superintendent of the New Jersey State Police, and William "Wild Bill" Donovan, a World War I hero who later headed the OSS (Office of Strategic Services), the World War II precursor to the CIA. President Herbert Hoover authorized the Bureau of Investigation (soon to be renamed the FBI) to work the case, even though at that time kidnapping was not a federal crime.[74]

In the weeks that followed, additional ransom notes arrived by mail, demanding first fifty thousand dollars, and then, after news of police involvement, one hundred thousand dollars. The state of New Jersey offered a twenty-five-thousand-dollar reward, with the Lindberghs adding another fifty thousand dollars—a stupendous sum in the darkest days of the Depression.[75] An intense, if haphazard, investigation followed. By today's standard, the crime scene was badly compromised, with not only Lindbergh but also police handling the initial ransom note, making it useless for fingerprinting purposes. Oddly, no fingerprints were found in the nursery—not even those of Lindbergh, his wife, or the nursemaid.[76] The ladder, however, had four hundred partial fingerprints, but they proved of little value. Edmund de Long, a reporter for the *New York Sun*, later said that everyone at the scene, including himself, handled the ladder.[77]

Lindbergh took command of the investigation to an astonishing degree, even giving police the slip to go off on his own to pursue leads and meet with shady characters who claimed to have important information.[78]

Organized crime fell under suspicion, a theory favored by Lindbergh and Schwarzkopf, on the assumption that mobsters were the only ones nervy enough to commit such a crime.[79] This was not a ridiculous idea—kidnapping became such a growth industry in the 1930s that Lloyds of London offered ransom insurance, and some wealthy Americans, including Bing Crosby, purchased policies.[80]

Al Capone, sitting in prison on a tax evasion conviction, promised ten thousand dollars for information leading to the child's return and requested release so he could investigate. Authorities declined both offers.[81] Mickey Rosner, a "small-time bootlegger," swindler, and police informant, offered his services as a go-between with organized crime, which Lindbergh accepted enthusiastically on the recommendation of Schwarzkopf.[82]

Rosner brought in two speakeasy owners, Salvatore "Salvy" Spitale and Irving Bitz, who were supposed to have underworld connections. In a sense, they did—both were working for the *New York Daily News*.[83]

HISTORY LESSON

Some crimes are so notorious they would give even mobsters a bad name.

Weeks of intrigue followed, involving additional ransom notes (thirteen in all), protracted negotiations, and shadowy go-betweens.[84] A former Bureau of Investigation agent and fraudster named Gaston Means almost succeeded in conning one of Anne Lindbergh's wealthy friends out of one hundred thousand dollars by claiming to be in contact with the kidnappers.[85]

A retired Bronx school principal, John Condon, volunteered as a messenger and proved satisfactory to both Lindbergh and "the kidnappers." Condon met several times with a man who at one point produced a baby's sleeping suit as proof he had the child. Lindbergh confirmed it as his son's. Eventually Condon delivered a fifty-thousand-dollar ransom to a man with a German accent who called himself "John." The final meeting came in a Bronx park. Taking the money, "John" handed Condon a note saying the baby could be found at Martha's Vineyard aboard a boat named *Nellie*. No such boat could be found.[86] Seventy-two days after the disappearance of Charles Jr., a truck driver discovered the corpse of a baby, covered in leaves and insects,[87] about two miles from the Lindbergh home. Lindbergh and Betty Gow, the nursemaid, identified the badly decomposed body as Charles Jr.[88] The head was crushed and some limbs were missing—apparently eaten away by animals.[89] On the orders of Lindbergh, the remains were cremated a day after they were identified.[90]

Within twenty-four hours, country music singer Bob Ferguson had released two new songs,[91] "Charles Lindbergh Jr." and "There's a New Star up in Heaven."[92] The site where the baby's body had been found became a roadside shrine. Crowds gathered with cameras and scoured the ground for anything that could be carried away. Enterprising vendors sold hot dogs, peanuts, and popcorn. In response to the tragedy, Congress passed the Federal Kidnapping Act of 1932 (the Lindbergh Law), making kidnapping a federal crime, although primary jurisdiction for the case remained with the New Jersey State Police.

Meanwhile, as the kidnapping investigation became a homicide case, the domestic staff came under suspicion. Lindbergh disliked and distrusted J. Edgar Hoover and intervened in an interrogation of Betty Gow by a bureau agent.[93] Violet Sharp, a household servant from Britain, gave contradictory statements to police as to her whereabouts on the night of the baby's disappearance. Subjected to three unfriendly interrogations by police, she forestalled a fourth by swallowing a silver-polishing compound containing cyanide, which killed her. She was posthumously cleared of involvement in the kidnapping.[94] With scant evidence and no suspects, police devoted most of their attention to tracing the ransom payments. Although the bills were not marked, their serial numbers had been taken down. New York City Detective James J. Finn and Federal Agent Thomas Sisk tracked bills appearing randomly throughout the city. By 1934, they had followed the trail to the Bronx home of Bruno Richard Hauptmann, a German immigrant.

Hauptmann turned out to be a carpenter with a heavy accent who had a criminal record in his native Germany. He was so secretive that his wife did not know his first name was Bruno until he was arrested. When police searched his home, they found fourteen thousand six hundred dollars of the ransom money hidden in a tin can in his garage, which Hauptmann claimed was left there by a friend who had returned to Germany. Experts would testify that Hauptmann's handwriting was identical to that of the ransom notes and that parts of the ladder matched wooden floorboards in his attic.[95]

Before, during, and after the trial, both prosecution and defense spun an intense public-relations campaign, but largely the press drove the course of the trial. The Hearst newspapers hired Edward ("the Bull of Brooklyn") Reilly to defend Hauptmann. Reilly had a reputation for being able to mesmerize a jury, but he was not only well past his prime but also alcoholic and syphilitic.[96] Paid up front, his performance was arrogant, theatrical, and hollow.[97]

The trial was held in Flemington, New Jersey, then a rural village of three thousand. On January 3, 1935, the opening day of proceedings, its population swelled to sixty-five thousand, including celebrity reporters, such as Damon Runyon, Walter Winchell, Lowell Thomas, Edna Ferber, Dorothy Kilgallen, and seven hundred lesser-known newshounds. The century-old courthouse had a capacity of two hundred sixty, but twice that many crammed in every day, some climbing through the windows. For weeks, news organizations had been installing the most up-to-date communications equipment, with more than one hundred Western Union telegraph wires strung in the courthouse attic.[98] The atmosphere in the streets was a cross between the World's Fair and the Oberammergau Passion Play. Vendors sold everything: food, "locks" of baby Lindy's hair, miniature ladders, and "autographed" pictures of Lindbergh. The Union Hotel had only fifty rooms. The overflow of reporters rented rooms in private homes.[99]

Even the press questioned whether a fair trial was possible, given the circus atmosphere, the public affection for Lindbergh, and the relentless news coverage.[100] During jury selection, Reilly demanded to know if the very first candidate had read Walter Winchell's columns declaring Hauptmann's guilt.[101] Several prospective jurors were excused after admitting a Winchell-inspired bias. Once a jury was seated, Judge Thomas Trenchard ordered its members not to read newspapers, listen to the radio, or speak to anyone about the case. Jury sequestration was rare in 1932, but the intense media scrutiny left Trenchard no choice. He sequestered jurors in the Union Hotel across the street. Yet twice each day the jury crossed the street through mobs calling for Hauptmann's execution while newsboys hawked the latest headlines. Jurors dined in the hotel dining room with only a thin curtain separating them from civilians and reporters, and they could overhear conversations and radios as well as the clamor outside.[102]

Described by the press as "patient, grandfatherly, wise," Trenchard had never been reversed on appeal in a murder case.[103] He did his best to run an orderly courtroom, but it was impossible. When he wasn't in his library, reporters used it for games of craps. And although he had banned them from the courtroom, a movie camera pointing at the witness chair was secretly installed under a box with a microphone behind the jury.[104] Only when the judge learned of the films—which were being shown throughout the world—was there a crackdown. Trenchard also prohibited photography, but reporters smuggled cameras into the courtroom in their mufflers. These excesses resulted in the passage of a new rule in the Canons of Judicial Ethics by the American Bar Association in 1937. Cameras were barred from courtrooms until the 1970s.[105]

HISTORY LESSON

Cases involving celebrities take on a life of their own—sometimes it's wildlife.

Under these circumstances, Hauptmann had no chance. New Jersey Attorney General David Wilentz, trying his first criminal case, knew this was the trial for which he would be remembered. At thirty-eight, Wilentz was a sharp dresser with a sharp courtroom manner. During an eloquent five-hour summation, he declared, "We got the man and we have got his handwriting, and he has got the money."[106]

Wilentz was not above torturing the law to get the result he wanted. Some evidence suggested that the Lindbergh baby was not murdered but had died in a fall when the ladder broke under the weight of the kidnapper. At the time, kidnapping was not a felony in New Jersey, which meant accidental death in the commission of a kidnapping was not a capital offense. To get around this inconvenient detail, Hauptmann was charged with burglary in the theft of the child's pajamas, with accidental death resulting from *that* crime.[107]

In addition to the evidence against him, Hauptmann's cold demeanor made him an unsympathetic figure. The jury disliked him. The audience disliked him. The judge disliked him. His own lawyer disliked him. The enormous public pressure to bring someone to account for the kidnapping and murder of Charles Jr. amounted to a nationwide bloodlust. After deliberating for eleven hours, the jury returned a guilty verdict. Even Lindbergh, listening to the verdict on the radio and hearing the howls outside in the street, commented, "That was a lynching crowd."[108]

Hauptmann denied guilt right up to the day of his electrocution on April 3, 1936. Offered life in prison and seventy-five thousand dollars for his wife and child in exchange for a confession, he refused. Some people even then were troubled by the investigation and trial. New Jersey Governor Harold G. Hoffman forfeited his political career by granting a thirty-day stay of execution in 1935 and urging the state court of errors and appeals to reexamine the case. The court declined amid public calls for Hoffman's impeachment.[109] As with the John F. Kennedy assassination, an industry of conspiracy theories has grown up around the Lindbergh kidnapping. Books, movies, articles, and Web sites emerge like toadstools with various notions about what really happened. The most bizarre is that Lindbergh himself killed his son, either accidentally or in a fit of rage, then directed the investigation toward an innocent scapegoat.

Not even the clamor of the O. J. Simpson murder trial has eclipsed public interest in the Lindbergh kidnapping case. Fueled by fact, rumor, and endless speculation, the fascination will continue as long as the public imagination persists in being carried down that ladder one cold spring evening in March.

CHAPTER 3

THE O. J. REVOLUTION

THE WHITE BRONCO

People love a good car chase. Or at least television news producers think we do. That's why we're treated to endless coverage of the police pursuing one felon or another on the streets—or, more likely, highways—of some major city, most often Los Angeles or Miami. In fact, Bob Tur, the "dean of LA's media helicopter journalists," pioneered the form. By June 17, 1994, he had already broadcast 128 freeway pursuits for KCBS. But no one had ever seen anything like what unfolded in the late afternoon and early evening hours of that day when a white Ford Bronco containing O. J. Simpson and his friend Al Cowlings led a phalanx of twenty-five police cars on a bizarre low-speed chase on the freeways of Southern California.[1]

Simpson, who was wanted for the murders of his ex-wife, Nicole Brown Simpson, and her friend, Ronald Goldman, was either trying to escape justice or suicidal, or both; during the chase, he was holding a gun to his head, as Cowlings told police by cell phone. At first, Tur had exclusive footage of the Bronco's progress, but soon his helicopter was joined by six others. When the highway passed through black neighborhoods, people lined the overpasses, cheering, "Go, O. J.!" By the time the pursuit ended safely back in the driveway of Simpson's Brentwood mansion, where the former NFL great surrendered meekly to police, some 95 million Americans had watched all or part of the chase. Networks carried live coverage. NBC even broke into its telecast of Game Five of the NBA Finals.[2] It was, in some ways, a fitting media beginning of what became known as "the trial of the century."

From that day forward, until a jury declared Simpson not guilty on October 3, 1995, America and the world could not get enough of the O. J. Simpson murder trial. After Judge Lance Ito allowed television cameras into his courtroom, the proceedings became a kind of daily soap opera, visible anywhere a television was on—in homes, airports, and health clubs. Reportedly, the first question Russian President Boris Yeltsin asked US President Bill Clinton when he arrived for a summit was, "Do you think O. J. did it?"[3] The public became so transfixed by O. J.'s courtroom drama, according to one estimate, that US industry lost a reported $25 billion in productivity as employees set work aside to follow the trial.[4]

TRIALS OF THE CENTURY

Of course, this was not the first "trial of the century." The public had been fascinated by the Harry K. Thaw murder trial of 1906, the Scopes "Monkey Trial" of 1925, the Lindbergh kidnapping trial of 1935, the Nuremberg Nazi trials of 1945–46, and the Manson Family murder trials of 1970–71—and many others over the course of the twentieth century. The media provided massive coverage for them all, limited only by the technology of the day. By some estimates, more reporters attended the trial of Lindbergh baby-napper Richard Hauptmann than covered World War II. In a bit of hyperbole that sounds oddly contemporary, H. L. Mencken called it "the greatest story since the Resurrection."[5] But for spectacle, for sheer numbers of eyeballs, the O. J. Simpson trial defined a new order of magnitude. Two thousand reporters covered the proceedings, although only a handful actually sat in the courtroom. Eighty miles of cable snaked out of the Criminal Courts Building in downtown Los Angeles where the trial took place. The *Los Angeles Times* alone published more than one thousand articles on the case. An average of 91 million viewers tuned in every day. When the verdict was read, some 142 million watched on television or listened on the radio.[6]

An entire book could be devoted to the Simpson murder trial, seeking to explain how a defendant with so much physical evidence against him could have won acquittal, and indeed, more than eighty books have. The racial explanation is the easiest—the jury, with nine blacks (eight of them women) among its twelve members—simply voted against the evidence in a textbook example of jury nullification. Blacks in Los Angeles had endured decades of conflict with the LA Police Department. Some saw it as an institutionally racist organization that, due to the city's unusual structure, operated independently of city hall oversight.[7] And so, in this view, the verdict was a "message" to the police department and to white America in general. Another popular narrative blames the prosecution, led by Marcia Clark and Christopher Darden, for being outgunned, outmaneuvered, and outclassed. And, of course, the flawed investigation by the LAPD, with its many procedural errors, not to mention alleged police perjury on the stand, left the prosecution's case vulnerable to attack by the defense, which succeeded in selling reasonable doubt to a friendly jury.

Judge Lance Ito also has come in for his share of criticism. Supposedly entranced by the television camera, he gave a televised interview—in the middle of the trial—about his Japanese immigrant parents, who were interned by the US government in World War II.[8] He greeted CNN star Larry King, among other celebrities, in his chambers. He invited lawyers from both sides to his chambers to share O.J. jokes and play videotapes of the running "Dancing Ito" bit from *The Tonight Show*, and he generally contributed to an injection of show biz that was badly misplaced in a double homicide trial.[9] He sent the jury on a pointless daytime visit to the crime scene—the murders occurred at night—and to the Rockingham estate that enabled O.J.'s house to be staged to make it more Afro-centric, replacing photos of O.J. and his white golfing buddies with family pictures; and a large nude photograph of Simpson's girlfriend, white model Paula Barbieri, with a copy of a famous Norman Rockwell painting depicting a black girl being escorted to a southern school by US Marshals.[10] To alleviate the sequestered jury's tedium, Judge Ito sent them on excursions, including one to Catalina Island. More damaging, many felt he lost control of the courtroom, allowed the defense to effectively take control, and made

loose and questionable rulings. Married to a high-ranking police official, he may have felt compelled to avoid any sign of favoritism to the
prosecution, which may have favored the defense by default. Vincent
Bugliosi, famous as the prosecutor in the Manson trials, wrote in his
scathing book *Outrage: The Five Reasons Why O. J. Simpson Got Away with
Murder* that Judge Ito made several "terrible" rulings, including the
decision to admit the Mark Fuhrman "N-word tapes."[11]

Although none of these narratives is wholly accurate, they do
describe and explain factors that played a role in the acquittal of O.J.
Simpson. What they neglect is the battle for the court of public opinion,
where the case may have been won and lost before the first witness took
the stand. From almost the beginning, both sides played the media for
all they were worth. The defense, though, proved more adept at getting
its message across to the public—or at least the public it was targeting
in this case: potential jurors from the African American community of
Los Angeles. If we look back with this in mind, the not guilty verdict
starts to look almost like a foregone conclusion.

BRUTAL MURDERS

The case began on the night of June 12, 1994, a Sunday when neighbors, responding to a large, barking dog, found Nicole Brown Simpson's
body on the walkway near the front door of her Brentwood condo-
minium. Nearby lay the body of Ronald Goldman, a twenty-five-year-
old aspiring actor and friend of Nicole who worked at a posh LA
restaurant, Mezzaluna. It was about midnight; the first police car
arrived at 12:15 a.m. Both victims had been stabbed repeatedly,
Goldman more than thirty times. Nicole's throat had been cut, nearly
severing her head from her body. She lay in a large pool of blood. A
single set of bloody shoe prints led down the walkway to the back gate
of the property. Next to Goldman, police found a bloody white envelope containing glasses belonging to Nicole's mother, which she had left
at the restaurant earlier in the evening. Goldman had come to the house
to return them, suggesting he was simply in the wrong place at the
wrong time, which also identified Nicole as the intended victim. Police

also found a single bloody leather glove, a beeper, a set of keys, and a dark knit stocking cap. Several of these yielded significant blood and hair evidence. Inside, the house was undisturbed. Nicole's children by O. J., Sydney (eight years old) and Justin (five years old), lay asleep in their upstairs bedrooms.[12]

Soon the scene swarmed with police, detectives, and forensic investigators. Photos were taken, video shot, and blood samples collected. Bloody spots were noted on the rear gate, and a pattern of blood drops alongside the bloody shoe prints suggested the killer had been cut in the commission of the murders. The seventeenth law enforcement officer who logged in at the crime scene was Mark Fuhrman. Detective Fuhrman would later figure prominently in the defense's argument that O. J. had been framed by racist police. His late arrival has implied to some, though—including Jeffrey Toobin in his book, *The Run of His Life: The People v. O. J. Simpson*—that Fuhrman could not have picked up a second glove to later plant at O. J.'s house. Too many trained eyes had already surveyed the area.[13]

At 5:00 a.m., four detectives, including Fuhrman, were dispatched to Simpson's mansion at 360 Rockingham Avenue, about two miles away in a richer portion of Brentwood. As the ex-husband, Simpson was, of course, inevitably a potential suspect. But police had as yet no evidence linking him to the crime. At this point, the detectives' mission was only to convey the news of Nicole's murder to Simpson in person. The LAPD was keenly aware of the sensitivities involved when celebrities or their families are involved in an investigation, and top department officials wanted to make sure Simpson did not learn of the crime from the news media. In fact, the police would later come under criticism for treating Simpson with too much deference in the early days of the investigation and even while he was in jail during the trial.[14]

Police, some at least, were not unfamiliar with the Rockingham estate. They had responded to domestic-dispute calls at least eight times during the Simpsons' seven-year marriage.

O. J. AND NICOLE

O. J. Simpson met Nicole Brown in 1977, when he was a fading NFL superstar of thirty-two and she was an eighteen-year-old waitress who was two months out of high school. They started dating even though Simpson was still married to his first wife, Marguerite. Raised in Oakland, California, Simpson had been an All-American football player at USC, winning the Heisman Trophy his senior year. Drafted by the Buffalo Bills, he enjoyed a hall-of-fame career in the NFL, setting a longstanding record in 1973, when he ran for 2,003 yards—the first running back to break the two-thousand-yard barrier. Every inch the superstar, Simpson was handsome and personable, cultivating a nice-guy image that netted him a high-profile series of commercials for Hertz, the leading rental-car company, and a minor acting career in television and movies. For a while, his football achievements and telegenic charisma made him an important public figure, a black man whose easygoing style did not make white people uneasy. In fact, upon achieving superstardom, Simpson separated himself from the black community. Rockingham was a rich white neighborhood, and most of his friends, like lawyer-businessman Robert Kardashian, were white. In 1968, the year he won the Heisman Trophy, he told a *New York Times* interviewer, "I'm not black, I'm O. J."[15]

After retiring from the NFL in 1979, Simpson became a respected announcer on *Monday Night Football* and settled into life as a Hollywood B-list celebrity. He continued to take minor acting roles, most notably in the popular *The Naked Gun* series of comedies. His most steady job, which earned him half a million dollars a year, was as a roving goodwill spokesman for Hertz. Under the Hertz banners, he played in a lot of charity and celebrity golf tournaments. Simpson's nice-guy public image was not altogether fake. He was known to tirelessly sign autographs for fans, and he gave Christmas presents to production workers at NBC Sports.[16] People who met Simpson liked him.

Nicole Brown, born in Frankfurt, Germany, moved as a child to Southern California with her family. She became an archetypal California girl—blonde, athletic, attractive, and a homecoming princess in high school. After she met Simpson, who transported her to a version of the pampered celebrity life, she never worked again.[17] The couple married in 1985, Nicole pregnant with their first child. The relationship was tumultuous, though, with fights and reconciliations and accusations of spousal abuse from almost the beginning. In 1985, an officer responded to a domestic-violence incident to find O. J. and Nicole in the driveway by a Mercedes with a shattered windshield. O. J. paced and screamed; Nicole cried. O. J., it turned out, had smashed the car window with a baseball bat. Nicole declined to file a report. The officer, amazingly enough, given later developments, was Mark Fuhrman.[18]

In one call to 911, Nicole told a dispatcher, "He's going to beat the shit out of me." During another, yelling could be heard, accompanied by sounds of slapping. In all but one instance, police came and left without arresting Simpson. He was a celebrity, after all. O. J. was liked, and some would say even pampered, by the LAPD. And O. J. always liked cops; he cultivated a friendly relationship with local police over the years, inviting officers to drop by and use the pool, attending police Christmas parties, and autographing footballs for officers. "You come out, and you talk to him, but you never do anything to him," Nicole told a 911 dispatcher on January 1, 1989. This time, when police arrived, they found Nicole—her face bloody and swollen, a bruise in the shape of a handprint visible at her neck—screaming, "He's going to kill me! He's going to kill me!" Simpson denied beating his wife, claiming he'd only pushed her out of bed. For once, Nicole signed a police complaint and O. J. was arrested. By the following day, however, she told authorities she did not want to prosecute her husband. Prosecutors brought the case to trial anyway. Simpson pled no contest and was sentenced to twenty-four months of probation, fines totaling four hundred seventy dollars, and one hundred twenty hours of community service—which he discharged by organizing a charity golf tournament.[19]

The marriage rollercoaster ground to a halt in 1992, when O. J. and Nicole finally filed for divorce. Nicole received a one-time payment of $433,750, plus ten thousand dollars a month in child support, and a rental condominium in San Francisco worth half a million dollars. She bought the condo at 875 Bundy Drive in Brentwood, where she lived with her children. Although the couple attempted reconciliation several times, O. J. had girlfriends. Meanwhile, Nicole seemed intent on making up for lost time on the LA party and dating scene, seeing, among others, O. J.'s friend and football rival, Marcus Allen. Nicole was a self-described party animal. Despite this and the years of spousal abuse, Nicole usually was the one seeking reconciliation. As late as April 1993, she sent an imploring letter to O. J., along with videos of their marriage ceremony and the births of their children.[20] Five days before her death, however, Nicole called the Sojourn Counseling Center, a Santa Monica shelter for battered women, to complain O. J. was "stalking her."[21] At the time she was murdered, Nicole Brown Simpson was thirty-five years old.

THE FATAL NIGHT

O. J. and Nicole, divorced for two years at the time of the murders, were last seen earlier in the evening, when they attended a dance recital at Sydney's middle school. They had appeared distant. O. J. chatted with Nicole's father and sister before going home. Nicole's party of nine proceeded to dinner at Mezzaluna, where her mother left behind a pair of glasses. Afterward, Nicole returned to Bundy Drive and put her children to bed. She called her friend Ronald Goldman, who was working that night, and asked him to bring the glasses to her. He agreed.[22]

Meanwhile, O. J. drove with Brian "Kato" Kaelin, who lived in a small guesthouse on his estate, to the drive-through at McDonald's and returned home at 9:45 p.m. They ate separately. At 9:50 p.m., Goldman left Mezzaluna to take the lost glasses to Nicole. Neighbors began to hear a dog barking on Bundy Drive at 10:15 p.m.[23] Allen Park, a limo driver, arrived at the Rockingham estate to drive Simpson to the airport for a red-eye flight to Chicago, where O. J. was to appear on behalf of Hertz the following day. Park rang the doorbell, but no one answered. Inside the guest house, Kaelin was on the phone with his girlfriend at 10:40 p.m., when he heard three loud bumping sounds—so loud he thought it might be an earthquake. At about 10:56 p.m., Park observed a black man walking up the driveway. At 11:01, lights come on inside the house, and Simpson came out to greet Park, saying he had been in the shower. At 11:15, Kaelin helped load Simpson's bags in the car, and O. J. left for the airport.[24]

Much would be made, by prosecution and defense alike, over this timeline and whether Simpson could have driven the two miles to Bundy Drive, murdered Nicole and Goldman, and made it back to Rockingham Avenue—all between 9:40 p.m., when he was last seen by Kaelin, and 11:01 p.m., when he opened the door for Park.

Mark Fuhrman, Philip Vannatter, and two other detectives arrived at Simpson's estate at 5:30 a.m. on Monday. A white Ford Bronco was parked, "slightly askew" on the street outside.[25] Lights were on inside the house, but the buzzer went unanswered. So did the telephone. Fuhrman, inspecting the Bronco, found what might be a bloodstain on the car door. Deciding someone might be hurt inside the house, Vannatter sent the younger Fuhrman over the wall to open the gate.[26] This is the police story, at any rate, but it later came under widespread derision as what many called a case of "police perjury" when Detective Philip Vannatter used it in his testimony. The defense later claimed it was a flimsy excuse to gain access to Simpson's home without the benefit of a search warrant.

As crime novelist Scott Turow, a prosecutor himself, scoffed, "If veteran police detectives did not arrive at the gate of Simpson's house thinking he might have committed these murders, they should be fired."[27]

The four detectives awakened Kaelin and Arnelle Simpson, O. J.'s daughter from his first marriage, who lived in another guesthouse. She told the police that O. J. was in Chicago, and she opened the main house. Inside, Detective Ron Phillips phoned Simpson's hotel and informed him of Nicole's death, not mentioning she had been murdered. Simpson volunteered to fly back to Los Angeles at once, but police took note that he did not ask how Nicole had died.

Meanwhile, Fuhrman, inspecting a narrow passage outside the guesthouse where Kaelin heard "bumps," discovered a bloody leather glove that seemed to be a match to the one at the murder scene. By noon, the police obtained a search warrant for Simpson's estate. Inside the house, they found blood in the foyer and master bedroom (two months later, they would find a sock with a bloodstain).[28] Blood was also found in the driveway and inside the Bronco. Simpson, arriving during the search, found his estate cordoned off by crime-scene tape, the grounds and house swarming with cops and criminalist technicians, and the streets crowded with reporters and television news crews. Police briefly handcuffed Simpson, a sight witnessed nationwide by television viewers.[29] He agreed to go to a police station and submitted to questioning—about, among other things, a fresh cut on his left hand. He claimed he could not remember how he cut himself but said he reopened the wound when he smashed a glass upon receiving word of Nicole's death. Amazingly, Simpson waived his rights to have counsel present, and his lawyer, Howard Weitzman, left him alone with police interrogators. Even more remarkable, the police treated Simpson gingerly, asking him no hard questions, concluding the interview after only thirty minutes, and then letting him go.[30] He attended Nicole's funeral two days later, July 16. On the advice of friends, he hired celebrity lawyer Robert Shapiro to replace Weitzman.

Simpson was arrested only after the infamous low-speed chase, by which time authorities believed they had built an airtight case of physical evidence against him. After all, they essentially had a trail of blood from the scene of the crime at Nicole's condo right into O.J.'s house. Simpson's blood was found at the crime scene, while the victims' blood was found in his car and home.[31]

NIGHTMARE CRIMES AND DREAM-TEAM DEFENSE LAWYERS

While police searched for the absent O.J., Robert Shapiro held a press conference at which Kardashian read a handwritten note that Simpson had left behind—universally construed at the time as a suicide note. It included the words: "Don't feel sorry for me. I've had a good life, made great friends. Please think of the real O.J. and not this lost person."[32] At the conclusion of the Bronco chase, police found eight thousand seven hundred fifty dollars on Cowlings, and a plastic bag containing Simpson's passport, a fake goatee and mustache, and a loaded .357 Magnum, all of which could be taken as evidence of an attempt to avoid arrest and flee the country. Before news helicopters focused on the Bronco, it was headed in a southerly direction, which many have construed as an intention to cross the border into Mexico.[33] In what Bugliosi listed as among the many mistakes made by the prosecution, neither the letter nor the escape kit, though seemingly incriminating, were presented as evidence by the prosecution.[34]

During the trial that followed, the flamboyant and effective Johnnie Cochran appeared to be the leader of the Simpson defense team—and he certainly was by the end of the trial. But Shapiro was reportedly the real architect of the racial strategy that won the case.[35] Never shy about media exposure, Shapiro's celebrity clients included Darryl Strawberry, Jose Canseco, Robert Evans, and Vince Coleman. Shapiro had successfully defended clients in court, but the main reason his high-profile defendants almost never went to jail was in his skill as a master negotiator of plea deals. He recognized that it would take a village to raise a successful defense of O. J. and quickly set about assembling a team of what would eventually be eleven lawyers, including his old friend F. Lee Bailey, DNA expert Barry Scheck, esteemed constitutional scholar Alan M. Dershowitz, and, of course, Cochran. And, as Toobin notes, "Johnnie Cochran had perfected the art of winning jury trials in downtown Los Angeles."[36]

Over time, Shapiro reluctantly ceded leadership of the defense team to Cochran. Dershowitz, for one, gives Shapiro great credit for establishing the pretrial strategy by hiring the best technical experts in the country—forensic scientist Dr. Henry Lee proved particularly effective to the jury—thereby gaining enough defense ammunition so the jury could witness a crossfire between the two sides rather than just a prosecution firing squad armed with physical evidence.[37]

"Almost from the day of Simpson's arrest," writes Toobin, his lawyers sought to portray him as "the victim of a wide-ranging conspiracy of racist law enforcement officials who had fabricated and planted evidence in order to frame him for a crime he did not commit." This "fictional version was both elegant and dramatic," and it was developed and in motion well before Cochran joined the defense team.[38]

From the very beginning, Shapiro seemed to have had no illusions about Simpson's guilt. In an informal strategy session with other successful, if less famous, LA lawyers, a medical examiner observed that the autopsy results showed evidence of possibly more than one assailant. Shapiro stunned the room when he said, "So, that means O. J. and who else did it?"[39] But he saw at once that race could offset the mountain of evidence against Simpson. The linchpin of this defense would be Mark Fuhrman, the detective who had discovered the second bloody glove at Simpson's estate.

Shapiro scored a resounding early public-relations victory when Toobin, working on a story for the *New Yorker*, showed up at his office unannounced one day. Acting on a casual remark from Dershowitz,[40] Toobin had looked up Fuhrman's records in the basement of the LA County courthouse. The journalist—a former prosecutor himself—was looking for any judgments that might have been rendered against Fuhrman for violating the civil rights of suspects. The city of Los Angeles paid out millions in judgments against the LAPD each year. In the decade preceding the Simpson trial, Cochran's firm alone won more than $40 million in such cases. Instead of court judgments, Toobin found the file of Fuhrman's 1983 suit against the city in which the detective had sought an early retirement and disability pension. It was a remarkable document. The stress of working in minority neighborhoods, Fuhrman argued, had made him a "dangerously unbalanced man"—had turned him, in effect, into a racist. Citing his record as a competent officer, the city countered successfully that Fuhrman was exaggerating his symptoms of psychopathology. Fuhrman lost and stayed on the job.[41]

Toobin's many skills included news reporting. He immediately went to Shapiro's office unannounced and talked his way into an interview. Shapiro not only knew about the Fuhrman file, but he told Toobin there was "worse" to come. "This is a guy who used to wake up every day and say to his ex-wife, 'I'm going to kill some niggers this morning.'"[42] Toobin saw at once the brilliance of Shapiro's strategy. He wrote a *New Yorker* story reporting that Simpson's defense planned to argue their client had been framed by an elaborate police conspiracy centered on Fuhrman and the "planted" bloody glove. This story, and a similar one by Mark Miller in *Newsweek*, thrust the issue of race into the center of public perception of the Simpson case.

Shapiro was so pleased by these developments that he phoned F. Lee Bailey and said, "It's over, I won the case."[43]

THE POLICE FIRE BACK

To be sure, prosecutors and police attempted to influence public perception of the case, too, partly through leaks to the press, partly through press conferences. The Los Angeles City Attorney's Office (a separate entity from the DA's office) released the recording of Nicole's 1989 call to 911 and other documents relating to Simpson's history of domestic violence. The *Los Angeles Times* noted, "Even though the press had been seeking access to the tapes, the timing of the material's release—just in time for Wednesday's early evening newscasts—reeked of advance planning by the prosecution."[44] Other early leaks included the news that police had found a bloody ski mask in Simpson's house (wrong); that police had found a "sharpened trenching tool" they believed to be the murder weapon (it wasn't); that potentially damaging evidence had been found in Simpson's golf bag (again, no); and that a man resembling Simpson had been seen in a wooded area near the O'Hare Plaza Hotel in Chicago (presumably disposing of the weapon and bloody clothing).[45] Prior to the Bronco chase, police leaked that Simpson was about to be arrested on charges of double murder.

"There was a leak nearly every single day," Cochran told *Jet Magazine.* "It was very calculated. They didn't come from the top brass, but they were calculated and orchestrated. It was done to prejudice the case."[46] Complaining that the torrent of leaked information would make it difficult for Simpson to receive a fair trial, Cochran asked, "Whatever happened to waiting for evidence to come out? People should wait until both sides make their presentations in court."[47]

Neither side was waiting for trial. Because both sides knew, as Dershowitz observes in his book about the case, "The way the media covers cases influences the way the public thinks about them."[48] Even though the attorney's job is to persuade judges and juries, "not the public or the pundits," public relations is still a critical consideration—jurors, after all, come from that same public. Prosecution and defense jostled for control of the message. The defense soundly won this contest at almost every turn. Dershowitz writes, "The outcome of the Simpson case was largely determined *outside* the courtroom in the first few weeks following the murders." True, the defense could have fumbled victory away by a poor performance in court. "But without the efforts orchestrated by Robert Shapiro well before the actual trial began, it is unlikely that any trial team could have won the Simpson case."[49]

THE DA JOINS THE MEDIA FRAY

Gil Garcetti, the district attorney, not only held press conferences but also appeared on *Nightline, Good Morning America, Today,* the *NBC Nightly News,* and the *CBS Evening News.* In an interview on *This Week with David Brinkley,* Garcetti even predicted that Simpson, like the Menendez brothers, would eventually admit to committing the crimes but still claim he was not responsible.[50] If, what to me is considered likely, Garcetti's ill-considered public statements alienated black Angelenos, then he played into the hands of the defense and its racial strategy. Oddly, Garcetti's prophecy came true, although not as part of Simpson's defense, as the DA speculated. A decade later, in the bizarre book called *If I Did It,* O.J. would present a hypothetical version of the crime that many would view as his confession.[51] By then, of course, he could not be arrested for the murders of Nicole Brown Simpson and Ronald Goldman, due to double jeopardy.

Despite all the defense commotion, old-school prosecutors might decline to launch a media counteroffensive. After all, the DA represents the people of California, and, by the way, every defendant is entitled to a presumption of innocence. Any such traditions, though, melted away under the glare of swarming cameras.

According to some observers, public-relations considerations guided many of Garcetti's other actions, including his decision to allow Marcia Clark to head up the prosecution team.[52] In the aftermath of the trial, some criticized Clark, and her selection became a source of controversy. Some jurors would later express an intense dislike of Clark, which may have contributed to the outcome of the trial. After a major defeat, losing lawyers are often transformed into lesser lawyers, as if portions of their brain or experience suddenly disappeared. At the beginning, however, Marcia Clark seemed a solid choice, if not the best possible one. At forty, she was a proven prosecutor "highly qualified" for the job, with a sterling record of nineteen homicide convictions. She was viewed as tenacious, aggressive, well-prepared, professional, and an expert at DNA evidence and violence against women.[53] She had faced off against celebrity attorneys, including Shapiro, and she won a conviction of stalker Robert John Bardo in the shooting death of television actress Rebecca Schaeffer, a case that received national attention.

Even if there were a few prosecutors with more experience than Clark in high-stakes cases, the selection of the prosecutor elicited a mild critique compared to all the heat over the selection of the courthouse. Almost every commentator viewed Garcetti's decision to try the case in downtown Los Angeles, rather than in Santa Monica, as the "crucial miscalculation" that most contributed to Simpson's acquittal.[54] In Santa Monica, the jurisdiction where the murders took place, the jury pool would have consisted primarily of whites, who presumably would have been less receptive to the race-based defense reportedly conceived by Shapiro and perfected by Cochran. Indeed, the wrongful death suit brought by the Goldman and Brown families was tried in Santa Monica, resulting in a $33.5-million judgment against Simpson in 1997. Many observers assumed Garcetti wanted to avoid convicting Simpson before a jury that did not include a majority of minority members. Just two years before, riots had erupted when an all-white jury in Simi Valley acquitted four white police officers in the beating of motorist Rodney King, despite a videotape showing police taking turns attacking King as he lay on the ground. Although Bugliosi would later argue that no one would have rioted over a Simpson conviction, Garcetti may have wanted to avoid the spectacle of a largely white jury convicting one of America's best-known black celebrities.[55] Professor Dershowitz concluded that, notwithstanding the outcome, "it was not a mistake, but a strategic decision made for decent reasons."[56]

Garcetti and others have given many reasons for filing the case in downtown Los Angeles. The central courthouse was better suited for the expected media onslaught; the Santa Monica courthouse was still under repair from an earthquake; the grand jury, in which prosecutors originally sought to indict Simpson, convenes downtown; prosecutors did not want to commute to the outlying venue; and Garcetti wished to keep the trial close to his office, both to supervise the prosecution and also likely to take advantage of opportunities for media exposure. In *Outrage*, Bugliosi seeks to demolish such factors, saying the downtown location was simply "a monumental blunder, one that all by itself was a reason for the miscarriage of justice in the Simpson case."[57] Overconfidence may have played a part in the decision. Marcia Clark said the evidence would result in a "clear-cut guilty verdict regardless of where O.J. was tried." Bill Hodgman, originally lead prosecutor in the case until illness forced him to step aside said, "Nobody even thought about it at the time."[58]

Whatever the reasons—if any—for trying the case downtown, Garcetti made public remarks suggesting racial sensitivities were the deciding factor. A downtown jury pool, with its much greater African American representation, would have more credibility, contributing to the "perception of justice," he said.[59] Later, when race became a central part of the defense strategy and things started to look more challenging for the prosecution, reporters pelted Garcetti with questions about why he gave up the strategic advantage of a white jury pool in Santa Monica. He responded by referring to earthquake damage to the Santa Monica courthouse and other mundane considerations. "Any time you have a tactical advantage, you're a damned fool if you give it up," veteran LA prosecutor Harvey Gliss told Bugliosi. "You argue like crazy to remain in a particular locale if you think it is to your advantage."[60] Losing makes many wise decisions seem foolish. Had O.J. been convicted, Garcetti would have been widely lauded for his decision to elevate public interest concerns over trial tactics. But he lost, so he wasn't.

SKIRMISHING INSIDE AND OUTSIDE THE COURTROOM

Garcetti's concern for venue did not mean that prosecutors were trying to make things easier for the defense. In fact, the prosecution maneuvered to avoid a preliminary hearing in the case by seeking a grand jury indictment of O.J. instead. In California, criminal cases are brought to trial via two avenues: grand juries or preliminary hearings. Grand jury deliberations take place in secret, with defense attorneys not present, enabling prosecutors to obtain indictments without revealing much, if any, of their evidence. Preliminary hearings, by contrast, are held in open court before a judge and essentially amount to "miniature trials," forcing prosecutors to reveal evidence and present witnesses for cross-examination by defense attorneys.[61] Presumably to avoid the defense benefits of a preliminary hearing, the DA originally sought to indict Simpson before a grand jury.

Dershowitz and Gerald Uelmen, a law professor and fellow member of the dream team, filed a motion charging that pretrial publicity released or leaked by police and prosecutors, including Nicole's inflammatory 911 call of 1989, had poisoned the minds of the members of the grand jury. The defense lawyers also cited Garcetti's multiple remarks speculating Simpson would eventually admit to the murders while still seeking to evade culpability. The defense motion discombobulated the DA's office. Garcetti, apparently worried about black voters, criticized the city attorney for releasing the 911 tapes. After grand jurors were overheard discussing the tapes not yet presented in testimony, prosecutors saw nothing but problems in continuing to pursue a grand jury indictment. In an astonishing strategic retreat, the DA's office joined in the motion to disband the grand jury, therefore conceding the need for a preliminary hearing.[62]

In the preliminary hearing, the defense argued the bloody glove found by Fuhrman at the Simpson estate should be excluded from the trial on the grounds police entered the property without a search warrant. Simpson's defense team, which had been appealing to the public through press conferences, filed some motions knowing they would likely fail—but also would receive wide press coverage. Judge Kathleen Kennedy-Powell, presiding at the preliminary hearing, ultimately ruled that the glove stayed in, but the proceeding enabled defense attorneys to try to portray Detective Philip Vannatter, a key witness, as "incompetent at best, sinister at worst."[63] As Toobin observes, "the defense lawyers planted the idea with a pool of potential jurors that the police had a secret, nefarious agenda to get Simpson."[64]

Defense attorneys also kept up the pressure in pretrial motions once the case reached Judge Ito, for example, asking him to suppress the bloody glove, attacking the state's DNA evidence, and arguing prosecutors had not provided blood samples for defense experts to test. "The court hearings over the summer raised a continual drumbeat of accusations against the police—amplified by intense media coverage—for the benefit of prospective jurors in the case," Toobin writes. While losing all these suppression motions, the defense managed to further tarnish Vannatter as a witness. Even Judge Ito criticized Vannatter for an affidavit filled with factual errors, calling it "at least reckless."[65]

AIRING DREAM-TEAM LAUNDRY IN PUBLIC

The defense lawyers did not always manage the media with such skill and precision, however, especially when the conflict turned to fighting among themselves. After assembling the dream team, Shapiro became increasingly uncertain about his position as its leader. Even his old friend F. Lee Bailey seemed less than steadfast. Bailey had once hired Shapiro to defend him on a charge of drunken driving. Things change, though, in supersized cases, sometimes even friendships. Adept at media manipulation, Bailey appeared on *Larry King Live,* where he said he wanted to "make it perfectly plain that [Shapiro] is the lead counsel in this case" and defended Shapiro against "all the sniping that someone has been sponsoring, saying Bob Shapiro couldn't handle this case."[66] At that point, however, Shapiro had come in for very little criticism. Some felt publicly defending Shapiro against nonexistent charges allowed Bailey to undermine him.

When it became clear that Johnnie Cochran was taking control of the defense, Shapiro tried but failed to enlist Bailey as an ally in his fight to remain lead counsel. By December 1994, Shapiro was indeed coming under sharp press criticism over issues including, ironically, his enthusiasm for speaking to the press. Shapiro struck back, first leaking word to *Newsweek* that he was no longer on speaking terms with Bailey. In January, he went on record in a *New York Times* story criticizing Bailey as disloyal and adding that Bailey added nothing to the defense team. Bailey responded by releasing a statement that said, "This case is not about Mr. Shapiro or Mr. Bailey. It is about O. J. Simpson."[67]

Simpson called a jailhouse meeting, where he demanded his lawyers stop feuding in public. Shapiro was forced to apologize to

Bailey. After this incident, Cochran was the undisputed captain of the defense team.[68]

THE MEDIA "TSUNAMI"

While defense and prosecution worked the press like gamblers work the slots, the media inserted itself into the case to an unprecedented degree. The O. J. trial marked a sea change in the relationship between the press and the courts because its spectacular media appeal coincided with the arrival of advances in television and Internet technology that spawned a multiplicity of new media outlets. In the past, traditional news outlets, like local television stations, broadcast networks, and newspapers and magazines, served mega trials to a ravenous public. But in the O. J. trial, the attorneys, police, parties, and court personnel also came under intense pressure from twenty-four-hour cable news channels, tabloid newspapers and television shows, as well as the speed and ubiquity of the World Wide Web. None of them, not one, was fully prepared for the ferocity of media probing. "It was like being smacked by a tsunami," said Jerrianne Hayslett, media coordinator for the LA Superior Court, who worked closely with Judge Ito during the Simpson trial.[69]

As William E. Loges, a professor at Oregon State University and coauthor of *Free Press vs. Free Trials*, told an interviewer, celebrity trials foster a "breathless" kind of coverage. "The media feel they can get away with more now than before," Loges said, "and the competition is frenzied. The distinction between legitimate news coverage and tabloid journalism got blurred during the O. J. trial because outlets like the *National Enquirer* were breaking stories. The *New York Times*, trying to double-check sources and facts, found itself getting burned."[70]

In a way, the media can hardly be faulted for its frenzied efforts to satisfy the public's interest in the Simpson murder case—it paid off handsomely. As *Broadcasting & Cable* magazine reported in 1995, ratings nearly doubled for news and talk radio stations broadcasting gavel-to-gavel coverage of the trial. Arbitron ratings for all-news KNX (AM) rose from a 2.2 share to a 3.7. And that's just one example of the nationwide groundswell.[71]

WITNESS STORIES FOR SALE

In addition to covering events, reporters can also make them happen, as Toobin did when he broke the story of the defense lawyers' plan to portray Fuhrman as a corrupt racist bent on framing their innocent client. Media organizations can weaken or strengthen the teams on the field in other ways. Prosecutors are understandably reluctant to use witnesses who receive any form of a payoff for their version of events. Witness bribing is, of course, despicable and indictable. But some of the same odor clings to witnesses who have sold their stories to tabloid newspapers and television shows before taking the stand. In the eyes of the prosecution, several potentially important witnesses disqualified themselves in this way. Shortly before 11:00 p.m. on the night of the murders, a young woman named Jill Shively narrowly avoided colliding with a Ford Bronco not far from Nicole's house. Not only did Shively recognize O. J. Simpson as the driver of the other car, she also memorized the license plate number. Despite being warned by prosecutors to give no interviews until after she had testified, Shively immediately sold her story to *Hard Copy* for five thousand dollars, plus another twenty-five hundred dollars for letting the *Star*, a supermarket tabloid, use the transcript of the interview. Outraged, Clark chose not to use Shively's testimony and directed the grand jury to disregard it.[72]

But Clark would encounter tabloid-tainted testimony again, and soon. The first witness called in the preliminary hearing was Allen Wattenberg, who ran Ross Cutlery, a knife store in downtown Los Angeles. Wattenberg testified that Simpson had bought a fifteen-inch knife on May 3, 1994, which the prosecution obviously intended to portray as the missing murder weapon. But Wattenberg also blithely testified that he planned to split a twelve-thousand-five-hundred-dollar jackpot with his brother and an employee, Jose Camacho, who had been paid for an interview by the *National Enquirer*. Although all three store workers corroborated the story of O.J.'s knife purchase, prosecutors eventually decided against using their testimony.[73]

Nicole's friend Faye Resnick became another casualty of intrusive media attention; in this case it was book publishing. Like Nicole, Resnick was an attractive, athletic woman in her midthirties, recently divorced from a rich husband. She led a hard-partying life, and at the time of the murders was in a tony drug rehab facility. She was well acquainted with O. J. Simpson, claiming she had mediated between Simpson and Nicole in their turbulent reconciliation attempts. She should have been an excellent witness for Clark, who sought to paint Simpson as a rage-prone wife beater whose violence escalated into murder. Instead, Resnick wrote a quickie book, *Nicole Brown Simpson: The Private Diary of a Life Interrupted*, cowritten by Mike Walker, a reporter for the *National Enquirer*. In it she asserted her conviction that O. J. was guilty. She reported, for example, a conversation with Simpson in which he said, "I can't take this, Faye. I can't take this. I mean it. *I'll kill that bitch.*"[74]

Not only did this book disqualify Resnick as a witness for prosecution purposes, it badly spooked Judge Ito. Instead of doing the sensible thing—ignoring the book and letting the furor run its course outside the courtroom—Judge Ito suspended jury selection for forty-eight hours, telling the jury pool "the publication of a book [has] caused the court great concerns about the ability of Simpson to get a fair trial." [75] He then wrote letters to the television networks and news channels asking them to cancel interviews with Resnick. Only one, CNN, agreed. Judge Ito's overreaction was the biggest favor he could have done for Resnick. The extensive coverage of his actions incited so much public curiosity about Resnick's book that its sales took off, and it promptly became a number one *New York Times* bestseller.

THE TRIAL OF O. J. SIMPSON

O. J. Simpson entered a not guilty plea on June 22, 1994, twelve days after Nicole Brown Simpson and Ronald Goldman were murdered. The trial began on January 24, 1995, and lasted for nine months. It was the longest trial in California history. His defense cost an estimated $6 million, while the state spent $9 million prosecuting him, $2.6 million of which went to feed, house, and entertain the sequestered jury.[76]

The defense had argued relentlessly, inside and outside the courtroom, that Simpson had been framed by a shadowy and indistinct police conspiracy spearheaded by the racist cop Mark Fuhrman. The prosecution tried hard to protect Fuhrman, who denied on the stand he had uttered "the N-word" in the preceding ten years. But that protection collapsed when the defense produced twelve audiotapes of interviews Fuhrman had conducted with an aspiring screenwriter in 1985. In the tapes, Fuhrman can be heard using the offending word—and worse. This disclosure gave Cochran opportunity to demonstrate his skill at manipulating public opinion. It may have been the turning point in the trial.[77]

The trial ground to a halt for a week as the defense fought to get the tapes entered as evidence and the prosecution fought to exclude them. Cochran, who "assumed jurors were receiving information about news coverage despite sequestration," knew that he needed "a public airing of the tapes. In other words, he needed their contents leaked to the press."[78] With the tapes ordered "under seal" by Judge Ito until the matter of their admissibility could be resolved, defense lawyers could not directly leak them to the press without risking contempt. So another leakster was needed. Larry Schiller, Simpson's advisor and the writer behind O.J.'s jailhouse bestseller, *I Want to Tell You*, reportedly leaked the tapes.[79] But getting the tapes to the press was not enough for Cochran. Taking the art of litigating in the court of public opinion to a new level, Cochran organized a news conference with leading black clergymen and civil rights groups demanding the release of the tapes. Ominous references were made to the events of 1992—a veiled threat of more rioting if the tapes were not released.[80]

Judge Ito decided to allow the defense to play whatever portions of the tapes it wanted in open court, but with the jury absent. Present, of course, was the press, which picked up the narrative of Fuhrman's racism and ran with it.[81] But when Judge Ito ruled only two brief excerpts could be presented to the jury, Cochran held a news conference that accused Ito of participating in a "cover-up," calling the ruling "perhaps one of the cruelest, unfairest decisions ever rendered in a criminal court." Judge Ito held to his decision, but he became even more cowed by Cochran. When Cochran refused to present evidence the next day in protest of the ruling, Judge Ito called an early Labor Day recess.[82]

On October 2, after only hours of deliberation, Orenthal James Simpson was acquitted of the murders. Simpson is said to be the most famous person tried for murder in American history. And so, inevitably, there was plenty of drama during the actual court case—Barry Scheck's brilliant obfuscation of DNA evidence; the Fuhrman flap; Christopher Darden's boneheaded decision to have Simpson try on the bloody glove; the seemingly damning procedural errors by police and criminalists; and Cochran's melodramatic closing argument ("If it doesn't fit, you must acquit"). And yet, in retrospect, observers typically cite two main factors that produced the acquittal verdict: a combination of prosecutorial missteps and the ability of Shapiro and Cochran to control the public narrative of the crime throughout the entire ordeal. Although the two lawyers came to dislike one another, they proved equally adept at public relations.

The conventional wisdom was that the dream team "out-lawyered" the prosecution, thus securing acquittal for an obviously guilty man. There are some who dissent from the majority opinion. In Bugliosi's *Outrage*, he argues strenuously that the defense, with the exception of Scheck, was "spectacularly ordinary throughout the trial."[83] O.J. went free, Bugliosi asserts, mostly because the prosecution was worse. Bugliosi claims that cross-examination techniques were often poor and preparation was inadequate at times, including a failure to interview opposition witnesses prior to trial. But because the Simpson lawyers were lionized as "brilliant" by a bedazzled press, jurors "likely" perceived their performance as better than it actually was. "If they were the dream team, they must be scoring a lot of points," Bugliosi writes, "and this all helps add up to reasonable doubt."[84]

Many will dispute Bugliosi's opinion, since the public held an exalted view of the dream team's exploits. One dream teamer whom the critics did not attack was Dershowitz, whose explanation for the verdict emphasized the fact that "we kept O.J. off the witness stand and put the LAPD on trial."[85] Even skeptics agree that O.J.'s lawyers succeeded with a reverse form of police brutality. They beat up the LAPD and wrung a not guilty verdict from a largely black jury with imbedded feelings and even perhaps bad experiences with a controversial police department. All the black jurors later denied race had played a part in their deliberations.[86] And yet juror Gina Rosburough admitted, "I believed from the beginning he was innocent."[87] Carrie Bass, immediately after the jury delivered its verdict, purportedly said to her fellow jurors, "We have to protect our own."[88]

When the trial was over, prosecutors appeared exhausted, dispirited, and, in the eyes of many, discredited. Actually, though, almost all the principal players in this biggest of all courtroom dramas benefited handsomely from being associated with it. Simpson, of course, lost his reputation and his lucrative careers as an actor and pitchman. But he avoided a lengthy prison sentence. Despite the $6 million he paid to his lawyers, he was not exactly poor. His NFL pension, about $25,000 a month, was protected by California law from the wrongful death judgment resulting from the 1997 civil trial brought by the Goldman and Brown families. But O.J.'s luck ran out in Las Vegas. In January 2008, Simpson was convicted of armed robbery at a Las Vegas memorabilia show (Simpson claimed he was trying to retrieve property that belonged to him). He was sentenced to thirty-three years in prison. He will be eligible for parole in nine years. Lawyers have appealed his prison term. And yet, even if he serves the full sentence for his souvenir raid, his acquittal for murder won him freedom and a lavish lifestyle for twelve years after the murders of Nicole Brown Simpson and Ronald Goldman.

Many key figures involved in the O.J. Simpson case wrote books. Some, like Marcia Clark, Johnnie Cochran, Robert Shapiro, and Christopher Darden, received multimillion-dollar advances and had bestsellers. Dershowitz wrote a book about it (in addition to his many other books); so did several jurors; and so, interestingly enough, did Mark Fuhrman, who, after telling his side of the story with *Murder in Brentwood*, reinvented himself as a successful true-crime writer.

About the only player in the O.J. drama who has not cashed in is Judge Lance Ito. Though he has continued to serve as a Los Angeles superior court judge, he has written no book, has granted no interviews, and has consistently declined offers of promotion. As Jerrianne Hayslett observes in her book, *Anatomy of a Trial*, "When Ito got the Simpson trial, he was considered one of the Los Angeles court's brightest rising judicial stars, destined for advancement to either a state appellate or federal judgeship. By the time the trial was over, his judicial reputation was tattered and his health battered."[89]

Just as lawyers in subsequent high-profile cases noted the many benefits to winners and losers alike, future judges would not forget the painful ordeal of the Honorable Lance Ito.

CHAPTER 4

ELIAN GONZALEZ
The Battle for the Child and for Public Opinion

THE RAID

A ny hope that the torrent of shouting was something other than an INS raid ended when the tear gas billowed into my face. As my eyes stung and my throat tried to close, I could hear a pleading voice—that of Marisleysis—crying out that she could not see and imploring the agents storming through the house not to hurt anyone. She begged them to stop aiming their guns at people. "We will give you the boy," she shouted. "Don't hurt him! Don't do this!" More words and shouts and the heavy fall of booted feet. Armed men in military-style gear had broken down the door of a defenseless and law-abiding home to seize a six-year-old boy at gunpoint.

I sat with two mediators in a back room where we had been working through the night to finalize negotiations with the Justice Department that might have brought the saga of Elian Gonzalez to a peaceful and dignified conclusion. We thought only a few details separated us from Attorney General Janet Reno. Now all that seemed foolish. For a few seconds I flashed on the SWAT raids I had approved years before as US Attorney—in an earlier life. More than the irony of seeing myself, now a private lawyer, on the receiving end of so much raw force, I was sickened by the sense of ambush. We had been played and betrayed.

Somehow the door to the yard had come open, and so I stepped outside. To the left was the swing set where Elian had laughed and played the day before while the rest of us prepared for the Easter weekend. Now, instead, dazed people stumbled about the yard, some sinking to the ground, coughing, gasping, unable to move. To my right, Lazarito, Elian's five-year-old cousin shrieked in pain and terror, tears flowing down his face from the gassing. His father placed him next to a tub of water and tried to rinse the chemicals from the boy's face, hair, and arms.

Across the small yard toward the street, I saw dozens of people in obvious pain and shock. Quickly, I placed a 911 call, reaching a dispatcher who seemingly tried to help. I was struck that she was completely unaware of the chaos taking place on this quiet residential street in Miami's Little Havana. Then a friend and supporter of Elian's cause told me that a leading activist, a member of the human rights group Mothers Against Repression, urgently needed a doctor in the house next door. As I hurried through the front door of that house, I saw her on the couch, her husband and friends by her side. Her body was wracked with convulsion that lifted her from the couch with a rapid-fire flailing of arms, legs, and head. Not long before she had been outside, peacefully demonstrating against those who wanted to return Elian to Cuba.

I rushed outside in search of a medical rescue unit. To my astonishment, none was in sight. I called 911 again and was told a unit was on the scene. Hurrying back to the street, I found an ambulance and demanded assistance for Mrs. de la Cruz. A crowd surrounded me, also urging help for their friends or family. The rescue staff in the ambulance told us to stand back so that they could close the door and leave.

Returning to the backyard, I stood by the swing set where, for the first time, bits of scattered anger began to crystallize. Weeks earlier President Clinton had assured Senator Bob Graham that the government would conduct no dark-of-night raid to snatch Elian from his relatives' home. Just the day before, we had agreed to the settlement proposed by the attorney general. We had spent the entire night in negotiation, trying to resolve what seemed like a few minor details. We later learned a federal magistrate had signed a warrant for the raid hours before, which meant Reno's negotiations had been nothing but a ruse to mask a surprise paramilitary raid. We had been set up by the highest levels of the American government. Our government.

THE TRAGIC VOYAGE

The odyssey of a six-year-old Cuban boy through a sensationalized American court case began on the shores of Cuba before dawn on Monday, November 22, 1999. Elian; his mother, Elizabet Brotons Rodriguez (twenty-eight years old); her second husband, Rafael Munero Garcia; and eleven others left Cardenas aboard a sixteen-foot aluminum skiff, with only three life jackets plus three inflated inner tubes that were towed behind the boat. Starting around midnight, waves ten feet high pounded the boat. The motor stopped working. For hours, the passengers bailed water, but the deadly tandem of wind and waves eventually capsized the skiff, tossing everyone into the sea.

As the hours passed, the refugees began to succumb to exhaustion and hypothermia, slipping one by one beneath the surface. As they struggled helplessly in the cold night ocean, Elian's stepfather, whom he knew as "Munero," lashed the boy to one of the inner tubes. Marisleysis later said Elian told her he fell asleep on the inner tube, and when he awoke, his mother was gone. "I think she, too, drowned because she didn't know how to swim," Elian said.[1] All told, eleven of the fourteen people aboard the boat died that night. One of the survivors, Nivaldo Fernandez Ferran, told reporters, "Elizabet protected her son to the end."[2]

For the rest of that terrible night, and for two more days, Elian drifted alone. On Thanksgiving morning, November 25, Donato Dalrymple and Sam Ciancio, two South Florida sport fishermen, spotted a dark circular object off the coast of Fort Lauderdale. As their boat drew near, they found Elian barely alive. Fernandez and his girlfriend, Arianne Horta, were rescued floating on another raft off Key Biscayne that same morning.

Brought ashore, Elian was hospitalized. After recovering from his ordeal, he was released by the INS to his great-uncle, Lazaro Gonzalez, who took him to the small, two-bedroom family home in Little Havana. Elian shared a room with Marisleysis Gonzalez, his twenty-one-year-old cousin. Marisleysis became Elian's principal caretaker, or what the media came to term his "surrogate mother."[3] She would also become a central figure in the controversy to follow, a frequent family spokesperson in newspapers and on local and national television. The

Gonzalez family instantly bonded with Elian and petitioned the INS to grant the boy asylum.

On the day the boat carrying Elian set sail from Cuba, his father, Juan Miguel Gonzalez, phoned Lazaro asking him to keep an eye out for Elizabet and Elian in Miami.[4] But now that the boy was safe with relatives in the United States, Juan Miguel remained in Cuba for months, demanding his son's return. Elian's father and mother had divorced in 1991 after six years of marriage but remained close and continued to try to conceive a child until 1993, when Elian was born. The couple finally broke up in 1996, with most press accounts portraying them both as loving and attentive parents. Elizabet moved in with Munero, and Juan Miguel formed a new family with common-law wife Nelsy and their infant son, Giani. Accounts vary concerning Juan Miguel Gonzalez's character and treatment of Elizabet. In the interviews that INS conducted, Juan Miguel's presentation of himself as a devoted father was taken at face value. Other information and evidence, however, painted a darker picture, with some sources suggesting he mistreated Elizabet.[5] Conflicting information also surrounded Juan Gonzalez's reported desire to leave Cuba and relocate to the United States. According to some family members, he declared a wish to leave Cuba, saying that he would come to the United States even if it meant coming in "a tub."[6] Whatever his real feelings may have been, Juan Gonzalez refused for months to travel to the United States to claim Elian. He refused even though the United States offered him a visa in November and again in December of 1999 to come for his son. In fact, in a written questionnaire submitted by US interviewers, Juan Gonzalez marked *no* in response to the question "Do you want to go to the United States to see Elian now?"[7]

FROM MIRACLE TO MEDIA SENSATION

Cubans in Miami embraced Elian as a "miracle child" delivered from the sea as a symbol of hope and opposition to the hated tyrant, Castro. For them there was no question: the boy should remain in the United States with Lazaro and his family, where he could grow up with the advantages of America—freedom, education, and opportunity. Prominent Cuban Americans, Gloria Estefan and Andy Garcia among them, stepped forward in support of the family's cause. Anglos in Miami, and most people in the rest of the nation, however, saw the situation differently. For them it was a matter of parental rights. If the boy had a father who wanted him back, then he should be returned to Cuba—even if that meant life under a communist dictatorship. The rights of the father trumped all other concerns. Meanwhile, on the streets of Little Havana, the already extraordinary facts of Elian's survival began to take on legendary qualities, with stories of dolphins protecting the boy at sea and leading him to safety.[8]

Such elements lifted Elian's saga above the average human-interest story that, no matter how compelling, rarely maintains public attention beyond a news cycle or two. This story had everything—a darling young hero, telegenic relatives, a supposedly loving father back home, and several layers of conflict. One center of conflict crystallized between the Cuban American community and the Castro regime that used Juan Gonzalez as its proxy. But conflict also emerged between the Cuban American community and the larger American public's opinion in favor of the father. And most of all, conflict flared between Lazaro and his supporters, and the might and power of the US government, which increasingly seemed bent on turning the boy over to a tyrant it had opposed for four decades. No wonder Elian dominated local, national, and international media for the next eight months.

CASTRO'S COURT OF PUBLIC OPINION

The intervention of the US government against the interests of some of its own citizens developed gradually. In the beginning, federal authorities declared an intention to stay out of the custody dispute. Indeed, a week after Elian arrived, the INS issued a statement saying it considered Elian's custody situation to be a matter best resolved in the usual way—in state family court, where child-custody issues are almost invariably resolved, even when foreign parents are involved. The INS's initial position rested on a traditional foundation of law and precedent.

Castro likely saw how Elian's case could be used to outsmart Washington, embarrass and enrage his old adversaries in the Miami exile community, and divert the attention of his own citizens away from the bleak, everyday realities of their lives in communist Cuba. Fidel may not be able to run his country in a way that allows for a decent economy, but his political skills are formidable. What's more, his public-relations acumen is second to none, as he was about to prove again. First he orchestrated rallies in the streets of Havana, with crowds angrily denouncing the United States and demanding Elian's return.[9] But this was only the opening gambit.

Since the United States had designated Cuba as a terrorist state, at odds with Castro for forty years, it might have seemed peculiar for Washington to side against Lazaro and his family. But Elian's story played out under the full weight of history—specifically that part of history that included the 1980 Mariel Boatlift, in which some one hundred twenty-five thousand Cubans fled to Miami after Castro briefly pulled his security forces from the island's ports. This wave of immigrants included not only legitimate refugees fleeing oppression and seeking freedom but also criminals and the mentally unstable, as Castro emptied his prisons and mental hospitals. Mariel spelled a political disaster for the Carter administration that would not be forgotten in Washington.[10]

Succeeding US presidents have avoided confrontations with Castro that might prompt him to again allow a mass migration of desperate Cubans to flood the shores of Florida. President Clinton had already weathered the "*balseros* crisis" of 1994. Frustrated by a worsening economy after the fall of the Soviet Union, Cubans increasingly set out on homemade rafts, launching waves of rafters known in Spanish as *balseros*. They hijacked boats and ferries for the voyage to Florida. Riots broke out in Cuban streets. Finally, Castro opened the coast for fifteen days, an invitation to everyone who wanted to leave. Somewhere between thirty thousand and fifty thousand accepted, most on rafts. After only a few days, Clinton ended the open-door policy Cuban refugees had enjoyed since the Cuban Revolution of 1959. *Balseros* rescued from the ocean were not taken to Miami or to Key West; instead they were interred at Guantanamo Bay, although most were eventually allowed into the United States. The crisis played heavily in Castro's favor. Clinton established the "wet foot–dry foot" policy, which repatri-ates rafters rescued at sea but allows those who reach land to stay.[11] The American government also agreed to allow twenty thousand Cubans to immigrate legally to the United States each year—a policy some scholars say has saved the Castro regime by providing a "release valve" for the most disgruntled of Cuban citizens, who might otherwise foment rebellion.[12]

Clinton, no doubt, wished to avoid another messy wave of Cubans rafting to Florida. And Castro, no doubt, knew it—giving Havana leverage over Washington. In mid-December, the US government did an abrupt about-face on Elian's custody case. The Department of Jus-tice (DOJ) and its subordinate agency, the INS, began to orchestrate a legal case for requiring his return to Cuba—disregarding their own prior statements about the best interest of the child or the primary role of state family courts. Now the official message emphasized "the rights of the father," and "upholding the law."[13] With Juan Miguel unwilling or unable to travel to Miami to fight for his son, INS officials obligingly went to Cuba to interview him. Predictably, they came back with only the most positive information, showing the man as an ideal father anx-ious to be reunited with Elian.

FROM OUTSIDER TO INSIDER

At the turn of the new year—and the new millennium—I was not involved in the fast-developing story, but like most people I readily consumed the message in the media that the conflict centered on Cuban American opposition to the communist regime. It was a battle of wills between the exile community and Fidel Castro. Still, I entertained my own speculations about the case, and I thought I saw a strategy for those fighting to keep Elian here.

In custody battles over minor children, courts routinely appoint independent officers of the court called *guardians ad litem*. They are usually attorneys who are authorized to make independent recommen-dations concerning what's best for the child. Increasingly fascinated, I found a federal appeals case from years earlier in which a guardian ad litem was appointed in a dispute over a young Mexican girl.[14] With this as a precedent, I thought, surely such a guardian could be appointed for Elian. Once this officer made sound recommendations in Elian's behalf, the knotty court case might be resolved.

Then I received an unexpected phone call inquiring about my interest in joining Elian's legal team. After speaking with Armando Gutierrez, the family's spokesperson and representative, I met with some of the lawyers. To my surprise, they voiced universal support for the guardian ad litem idea, but the decision, they said, would have to be made by Lazaro. Lazaro immediately embraced the strategy, unhesitatingly declaring he would accept whatever determination a guardian might reach, even if it meant returning Elian to Cuba. Of course, he was confident any neutral, fair-minded person who examined the facts would agree that Elian was best served by staying in this country. It seemed apparent to me that, contrary to what I viewed on the evening news or read in the papers, Lazaro did not see himself in a historic struggle with Castro, but as a man duty-bound to honor the wishes of Elian's mother, who gave her life to bring the boy to the United States. He believed that Juan Gonzalez also wanted to leave Cuba, but with a new wife and small child, he faced unimaginable pressures. When a Cuban defies Castro by leaving, the regime retaliates against any family members who remain behind.

Encouraged by Lazaro's honesty and passion, I joined the team. So did my law partner, Manny Diaz, who would become one of our principal negotiators and advocates with the press. I immediately filed a detailed motion for the appointment of a guardian ad litem. Middleground solutions, though, are not sexy, and the filing was ignored. Instead, the media focused relentlessly on the perception of a battle pitting angry exiles against the legitimate rights of Elian's modest and justified father.

IN MIAMI FEDERAL COURT

I joined the legal team in early February 2000, shortly after a lawsuit had been filed on Elian's behalf in Miami federal court. The suit asked the court to declare that Elian had a right to seek asylum on the grounds of a relevant statute authorizing "any alien who is physically present in the United States" to invoke this right.[15] It was a bold move for a custody battle.

On March 9, US District Judge Michael Moore listened attentively to oral arguments from both sides. Barbara Lagoa, who later became an appeals court judge, presented a superb argument on the merits of Elian's right to seek asylum. Judge Moore aimed pointed questions at government attorneys, including why the language of the statute—"any alien"—necessarily excluded a child. I argued on behalf of the need for a guardian ad litem and decried Juan Miguel's failure to come fight for custody in Florida even now, one hundred days after his son's arrival. Judge Moore seemed receptive to appointing a guardian but hinted that the father's appearance in the United States might change the outcome of the case.

For days we awaited the court's decision with guarded optimism. But while Judge Moore's ruling favored our side on several helpful procedural points, he rejected Elian's right to seek asylum. It was a clear victory for the government.[16]

APPEALING TWO APPEALS

From that moment forward, my role expanded greatly. I became lead appellate counsel and occasional spokesperson for the team before the national press corps. In consultation with Elian's other lawyers, I rejected strategies that attempted delay; instead we immediately filed an appeal rather than wasting time filing for a rehearing—a common, but generally futile, tactic. Asking a judicial officer like Judge Moore to reverse himself despite the extensive consideration he had already given the issue rarely works. Meanwhile, DOJ lawyers pressured us to accept an unrealistically short timetable of two weeks for the appeal, with no right to seek supreme court review. We countered by asking the appeals court to create a prompt but more reasonable timeline. Our request was granted—a small victory, but our first success in federal court.

Although the legal work was difficult and exhausting, it was easier than dealing with the media. Engulfed by requests for interviews, Armando coordinated our media efforts by assigning team members on a daily basis to handle particular interviews. We met most of the national television requests, but we had no time to engage the media strategically to sell our legal themes. We unfailingly responded to the *Miami Herald*, but it was impossible to speak to the hundreds of other newspapers that were closely following the story in this country and around the world.

Although different faces and voices appeared from the members of the Elian team throughout the saga, our best ambassador was Marisleysis, Elian's cousin. She emerged as a maternal figure for Elian, and although only twenty-one years old, she was a telegenic and compelling presence. We also had media help from unofficial supporters. I appeared alongside Gloria Estefan on CNN's *Larry King Live* as she presented a strong argument for Elian and for the Miami Cuban community.

Attorney General Janet Reno, with her homespun persona and seemingly artless press conferences, became the face and voice of the administration. Nothing about her demeanor suggested a sophisticated lawyer who was media savvy. Raised by parents who both worked for the *Miami Herald*, she trained at Harvard. Unlike most political veterans, she actually liked reporters. In the 1960s and 1970s, she was a fast-rising prodigy of legal icon Talbot D'Alemberte, who made her a major force in his work revising Florida's Constitution in 1968–70. She was a presence with no frills but great skills.

Reno sounded simple themes. Her relentless invocation of the "rights of the father" was not catchy nor clever but held sway with the American public. If motherhood is the ultimate in popularly acclaimed virtues, fatherhood is a close second. And the daily repetitions of "uphold the law" drilled home the imagery of an unflinching commitment to duty and order. Along with targeting everyday values of everyday people, Reno's sound bites avoided the slickness that reporters distrust. To be sure, others in the government worked the media behind the scenes. Her subordinates had the added tactical advantage of not only spinning the news but breaking it, too. DOJ regularly slipped copies of government letters, ultimatums, and pleadings to media sources before we received them. Almost invariably, we learned about the government's next step when reporters called for reaction.

In times of peace, no federal agency has more delicious news to dole out to the media than the Department of Justice. As a result, reporters are more likely to curry favor with DOJ gatekeepers than to challenge its positions. What's more, DOJ lawyers are usually among America's finest, prosecuting many of the nation's worst malefactors. All this meant Reno's simple, consistent message on Elian's case went to reporters primed to accept it, with little incentive to examine our version of a two-sided controversy.

Against the media power at the disposal of the US government stood Armando, a local political consultant. Mostly because he adored Elian and the Lazaro Gonzalez family, he served tirelessly and without compensation from almost the beginning of the struggle to keep the boy in Miami rather than send him back to Cuba.

Armando had a keen awareness of the local community and local reporters, and he proved remarkably astute about the national arena. Under his lead, we sought simple messages of our own. We tried "*any* means *any*," referring to the law guaranteeing an asylum hearing to "*any* alien." If *any* means *any*, then even a child like Elian must have the right to his day in court. But in the battle to control the media message, just as in legal cases, you can change your spin, but you cannot change the facts. And the fact was that technical concepts like "any alien" and "day in court" lacked the punch needed to counter public sympathy for a father who wanted to be reunited with his child.

THE SAWYER INTERVIEWS

America Meets Elian and Marisleysis

To counter the lopsided coverage in favor of the government, Armando decided Elian should appear on television with Lazaro and his family. An exclusive interview with a major news show would provide a high-profile chance for America to meet Elian and hear our side of the story. In big cases, though, exclusivity is likely to incite resentment among the reporters and news organizations left out. But with the tide of public opinion turning against us, we were not in a position to follow conventional media strategy. In such circumstances, whether dealing with the media or a jury, a lawyer has to rely on risky alternatives. The exclusive interview became a spectacular coup for ABC's *Good Morning America* and its star, Diane Sawyer. Inevitably, though, it was a disappointment for other networks. And while Sawyer and *Good Morning America* were sensitive and fair, they made considerable effort to avoid accusations of bias and, unfortunately for us, remained pointedly neutral. Nevertheless, ABC received some criticism of its handling of the interviews, causing the network to be even more cautious in its future coverage of the Elian story.[17]

Even so, the immediate effect of the *Good Morning America* interview was clearly positive. Not only was Elian himself presented to the American people in their living rooms with all his six-year-old charisma, but the other members of Elian's family were humanized. For the first time, this became a case about a family and a child rather than a Cuban American rant against Fidel Castro. And while Sawyer did not endorse our position, on March 28, she accurately reported that Elian himself expressed a preference to remain in the United States.[18] Armando's gamble seemingly paid off. On the heels of the Sawyer interviews, Florida's House of Representatives passed a resolution of support for Elian. More important, support in the US Congress for granting him residency picked up steam. On March 31, *USA Today*'s lead headline announced "Gore Splits with Boss over Elian."[19] Marking a peak in public support, the vice president and presumptive Democratic presidential nominee announced his support for permanent residency for Elian.

But perhaps we were peaking too soon, because the gains following the Sawyer interview were not ignored by our opponents. It had become apparent that the television visual of a family portrait seemed to compete effectively with Reno's verbal message about the father and upholding the law. They still held the cards, though, to trump virtually any that we might play. And so the administration responded with its own strategy for visuals, a strategy that cast Elian's father in the starring role.

A FATHER MAKES NEW TRAVEL PLANS

I can still recall watching the television coverage of the departure of Juan Miguel Gonzalez from Havana on April 6, 2000. Other setbacks and frustrations were minor compared to the problems we soon confronted with a photogenic father launching a television campaign to reclaim his son.

When I initially signed on, team members were certain that Juan Miguel would never be allowed to come to this country. According to our sources, he wanted to live here and would try to defect the moment he stepped on US soil. What we apparently underestimated, however, was the ability of Castro, perhaps using the intervening months after Elian's arrival, to take steps to guarantee that Juan Miguel would not defect—most likely a combination of threats to family members left behind as well as promises of reward upon his return. Whatever replaced Juan Miguel's nonavailability in November with his new travel plans in early April, his coming to America reenergized the fatherhood theme and quickly displaced the gains in public opinion we had made through the Sawyer interview.

For the first time since I joined the team, I sensed that we might lose Elian without even getting an asylum hearing, the core of our strategy. The following day, our home-field advantage in Miami deteriorated. The *Miami Herald* had previously acknowledged that "the leading presidential candidates" and "the vast majority of Americans" supported resolving the case based on "the best interest of the child." But upon Juan Miguel's arrival, the *Miami Herald* called for the Gonzalez family to agree to have Elian "rebond with his father."[20]

Emboldened by rising public support that accompanied Juan Miguel's appearances in the United States, the administration intensified its pressure on Elian's Miami family. Increasingly strident demands pounded us for the delivery of Elian to the INS. Even President Clinton spoke of the risk of "a train wreck for all concerned."[21] The pressure, constantly stressful, now became excruciating. It is difficult to convey the utter exhaustion of people caught in the eye of a media storm. An army of cameras surrounded Lazaro's home night and day. Rumors bombarded the family incessantly, ranging from far-fetched schemes to take Elian to sanctuary in foreign consulates to ominous reports that helicopters were gathering to launch a raid on the home.

THE PRESSURE MOUNTS ON A SLEEPLESS FAMILY

The family feared most the threat of an armed raid. Sitting in my office in early April, I received an unexpected phone call from US Senator Bob Graham. A Florida icon, he called as he was literally walking into the White House and asked me to suggest the one request he should make of President Clinton with respect to Elian. Startled and humbled by the call and realizing that the administration's ultimate position on Elian's return to Cuba was non-negotiable, I was somehow able to identify the one realistic request that mattered the most: an assurance from the president that there would be no dark-of-night raid upon Lazaro's household. This anxiety was not only an hourly source of torment for Elian's Miami family, it was jet fuel for the rumor mills churning throughout the Cuban American community. As events would unfold, Graham secured the president's promise in the Oval Office. But that promise would not be kept in the streets of Little Havana.

In the meantime, Lazaro and Marisleysis struggled to maintain a happy household for Elian amid the surrealism of 24/7 television coverage. Continually responding to friends, politicians, supporters, and, of course, reporters, they subsisted on two to three hours of sleep each day. Unforgiving physical exhaustion is the reality of such ordeals, but even though it should be understandable, neither the press nor the public will accept it as an excuse for mistakes. Those on camera must perform flawlessly—or else. In 1972, for example, the late Senator Edmund Muskie doomed his presidential candidacy when his exhausted tears were televised. Today, I counsel clients to go nowhere near reporters or any other venues that record their words unless they are fully rested. In such instances, I advise the family that if they cannot sleep due to the pressure of the media glare, they should consult with doctors about prescription sleep aids.

Fatigue certainly took a toll on the presentation of our message to the media. At times, the family's exhaustion reached a point of a virtual illness. Lazaro and Marisleysis had media moments that were broadcasted repeatedly, with damaging results. None of the reporters reminded the public of the many times Lazaro and Marislyesis had conducted themselves admirably, despite the excruciating pressures. Nor did any news show make the slightest acknowledgment that Elian's Miami family, once the government's threats accelerated in early April, never got a full night's sleep.

On April 12, a much-heralded meeting between Janet Reno and family members at the house of Reno's longtime friend, Sister Jean O'Laughlin, president of Barry College, failed to result in an agreement. This left Lazaro demoralized. That night, before a sea of cameras, he launched into an exhausted harangue that was widely portrayed as a proclamation of defiance of the United States and its laws. His fatigue played into the government's hands while whetting the media's appetite for an imminent showdown.

The issue of supposed defiance was highly useful to Reno. The government could not use paramilitary force in Little Havana against nothing more than a small family defended by lawyers with briefcases. The image of a lawless family in a lawless community was needed to justify such an unprecedented and extreme measure. Lazaro's tired tirade bolstered the government's message. And the media helped by repeatedly portraying our disagreements with the INS as if they were a willful disobedience with orders of the court. We declared at every turn that the family would comply with any orders issued by a judge, even as we continued to challenge directives issued in INS letters.

And we never spoke of resistance. As Manny Diaz emphasized continuously, "If INS shows up tomorrow and says 'We are here for Elian,' we will, of course, comply."[22] Lazaro Gonzalez steadfastly declared that he would allow INS to knock on his door to remove Elian but would not deliver him to a "neutral site" unless commanded to do so by court order. Still, the image of the family, humanized in the Sawyer interview, was now twisted into something like a clan of outlaws.

In the process, waves of negative publicity tarnished Miami's image, which did not aid our cause. Several years earlier, one prominent correspondent had compared Miami to a "banana republic" on CBS's *60 Minutes*, and as the cameras repeatedly played up scenes of the crowd around Elian's home, a *New York Times* quote prominently reprised that label.[23] Local politicians did not help matters. Several mayors in Dade County announced that the county and some cities would not provide police assistance for any armed INS action against Elian's home in Little Havana. Well-intentioned, the statements backfired. Rather than decrease the risk of a raid, they made one more likely by inadvertently contributing to the picture of a defiant family in a lawless community, where a raid by heavily armed federal agents would be justified.

SURPRISING COURT SUCCESSES

Following the collapse of the negotiations, the INS continued to deliver demands (which we continued to learn about first from reporters) for the delivery of Elian. It was evident to us, faced with endless rumors and the very real prospect of an INS raid, that the government might act to return Elian to Cuba even before our appeal could be decided. Any such removal would render the appeal meaningless since, if Elian were back in Cuba, no US court had the power to force Castro to return him to the United States. To prevent this, we attempted an extraordinary legal strategy and asked the appeals court to order that Elian not be removed from this country during the time needed for our appeal.

To my surprise, a judge of the Eleventh Circuit Court of Appeals quickly granted the temporary order. The order keeping Elian in the United States, however, was to last only for a few days. Both sides were ordered to submit extensive papers to a court of three appellate judges to argue the issue of whether the United States should be prohibited from returning Elian to Cuba throughout the rest of the appeals court process.

The stakes were high. If our request were denied, it would be tantamount to inviting the INS to immediately seize Elian and turn him over to Castro. Our chances of winning an order against the US government seemed low. And yet, remarkably, the three judges of the appeals court ruled in our favor, issuing an opinion that not only ordered the government to allow Elian to remain in the United States for the time being but also strongly suggested a favorable view of our position on the critical issues.[24] *USA Today* described the ruling as a "strongly worded decision that challenged the government's handling of the Elian Gonzalez case," adding that the judges criticized the INS "for not considering the boy's stated wishes to remain in the United States."[25] Hope surged with this stunning victory.

HOPEFUL SIGNS FOR THE EASTER WEEKEND

Without our knowing it, community leaders had quietly designated four prominent leaders, two Anglos and two Cubans, to negotiate directly with Janet Reno, their longtime friend from her tenure as US Attorney in Miami. They were concerned for Elian and deeply worried about the damage to the city's image. I received their calls at home early in the morning, two days after the appellate victory on April 19. We were thrilled. As the day progressed, it became clear that a settlement based on the six basic elements suggested by the four leaders and Reno might be attainable. The scenario called for bringing the Miami relatives and Juan Miguel into the same housing complex and allowing phased-in visitation.

I was contacted to secure and confirm the approval of the Gonzalez family. The attorney general did not want to be embarrassed during negotiations—ironic in light of subsequent events—and demanded a document confirming the family's agreement with the six-point plan. Manny Diaz typed up our handwritten notes summarizing the agreement. By midafternoon on Good Friday, the Gonzalez family met with us and assented. Believing they had reached an agreement in principle, the negotiators faxed a "term sheet" in time to meet Reno's 5:00 p.m. deadline. Reno asked for a signed copy, which we faxed at 8:30 p.m. The family added a single request that a spiritual advisor be allowed in the housing complex during the reunification process. Although we had an agreement in principle, details had to be worked out between Reno and the community leaders during the night that followed.

By 1:30 a.m. we were confident a deal was in the process of being finalized. The negotiators and the Miami leaders waited for confirmation to come from the attorney general. With a sense the tumultuous case was finally resolved, I relaxed for the first time in months and fell asleep on the living room couch in Lazaro's home.

AMBUSH

Having your foot shaken by a prominent leader like Miami's Carlos de la Cruz would normally be an honor of sorts. But in the circumstances of that night, it was unsettling. He awakened me to say that there was still no final approval from Reno. It was baffling. Whenever a supposedly unresolved detail was raised by Reno's staff, our side simply gave in. Nothing, we thought, should keep us from reaching a tolerable solution. Even when Reno's team backed off its agreement that the housing complex for the families would be in Florida, the family agreed to a transition location in Georgia.

We did not know that a countdown to a raid had already started. While we negotiated in good faith, close to a hundred agents and police were already on their way. It was the last thing I expected that night. After the president's promise of no dark-of-night raid, we believed that the government would rely on judicial process in the event talks broke down.

High-profile cases, though, take on a life of their own. And with the extraordinary profile of Elian's case, the media's expectation of confrontation involving a show of force had become a self-fulfilling prophecy.

Around 4:00 a.m. on Saturday, prominent attorney Aaron Podhurst, the mediator, called. He had the attorney general on the other line. Her tone of voice had changed; Podhurst indicated that she seemed to him under enormous pressure and that the deal had changed substantially. Shortly afterward, he called again, saying we had five minutes to agree to the new conditions. At 4:15 a.m., as Podhurst relayed Reno's latest demands, Miami Police Chief William O'Brien received a call at home apprising him that federal agents would storm the house at 5:15 a.m. At 4:30 a.m. Podhurst conveyed Reno's abrupt message that we were running out of time. We repeatedly assured them that there would be no sticking points. On the contrary, we conceded to every new demand.[26] Shortly after 5:00 a.m., INS forces burst through the door.

Dressed commando-style in helmets and Kevlar and brandishing weapons, they terrorized the unarmed men, women, and children in the house. After ramming the door off its hinges, these officers of federal law enforcement shot off nonincendiary tear gas, wounding innocent and disoriented citizens, none of whom offered the least resistance. No one inside was suspected of any crime, yet all were subjected to shock assault tactics ordinarily reserved for drug dealers and violent offenders. At the time of the raid, Reno was still on the phone with Podhurst. As far as we knew, the final few details were all that remained.

Along with the negotiators and other members of Elian's team, I was inside the house but blocked in the back room by INS raiders and subjected to the gassing that flowed throughout the house.

Agents stormed through the house, guns at the ready. Finding Elian cowering in a closet, one INS officer pointed an MP-5 submachine gun directly at the boy's head, forcibly prying him from the arms of Donato Dalrymple, who had become a family friend since rescuing Elian from the sea months earlier.

This image, taken by an Associated Press photographer who rushed into the house behind the agents, appeared on television broadcasts and newspaper front pages all over the country. The armaments wielded by the INS are not designed for ordinary police work, as the *Washington Post* would report, but for "killing situations, in high-risk raids, where commands of law enforcement officers are likely to encounter opposition that must be stopped quickly and powerfully."[27]

After snatching a terrified Elian from Dalrymple, the agent tossed the boy to another INS agent, who covered his head with a towel and hustled him out of the house and into a waiting van. Elian screamed in English, "Help me! Help me!" and in Spanish, "Que pasa? Que pasa?" which means, "What is happening?" Dalrymple, who was obviously unarmed, followed, pleading with the INS agents not to hurt Elian; he was met each step of the way by the barrels of INS machine guns and with the agents' threats: "Stay back, mother——er, or we'll shoot."[28]

The irony: our negotiations created the perfect scenario, from a law enforcement perspective, for the use of overwhelming force. Precisely because we were immersed in talks with the attorney general, the last thing we anticipated was an armed assault on Lazaro's house. Critically for the INS, the crowds of supporters that had swarmed the streets around Elian's home for months had largely dispersed after midnight. They, too, thought a deal was imminent between the family and the Department of Justice.

For us the raid may have been the ultimate in bad faith, a shocking use of unnecessary military-style force. But for the INS it proved a spectacular success. In fact, the INS's great feat in wrenching a small boy from an unarmed household resulted in an orgy of self-congratulation. The heroes conducting this operation, wearing t-shirts emblazoned with *180*—the number of seconds the raid required—received honors and awards from Reno herself in a closed-door ceremony.

PUBLIC OUTCRY MEETS FATHERHOOD

Following the raid, we headed to my law office and found plenty of cameras waiting for our blistering denunciations of the government's duplicity and excessive use of force. By far, though, the most important visual of the day was the AP photograph of a terrified Elian, held by Dalrymple, with a heavily armed agent pointing an automatic weapon at him. For hours, this image dominated every news report about the raid, giving rise to public outcry. That following Sunday morning, I had the privilege of being interviewed side by side with Senator Graham, who described the promise that President Clinton had made to him in the Oval Office as "a clear commitment which was violated."[29] One of the Senate's most thoughtful members, he described the raid as "a gross, excessive use of force."[30]

But the government countered with its own visual—a photo op of a smiling Elian held by Juan Miguel. With Elian in his father's arms, public opposition to the raid wilted in the overwhelming support for a father reunited with his son, never mind the means. Things got worse. On Monday, devastated by the loss of Elian, Marisleysis went to Washington in the hopes of seeing the boy. She was refused by authorities. Distraught, worn by fatigue and anguish, Marisleysis's disorganized and emotional outburst before the cameras that day likely damaged her previously positive public image.

The happy snapshots of father and son orchestrated by the government belied their setting. As a few news reports described matters, "Castro's government erected a virtual Cuban village in and around Washington." Cuban handlers, in fact, surrounded Juan Miguel and

Elian, with the Clinton administration's blessing, guaranteeing that both would remain snugly in the grip of the Havana regime. Enforcing this arrangement, the US Marshals Service racked up overtime and travel that cost US taxpayers more than $1.8 million. And that figure is only a small fraction of the US investment made to protect Elian from Lazaro and Marisleysis. Castro's Washington compound never made it onto the radar of public opinion, but the exile community in Miami viewed it with disgust. When photographs appeared showing Elian in the uniform of the Pioneers—a communist youth group—disgust turned to rage. Elian's indoctrination seemingly began while still on American soil.

Once more, I attempted a motion for appointment of a guardian ad litem. Initially, the court's reaction seemed encouraging as they ordered the government to explain why such a request should not be granted. Ultimately, however, the request was denied. From the time that Elian was taken from Lazaro's home until his eventual departure to Cuba, we experienced nothing but defeat.

A COMMUNITY'S COURT OF PUBLIC OPINION

In the Elian case, those of us on the legal team made strategic mistakes in managing the court of public opinion—some through inexperience, others because of exhaustion, still others due to lack of human and financial resources. The might and sophistication of the US government is almost impossible for a private citizen to resist, even, as in this case, when aided by able and diligent counsel, many working for free. But the government spin machinery failed to heed one fundamental principle when trying cases in the press—more than one jury is seated in the court of public opinion. This failure would have consequences on a national scale in the 2000 presidential election.

In the streets of Little Havana, the impassioned beliefs of the Cuban American community are a world away from the main street where the administration's themes resonated so strongly. One survey showed that 76 percent of white non-Hispanics and a whopping 92 percent of African Americans supported Elian's father.[31] Among Cuban

Americans, some 83 percent believed that Elian should remain in Miami. Media coverage similarly diverged. Following the day of Elian's seizure, the *Miami Herald*'s banner headline proclaimed "Raid," while the Spanish-language counterpart *El Nuevo Herald*'s corresponding words were "Que Verguenza," meaning "How Shameful."[32]

In the aftermath of the raid, thousands of Cuban American Democrats reregistered as independents, including my partner, Manny Diaz, who would become Miami's mayor the following year. Sensing the implications, one pollster, Neil Newhouse, predicted this would pose a serious setback for the presidential aspirations of Al Gore. The government's handling of the Elian case "solidified the Cuban vote against the Clinton administration and Gore," Newhouse observed. That Gore had earlier broken with the administration regarding Elian became lost amid the angry voices on Cuban radio, inciting listeners against the administration. Some Democratic insiders recognized the peril.[33] I began to get sympathetic calls from Energy Secretary Bill Richardson, the administration's highest-ranking Hispanic. Richardson was thoughtful and concerned and made several tries at limiting the damage. But unless Elian could be returned to Little Havana, Richardson's attempts at reconciliation between Cuban Americans and the administration—and the Democratic Party—were doomed.

THE VERDICT IN THE COURT OF LAW

When the day came to present oral arguments before the Atlanta appeals court, both sides faced tough questions, and many observers handicapped the odds as even. Privately, however, my spirits sank when the Chief Judge J. L. Edmondson emphasized his concern about the legal principle known as "separation of powers."[34] Separation of powers describes a rule by which one branch of government accepts the right of other branches to make the decisions concerning the issues entrusted to that part of the government under the Constitution. In immigration cases, a court's focus on separation of powers almost always leads to a decision accepting action taken by the INS, which is part of the executive branch.

I was therefore deeply worried on June 1, 2000, the morning the appeals court was to release its decision. In Miami, police and other security personnel were placed in a state of alert, anticipating protests—or even riots—if the Cuban community received bad news. Such anxieties were unfounded and unfair. In fact, the only time throughout the case that Cuban Americans had taken to the streets in anger—despite the succession of setbacks—came immediately after the raid on Lazaro's house.

While not unsympathetic to our issues, the court's thoughtful and well-written opinion nonetheless concluded that the immigration service had the power under our legal system to decide Elian's future and to return him with his father to Cuba. The decision did not rubber-stamp the administration's actions, however. Indeed, in a footnote, the court seemed to criticize Reno for her relentless insistence that she merely followed the law. As the court observed, "it has been suggested that the precise policy adopted by the INS in this case was required by 'law.' That characterization, however, is inaccurate."[35] Rather than following the law, Reno was in fact the decider of the law and, due to the principle of separation of powers, the court was deciding to accept her decision as the "sole prerogative of the executive branch." In explaining the opinion to reporters, we pointed out some of its favorable features, but we knew the truth. There was no middle ground or moral victories in a case like this. We had simply lost.[36]

Few options remained. Motions for rehearing, requests that the court change its mind, are very rarely granted. Securing a different result from the Supreme Court equates to one chance in a thousand. For once, we could privately agree with the media, which projected no hope for the future of our case.

THE FINAL STEPS IN A LEGAL ODYSSEY

The only good news to arrive after the appeal came with an unexpected offer of help from two outstanding Washington lawyers with the prestigious firm of Kirkland & Ellis, who volunteered to present our case to the US Supreme Court. After reviewing the file, they determined that a motion for rehearing should be submitted, and their submission demonstrated with great skill that a newly decided Supreme Court case concerning the amount of latitude granted to federal agencies such as the INS should prompt the appeals court to reconsider its decision in our case. Even so, no one was surprised when the motion for rehearing filed on June 15 was denied. The papers they prepared and filed on June 26 seeking Supreme Court review were equally brilliant, but our cause grew increasingly unpopular.

Two days later, Lazaro and Marisleysis and our legal team gathered in a Miami chapel, La Ermita de la Caridad, to await the news of the Supreme Court's decision. Situated near Biscayne Bay, the chapel was built to honor Cuban refugees, and it was an appropriate place for the final hopes for the relatives of the most famous of all Cuban refugees. The gentle call I received that morning from co-counsel, Brett Kavanaugh, though, let us know that the Supreme Court had chosen not to hear Elian's case. It was over. Hours later, as the networks featured video of Elian and Juan Miguel departing Washington and heading to Cuba, a few accounts would describe the hundreds of flag-waving students the regime assigned to await his arrival in Cuba.

The following morning I made what was to be my last appearance on a network morning show to discuss the Elian case. An unhappy event under the circumstances, the interview centered on the kind of second-guessing that is fair game for losing lawyers.

AN UNEXPECTED LEGACY

Elian was gone, and the sense of loss was deep not only for Lazaro's family but also for anyone associated with the case and its cause. For a time, though, it seemed that perhaps some good might come of it after all. There were signs that Elian's case had shed light on the previously invisible tragedies of other refugee children. Legal papers submitted in our case by children's advocates indicated that, at any given moment, more than twenty million children around the world are refugees, and some two hundred fifty thousand of these displaced, extremely vulnerable children are separated from their parents.[37] In the United States alone that year, more than five thousand refugee children were in INS custody with no parents in sight.[38] Articles were written about the startling inhumanity endured by these children. Legislation was formulated to create safeguards such as appointing guardians, the remedy we had futilely sought for Elian.[39] Unfortunately for these children, much of this positive momentum was lost in the wake of the anti-immigrant forces unleashed by the 9/11 atrocities.

Although a devastating defeat for the legal team, the consequences for members were not entirely negative. When I originally considered joining Elian's legal team, I was counseled against it by friends who said that it was an unwinnable case and that the Cuban community would forever blame the attorneys who participated in Elian's defeat. While the first part of that admonition may have been correct, the second was not. Cuban Americans respect those who battle for their cause, even in defeat. Meanwhile, the constant spotlight, even in defeat, adds to a lawyer's visibility, especially at a local level. Two members of Elian's team went on to hold judicial office, and Manny was elected to two terms as Miami's mayor. Meanwhile, I was, for months, warmly received by Cuban Americans. Some of that appreciation, though, disappeared abruptly during the 2000 presidential recount litigation. One of the most momentous cases in US history, it resulted from a startling turn of events that, ironically enough, included the legacy of that six-year-old Cuban boy.

CHAPTER 5

POLITICAL LITIGATION AND CHANGING HISTORY
From Hanging Chads to Missing E-Votes

PART ONE

The Florida Recount

I was really tired after a long day's work on November 7, 2000, and I was pleased that I could go to bed without staying up late to watch the election returns. Right after Florida was called for Al Gore, I went to bed happy. I did not know Gore well, but I had met him a few times and really liked him and his concepts for making government more accountable. And maybe for the first time in history, and just when we really needed it, America would have a true environmentalist as president.

What a difference a few hours can make. By the time I woke up the next morning shortly before 5:00 a.m., everything had changed. While I slept—along with most of the country—the networks recanted their predictions of a Gore win. With 85 percent of the vote counted, George W. Bush, governor of Texas, was declared winner of Florida's 25 electoral votes—and with them, winner of the presidency.[1] In fact, by 4:00 a.m. on November 8, Gore had called Bush to concede. However, that 85 percent didn't include a significant number of votes yet to be counted in three heavily Democratic counties: Broward, Miami-Dade, and Palm Beach. Things were getting intense. Within hours, Gore had closed Bush's Florida lead from one hundred thousand votes to just over two thousand votes—a whisker-thin margin.[2] A short time later, after watching the Republican lead dwindle to 1,784 votes, Gore called Bush back to rescind his concession.[3] Exhausted after having

111

gone almost forty-eight hours without sleep, Gore went to bed in his suite at the Lowe's Vanderbilt Plaza. His top aides met at their Nashville headquarters to plot their next moves.[4]

As a result of the narrow margin, a mandatory machine recount went into effect in all sixty-seven Florida counties.[5] A machine recount means that the same mechanical process utilized to count ballots during the election is used a second time after Election Day, and so the changes are minimal.[6] For example, the punch-card machines used for Miami-Dade, Broward, and Palm Beach Counties used heavy paper ballots on which voters, using a needlelike stylus, would "punch" through the square designating their candidate. In a machine recount, election officials would feed ballots back into the same counting machines used on election night. In truly rare situations, Florida law allowed for a manual recount in which individual elections workers would visually inspect the ballots, determine the candidate whose name had been punched by the voter, and hand count the totals. Machines could read clear holes, but only human eyes could see a partially punched circle where the "chad"—the bit of paper adhering to the ballot—might still be intact. For that reason, a manual recount by human beings would retrieve additional votes that the electronic machines could not read.[7]

By 6:30 a.m. on Wednesday, Donnie Fowler, Gore's national field director, had dispatched a number of volunteer campaign workers to monitor the machine recount that Florida would immediately perform.[8] Ronald Klain, the former chief of staff to Gore, and a brilliant Washington lawyer, was being charged with heading the Democratic legal effort. Senator Joe Lieberman's plane had been assigned to carry everyone to Tallahassee.[9] Carter Eskew, a top campaign aide and long-time Gore friend, and William Daley, Gore's campaign chairman, called to wake Warren Christopher, former US secretary of state. Within three hours, Christopher was airborne, on his way to Florida as well.[10]

Elsewhere that day, in the state capital, Tallahassee, the Florida secretary of state, Republican Katherine Harris, said she would probably declare a winner by the end of the day based on the machine recount of six million votes and a final tally of absentee ballots.[11] Few shared her confidence that the election would be over so swiftly.

Around the same morning hour that Fowler was assembling a

national team, I received a call from a close friend and fellow election lawyer, Ben Kuehne, who said to me, "We've got to get moving and help." We immediately began to analyze the possibility of a full-scale election law battle. Experienced election litigators were a rare breed in Florida, where only a small number of people engage in this seasonal practice. I had been lead counsel in 1998, when Joe Carollo successfully challenged his mayoral defeat in court on grounds of voter fraud. Kuehne had also played a major role in the litigation.[12]

Soon I received one call after another from Democrats around Florida who were reporting a flood tide of election mishaps and trying to figure out what to do about them. There were numerous irregularities in Miami-Dade County, but it seemed the most spectacular problem had arisen with the butterfly ballot in Palm Beach County.[13] The ballot presented all the presidential candidates side by side, in two columns—hence the nickname "butterfly"—rather than the usual design with a single vertical list on the same page. Due to the unusual layout, several thousand Gore voters had inadvertently selected Pat Buchanan. Because the two names were on virtually the same level on either side of the ballot, with the middle column containing the squares to be punched, it was difficult to know which square was for Gore and which would be a vote for Reform Party candidate Pat Buchanan. A study that would later be conducted by a local newspaper indicated that more than five thousand Gore votes were lost when voters punched the card for both Gore and Buchanan.[14]

By midmorning, I fielded a call from Joseph E. Sandler, the general counsel for the Democratic National Committee in Washington, DC. Someone at the White House had mentioned my name, Sandler said. They evidently knew not only about the work on the mayoral voter fraud case, but also that I had managed to survive the frenzied, high-profile Elian Gonzalez controversy when I had helped represent Elian's Miami family in opposing his return to Cuba. By Wednesday evening, I was on a flight to Tallahassee. When I arrived at the state's capital, I realized that, for the first time in more than a century, a full day after polls closed, the identity of the nation's president-elect was up in the air.

Both sides scrambled to muster their legal talent, political muscle, and sophisticated spin machinery. In the first twenty-four hours, six of

Florida Governor Jeb Bush's senior political operatives took unpaid leave to join the fight for George W. Bush, his brother. Within forty-eight hours, the Bush-Cheney campaign had James Baker III, Ronald Reagan's secretary of state, on the ground in Florida to lead their legal charge.[15]

Early the second morning after the election, a Thursday, I found myself in a Tallahassee hotel conference room briefing Daley and Christopher on Florida election law. The immediate focus was the butterfly ballot controversy that was setting off a wave of voter outrage. Starting Wednesday morning, a spontaneous surge of lawyers and voters would quickly gather more than one thousand affidavits in Palm Beach County attesting to the confusion and mistaken votes. Even Buchanan agreed that many of his votes were intended for Gore.[16]

But moving votes around, switching them from one candidate to another after an election, even based on voter affidavits, is not a remedy courts would allow.[17] The only possible solution for the Palm Beach fiasco was to discard all the votes in that county and do a revote, that is, to do the Palm Beach balloting over with a ballot that would not fool people. When the Gore camp originally engaged me, the focus was on the idea of challenging the butterfly ballots. In the first two days after the election, bringing an election contest to challenge the cockamamy configuration that threatened to transform a nation seemed to be a viable option.

On Thursday, November 10, I stood behind Daley and Christopher at a remarkable press conference. I thought I'd faced a lot of cameras during the Elian Gonzalez saga, but this was like nothing I'd ever seen. I made two comments at the microphone, explaining some of the mechanisms of an election contest. Meanwhile, the automatic machine recount, completed that day, narrowed Bush's lead from 1,784 votes to a mere 327.[18]

By then, the butterfly ballot issue was losing steam in no small part because of the logistical problems of filing a case, winning it, winning the appeal, and conducting a new election exclusively for Palm Beach County, all before mid-December. Instead, the leadership's thinking was fast shifting toward a purely recount strategy. Election law is a specialty itself, but when recounts are litigated, fewer than a dozen lawyers in the entire country occupy the subspecialty of election recounts. The

Gore team immediately brought in two of the best, who advised the leadership to pursue a recount in all sixty-seven counties. The recommendation was rejected, a decision that has been second-guessed more times than Pickett's Charge at the Battle of Gettysburg. Only four counties at that time had been identified problems—Palm Beach, Miami-Dade, Broward, plus the most extreme example, Volusia, where they had experienced a complete system failure.[19]

On November 9, Gore requested manual recounts in Miami-Dade, Broward, Palm Beach, and Volusia Counties. The Volusia supervisor of elections was the only one who joined the suit for a recount. Supervisors of elections generally resist recounts, apparently believing that their systems and people are virtually infallible.[20]

The Democrats would continually face accusations that they cherry-picked the best Democratic counties, but that's not accurate. The four counties were chosen because they had real voting problems that had been identified. Certainly there were other strongly Democratic counties. Hillsborough, Leon, Alachua, and Gadsden, to name a few, would have generated pro-Gore margins sufficient to carry the election. But there was simply no information to suggest that irregularities occurred in those counties and, under Florida's law, a razor-thin margin without identifiable mishaps was not enough for a manual recount. Plus, we were walking on eggshells from the very beginning. There was constant trepidation about moving too far, too fast. If any missteps incited a public outcry of sore-loserism, the rug would be pulled out from under us in the court of public opinion, and the legal case would end immediately.

The Thursday and Friday after the election were exhilarating and momentous, but, for me personally, they came at a cost. When it became public that I had signed on with the Democratic team, I got a tidal wave of complaints from the Elian-faithful in Miami, who blamed Democrats for sending the boy back to Cuba. In a single year, I had succeeded in alienating almost everyone I knew—one half by representing Elian, the other half by working for Gore and Lieberman. At such times, it certainly helps to come home to one's rarely critical family and never-critical golden retriever.

On Saturday, after Palm Beach County announced that it would proceed with a manual recount of all 462,675 ballots, the Bush camp filed suit in US District Court in Miami to stop the counting.[21] I received the copy of the federal lawsuit from Marcos Jiminez, a long-time friend and GOP lawyer who would be named South Florida's US Attorney the following year. The Republicans had hoped to get a conservative Reagan-appointed judge, but the case was assigned to Judge Donald Middlebrooks, a Clinton appointee. By Sunday, I was back in Miami to prepare for the federal court hearing, huddling with Harvard Professor Lawrence Tribe, one of the most respected constitutional law experts in the country. As we drafted papers and outlined oral arguments for the federal hearing on Monday, we focused on the Republican argument that the hand recount should be shut down because the lack of uniform standards for a recount in Florida would violate the equal-protection clause of the Constitution.

At the time, the argument seemed more of a political attack than a serious legal argument. The Democrats as well as the press were underwhelmed by the Republicans' theory—with so many different voting systems in the state and around the nation, it seemed hopeless for Bush-Cheney lawyers to argue that the US Constitution imposed a requirement of uniform standards for examining ballots. Elections were conducted not by the state but by local elections officials, each county choosing its own system.[22] Most Florida counties used punch cards, which, through voter error or problems with the ballot paper, resulted in hanging, dimpled, or pregnant chads, which caused these ballots to be disqualified as "undervotes" in the original tabulation. Other Florida counties used optical-scan systems—filling in the oval on a paper ballot, which, in turn, would be read and recorded through electronic tabulation using laser scanners. The punch-card counties had many more undervotes, where a voter's ballot recorded no vote in a particular race, than those jurisdictions using optical scanners.[23] Most Florida counties had punch-card machines; some used optical scanners, one used old-fashioned paper ballots.[24] With different systems being a long-accepted practice in Florida and throughout the country, almost no one believed at the time that each county had to use identical standards.

In fact, the Republican equal-protection argument was viewed as so slim that I was allowed to do a significant portion of the argument on behalf of Gore-Lieberman. In federal court that Monday morning, my assignment centered upon Florida election law, and I compared the different voting systems in Florida, describing the optical-scan or punch-card systems and explaining what undervotes were, as well as the different levels of undervotes yielded in different systems. An undervote, I noted, means that in an election where the voter appeared to cast a ballot, no vote was recorded in a particular race. Of course, as I explained, each Florida county is allowed to choose its own systems. And there are simply many more undervotes with punch-card systems. Is it because the voters in the punch-card counties are less likely to vote? Of course not. It's the mechanics. Sometimes the voters unwittingly fail to punch all the way through the card and, absent a manual recount by election workers, such votes are lost.

Arguing this case in the central courtroom of the old courthouse in Miami, with its grand mural of old Florida, would be a dramatic moment for any lawyer. I was surrounded by all that legal tradition, and I was making a major portion of the argument in the first hearing of a case that involved who would become the next president of the United States. Along with Professor Tribe, another legal giant, Harvard Professor Alan M. Dershowitz, joined me in the oral arguments that morning. It seemed evident at the time to us, and to many others, that if the Republican equal-protection argument prevailed due to a lack of "uniform standards" for manual recounts, it would mean that virtually every election in Florida violated the US Constitution. Yet, by the time it was all over, five weeks after the general election, that was the same argument the Supreme Court cited in its decision to shut down the Florida recount.[25] And therein lies the chronicle of how, in five weeks, a weak constitutional argument grew to a legal force powerful enough to transform our lives and rewrite our history.

As soon as we completed our arguments that Monday morning, Judge Middlebrooks rejected the Bush suit and refused the demand for ending the hand recount in Palm Beach County. Several of his findings—uncontroversial in their correctness at the time—rejected the same theories that the Supreme Court would halfheartedly adopt in later litigation.

Florida's state election scheme is reasonable and nondiscriminatory on its face.

Florida's manual recount provision is a "generally applicable and evenhanded" electoral scheme designed to "protect the integrity and reliability of the electoral process itself," the type of state electoral law often upheld in federal legal challenges.

While discretionary in its application, the provision is not wholly standardless. Rather, the central purpose of the scheme, as evidenced by its plain language, is to remedy "an error in the vote tabulation which could affect the outcome of the election."[26]

Following Judge Middlebrooks's ruling, another federal judge also quickly dismissed a similar challenge brought in Central Florida.[27] Meanwhile, the spin machines were whirring at breakneck speed in both camps. Bush continued to claim victory in Florida, and thus the nation. As usual, Gore struck a more cautious tone. "Because of what is at stake," Gore said, "this matter must be resolved expeditiously, but deliberately, and without any rush to judgment. No matter what the outcome, America will make the transition to a new administration with dignity, with full respect for the freely expressed will of the people, and with pride in the democracy we are privileged to share."[28]

These positions reflected legal strategies whose broad outlines had already been mapped out. From the beginning, the Republican themes emphasized the need to close the book on the election to avoid the instability—even the chaos—of having an empty chair in the Oval Office. Baker and company understood how powerfully the state deadlines worked in the Republicans' favor. In response to Judge Middlebrooks's November 13 ruling that rejected the equal-protection challenge and allowed the Palm Beach manual recount, Katherine Harris announced she would reject any revised totals from counties conducting hand counts if they missed the November 14 statutory deadline. Her position, while invoking a statute, still seemed like a technicality. The Republican team knew that the arguments for enforcing such deadlines would be much stronger if there were a realistic need for a quick cutoff, for instance, if the situation in Florida appeared potentially chaotic.[29]

To that end, Baker's aides alerted reporters to any symptoms of uncertainty or instability. Repeatedly, Republican spokespersons went on television to comment on images of the unrest and to warn that the nation was growing alarmed at the deteriorating spectacle in Florida. The shrewd public-relations ploy paid added dividends when major news outlets played up election chaos in Florida and hinted that the nation was on the verge of disaster. Ted Koppel, for example, intoned ABC's election coverage slogan, "A Nation Waits" with the added line, "in a solemn cadence suited to imminent nuclear disaster."[30] Tim Russert warned that "we could have chaos and a constitutional crisis" if Gore won the Florida recount, but the Republican-dominated state legislature moved to certify Bush as the winner anyway.[31]

Adding to the imagery of uncertainty, Republican Harris insisted Gore wasn't legally entitled to those recounts based on her reading of the statute, while a contrary opinion letter was issued by Florida's Attorney General Robert Butterworth, a Democrat.[32]

Although several counties had agreed to Gore's request for a manual recount, they soon saw they might not be able to finish before November 14. Additional time was lost when Palm Beach County, following advice of counsel, waited until the state circuit court resolved the legal disagreement between Republican Harris and Democrat Butterworth. Broward County initially followed Harris's reading of the statute and declined to conduct a recount, until Butterworth issued his opinion. The delay meant Broward, like Palm Beach, almost certainly could not complete its recount before the November 14 deadline.

Volusia County, chagrined at the malfunctioning of its optical-scan system, brought an action that was soon joined by the Palm Beach County Canvassing Board, the Florida Democratic Party, and Gore. The suit was intended to force Harris to accept revised totals from the recounts, even if they came in after the 5:00 p.m. deadline on November 14.[33]

Gore finally made his first public statement on the matter. He said it was important to "spend the days necessary to determine the winner" in this bitterly contested race. "I would not want to win the presidency by a few votes cast in error or misrepresented or not counted, and I don't think Governor Bush wants that either. While time is important, it is even more important that every vote is counted and counted accurately."[34]

Karen Hughes, spokesperson for the Bush campaign, decried Gore's efforts to obtain a recount, once again playing the GOP's stealth equal-protection strategy. "To produce a fair and accurate count, votes need to be counted fairly and accurately," she said. "Because there are no uniform standards governing this manual recount in four heavily Democratic areas, the votes in those four selective counties are not being counted accurately or fairly. They are being counted subjectively and selectively."[35]

In hindsight, it was clear that the Republican legal strategists understood all along that they needed to get their case to the US Supreme Court rather than let it be decided under state law by Florida's courts. To get their case there, they needed a federal issue because the US Supreme Court could not decide the case if it involved only state law questions. For their purposes, a weak equal-protection challenge concerning lack of uniform standards was infinitely better than no federal issue at all.

We thought the real issues were Florida matters and kept our focus on the four recount counties. While butterfly ballots, hanging chads, and the performance of Supervisor of Elections Theresa LePore were being debated in Palm Beach County, I was in Miami-Dade.[36] As soon as we won the federal court hearing that Monday morning, by afternoon I was enlisting the help of Steve Zack, an immensely talented lawyer who would be selected to become the first Hispanic president of the American Bar Association in 2010. Our assignment was to help convince the canvassing board to conduct a manual recount. Initially, on November 14, the board agreed to a sample recount of three precincts. But later that day, the board refused to do a manual recount for the whole county. It was a crushing defeat . . . or was it? Although we were confident that recounts in the heavily Democratic Broward and Palm Beach Counties would yield more votes for Gore, some political veterans told me that a recount in Miami-Dade might favor Bush. After all, ballots with hanging chads, the kind that get counted by hand but lost in the machines, are often produced by elderly voters. Since elderly Cuban Americans in Miami were not Gore voters, perhaps Miami-Dade's turndown might turn out to be a blessing in disguise.

In other Florida counties, the struggle was with deadlines. Terry P. Lewis was the Leon County Circuit Court judge hearing the state case brought by the counties over extending the deadline for recounting votes. He initially expressed skepticism toward the Bush camp's arguments. The judge demanded of a Bush campaign lawyer, "How could you conceivably do a manual recount in a large county without enough time?"[37] But in the end, Lewis ruled that Harris could stand by the deadlines and ignore late returns, so long as it was done not "arbitrarily" and she exercised proper discretion "after consideration of appropriate facts and circumstances." Easily enough, Harris responded by stating that any county wishing to file amended returns based on manual recounts would have to explain its reasons in a letter to her the following day.[38] By now the Volusia County hand recount was completed, shaving Bush's lead to an even three hundred votes. Manual recounts were under way in Palm Beach and Broward.

Throughout the recount litigation, and especially after we lost, the Democratic effort was widely seen as not aggressive enough. The Republicans attacked everything, many said, while we were too cautious. We were widely criticized for asking for recounts in only four counties. Gore also did not embrace the challenge to the butterfly ballots in Palm Beach or the attempt to invalidate the questionable pro-Bush absentee ballots in Martin and Seminole Counties.[39] And yet, the central consideration in our decision making—and our message to the American people—was counting all the votes rather than discarding any Election Day ballots. Because we valued democracy, we valued, above all, a citizen's right to vote. At the same time, every day we labored under the cloud of being considered sore losers. We realized that if the press really came down on us, there might well be a mass defection of Democrats calling on Gore to throw in the towel.

Throughout the five weeks, Klain's legal work and management skills were superb. We also had the perfect clients. Despite his understandable caution, Gore was always upbeat and focused throughout the many conference calls. He and Lieberman provided just the right blend of oversight, attention, and respect for their professional team. If only all clients were like Gore and Lieberman, lawyers would have fewer gray hairs and psychologists would have fewer patients.

I was also incredibly impressed by Gore-Lieberman press operations. Both sides had spin machines, and each was a thing to behold. We had two major phone conferences daily, each day having its specific messages and talking points developed whenever needed. Our highly focused press team constantly monitored the news (good and bad), formulated the message, and coordinated its delivery—including the decision of who would deliver each message. Often, by speaking with reporters who had spoken with Republican lawyers, our press people would get a heads-up on the opposite camp's next move in the constantly shifting, multidimensional chess game that was always in play. It was an eye-opener. I saw for the first time what kind of operation we had been up against in the Elian Gonzalez case, where relentless press demands wore down the handful of players on our side. From my perspective, the successful work of the Gore press team enabled us on the legal team to do our work, always pushing our cause and keeping our case alive in the legal system long enough to travel all the way through the courts.

In an isolated departure from our "count all the votes" theme, we eventually challenged overseas military absentee ballots. Lieberman distanced himself from the effort, and his misgivings would be validated.[40] The whole move to challenge military overseas votes was doomed from the start and soon evaporated. Attacking the ballots of our men and women in uniforms was simply not smart. It was seen as unpatriotic, with Democrats failing to stand up for our brave soldiers. Whether in the court of public opinion or in the courtroom itself, you can't talk out of both sides of your mouth. We were either for counting every vote, or we weren't.

On November 15, Al Gore and George W. Bush engaged in a long-distance televised exchange. Gore took the initiative in a press conference timed to coincide with the network news. He made a brief speech proposing a meeting with Bush to agree to extend the recount to all sixty-seven Florida counties and promised in return he would not pursue any further legal action to overturn the result. "The campaign is over," said Gore, in words that seem more eloquent with the passage of time, "but a test of our democracy is now under way. It is a test we must pass. And it is a test we will pass with flying colors. All we need is a common agreement that what is at stake here is not who wins and who loses in a contest for the presidency, but how we honor our Constitution and make sure that our democracy works as our founders intended it to work. This is a time to respect every voter and every vote."[41]

Bush brushed him off. "The outcome of this election will not be the result of deals or efforts to mold public opinion," Bush said in nationally televised remarks. "The outcome of this election will be determined by the votes and by the law."

While this exchange took place, Katherine Harris received the petitions from the counties to submit amended returns based on manual recounts—and denied them all, in an action that seemed to me the very definition of the arbitrariness Judge Lewis had prohibited.[42] The *New York Times* termed Harris's announcement "a clear tactical move to freeze the election results in Mr. Bush's favor, and she was under no legal compulsion to make it."[43] In response, Broward and Palm Beach Counties sued Harris on November 17, and late that same day, the Florida Supreme Court agreed to hear the case and enjoined the secretary of state from certifying the election until further order from the court.[44] Bush, meanwhile, appealed the ruling denying him the federal court injunction he had sought in Miami, and the federal appeals court in Atlanta agreed to hear the case.[45]

All that week, while lawyers for both sides fought in the courts, the simultaneous battles continued to rage in the court of public opinion. Democrats accused Harris of trying to call the election prematurely, thereby subverting the meaning of democracy, while the Republicans blasted Democrats' efforts to get manual recounts as an attempt to rig the results for Gore with the subjective judgments of ballot workers in blue counties.[46]

Tom Cole, chief of staff of the Republican National Committee, articulated the Republican theme: "Our message is, first, that we won the count, we won the recount, and presumably won the absentee counts."[47] In fact, by November 18 the overseas absentee ballots had been counted, pushing Bush's margin up to nine hundred thirty votes. But with recounts continuing in Miami-Dade, Broward, and Palm Beach Counties, the contest seemed far from concluded.[48]

Nonetheless, Democratic strategists recognized the strength in Cole's tack. Bush had enjoyed a huge public-relations edge ever since being named the winner on election night. Like being a little pregnant, winning by a little, even by a submicroscopic margin, is all it takes to be a winner of public opinion even as the legal wars rage on. Gore had, of course, won the nation's popular vote, a fact that seemed politically relevant but was legally meaningless and never matters much to judges or reporters.

Republicans could afford to adopt a harsh tone. Marc Racicot, governor of Montana, accused Democrats of counting ballots that had been used as fans, that had been stepped on, and that had been counted by people using flashlights. Speaking at a press conference organized by the Bush camp, Racicot asserted the electoral process had suffered "irreparable harm," and that if Americans knew which votes were being counted, they would be "flabbergasted."[49]

The Democratic response was characteristically cautious. "The Bush campaign does not need to rush this and shut this down," said Democratic Senator Tom Harkin of Iowa. "The country is doing just fine. People are getting up and going to school every day. People are planning their Thanksgiving dinners."[50] At the same time, Gore's camp focused much of its PR energy on persuading the public to remain patient while key Florida counties retabulated votes by hand. They also lobbied editors at the newsweeklies and anchors at network and cable news channels to persuade them not to declare Bush the winner before all the votes were counted.

As the supreme court of Florida was deciding whether to extend the deadline for submitting recounted ballots for three counties, we attempted a motion for reconsideration in Miami-Dade, asking that the canvassing board reverse itself and conduct a countywide recount.[51] I had filed only two motions for reconsideration in more than two decades of practicing law because asking tribunals to change their minds after fully considering and deciding a significant issue is almost always a waste of time.

But usual assumptions mean little when you are litigating over the presidency. On Friday, November 17, Steve Zack and I appeared before the Miami-Dade Canvassing Board to deliver some of the most emotional and personal arguments lawyers could make. Steve talked about his Cuban grandfather's love of American democracy and faith in the right to vote. I focused on the legal points but also described how the startling swirl of events had summoned the three board members to answer history's call. I recall vividly the intensity in the eyes of Judge

Miriam Lehr, the likely swing vote of the three members, as she absorbed the momentous occasion and searched for the right decision. Nothing would seem to reach the supervisor of elections—the following morning's front page showed him with arms crossed, and he voted against the recount. But with Judge Lehr joining Judge James Lawrence King Jr., by a two-to-one vote the board reversed itself and ordered a countywide manual recount.[52]

That very weekend, after the Miami-Dade Canvassing Board ruled for us, the Republicans filed another suit to stop the recount.[53] The judge on duty, who was in the Florida Keys, was reached by telephone, and she immediately rejected the Republican request.[54] I thought at the time GOP lawyers were wasting time. Rather than legal argument, their lawsuit seemed like trash-talk, and literally speaking, it was. This latest lawsuit complained, yet again, about chads, saying that they were falling on the floors of the election office and being swept into dustpans. But the Republicans weren't crazy. They had a weak legal argument and needed to make it more acceptable by combining the public messages of "chaos" resulting from the ongoing uncertainty about the presidency while heaping ridicule upon hanging chads. So they planned to trash-talk all the way to the US Supreme Court, where they could be confident of a conservative majority. To me, and to everyone on the Gore side, the election was all about issues of state law. But the Republicans never questioned whether the Supreme Court would decide the election. They truly got it—this battle was for the presidency, and there was no way the Supreme Court would sit it out and let Florida's state judges decide America's future. And they were right.

As the Miami-Dade recount commenced on Monday, November 20, results throughout the day indicated that Gore was gaining ground in Tallahassee.[55] Lawyers from the two camps appeared before the Florida Supreme Court to argue the critical issue of whether the deadlines for counting and submitting votes could be extended. In legal terms, the question was whether the law gave Secretary Harris discretion over the matter, and, if so, what rules governed her discretion.[56]

The Florida Supreme Court ruled that the secretary's ability to reject late-filed tallies was sharply circumscribed by a state constitutional mandate for counting as many votes as possible. As a result, the ounts should continue so that the loser of the hand recounts should have time to contest the results, and that contest should be concluded by December 18. The court ordered Harris to accept manual recount results until 5:00 p.m. on November 26.[57]

The supreme court cited an earlier decision from Illinois for the proposition that an accurate count was of primary concern: "Voters should not be disenfranchised where their intent may be ascertained with reasonable certainty, simply because the chad they punched did not completely dislodge from the ballot.... Such a failure may be attributable to the fault of the election authorities, for failing to provide properly perforated paper, or it may be the result of a voter's disability or inadvertence. Whatever the reason, where the intention of the voter can be fairly and satisfactorily ascertained, that intention should be given effect."[58]

That night I appeared on Brian Williams's MSNBC show opposite James Baker III—which, I have to admit, was pretty cool, going one-on-one with someone as important and impressive as the Republican team leader. He was trying to beat up on the Florida Supreme Court, hitting all the typical Republican themes—the court was interfering with the elections and practicing judicial activism. I had a much simpler job—whatever argument he made, I simply came back with the position that we stood for counting every vote. I talked about the judicial duty being not to select candidates but to protect voters, the people who stand in long lines to make their ballot decisions because their votes really matter to them. I was told it went really well for us, and I hope it did. When you have a clear and simple message, your risk of misspeaking or drifting off topic is greatly reduced. I believe the powerful simplicity of our message—protecting the right to vote—got through, at least that evening.

The court's ruling was a crucial victory; the Florida Supreme Court ruled unanimously in our favor that hand counts in Palm Beach, Broward, and Miami-Dade must be included in the final tally, and it extended the deadline five days.[59] Even so, I was deeply concerned. I was at a team gathering that night when word came down from the state supreme court. Others were jubilant, but I was hit with a sinking feeling: *that's not enough time.* Maybe that's all the time our lawyers could get, but it troubled me. Representing Gore-Lieberman before the Miami-Dade Canvassing

Board, I made a public statement that the board was committed to finishing its recount. But now I feared that Republicans would try to tie up the recount process until the November 26 deadline expired. David Leahy, supervisor of elections for Miami-Dade, was also worried. "Certainly the question that we must answer," he said, "is what additional resources we need to consider if we are to meet the deadline."[60]

The next day, Tuesday, November 21, the radio airwaves of Miami were buzzing as callers phoned in with absurd accusations about the canvassing board members, two of whom were state judges who would need to stand for reelection. But the real counterstrike was far less predictable and much more sinister.

Bush operatives sent out a call nationwide for Republican supporters to flood into Florida and do anything they could to disrupt the recount.[61] Bush's investment paid enormous dividends in Miami on Wednesday, November 22, when a demonstration against the Miami-Dade manual recount turned into a riot—what has come to be called "the Brooks Brothers Riot," after the preppy clothing worn by most of the protestors.[62]

Struggling to comply with the November 26 deadline established by the Florida Supreme Court, the county canvassing board had decided that morning not to recount the entire six hundred fifty-four thousand votes cast in Miami-Dade County. Instead, only the eleven thousand undervotes, those ballots that machine tabulation had not registered a vote for president, would be counted by hand. These votes were believed by many to be heavily in favor of Gore. While the canvassing board proceeded with its truncated recount on the nineteenth floor of county hall, about one hundred fifty protestors gathered outside the room, chanting "Shut it down!" and "Stop the count, stop the fraud!" The crowd, morphing quickly into a mob, began pounding the doors of the County Elections Department.

Joe Geller, Miami-Dade Democratic Party chairman, was in the office to pick up a sample ballot, but when he attempted to leave, protestors shouted he was stealing a vote, and chased him down, pushing and manhandling him. "Suddenly, I was surrounded by a screaming, shoving, insane crowd, shouting that I had done something I hadn't done," Geller says. "People [were] grabbing at me and my clothes, and there was almost no security. I couldn't believe those people weren't arrested."[63]

The rioters warned the canvassing board that one thousand angry Cuban Americans were marching on the building to join the protest.[64] Indeed, some of the Spanish-language radio stations were broadcasting inflammatory calls to the Cuban community, which, still outraged by the Elian Gonzalez incident, had voted more than 80 percent for Bush. The riot was largely portrayed in the media as a typical example of Miami "tantrum politics"—street riots had broken out only a few months before when Elian was taken from his uncle's home in Little Havana. But it was in fact a carefully orchestrated operation by the Republicans and the Bush camp. Contemporary accounts of the riot appearing in *Time Europe, Salon,* and the *London Sunday Times,* the latter of which had a correspondent at the scene, reported that most of the protestors were well-dressed Anglo-Americans.[65]

It was an astonishing spectacle of brute intimidation, almost unbelievable in the world's leading democracy. To those on the receiving end, the threat of violence during the melee seemed very real. "I'm all for anyone's right to protest," Geller told *Time Europe.* "These were brownshirt tactics." And *Salon* quoted him as saying, "This was not a Miami moment. It was outsiders, Hitler youth, sent in by the Republicans to intimidate the election officials."[66]

But it worked. Within two hours of the lawless protest, the canvassing board voted to halt the recount. Board members denied they were cowed by the protest and claimed the decision came in response to the Florida Supreme Court's tight deadline. I arrived minutes after the recount was halted. We launched an emergency appeal to try to restart the recount, but to no avail. Strikingly, the supervisor of elections changed the reason for why he chose to walk off the job. In the morning, before the mob scene, the supervisor estimated that the board had enough time to complete the recount of undervotes, but after the pandemonium, he revised his story.[67] This dramatic and deeply troubling incident may have been the key event in the entire 2000 presidential election struggle. Ending the Miami-Dade recount may well have cost Gore hundreds if not thousands of votes—enough to obliterate Bush's slim lead.

During the riot, I was in my office preparing papers for the next Republican lawsuit, and I arrived at the courthouse immediately after the protestors dispersed. I was so immersed in the legal battles at the time that I didn't fully comprehend the significance of the Brooks Brothers Riot and how utterly cynical it was. While the Bush lawyers we battled were honorable, this was far different; and the over-the-top, below-the-belt tactics of the "mob" portended something ominous. In retrospect, the brute exercise in disruptive tactics, like the Brooks Brothers Riot, signaled what turned out to be a darkening era of the bloodsport that now routinely characterizes high-stakes political battles.

We sued to force Miami-Dade to resume the manual recount, but the intermediate appellate court and then the Florida Supreme Court refused with a ruling received the next day, on Thanksgiving.[68] As a result, Miami-Dade certified its numbers from November 14. Harris accepted this tally and certified Palm Beach County's numbers from the fourteenth as well. Only Broward was able to certify numbers from the manual recount, yielding a net gain of 567 votes for Gore. Harris announced the new vote totals on November 27 and certified Bush as the winner.

Bush took his cue. "The election was close, but tonight, after a count, a recount, and yet another manual recount, Secretary Cheney and I are honored and humbled to have won the state of Florida, which gives us the needed electoral votes to win the election," he said.[69]

Far from throwing in the towel, an energized Gore sued to contest the Florida election. "The hand counts will still be valid evidence in the contest action, no matter what the Supreme Court rules," said Klain, a senior Gore legal advisor. "In fact, it could be very powerful evidence as to who got the most votes."[70]

I was selected as one of the members of the trial team appearing before Circuit Court Judge N. Sanders Sauls in Leon County.[71] But we knew it would be almost impossible to win before a conservative judge like Sauls. It's not that conservative judges are for you or against you in partisan terms, but that they are extremely reluctant to change whatever the tally was on Election Day. Based on my past experiences in election cases, so much of what happens in these cases begins with the judge's own philosophy concerning whether judges should ever intervene in democratic elections.

When you know you can't win at the trial level, the fewer witnesses the better. I turned in a witness list with twelve names on it. Lead trial counsel, David Boies, marked through each of my suggestions. He knew better. When the trial turns on witness testimony, and the keys are matters of fact rather than law, an appeals court can't do much. The supreme court cannot revisit a decision a trial court makes regarding disputed witness testimony. Boies's strategy—rightly—was to have as few witnesses as possible. It was all about law and documents. There's not enough time, he said, and he understood that no one on our team believed this judge would rule for us. (I did have the opportunity to cross-examine one Republican witness. We knew he had been involved in the mob actions orchestrated by the Bush camp. He was caught in the act in a photo. We put up the photo in the middle of the cross-examination—another memorable moment, in my opinion.)

At least the legal battle moved swiftly. Judge Sauls of Leon County Circuit Court, after two days of hearings in favor of Bush, turned down Gore's request for a resumption of manual recounting in Miami-Dade and Palm Beach Counties.[72] The evidence, he ruled, did not present a reasonable probability the rejected votes would change the outcome of the election. He further ruled that Gore had failed to prove any illegality or abuse of discretion. If a losing candidate wished to contest an irregularity, he ruled, that irregularity must be corrected across the state.

When we went before the Florida Supreme Court, Boies's strategy was fascinating and his skills were remarkable. His theory was that once the ballots were moved into evidence, the court had no choice but to count them. The view of the Florida lawyers, however, was that you had to show more solid reasons to conclude that the result of the election was "in doubt." Boies began his oral argument on this theory, but when the judges started pushing him, asking if he didn't have reason to believe the election was in doubt, he turned like a figure skater. He argued that the partial recount in Miami showed increased numbers for Gore, as did the recounts in Broward and Palm Beach. Miami-Dade provided one of the strongest reasons to believe that if you did a recount, you'd get a different outcome. Voting machines couldn't see the votes, but human eyes could. That's a large part of what carried the day for us before the Florida Supreme Court.

By a four-to-three vote, the Florida Supreme Court rejected Saul's opinion almost entirely, ordering 383 votes back into Gore's column.[73] The court also held that Gore was entitled to have the eleven thousand undervotes in Miami-Dade counted. The court called for an immediate recount of all undervotes in the state, something like forty-five thousand ballots.[74] To some extent, the court's own decision to recount all sixty-seven counties erased some of the painful doubt concerning the earlier failure to seek an all-counties recount throughout Florida.

As the final chapter moved to the US Supreme Court, I drove to Sarasota to represent Gore at the local canvassing board's recount. We had divided up the counties very quickly following the decision on December 8, the day before. It was inspiring to be on the conference call early that Saturday morning as the voices of dozens of volunteer attorneys appeared from nowhere to join the cause all across the state. Perhaps a little melodramatically, it reminded me of American minutemen answering the summons of duty centuries earlier. I was excited when I met with the Sarasota Canvassing Board in the morning, as they planned to start their recount in the afternoon. For more than an hour, I was getting phone calls indicating that, around the state, we were gaining ground.

There is one phone call I will never forget. While I was in the car during the board's lunch break, I got the call that the Supreme Court had halted the recount.[75] At first I was in shock. It was a jarring end to the biggest roller coaster ride of my life. Just the night before, the Florida Supreme Court reversed Saul, one of the most exhilarating moments imaginable. And now, less than twenty-four hours later, we were dropped from the mountaintop into the deepest crater. But you can't stay down when you have bad news. I started thinking about what we could do to recover, what legal steps we could pursue.

My instinctive reaction to any setback is to think how best to climb out of the hole. Sometimes, though, even with a long climb up, there's no way out. As the ruling sank in, my other reaction was a sense of profound discouragement. It seemed like the cynics among us had been right all along. We'd heard rumors from around the US Supreme Court that there was interest in rounding up the five votes needed to give Bush the win. I had dismissed the rumors. I assumed the conservative judges would abide by their principles and not intervene in state law issues. But they ignored the traditional respect for state processes that conservative jurists had so long championed. The result-oriented decision by the Supreme Court profoundly denigrated what I thought were the core principles of respect for the rule of law. It was devastating in every sense of the word.

After hearing oral arguments on December 11, the US Supreme Court ruled, one day later, in favor of Bush, overturning the Florida Supreme Court's ruling and ordering an end to the recounts.[76] That was it. Game over. Bush won.

But at the time, and now, looking back a decade later, I am still proud of the work we did on the Gore-Lieberman legal team. If we had known it was going to come down to five votes on the Supreme Court, there would have been very little we could have done differently. Once you make it as far as the highest court in the land, you can go no further. Not that we couldn't have done some things better along the way, but in the big picture we did our best, and we were all proud of those five extraordinary weeks.

As I packed up my papers to return home to Miami, I reflected on an early meeting with the legal team when one of the attorneys joked that if it were not for me, we wouldn't be there. He meant the Elian Gonzalez case, which turned Miami's Cuban population fiercely against the Democrats, even though Vice President Al Gore had broken with President Clinton on the question of sending the boy back to Cuba.[77] With so small a margin in Florida's vote totals, there were other mishaps, like the butterfly ballot and the shutting down of the Miami-Dade Canvassing Board, that could have saved the election for Gore. Elian really had been a tipping point, though, costing him thousands of votes in Miami-Dade County. Without it, Gore might well have become president, altering in ways we can only imagine the first eight years of the twenty-first century.

PART TWO

The Case of the Missing E-Votes

Losing the Courtroom Battle but Winning the Public's War

Six years after I received the history-transforming news in Sarasota about the halt of the 2000 presidential recount, I was back. On Election Day 2006, I had returned to Sarasota, but this time things would be different. As campaign counsel for Christine Jennings, the Democratic nominee for Florida's Thirteenth Congressional District, centered in Sarasota, I had every hope that her strong candidacy might be a historic difference-maker. Polling data placed her in the lead over Republican Vern Buchanan and, if elected, Jennings might be the additional Democrat needed in Congress to provide a Democratic majority. Everything about the Jennings candidacy was compelling. A personable, classy, and articulate former bank president, her hard work and integrity had taken her all the way from bank teller to the top of her industry. She was from central casting for the American dream.

But by midafternoon on Election Day 2006, Chris and I were on stage for a press conference that should never have been needed. For days prior to the election and with disturbing frequency throughout Election Day, we were getting inundated with reports that votes for the congressional seat were being cancelled by Sarasota's paperless touch-screen voting machines. Although the scenarios varied, a frequent eye-witness account was that after a voter selected Jennings, her name did not appear on the ballot summary screen that lists all the voter's selections when voting is completed. Some of the people contacting us with this disturbing news had corrected the erasure of the Jennings vote by going back to the District Thirteen election page and voting for her again. Many voters did not double check by reviewing the ballot summary page when they finished voting. Although dozens of reports of malfunctions had been pouring in, by Election Day it had become a flood of trouble. We had written about these concerns to the Sarasota elections office the week before but had been ignored. By midafternoon on Tuesday's election, when we stepped in front of television cameras to alert voters to the chronic computer problems, things seemed to be getting worse, much worse.

By evening, our fears were confirmed all too well. It became apparent that thousands had not reexamined their vote summaries and that many thousands of votes were missing from the District Thirteen Congressional election. It was a painful evening for Chris and the campaign team as the initial tally showed her well behind her opponent, Vern Buchanan. As more votes came in from Sarasota County, her hometown as well as the largest community of voters in District Thirteen, though, the race kept tightening. Remarkably, by the time the final tallies came in, she was fewer than four hundred votes behind Buchanan out of the nearly two hundred forty thousand votes cast for that race.

But the most striking number was the total of voters for whom no vote was recorded for the US Congress: 18,412. The shortfall of 15 percent from the more than one hundred thousand votes cast in Sarasota was stunning, given the intense national interest in her race. There was no precedent for so many missing votes in a hotly contested congressional election, and this campaign had been red hot. Not only was this the nation's second most expensive congressional race of the year, but interest was further accentuated by the fact that it would fill the vacancy left by incumbent Katherine Harris, the polarizing heroine/villain who helped the Republican cause so mightily during the 2000 presidential recount. Moreover, because the Democrats needed a net gain of only fifteen seats that year to seize control of the US House of Representatives from the Republicans, the Jennings-Buchanan race could determine which party had control. In light of the flood of complaints about votes missing from the touch-screen machines, the most likely explanation was that a computer glitch, such as a bug in the software, had erased thousands of Sarasota votes. Starting on election night, we immediately launched a legal and political campaign to challenge not only the election results but also the paperless election system itself.

Before proceeding to court, there was one formality to be observed—ironically enough, it was the recount. The good news was the fact that the microscopic margin between Buchanan and Jennings required under Florida law that a manual recount be conducted. The bad news was that there is no meaningful way to conduct a manual recount of a paperless voting system. In a surreal exercise in futility, the Sarasota Canvassing Board proceeded with the oxymoronic manual recount of purely electronic voting. Because there was no paper trail of physical ballots to count, the "recount" consisted simply of rerunning the computers with the same data as before, printing out pages from the computer's data bank that mirrored the existing electronic data, and counting those pages. Needless to say, the same totals as before were essentially repeated. None of the missing votes could be retrieved because the actual voting was paperless, and so there were no actual ballots to manually recount.

On November 20, 2006, when the state of Florida officially certified that Buchanan had won the election by 369 votes, Jennings immediately filed an election contest under Section 102.168 of the Florida Statutes, alleging that malfunction of Sarasota County's iVotronic system had cost her the election. Several hearings later, though, the trial judge in Tallahassee refused to allow any examination by our experts of the computer system that had accounted for the disappearing votes. The manufacturer of the voting machines, Election Systems & Software, had succeeded in claiming that its right to protect its trade secrets prevented an examination of election hardware and software. As a result, our computer experts would have no opportunity to locate the software bug that we believed erased so many votes.

One reality was not a secret. As the parties litigated the issue through November and December 2006, the experts for both sides agreed that, but for the missing votes from Jennings's Sarasota stronghold, she would have won the election. In fact, by applying her margin of victory in Sarasota to the number of missing votes from that county, the net gain to Jennings would have given her a clear margin of victory estimated from more than six hundred votes to as many as two thousand.

In light of the obvious reality of an election gone wrong, limited testing of the ES&S voting machines was undertaken by the state elections department. But these were the same bureaucrats who had previously assured the public that these machines were flawless. Not surprisingly then, the people who had already given the touch-screen machines their validation earlier did not invalidate them now. We complained bitterly about the preordained results of the modest testing, but to no avail.

We ultimately fared no better in court or even in Congress. In a congressional or senatorial election, state court proceedings are often pursued but are never binding. The US Constitution decrees that any dispute over an election of members of the US House or Senate must ultimately be determined only by the respective House or Senate.[78] For that reason, the House of Representatives itself was the ultimate decision maker over the Jennings-Buchanan dispute, a process governed by federal law pursuant to the Federal Contested Elections Act, Title 2 of the US Code, sections 381–96. Even though the Democrats held a majority in the House, too, they authorized only limited testing of the voting machines, never solving the missing-votes mystery and leaving Buchanan in the congressional seat Jennings had rightfully won.

Although neither the courthouse doors nor the halls of Congress were truly opened to the Jennings case, our efforts struck a powerful chord with the public. Florida needed a voice for the cause of restoring confidence in voting, and Chris Jennings accepted that role. In an attempt several years earlier to challenge Florida's paperless systems, a US Democratic congressman, Robert Wexler of Palm Beach, had gone to federal court to challenge the legality of the touch-screen voting. Although unsuccessful, his efforts proved to be a critical foundation for the campaign we brought later. Wexler had presented the right issues, but he did not have the actual example of a disastrous election mishap. By providing a statistically overwhelming case that, as a result of eighteen thousand missing votes in Sarasota, the intended outcome of an election was thwarted, our efforts became the poster child for the cause of requiring verifiable paper trails.

In our campaign against paperless voting, Chris and I visited newspaper editorial boards throughout the state and garnered a remarkable sweep of supportive endorsements. We had the facts—eighteen thousand missing votes as well as a consensus of experts that the lost votes meant a lost election—and we had the message. As we had emphasized from the beginning, we told editors about the "crisis of confidence" and underscored the paramount need to restore confidence to a Florida electorate that was still disillusioned from the 2000 recount. As we kept emphasizing, from hanging chads to missing votes, Floridians needed a voting system that would restore their faith in the principle that every vote would indeed be counted. As one editorial expressed things about Christine Jennings, "Good for her. She kept the state and the nation paying attention to the hazards of touch screens."[79] Some editorials, such as those from the *Tallahassee Democrat*, not only criticized paperless voting but also called upon the courts in our case to allow experts for the parties to examine the software. Yet the focus on the larger issue of paperless voting was for many more energizing than the undoubtedly critical court battle for Chris Jennings. In June 2007, the Associated Press observed that "her claim of a computer malfunction in Sarasota County gained attention as far away as France and fueled Florida's move to require a paper trail in future elections."[80]

Our litigation in court and Congress did not succeed, but our case before the public could not have been more successful. In 2007, in the wake of our media campaign, the governor of Florida, Charlie Crist, a reader of newspapers with an instinct for good government causes, cited the Jennings-Buchanan race as a contributing factor to his decision to support the requirement of verifiable paper trails. On May 21, 2007, Governor Crist signed into law House Bill 537 requiring that all votes in Florida be cast with optical-scan paper ballots. By 2008, paper trails were a reality in the state of Florida, and the state surprised many by landing in the win column for Barack Obama.

During that same election, Chris Jennings lost her second campaign against Republican Vern Buchanan, this time by a much wider margin, as Buchanan had shrewdly used his time in Congress to strengthen his once-shaky support. She had lost her battles for a US House seat, but she triumphed in her war against paperless touch-screen voting. As one of District Thirteen's newspapers summarized the Jennings quest, "Give Christine Jennings credit for sticking to her guns and risking her political future to seek change. It is a goal she has embraced from the beginning—always telling interviewers the issue is not just about her. Now we can see it is indeed not just about her."[81] The people of Sarasota might have lost their choice for Congress in 2006, but at least the people of Florida finally gained an election system they could believe in.

CHAPTER 6

OPEN TRIALS
Press Freedom or Press Free-for-All?

THE TRADITION OF TRANSPARENT TRIALS

In the sensational 2004 trial of Scott Peterson, accused of killing his wife and unborn child, a public-opinion survey indicated that more than 50 percent of the community already believed he was guilty, based upon the media blitz that continued to blast him. And yet the Peterson percentage of toxicity fell well short of record levels. In one landmark case decided in the early 1960s, a small Indiana town convicted the defendant charged with six brutal murders in the court of public opinion before his trial even started. Out of the four hundred thirty people summoned for jury duty for his trial, 80 percent had already concluded that the defendant was probably guilty.[1]

The pretrial poisoning of the very people who are to serve as fair and impartial jurors has triggered a debate over open trials that has raged for centuries.

Anglo-American tradition predating the Norman Conquest reveals court proceedings in England that resembled modern-day town hall meetings where locals would enthusiastically decide the guilt or innocence of a defendant, in effect by voting thumbs-up or thumbs-down. That was the earliest form of open trials, and the evolution of the jury system brought no diminution of public access.[2]

While neither the English monarchy nor fish-and-chips were big hits in the thirteen colonies, the pilgrims embraced open justice more enthusiastically. "Open proceedings enhanced the performance of all involved, protected the judge from imputations of dishonesty, and served to educate the public," noted one historian.[3]

Today, the US Supreme Court continues to support openness because it "guards against the miscarriage of justice by subjecting the police, prosecutors, and judicial proceedings to extensive public scrutiny and criticism."[4] An open trial also fosters respect not only for those who enforce the law but also for the rule of law itself. When crimes are committed, especially acts that provoke outrage or protest, society demands that the wrongdoers be brought to justice. But vigilantism is a bad idea.

At a primal level, we have long believed that by openly trying the accused and punishing the guilty we obviate the need for vengeance, despite the allure of Charles Bronson roaming the streets or Uma Thurman trying to "kill Bill." When inflamed by crimes of violence such as a brutal homicide, open justice can offer a community the catharsis that invisible verdicts fail to evoke.

Even injustice is also better when it is public. Not every judge or juror is King Solomon, and mistakes happen, but a troubling result can create more harm if it is never explained. As courts recognize, "People in an open society do not demand infallibility from their institutions, but it is difficult for them to accept what they are prohibited from observing."[5]

In addition to building a foundation of respect for law and relegating vigilantism to action movies, openness helps to educate the public about the legal system. Famed Supreme Court Justice William Brennan emphasized that access will "contribute to public understanding of the rule of law and to comprehension of the function of the entire criminal justice system."[6] Television shows like *Judge Judy* have their moments, but the proceedings inside real courtrooms are apparently what our nation's founders had in mind. It was a firm faith in open access to justice that prompted them to incorporate freedom of the press into the Constitution. Even at times when all the parties and lawyers want to close courtroom doors, the First Amendment keeps them open to the public and to the press. While these safeguards are vital for society as a whole, they can create risky business for the defendant in a high-profile case.

PRETRIAL PUBLICITY AND PRETRIAL PREJUDICE

Robert Morvillo, attorney for Martha Stewart, describes coverage of a high-profile defendant's prosecution as "overwhelmingly negative."[7] Publicized court proceedings often create personal injury as surely as they offer societal gain. When accusations resound from television voices and newspaper pages, "presumption of innocence" does not always ring true because the appearance of guilt is generated by chronic repetition of the accusations. Defendants deny early and often. Their denials, however, are professions of self-interest. In contrast, the accusations of the prosecutors and police are seen as unbiased testimonials by the guardians protecting us from criminals.

For that reason, pretrial publicity is never a defendant's friend and can often be a crushing adversary. For decades, empirical studies have repeatedly shown that negative pretrial publicity can contribute to a negative trial result.[8] That said, not all publicity is created equal. Some published studies have suggested that weaker prosecution cases benefit less from pretrial publicity than do more compelling cases.[9] According to a 1999 survey, any bias generated by pretrial publicity in marginal prosecution cases was reduced, and even eliminated, through the course of jury deliberations. With stronger cases, however, the initial predisposition created by adverse publicity persisted and ultimately contributed to guilty outcomes.[10] Perhaps significantly, exposure to pretrial publicity laden with emotional content appeared more likely to negatively affect the jurors' deliberations at trial.[11]

Whatever may be the variations in the studies, they generally comport with the common sense that pretrial publicity can be hurtful and is almost never helpful for defendants.[12] As one real juror candidly admitted in a high-profile case, "You can't forget what you see and hear."[13]

THE DILEMMA

This negative impact of an open trial imperils a defendant's constitutional right to a trial by an impartial jury. Even the nineteenth-century hanging judge, Roy Bean, who heard cases in his saloon along the Rio Grande in the western Texas desert, purportedly insisted that defendants would get a fair trial before the hanging. In the century since Judge Bean presided, the American instinct for a fair trial has remained a cornerstone of our legal system.

This free press–fair trial dilemma represents a collision between two cherished American values. The Supreme Court explained, "But when the case is a 'sensational' one, tension develops between the rights of the accused to stand trial by an impartial jury and the rights guaranteed others by the First Amendment."[14] Like a parent asked to choose between two children, the court has declined to elevate one value above the other. In the milestone Nebraska Press Association case, the court considered the constitutionality of an order that prevented the media from publishing or broadcasting information about a man accused of murdering an entire family in a small town in Nebraska. The court wrote, "The authors of the Bill of Rights did not undertake to assign priorities as between the First Amendment and Sixth Amendment rights, ranking one as superior to the other.... It is not for us to rewrite the Constitution by undertaking what they declined to do."[15]

JUDGES DO NOT GO NUCLEAR

In fact, court decisions almost invariably view silencing the press as the nuclear weapon in a judge's arsenal, too drastic for actual deployment. Courts almost never muzzle the media because such an order would constitute a "prior restraint," that is, judicial censorship of the press. The refusal to allow judicial intervention to control the press is a tradition that has endured for centuries.[16]

In the nation's first "trial of the century," future president John Adams successfully defended British officers accused in the Boston Massacre, amid the "passions of the populace that sometime play in influencing potential jurors." Thomas Jefferson lamented the fact that a public servant "should not be arraigned in a newspaper," but concluded that it is "an evil for which there is no remedy."[17]

In modern times, there have been few exceptions to these principles, and the exceptions were short-lived. When Panamanian dictator Manuel Noriega was prosecuted on charges of drug trafficking, the federal judge initially prevented CNN from broadcasting a conversation between Noriega and his defense lawyers. The federal appeals court allowed the temporary order to remain in effect, largely due to concerns of exposing the contents of the attorney-client conversation. Ultimately, however, the federal trial court found that the attorney-client contents had already been broadcast by CNN and permitted its use.

During the Colorado rape prosecution of Kobe Bryant, confidential materials implicating the privacy rights of the accuser were briefly released when clerical personnel accidentally posted them on the court's Web site. The trial judge ordered the media not to use the information it had obtained, and a divided Colorado Supreme Court allowed that decision to stand. After a US Supreme Court justice expressed concerns about the prior restraint, however, the trial judge withdrew his restraining order.

The decisions in the Noriega and Bryant cases, far from representing a judicial mainstream, swam upstream—and only briefly—against the strongest of constitutional currents. Due to the overwhelming policy against prior restraint, allowing the press to report the news as it sees fit is almost always the law of the land.

THE SUPREME COURT HANDBOOK ON PRETRIAL PUBLICITY

The 1954 trial and conviction of osteopath Sam Sheppard for the murder of his wife ignited a press sensation, a courtroom disaster, and, ultimately, a set of guidelines for dealing with media frenzies of the future. Sheppard had drowned in a media downpour that saturated the community with allegations about the bludgeoning death of his pregnant wife.[18] Decrying everything from his lack of cooperation with police to his refusal to take a lie-detector test, front-page editorials proclaimed that he was "getting away with murder." News reports about his cheating on his late wife were, of course, lapped up.

Just as bad as the howl outside the courtroom was the media's commotion on the inside. According to the Supreme Court "bedlam reigned…and newsmen took over practically the entire courtroom," with twenty reporters setting up at a table just a few feet from counsel. This created constant disruption and prevented the defendant and his counsel from engaging in confidential discussions. Even the jurors were drawn into the media's glare, with some featured in the newspaper.

Lambasting the "carnival atmosphere" that dominated the trial, the Supreme Court reversed the conviction after Sheppard spent a decade in prison. To keep courtroom circuses from coming to town again and again, the written opinion in *Sheppard v. Maxwell* listed steps to minimize the collateral damage that intense media coverage inflicts upon on a trial. These measures include: (1) changing venue, that is, transferring the trial to a different location; (2) postponing the trial until the local furor subsides; (3) screening out jurors with fixed opinions as to guilt or innocence; and (4) providing judicial instructions on the juror's sworn duty to decide the case solely on the evidence presented inside the courtroom. Additionally, courts can consider sequestering the jury, for example, by requiring that they stay in a hotel without access to television or newspapers during court proceedings; and if all else fails, they can consider ordering a new trial so that the defendant might finally get a day in court that is fair. In fact, in a 1966 retrial where he was represented by F. Lee Bailey, a jury acquitted Sheppard.[19]

The case was an extreme combination of a weak judge and a rambunctious press. Even so, courts continue to adhere to their guidelines in attempting to balance the dilemma of a free press versus a fair trial. Although the Supreme Court found it necessary to erase Sheppard's conviction, in other trials where the proceedings resemble a courtroom more than a circus, the potential harm that pretrial publicity inflicts upon the defendant may not be enough to wipe out a conviction and bring on a new trial.

MEASURING HOW MUCH BECOMES TOO MUCH

The Supreme Court, for instance, did not intervene to reverse the conviction of Jack Roland "Murph the Surf" Murphy, who had been convicted of robbery and burglary amid relentless news coverage during the 1970s.[20] Notorious for his role in the theft of the Star of India years earlier, Murphy had also been indicted for murder, along with other crimes. Transcripts of the court proceedings showed that, in response to questioning, some jurors confirmed that they had learned about the Star of India convictions and other arrests from press reports. Troubled by such circumstances, Chief Justice Warren Burger—hardly a liberal flame-thrower—wrote that the "trial judge was woefully remiss in failing to insulate prospective jurors from the bizarre media coverage of this case."[21] In allowing the guilty verdict to stand, the Supreme Court's test for whether constitutional rights were violated depended on whether there were any indications that the trial was not fundamentally fair.

Based on that standard, judges are encouraged to do everything realistically possible under the law to minimize the impact of adverse publicity. Providing a trial that is "fundamentally fair" means essentially a judge's "best efforts" to protect against poisoned publicity.[22] It is not a standard of perfection.

NOT EMPTY MINDS, JUST OPEN ONES

Just as perfect trials are unattainable, jurors are not flawless. Nor do they need to be mindless. In confronting pretrial publicity, the trial judge is not obliged to search the highways and byways to find trial jurors who have never heard a thing about a publicity-charged case. In fact, as the Supreme Court once observed, "Scarcely any of those best qualified to serve as jurors would not have formed some impression or opinion as to the merits of the case."[23]

As a result, trials of the rich and famous do not require jurors with an empty mind, just an open one. To find those jurors, during jury selection judges and attorneys try to ask the most penetrating questions possible about the diet of news coverage that jurors have consumed, especially the spicier entrées (such as shocking greed, horrific violence, or any kind of sex). But jurors can be closemouthed about whether they are truly open-minded. Inevitably, whatever may be their predisposition, most jurors insist that they can be fair and decide the case based solely upon the evidence at trial. Even if they have been studying every tabloid at the supermarket, most believe they can erase it all with one finger tap on the mind's *delete* key.

Jurors infected by pretrial publicity may not manifest symptoms. Except for cases that include bloodcurdling atrocities, most of us want to say that we can judge without prejudgment. Even if jurors tell the truth when they promise spotless impartiality, the actual impact of prejudicial infusions is hard for even the jurors themselves to know. For that reason, one leading study of simulated juries concluded that the jury selection process was largely ineffective in weeding out jurors with publicity-induced biases.

THE POISON PILLS

Since jurors are allowed to decide cases even if they have read about them, and most will say that their readings do not diminish their fairness, it can be difficult for judges to draw the dividing line between the media-exposed and media-infected. To assess how curable the news disease may be, courts often focus upon the character of information received by juries. Unsurprisingly, one of the most explosive of all bombshells is a defendant's confession. Its seismic impact is all the more harmful to a fair trial if the publicized confession is one that the defendant later retracted or one that a judge could throw out for technical reasons.

In a case of kidnapping and murder in Louisiana, the defendant's incriminating interview with the local sheriff had been broadcasted repeatedly throughout the community. After the inevitable guilty verdict, the Supreme Court threw out the conviction. Because the community had been infected by the "spectacle" of the confession, the court found that the defendant's trial was not a fair day in court, but instead "could be but a hollow formality."[24]

Severe publicity contamination also occurs when potential jurors learn about a defendant's prior criminal history. When defendants are tried in a court of law, surprisingly little information is usually permitted about a defendant's criminal past. Arrests that do not result in a conviction are almost never presented to jurors, unless they involve acts very similar to the criminality on trial. Even prior felony convictions are barely mentioned. Unless the defendant steps up to the witness stand, a vast amount of personal baggage is never delivered to the jury.

In the court of public opinion, however, prior convictions, arrests, and even rank accusations constitute live ammunition that jurors may not forget once the real trial begins. As a result, judges have long been concerned with the "high potential for prejudice" inflicted by publicity about a defendant's criminal past.

In a case involving the illegal dispensing of a narcotic, the trial judge correctly refused to allow the jury to consider the defendant's prior conviction for practicing medicine without a license. Several members of the jury, however, read about the conviction in local newspapers. After the jury returned a guilty verdict, the Supreme Court ruled that the defendant was entitled to a new trial because the unfairness is just as great when damaging information improperly reaches the jury through news reports as when it is presented by prosecutors in a courtroom.

Straightforward reports about the basic facts of a case are less troubling to courts because jurors will receive the same information at trial. In the case of a New England wife accused of enticing her fifteen-year-old lover to murder her husband, an avalanche of publicity piled onto the trial. The appeals court refused, though, to order a new trial because most of the coverage consisted of "straightforward, unemotional factual accounts of events."[25] Especially when courts find that pretrial publicity is little more than a preview of the feature presentations at trial, such information may not equate to contamination.

Sirhan Sirhan, who assassinated Senator Robert F. Kennedy in 1968, attempted to challenge his conviction based upon the pretrial blitz that included plenty of publicity about his confession. The supreme court of California found, however, that Sirhan's right to a fair trial was not violated because he never intended to deny the fact that he killed Robert F. Kennedy. At trial, his defense lawyer had not sought an outright acquittal but instead hoped for a conviction on a lesser form of homicide. Since the jury's pretrial exposure to the incriminating statements did not diverge greatly from the evidence at trial, the publicity was neither misleading nor unfair.

Bad publicity is unavoidable. After all, there is not much good to say about being criminally prosecuted. But our system demands that the judge imposes every reasonable safeguard to ensure a fair trial. In significant respects, when an appeals court determines whether pretrial publicity has so infected a proceeding as to require a do-over, it is the responsibility of the trial judge to treat the infection.

CHANGE OF SCENERY

Location, Location

Rather than attempt to find an open-minded jury in Oklahoma, when Timothy McVeigh, one of the most despised criminals in US history, was prosecuted for the bombing of the federal building in Oklahoma City where 168 people perished—including many children—the trial judge transferred the trial to Denver, Colorado. As recognized in the Sheppard case, one of the most important remedies when a defendant is already found guilty by the neighbors is to find a different neighborhood.

McVeigh's trial was a federal case. In federal cases, the judge can move the trial to a different part of the country, since the federal court system operates throughout the states and US territories. The vast majority of criminal cases, however, especially violent crimes, are prosecuted in state criminal systems where interstate transfers are not acceptable because the jurisdiction in a state judicial system extends only to the borders of that state. As a result, publicity storms can be harder to outrun.

For example, in the gruesome and spectacularly publicized murder trial of Charles Manson, he tried to secure a venue transfer away from Los Angeles, the scene of the crimes and the center of the publicity. After his conviction, Manson appealed and challenged the trial judge's refusal to change the venue of the trial. The courts found Los Angeles acceptable, though, in no small part because the rest of California, indeed the rest of the nation, had also been immersed in the downpour of publicity about the brutal cult slayings.[26]

In the 2002 prosecution of John Walker Lindh, the "American Taliban" who was accused of fighting against his own country in the fields of Afghanistan, his attorneys sought a transfer away from the Virginia Federal Court near the Pentagon in Washington, DC, the scene of one of the September 11, 2001, atrocities. In denying the move, the federal judge pointed out, "one would have to go to planet Pluto to find those who have not heard of this."[27]

While Lindh's case was resolved through a plea agreement, the problem of finding a better home for cases of national notoriety persists. Without the ability to identify a better venue, a bad venue is hard to escape, and there are no courtrooms available on Pluto.

Calling the Movers

Scott Peterson followed the classic strategy for securing a transfer to a different courthouse prior to his trial for murdering his wife, Laci, and their unborn child. The crime had already appalled the entire community in Modesto, California. Then things got worse. Peterson was hammered even more with the revelations of his mistress, Amber Frey, as well as Peterson's own strange assortment of incriminating antics. Understandably, his attorneys tried to move as far as possible from the populace that was denouncing Peterson as a "monster in chains." By presenting opinion surveys to confirm that Peterson had already been convicted in the local court of public opinion, his counsel succeeded in getting a transfer to a courtroom several counties away. Though no county had escaped the national media blitz, Peterson stood a better chance of a fair trial if the case were tried somewhere else, anywhere else.

In contrast to the public-opinion surveys that persuaded the court to move the case for Scott Peterson, another sensational murder case flunked the test for a venue change by failing to do the groundwork to prove community-wide contamination. The Stroble case, regarding the murder of a six-year-old child, was plagued by blistering coverage featuring reports of a confession.[28] Putting the nails in the coffin of a certain conviction was news coverage describing the defendant as a "were-wolf," "fiend," and "sex-mad killer." Although the defendant presented the court with plenty of newspaper articles documenting the blistering coverage, the appeals court refused to find that a fair trial in Los Angeles had been impossible because the defense submitted no evidence that any juror was actually prejudiced by the news stories.

For media-battered defendants, travel plans to faraway places are highly preferable. In a brutal murder and kidnapping case in Arizona, the court found that a transfer of a hundred miles was separation enough, even though the defendant wanted more mileage. Half the jurors in the new locale admitted to having heard about the case. Two years had passed, though, since the commission of the crime, and the judge took extensive steps to minimize the adverse consequences of publicity. Rather than a media "circus," the appeals court found that even with cameras inside the courtroom, the trial was conducted with the necessary "serenity and sobriety." As a result, the appeals court found that even if the venue transfer did not get what the defendant wanted, he still got the distance he needed for a fair trial.[29]

Sometimes, trials keep moving. In a Florida case where nine-year-old Jessica Lunsford was abducted, assaulted, and buried alive in February 2005, the judge initially moved the trial of defendant John Couey from Citrus County to nearby Sumter County. He soon found, however, that the community's outrage had spread throughout Central Florida. As a result, in the summer of 2006 the judge halted the Sumter proceedings when jury selection became an exercise in futility. The trial eventually landed in Miami, a totally different media market several hundred miles away from the scene of the horrible crime. In 2007, the child killer was tried, convicted, and sentenced to death.

In general, when venue transfers are requested in advance of the trial, the defendant's best ticket out of town is an opinion survey that demonstrates too much home-court advantage for the prosecution. At times, though, rather than decide about jury contamination before jury selection, judges want to try to start the trial and take temperatures before deciding whether local feelings are too heated. During the jury-selection process, the questioning often centers upon the exposure to pretrial publicity and predispositions toward the defendant. In high-profile cases, even before jurors report for duty, courts often send detailed questionnaires to the universe of potential jurors about their preexisting knowledge and tendencies.

In an Iowa case about a woman accused of killing one son and seriously injuring another, the defense used a creative strategy to move a case soaked in publicity to drier ground. The defense counsel wanted to transfer venue of the trial away from the relentless media blitz in Buchanan County, the community of the crime. The prosecution opposed the transfer, arguing that pretrial publicity concerns could be addressed through the traditional tools that combined careful jury selection with frequent warnings about media from the judge. Besides, the prosecution agreed that any bad news for the defense was news covering the entire state rather than just the locale of the killing.

The trial judge examined the piles of news articles. But to resolve the dispute, the court agreed to assemble a mock jury, local people role-playing as jurors, to hear from some human beings. After a majority of the simulated jurors said they could not be unbiased, the judge had heard enough and ruled that the trial should be moved to Grundy County.

Once the trial commences, judges, and generally attorneys, question the jurors in the presence of the entire pool of other jurors in an open courtroom. In the megapublicity trial of homemaking diva Martha Stewart, jurors were questioned individually inside the judge's own office, with the press excluded for the day. The exclusion of the press was later found to have been a legal mistake. On the other hand, Stewart's trial judge certainly pursued every avenue to explore what each juror actually knew about one of the most publicized federal trials in recent years.

JURY SHIELD

Another protective measure taken in the Martha Stewart case by Judge Cedarbaum to insulate jurors was less controversial than excluding their peers and the press from juror questioning. On the eve of the trial, she issued a sweeping order directing that "no member of the press may speak to, interview, or have any contact or communication with any prospective juror...or any family member of such juror."[30] Although not a press-pleaser, such an order was supported by prosecutors as well as defense counsel, and it contributed to a trial that kept dignity inside the courtroom even as an enthralled media surrounded the courthouse.

GAG ORDERS

The press can almost never be silenced, but sometimes others involved in the case can be. The silencers are referred to as "gag orders," which prohibit the attorneys, parties, and others associated with the case from discussing the trial with outsiders—especially reporters. A judge restraining the parties and their lawyers, though, indirectly restrains the media by cutting off their access to information. As a result, gag orders are disfavored and could violate the Constitution unless they are strongly justified.

In the Nebraska Press Association case, the Supreme Court ruled that a trial judge can issue a gag order only after establishing that such an order is necessary to preserve the defendant's right to a fair trial and explaining why no other measures would be sufficient to safeguard that right. Since gagging attorneys is more acceptable than censoring reporters, the practice is not as troubling as the nuclear weapon of prior restraint. Still, gag orders need to be justified and specific, the legal equivalent of a heat-seeking missile to combat harmful pretrial publicity.

In the Scott Peterson case, Superior Court Judge Al Girolami imposed a sweeping gag order on the attorneys, their staff, potential witnesses, court personnel, and police officers, emphasizing that violators could be held in contempt. Since gag orders require a specific explanation of their need, the judge found that "all the statements by the witnesses, all of the rumor and gossip would be rehashed shortly before trial, thereby making it extremely difficult to select a fair and impartial jury."[31] Judge Girolami also noted, among other things, that because the publicity waves immersed the entire country, other antidotes for publicity poisoning, such as moving the trial to a different city, could not provide a complete cure.

Gag Orders—Lite

Gagging the Lawyers

Even in the absence of a full-fledged gag order there are significant restrictions on what lawyers can say about a case being tried before a jury. Concerns about attorney-generated publicity prior to trial have a long history. At the beginning of the twentieth century, the American Bar Association (ABA) attempted to develop a rule that generally prohibited lawyers from feeding quotes to the newspapers prior to and during trials. The frustration with press-chasing lawyers also appears in leading court decisions. In the *Sheppard* case, the Supreme Court admonished not only the trial judge for his lack of control but also the prosecution and defense lawyers who jumped on the news bandwagon. Today's ABA guidelines prevent lawyers from spreading information about a case if there is a "reasonable probability" of interfering with the trial or prejudicing the administration of justice.

Attempts by state bar associations to tighten the lawyer's lips have been challenged before the US Supreme Court on First Amendment grounds. The *Gentile* decision was a good news/bad news case for lawyers who want to make news with out-of-court statements.[32] The Supreme Court found that the Nevada lawyer could not be punished for insisting upon a client's innocence because the rule was too vague for its prohibitions to be clear. The court also found, though, that the First Amendment permitted states to regulate attorney speech more stringently than the speech of others. As the *Gentile* decision explained, "Few if any interests are constitutionally more fundamental than the right to a fair trial by impartial jurors, and an outcome affected by extrajudicial statements would violate that fundamental right."[33]

Sometimes restrictions on attorneys have been ignored, at times famously so. Former Gambino family leader, the late John Gotti, was once known as "Dapper Don" for his flashy clothes and "Teflon Don" for his success in defeating three previous attempts by the government to end his career as a mob boss.

When he was arrested on racketeering charges on December 11, 1990, his lawyer, Bruce Cutler, launched an extraordinary press campaign attacking prosecutors as "publicity hungry" and accusing them of a vendetta to frame Gotti.[34] Cutler became a favorite of reporters to quote in New York's four major newspapers, and he did not shy away from television cameras. Among other interviews, he appeared on *Prime Time Live*, where he strenuously denied that Gotti was a mob boss. Although remarkably attentive to the press, Cutler did not heed the admonition of the federal district court in Brooklyn. He also seemed indifferent to its local court rule, which prevented a lawyer from making any public extrajudicial statements about a case from the time of an arrest through the trial.

More than once, the federal judge scolded Cutler. But even as he walked out of the courtroom, fresh from a judicial tongue-lashing, Cutler would step immediately into yet another press conference. He constantly denounced the government for having "thrown the Constitution out the window" and for falsely attacking Gotti with witnesses who were "bums."[35] More judicial admonitions followed, but the refusals to respect them continued.

From Gotti's standpoint, Cutler had succeeded in "presenting a compelling, sympathetic portrait of a notorious defendant as a victim of prosecutorial zeal."[36] From the court's standpoint, he had become a repeat offender. Well before trial, Cutler was disqualified as counsel due to the likelihood he would be called as a witness at Gotti's trial. Even when jettisoned as an advocate inside the courtroom, though, he continued his over-the-top defense of Gotti in the outside world.

In a one-hour live television show broadcast in New York, Cutler asserted, "[Gotti is not] a danger to any community other than federal prosecutors;...the prosecutors are doing everything they can to destroy John Gotti and are dealing in vendettas, on a witch hunt, and framing people."[37] Applying the venerable principle of "enough is enough," the district judge hauled Cutler into court on criminal contempt charges and found that the statements were made willfully with the intent of prejudicing prospective jurors. Cutler was found guilty of contempt and sentenced to ninety days of house arrest, five years of probation, and a six-month suspension from the practice of law in the Eastern District of New York.

Meanwhile, Gotti apparently did not benefit greatly from the media campaign. On April 2, 1992, following thirteen hours of deliberation, the jury found Gotti and his codefendant guilty on all counts. While serving a sentence of life imprisonment, he died of throat cancer in 2002. His dandy days had ended and all the Teflon was lost.

Gagging the Documents

Trial veterans like Robert Morvillo agree that closing the courtroom from the press is almost always a bad idea. Unless the privacy rights of children would be seriously compromised, it is rare for judges to lock out the media. Justice in the shadows promotes suspicion in the public's mind and makes defendants seem guiltier or arouses suspicion that the government is hiding something.

More common than sealing doors is sealing documents. Court papers are supposed to be public documents. When their contents are highly sensitive, though, judges can order them to be "sealed," that is, filed officially but secretly and not made available to the public or press.

In the megatrial of the late pop icon Michael Jackson, Superior Court Judge Rodney S. Melville ordered that most court pleadings be filed under seal so that prying press eyes could not see them. In justifying the extreme measures in the Jackson case, Judge Melville emphasized that due to the "combination of sensitive information involving minors with the notoriety of a celebrity defendant," the right to a fair trial was "imminently threatened with substantial prejudice."[38]

In the Kobe Bryant case, Judge Ruckriegel also directed that a large majority of court papers remained sealed and out of public view. Both judges drew heat from First Amendment fans. But they held a set of tight reins that avoided the criticism leveled at Judge Lance Ito in O.J. Simpson's trial for letting the leash on lawyers get too long and too loose. As Simpson lawyer Robert Shapiro noted, "A lot of judges learned from the Simpson case. They learned some lessons, and they learned very quickly." The strong measures in the Bryant and Jackson cases are usually denigrated by free-speech advocates but appreciated by fair-trial proponents. Advocating for stronger protection of parties and witnesses, Shapiro reasons, "What's going to happen to these individuals? The press is going to be camping out and doing background stories on them. It ruins people's lives."[39]

JUDGES WARN JURORS—BUT DO THEY LISTEN?

One of the biggest safeguards against publicity poisoning are the judge's use of cautionary instructions to jurors reminding them to avoid news coverage about the case. In the trial of Martha Stewart, Judge Cedarbaum continually counseled and cajoled jurors to stay away from the news blizzard. "If you see a headline about the case, turn the page; look at another story," she cautioned. "If you hear something about the case, change the channel."[40]

Such admonitions reduce misbehavior, but unless jurors are sequestered in a hotel, isolated from their families, and under the watchful eye of court personnel, they operate under an honor system. Odds are, if they cheat with some news peeks, no one will ever know. Trial mavens believe that while jurors mostly comply with a judge's stern warnings, they also mostly talk to their own families when they get home.

Famed Philadelphia lawyer Richard Sprague believes that judges are generally good about trying to admonish jurors, "but the real problem is, how effective are their admonitions?" He believes that jurors "talk about the case at home, and they do know what's being reported."[41] Criminal defense attorney Ben Brafman also believes that jurors "watch news reports about the trial, even though they are told not to." It is "almost impossible to avoid the coverage," Brafman concludes. "It is inconceivable that juries could completely insulate themselves," he adds.[42] Morvillo concurs that it is difficult for judges to control the jury's access to the media; he also worries that the pundits on cable news can spout misinformation about a case, enjoying a form of access to a juror's family, perhaps even to jurors themselves, that even the trial lawyers do not have.[43]

STEALTH JURORS

Los Angeles attorney Mark Geragos has represented a striking array of high-profile clients—Whitewater defendant Susan McDougal, actress Winona Ryder, pop icon Michael Jackson, Scott Peterson, and hip-hop artist Chris Brown. One of Geragos's biggest worries is the stealth juror in famous trials. These are the jurors who conceal the truth about their attitudes during jury selection in order to sneak on board a high-profile jury. The likelihood of prevaricating stowaways rises dramatically in supersized cases, with barrages of news coverage as well as calls to counsel's offices. Geragos says he knows when a new case is supersized because his law firm's receptionist, who fields the press calls, threatens to quit. He does not always know, however, when seeming sincerity masks a juror's stealth scheme.[44]

Geragos cites a woman who convincingly portrayed herself as an open book about Scott Peterson, willing to consider the evidence fairly, and then began e-mailing friends about her opportunity to nail the accused murderer. No accurate statistics are possible because most stealth jurors succeed in their concealment. Even so, with a supersized case, Geragos estimates that at least 40 percent of all prospective jurors lie some, and some lie a lot.

In addition to disguising their attitudes, some jurors conceal their past. In the Martha Stewart trial, a juror, who later voted to convict her for lying, lied himself by failing to disclose his financial problems as well as a past arrest for assault. Morvillo cited the lying juror in seeking a new trial, but a juror's shortfalls at candor generally fall short of getting a conviction discarded.

The many who dread serving as jurors on long trials might wonder what motivates people to become part of what Loyola Professor Laurie L. Levenson calls "the age of stealth jurors."[45] Such jurors may be seeking not only their own fifteen minutes of fame but also sometimes a book deal. Even apart from the occasional financial opportunities after the famous trial is over, there is simply the glory of it all. As Ben Brafman notes, jurors in celebrity trials later become "minicelebrities" in their own workplace and social circles.[46]

COURT TRADITIONS AND THE HIGH-PROFILE CASE

When courts laud the traditional benefits of a public trial, they speak of values such as educating the public about the legal system, enhancing respect for its participants, and fostering respect for the law. With high-profile cases, though, the results may be mixed. Charles Stillman, a New York veteran of high-stakes trials ranging from the Reverend Sun Myung Moon's tax-evasion case to Tyco's case notes that when the media is watching, "everybody is affected."[47] The good news is that judges and lawyers do their utmost to present the system at its best, and they usually rise to the occasion. Martha Stewart's lawyer, Bob Morvillo, concurs that all the trial participants "prepare arduously" for each performance, and with media in the courthouse, there is invariably a "better temperament in the courtroom."[48] When the public is watching, each participant usually is on his or her best behavior inside and outside the high-profile courthouse.

Morvillo questions, however, whether showcase trials reveal the truth about most cases. He suggests that "the public ends up coming away with more respect"[49] than might be warranted by a typical day in the county courthouses of America. As legal realists know, the overwhelming majority of cases are heard in a courtroom that may, at times, feature grouchy court personnel, unprepared lawyers, and an impatient judge showing up late and planning to leave early. These are not the impressions created by a day in the life of a celebrity trial. While the public indeed has the right to know about famous cases, there may also be a need to know about the everyday courtroom realities that are almost never featured on prime-time specials.

Stillman and Morvillo also worry that the legal education provided during high-profile cases may be an unaccepted curriculum fostered by television's talking heads—the so-called legal analysts who dissect and critique cases. While favorites of cable television, these analysts are rarely seen as a positive for the system by its insiders. Morvillo believes that "cable television has a huge impact on high-profile cases." He notes that typical television segments feature pro-prosecution analysts bashing the defense while defense lawyers fire back with potshots against the prosecution. "They want controversy," he observes about television shows, rather than explanation of the often-complex trial processes.[50]

Even when trial-savvy talking heads are talking, like other armchair quarterbacks, they do not know the players or the playbook nearly as well as the quarterbacks on the field. Further, as Morvillo points out, legal commentators describe their glimpse of a day in trial as if the entire case rested on a single episode. In reality, trial lawyers strategize like workers constructing a house, building the foundation and working methodically until the roof is finished, which is a continuous process over the weeks or months of a trial. Just as a single brick does not build a house, hyperventilating over a single witness does not tell the story of a two-month trial in which dozens take the stand. Not all super lawyers join in that criticism. Celebrity attorney Roy Black points to Court TV's daily reporting on the William Kennedy Smith "date rape" trial as a turning point with respect to the educational value of legal coverage and commentary.[51] Because of the many hours of televised proceedings and the depth of the analysis, Black believes that "for the first time it was really explained and made sense."[52]

Although the "show biz" of many talking heads may annoy some high-profile lawyers with all their second-guessing, the greater concern is for juries. Legal commentators can make outlandish remarks on television about an ongoing trial that might land one in jail if made by lawyers representing the parties. And yet gag orders do not gag talking heads. Nor do ethical rules constrain lawyers who are on the outside of a trial. Harvard Professor Alan M. Dershowitz suggests that standards are needed for legal commentators, not only to guide their conduct but also to validate their competency.[53] The extent of harm created by television commentary is not quantifiable, and Morvillo acknowledges that trial lawyers "don't know how much of that misperception gets to juries."[54] Yet the potential for damage is real. And some of the real players believe that the Monday-morning quarterbacks should exercise greater restraint so that television trash-talking does not add to the publicity poison that already contaminates high-profile cases.

CHAPTER 7

DEFENSE LAWYERS
The Underdogs and Their Uphill Strategies

THE UNDERDOGS

Criminal defense lawyers are the law's ultimate underdogs. Their odds of winning at trial usually range from a long shot to no shot at all. In fact, as one prominent former prosecutor explained it, the biggest difference in going from prosecution to private practice is that "before, I used to win all my trials, now I lose them." Another big difference is that private defense lawyers are ordinarily better paid than prosecutors—law is perhaps the only field of endeavor where losers are usually paid more than winners.

But inside the courtroom, defense lawyers are battling the odds. While underdogs at sporting events have fans in the stands rooting for them against the big dogs, for the defense lawyer there may be few cheerleaders and plenty of boobirds. When I was attending law school, I foolishly asked one of Florida's preeminent attorneys the clichéd questions that defense lawyers invariably get from clueless law students: "Are you able to defend people even if you believe they are really guilty?" Now a highly respected judge, he guffawed. "Heck, are you kidding? Almost all my clients are guilty." So not only are defense lawyers usually climbing uphill against a mountain of evidence, their typical goal at the summit is to plant a banner proclaiming the legal innocence of someone who is factually guilty.

The defendant's dream of acquittal may be shared only by his attorney (always), family (hopefully), and friends (both of them). While purists extol high-minded notions about fairness and justice for all, the rest of creation often wants a guilty verdict. By the time jurors hear the case, it is no longer a game of Clue to unravel the mystery of the perpetrator's identity. Instead, the forces of law and order have already selected Colonel Mustard for his day of reckoning. The issue changes to whether he will get his just deserts. Rather than an emotional connection with lofty aspirations, such as the "presumption of innocence," the prospect of punishing the wrongdoer is far more exciting. For many court watchers, the greater the defendant's fame, the greater the thrill when the mighty are felled by a conviction.

For that reason, if defense lawyers try to appeal to ethereal abstractions, they collide with a community's visceral instincts. This duel between value systems for justice is assuredly lopsided, and in the high-profile case it may be the least of the defendant's problems.

THE CHALLENGE

"Everything Is Different" under the Media's Microscope

Celebrities are different than the rest of us, and so are their legal problems. Two of New York's best lawyers, Charles Stillman and Bob Morvillo, have experienced plenty of high-profile cases. Both confirm that "everything is different" in cases tried under the media's microscope.[1]

"Everybody is affected by it" observes Stillman, while Morvillo confirms that when the glare of the media stares at courtroom participants, "it freezes them. Judges react differently—prosecutors, lawyers, witnesses all react differently."[2] No one wants to make mistakes or expose him- or herself to criticism in a media-exposed case, so the participants can become exceedingly cautious. Across the board, players in high-profile cases are "much more rigid," says Morvillo.[3]

Prosecutors, for example, know that if they entertain low-punishment plea deals with high-profile defendants, reporters may blast them for their leniency. On the other hand, prosecutors are never skewered for being tough on criminals. As Morvillo candidly acknowledges, "you get the best plea deal when no one is looking."[4] When the press is ready to second-guess, defendants often get no real deal at all.

Nor does press coverage inspire compassionate sentencing. When the trial participants all believe they must go by the book, the result is that judges often throw the book at defendants in deciding how many years to give. Post-Enron cases witnessed sentences so extreme that appellate courts have issued a string of decisions requiring reductions, including that of Enron's former president, Jeffrey Skilling. One of New York's top lawyers described the sentence imposed on fraudster Bernard Madoff as "a joke," and not because Madoff's record-setting ruthlessness deserved compassion. With the one-hundred-fifty-year term exceeding Madoff's life expectancy sevenfold, some suggest it had more relevance to the court of public opinion than to a legal proceeding.

Of all the dramatic differences between high-profile cases and trials of the not-so-rich-or-famous, the biggest challenge is the toxic tidal wave of publicity. When a client is under arrest, there is no good press. Negative press treatment is, of course, the reality for all defendants, including Joe Schmo (now known as Joe Lunchbucket or Joe Six-pack). For Joe or anyone else, an arrest or even bare accusations all add up to bad news, while denials are usually irrelevant news. At least for Joe, the news coverage may be only a paragraph or two inside the local section of a newspaper, with perhaps no television at all. In the high-profile case, though, Joe's woes may be multiplied a hundred, even a thousand, times. The publicity equation is simple: news about the accused will be bad news—and the higher the profile of the case, the worse will be the news coverage. In a high-profile case, "from the moment it starts, publicity is a bad thing that hurts the defendant," according to Stillman.[5] Morvillo also believes high-profile defendants are at a "huge disadvantage" and that the high levels of publicity can have a major impact on the trial.[6] In the eleven months of the two post-Enron/Tyco trials, Stillman recalls only a single favorable news report. After New York trial maven Ben Brafman successfully defended Sean "Diddy" Combs, he remembers one truly positive piece prior to the acquittal, and it fortuitously appeared. One weekend during the trial, Combs took his two young children to Central Park to play in the snow. A photographer happened to spot the celebrity defendant and took a picture of him with his children that appeared on the next day's front page. No one will know if this humanizing portrait was seen by jurors, but it underscores the reality that the only good press during a media-intensive trial happened by accident.

A veteran of many high-profile cases, Roy Black believes that "today's lawyer has an obligation to deal effectively with the media—it's a part of the job to take a proactive stance with reporters."[7] Before engaging the press, Black emphasizes the need to know the ethical rules as well as the media landscape, a perilous place for newcomers.[8] Professor Alan M. Dershowitz similarly emphasizes that careful judgment is needed to ascertain whether and when attorneys should enter the minefield of media communication, but "sometimes it's malpractice not to change the atmosphere" created by adverse publicity.[9]

ANOTHER CHALLENGE

Plea-Bargaining When the Press Is Ready to Second-Guess

No one really knows the full extent to which a verdict from the court of public opinion might influence decisions inside the court of law. And yet for all the insistences that judges and jurors do not decide under the influence, attorneys work the press for favorable coverage about their clients' side of the case. Although the courtroom benefits of press strategies are unknowable, most of the big-time lawyers seek even small-time advantages to add to their chances of winning, as surely as champion cyclists shave their legs just in case a few strands of hair could make the difference.

While unquantifiable, the impact on judges and juries remains a source of delicious intrigue. Brafman points out that, "it can't hurt," and suggests that an effective press strategy could be a factor in a close case.[10] Stillman emphasizes that the steep uphill climb for defendants requires "any edge you can get" within the rules.[11] Celebrity lawyer Black questions whether any press strategies ever help defendants in a criminal case with a jury and believes that their real value may be in reducing the reputational damage inflicted outside the courtroom.[12] With civil cases, on the other hand, where the contestants are more evenly matched, Black believes that a litigant's favorable press may occasionally contribute to a favorable outcome.[13]

For all the legitimate concern that pretrial publicity creates about prejudgment among future jurors, a jury's reactions to the press may be a small fraction of the reactions that matter.

STILL MORE CHALLENGES

Getting "Cover" for Plea-Bargain Coverage

In the legal scheme of things, jurors decide less than 10 percent of all state court criminal cases and even fewer civil cases due to out-of-court settlements. Criminal trials are becoming even more extinct in federal court. Due to plea bargaining, more than 96 percent of federal crimes are resolved out of court. Because plea bargains drop the curtain on cases before the opening act at trial, the judicial system does not pass its judgment. For that reason, in the real world, where relatively few cases are actually tried and guilt is usually not decided by judge or jury, the prosecutor has greater power over most defendants than either.

Because the overwhelming majority of arrests result in plea bargains, getting a real bargain is usually the endgame for defense lawyers. Rarely are defense lawyers negotiating from a position of strength. Yet the masters of this craft are extremely crafty in dramatizing alleged weaknesses in the prosecutor's case while humanizing the circumstances about their clients. Few prosecutors, though, will entertain plea deals that provoke public criticism. Especially in media-intensive cases, no sane prosecutor wants to be portrayed as being kinder and gentler toward a notorious defendant. For an elected district attorney, it could even hasten one's return to private practice by creating a potential campaign issue for an opposing candidate. Granting leniency toward a controversial defendant, popularly known as being "soft on crime," does for prosecutors what raising taxes can do for legislators.

Because justifying a plea bargain can sometimes be as difficult as explaining a tax increase, prosecutors often want cover. As in other government contexts, *cover* is the traditional code word for a public-relations sweetener to make the supposedly bitter pill of a plea bargain easier for a skeptical public to swallow. If it can be obtained, the victim's support for the defendant's plea bargain may be the sweetest antidote of all for potential criticism.

Harvard's Dershowitz recalls a high-profile case in which a prosecutor told him bluntly to work some media magic because the "press was on his neck," and he needed cover to make a fair plea deal with Dershowitz's client. Dershowitz got some good press, and then his client got a good plea agreement.[14]

CASE STUDY

A Tale of Two Wide Receivers

The National Football League's Donté Stallworth, a wide receiver for the Cleveland Browns, struck and killed a pedestrian while driving in the early morning hours of March 14, 2009. Initially it appeared that the inevitable outcome for driving drunk and causing a victim's death would be years in state prison. Instead, heavily emphasizing the support for the plea deal from the victim's family, several months later the Miami-Dade state attorney announced an agreement landing Stallworth in county jail, not state prison, and for only thirty days. The support of the victim's family followed weeks of media reports that included references to Stallworth's cooperation with police throughout the tragedy as well as to his expressions of remorse. Even the respected victim's rights organization Mothers Against Drunk Driving did not oppose the brief amount of jail time. An unusually light sentence for DUI manslaughter, the sentence was certainly neither glorified nor vilified in Miami. Some television punditry was skeptical, but the reputation of the state attorney's office remained intact. Under the circumstances, this amounted to a public-relations victory. When prosecutors have cover, they can withstand the coverage.

In Stallworth's case, however, there were no high-decibel voices calling for maximum punishment. Another NFL player, Plaxico Burress, was arrested in November 2008 for a less serious crime, but with more serious public outcry. Illegally taking an unlicensed gun into a Manhattan night club, Burress accidentally shot himself in the leg. Like Stallworth's case, the core facts for Burress were never in dispute. Burress undeniably brought a loaded gun into a night club illegally. Under such circumstances, the case could not realistically be defended before a jury. The only real decision maker for Burress, as for defendants in most cases, was the prosecutor. Since Burress took the bullet himself, one might say that he certainly had the shooting victim's support in his appeal for prosecutorial leniency.

Before Burress could even begin negotiations for a reasonable plea deal, though, public calls for tough punishment came crashing down, including some from high places. As Burress's attorney, Brafman, acknowledged, "How do you get around Mayor Bloomberg and the DA Morgenthau demanding incarceration?"[15] Newspapers joined the chorus demanding maximum punishment. Stallworth's DUI manslaughter resulted in thirty days of county jail, and after a year's suspension from the NFL, he was able to join the Baltimore Ravens for the 2010 season.[16] In contrast, Burress's publicity flogging left him lucky to get a plea agreement for two years in state prison.

Next best is a small-fry defendant's pledge to cooperate and testify against bigger fish, increasingly a rationale that members of the public—and certainly members of the press—can appreciate.

While savvy lawyers approach the press warily in high-stakes cases, the risks can soar off the charts when the clients themselves speak publicly. Interviews given by a defendant on television[17] as well as on radio[18] can and will be used against that defendant.

DAMAGE CONTROL

The Planning

Many of today's deans of defense have had to add a minor in press relations to their curricula. Even if defending villains does not make defense lawyers crowd pleasers, the top guns often become press favorites when reporters watch them in action. In cross-examinations as well as in closing arguments, the great ones perform the virtuoso's solos, even while being overwhelmed by the blaring band of the prosecution's evidence. And they know that more than just the jurors are watching.

Stillman recalls that in times past, speaking to the press was considered unprofessional. But now it may be unavoidable. As Brafman notes, "The avalanche of adverse publicity is so difficult that trying to level the playing field is as difficult as the case itself."[19] Recognizing that defendants are also human beings who need to survive professionally in the outside world, Brafman believes that judges will tolerate press strategies so long as any gag orders are strictly obeyed and "nothing is done to undermine the integrity of the process." But good press, he notes, "does not mean anything if you're guilty."[20]

That is not to say, though, that attorneys should not influence the media strategy. Stillman's remarkable legal career began in 1962, during times when the top lawyers ignored reporters. He believes that today, though, attorneys need a plan for dealing with media in high-profile cases. Financial resources permitting, a media consultant should be retained. Morvillo also advocates help from media professionals but cautions that there is only a "modest ability" to make bad legal news better.[21] LA public-relations guru Elliot Mintz agrees. He has had dozens of celebrity clients over the years and, among other things, is credited with helping to turn Paris Hilton from the subject of an Internet-video controversy to an international celebrity. While he regularly advises attorneys, his advice includes recognition that PR "can only do so much. At the end of the day it's not a media game, and the gavel comes down in the courtroom."[22] For that reason, expectations need to be realistic. And realism may not come easily to celebrity defendants. Savaged by the hostile coverage that follows arrests or nasty lawsuits, some believe if they simply find the right PR person with the right connections, harsh publicity can be transformed into puff pieces. Such magicians do not exist in the real world. Even the best media consultants cannot put a happy face upon a federal indictment.

Knowing the Jury in the Court of Public Opinion

LA's champion for the stars, Mark Geragos, a celebrity himself, believes that media planning requires a calculated decision in the beginning about the likely result in the end. "You can usually tell about a case," Geragos observes, and he recommends that attorneys assess whether a media strategy is warranted and "try to calculate early on, get into the first news clip or damp it down" if the case is a likely plea deal.[23]

Whatever magic a consultant may have is often centered upon particular media, so identifying the target audience for the campaign is vital. In the Elian case, we prioritized local radio and national television. As a result, the administration's spin machinery had a virtual monopoly on America's major newspapers—the principal news source, as it is, for the federal judiciary. There may not be enough resources to launch a press strategy upon every television and radio station, newspaper, magazine, and blog in the state. For that reason, Stillman urges that the target audience should be identified and the media priorities should be assigned. A longtime New Yorker who still rides the subways, Stillman rarely sees his travel companions reading newspapers. He concludes that, for jury purposes, such media are far less important than in times past. Judges, on the other hand, read newspapers.[24]

Even apart from the key decision making at the end of the case is a defendant's reputation while the case is pending. Stillman represented one of the nation's great law firms, Sullivan & Cromwell, in a discrimination case brought by an attorney formerly employed by the firm. Despite striking success in the legal proceedings, the defense was supposedly striking out according to some of the blogging buzz within the legal community—a prime determinant of a firm's reputation. Stillman therefore recommends that media plans need to consider not only the ultimate decision makers at trial, but also the reputation makers along the way.[25]

Not Getting Hung Up with Hangers-On

Along with choosing the right media strategy for the right audience comes the need to select professionals who understand that the "legal interest is paramount." The focus on winning is not always evident to the many voices in a celebrity's ear. Morvillo explained that "close friends, advisors, and relatives are constantly barraging the client" about ways to put good news back on the air. High-profile individuals, always used to great press before, become bewildered, even distraught when the media's smiles are transformed by criminal charges into unrelenting glares. And yet, as Morvillo notes, celebrities "can't spin things their way in a criminal case."[26]

When Silence Is Golden

Silence can be as important as any high-volume strategy. As the late comedian-philosopher George Carlin once said, "'No comment' is a comment." And it can be harmful. On the other hand, the ancient wise ones point to the many virtues of silence, including the avoidance of misquotes due to sloppy reporters, or, just as bad, accurate quotes that find attorneys misspeaking due to bad information or hip-shooting strategies. With all his experience in dealing with reporters, Roy Black only deploys press strategies "in self-defense" because "news focuses on the controversy, and the controversy is the accusation, not the defendant's claim of innocence."[27] Because news coverage is usually hazardous to a defendant's legal health, Dershowitz's advice about speaking on the record to reporters is: "when in doubt, don't do it."[28]

Lying low is an undervalued position. It is often the best prescription for minimizing a news overdose in the early stages of an investigation, before any court papers are filed or public action has been taken. Reporters who have no one credible to quote may have nothing that they can write credibly about the client. Lawyers need to avoid press when their clients' interests require it, but some are drawn to reporters like moths to flames—and it may be the client who gets burned.

Even after an arrest is made or a lawsuit is filed, it is better to give no comment than to blast the adversary if an out-of-court resolution is the goal. Occasionally, some civil settlements may thrive on press warfare, but usually, once the bullets have left the gun, the damage is done. In those circumstances, there may be less, rather than more, incentive for the opponent to settle. Geragos sometimes chooses not to speak to the press based, for example, upon a "calculated decision looking to plea-bargain out the case."[29] In fact, when a public official was exposed to high levels of publicity despite low levels of criminal exposure, Geragos's only public comments were expressions of regret about the leaks. Some battles are better fought behind the scenes, and Geragos won the best kind of victory for a client when no criminal charges were pursued by the district attorney.

Press-Wise or Publicity-Foolish?

Some press-friendly lawyers try to extract advantages not only for the client but also, in some instances, for themselves. Many in the media are troubled by publicity seekers who carry a law license. PR expert Elliot Mintz refers to a "greed factor" among publicity-hungry lawyers. Self-promotion, more benignly referenced as "marketing," has escalated dramatically since the Supreme Court decided in an Arizona case that lawyers have a right to advertise. The profession has never been the same, and the legal world's ever-increasing enthusiasm for legal marketing often targets the free advertising that comes when lawyers' names and faces appear in news stories about their cases. Many lawyers worry that some self-aggrandizers go too far. Philadelphia's Richard Sprague is one of the nation's preeminent trial lawyers; his career includes the epic prosecution of labor leaders for murdering rival Joseph Yablonsky along with his wife and daughter in the 1970s. In recent years, Sprague won a stunning dismissal of criminal charges against basketball superstar Allen Iverson. Over time, Sprague has witnessed a troubling trend by lawyers who grab ink by tipping off the reporters who hold the pens. "Disgusting" is Sprague's word for lawyers who push themselves into the limelight at the expense of clients who might be better served by dimming the lights.[30] To his dismay, news stories appeared with information about the ongoing investigation, and some items just happened to mention the names of lawyers. Naturally, the article might, in identifying the lawyer, report a refusal to comment. But savvy veterans like Sprague are not fooled by lawyers who hand out tidbits off the record so as to get their names in the news and then purport to decline comment so as to keep their fingerprints off the story.

Sprague has been making a list of such lawyers, to whom he will not refer cases again—and he will not have to check that list twice.

SPINNING WHEELS

The Press Conference

There is no sure antidote for toxic publicity during ongoing cases. Well-crafted press conferences, though, sometimes balance the bad news. Mark Geragos provided press briefings almost daily when President Clinton's friend Susan McDougal was tried in Arkansas in a case that sprang from the Whitewater Investigation. Along with highlighting any episodes from the trial in which the defense was beating the prosecution, Geragos's media messages kept beating the drums about the politically inspired vendetta of the special counsel, Kenneth Starr.[31]

Geragos also represented Michael Jackson, and following Jackson's arrest on child molestation charges, he went immediately on a counteroffensive to oppose the salacious charges: Jackson was "greatly outraged by the bringing of these charges," Geragos declared, and the charges were categorically untrue—"a big lie."[32] To shift the focus from alleged abuser to accuser, Geragos added, "Anybody else who knows anything about the history of these accusers, anybody who knows anything about the history of the investigators and the axes they have to grind, know [*sic*] that these charges are not only categorically untrue, but they're driven, driven by two things: money and revenge."[33] Still trumpeting the theme of putting the alleged victims on trial because Jackson was the real victim, Geragos said, "Michael Jackson is not going to be abused. Michael Jackson is not going to be slammed. He is not going to be a piñata for every person who has financial motives."[34]

Not only did Geragos know how to score quotability points, but also his stock with the media was high enough that the message he crafted was drafted by reporters.

Unless a press conference is assured wide coverage by national media, the press will select the quotes, and attorneys can only hope that the best rather than the least, weakest, or worst of their comments might be used. For that reason, some high-profile veterans repeat their key themes repeatedly to multiply the likelihood that the press will quote the armor-piercing bullet rather than a weaker pellet.

Another big-league lawyer wise in the media's ways is San Francisco's Harland Braun, who has represented American Taliban John Walker Lindh as well as Robert Blake, the former actor accused of killing his wife. Soon after Blake was arrested, the prosecution held a press conference about Blake's murder charges. Braun did not sit back with a bland denial but instead lunged forward, repeating the key theme for the defense, "The woman had an extensive history, and there are people in her past who have made threats to her." To ensure that his main theme would get the most steam, he restated it in different ways, everyone "who ever came into contact with her had a motive."[35] Putting the victim on trial seems risky, especially when the victim is the defendant's dead wife. But unless the defense could show that others wanted her gone, her accused husband would be the only viable suspect for the jury. Focused on his message, Braun knew it did not need a low-watt transmitter and turned up the switch: "...I'm not trying to besmirch [the late wife], but the woman had an extensive history, and there are people in her past [who] have made threats to her, people with motives."[36]

In the rare case when a press conference is greeted by a sea of cameras for a live broadcast, the lawyer's every word may actually be heard. As a result, a more complete message may reach the viewers.

In the Kobe Bryant case, defense lawyer Pamela Mackey opted to address not only her client's denial but also his explanation of the encounter as consensual. The points she made included chastising the Eagle County sheriff for his leaks and the district attorney for filing weak criminal charges. In conclusion, she repeated that she would "not try this case in the press" but before "a Colorado jury."[37]

Because Kobe Bryant was a major sports celebrity and the charges had just been filed, public fascination was sky-high and all her points reached a national audience. Usually, though, lawyers need to pick and choose their themes selectively because, otherwise, reporters will select the quote for them.

While many advocate press conferences so long as they are planned carefully and delivered by press-savvy lawyers, two of the biggest names in the business are reluctant to use them. Defense superstar Roy Black does not summon reporters for a press conference. "The only time I have a press conference is when there are a lot of reporters and photographers already standing and waiting outside the courthouse and it is easier to speak to make a statement at the same time to all the press."[38] Legal expert Alan M. Dershowitz believes that organizing a press conference is usually a mistake and will be seen by media "as a sign of weakness that creates an artificial situation."[39] Rather than pursue reporters to get them to come to a "transparently manipulative" press conference, Dershowitz recommends "letting them come to you" when there is real news to discuss, and especially when one-on-one discussions off the record would benefit the client.[40]

The Television Interview

Television interviews can be a great forum for getting a message to the public. But they sometimes offer pain as well as gain because, in many ways, the broadcast venue is less forgiving than a judge and jury.

During the Elian case, I appeared in dozens of national news interviews over a four-month period in 2000. As I discovered immediately, each interview required the same intense level of preparation that lawyers require for a closing argument, except that closing arguments rarely occur between 7:00 and 7:30 a.m.—that is, when network morning shows were starting their day with Elian. The time of day was manageable—no one on our team was sleeping much. As I soon learned, however, there were other factors that made television interviews and court appearances about as similar as Oz and Kansas.

Superficially, a reporter's interview consists of questioning lawyers about the client's case just as judges question them in a regular courtroom. And, like good judges, good reporters typically ask thoughtful questions that intellectually challenge the attorney's position, especially in high-profile cases where reporters can take the time to study the issues.

Judges and juries, though, while holding the actual power of decision, are almost always a more hospitable venue than the networks. In a courtroom, judges and juries actually want lawyers to do their best and are often uncomfortable, even frustrated, over courtroom stumbles. As judges and jurors watch a lawyer walk across the legal tightrope, they want to see him or her safely reach the other side, even if they do not agree with that lawyer's perspective of the case.

In high-profile cases, on the other hand, television interviewers might just as soon see the attorney stumble precariously on the tightrope with arms flailing, perhaps hanging on by a finger or maybe even falling. Legal missteps, like other unexpected twists, are simply more newsworthy.

And the court of law is more forgiving of mistakes than the court of public opinion. When attorneys misspeak during court proceedings, their corrections are routinely accepted. Regarding damage control for televised mistakes, however, there is usually more damage and less control. In contrast to ongoing court proceedings, there is no second chance for correction after the interview is concluded. And while all judges know that smart lawyers are capable of saying dumb things, neither the media nor the public seem sympathetic when ill-advised mouthings come from professional mouthpieces.

Also crucially different is the appetite for conflict. Judges and jurors rarely enjoy contentiousness between opposing attorneys. To the contrary, when judges ask questions, they often look for areas of agreement between lawyers and are usually gratified when opposing lawyers seem to agree on significant issues.

Talk shows, however, do not stage lawyers for a group hug. Conflict is the spice of legal life for television. From the standpoint of many news producers, the more contentious the interview, the better the segment. As a result, rather than a judge's question exploring concurrence between parties, news shows can be a relentless search for conflict where reporters try to accentuate existing disagreements or provoke new disputes. During one of my interview tapings with *Good Morning America*'s Diane Sawyer, she confronted me with the statement by an unnamed member of Elian's own legal team who said there was no chance of winning our appeal. Although I still stuck to my position that "any alien" included a child, I was caught off guard and was relieved when that exchange was not used in the actual news story. Whenever inconsistencies are made by a team's attorneys, the press pounce to hammer about "disparate statements." Through such experiences in Elian's case, we learned about the importance of weekly message consistency even if, at times, the message necessarily must evolve over the course of litigation.

Cameras in the Courtroom

Many of the nation's most closely followed cases are handled in federal courthouses, ranging from terrorism trials and post-Enron defendants to Martha Stewart's 2004 trial for lying and obstruction. For federal defendants, however, the only cameras inside the federal courthouse will be attached to a security system. Article Three judges do not want them, and, since judges get the final word under our Constitution, those final words are, "Forget it." The first court hearing in the 2000 recount litigation was in a Miami federal court, and the media beseeched the court to allow cameras for those historic moments. US District Judge Donald Middlebrooks practically apologized in denying the request, noting that as a First Amendment lawyer prior to joining the bench, he had made the same request himself. The federal rules, though, could not be ignored. Weeks later, the final hearing took place before the rule makers themselves: the US Supreme Court. Even though the future of America was about to be determined in the justices' courtroom, the cameras stayed out. In a concession to history, the justices authorized an audio feed so that the momentous arguments could be heard, if not seen. Unless the US Supreme Court becomes camera-friendly, televised trials will be found only in state courts.

The state judiciary of Florida, famous for its sunshine and strange legal cases, brought trials into the sunshine by televising the bizarre murder trial of Ronnie Zamora. Zamora was charged with bludgeoning to death an elderly woman in the course of a burglary. Facing overwhelming evidence of guilt, his defense lawyer came up with a theory that Zamora had been brainwashed by the endless violence on television into acting out the acts of violence. Zamora's attorney, the late Ellis Rubin, agreed to allow cameras to televise the case, perhaps hoping it might underscore the pervasive presence of television to foster the highly unorthodox television defense. Unsurprisingly, the jurors concluded that the human assailant—rather than inhuman programming forces—was to be blamed for the homicide, and Zamora was convicted. Although using television as a defense was a controversial bust, television in the courtroom was a success, and a new era was born.

The Supreme Court, while not embracing cameras for the federal courtroom, has found that state courts can allow them without violating the constitutional rights of state criminal defendants. During the 1980s and into the 1990s, televised trials gained increasing acceptance among the states, and a high tide was reached with the O.J. Simpson murder trial.

His controversial acquittal fueled further controversy about televised trials. In recent years, live cameras have not seen the inside of the super trials. Cameras in the courtroom may appear in medium-profile cases, but, since the heyday of O.J., they are rarely found in the celebrity's courtroom. In 2002, I appeared on a Fox News segment to discuss the issue and was intrigued to hear former LA District Attorney Gil Garcetti say that his opinion had evolved from support during the O.J. trial to a view that televised trials might be a mistake. I presented the opposing viewpoint, advocating for cameras based on the usual rationale that they promoted access without any documented downsides. Although Garcetti acknowledged that the studies on the impact of cameras in the courtroom failed to document harm, his own experience indicated that they detracted the jury's focus on the evidence from the witness stand.

The debate continues. Mark Geragos, in a candid look back at the Scott Peterson case, wondered whether it might have been a mistake to oppose the televising of that trial.[41] He points out that with cameras watching the entire proceeding, it would have transmitted a total picture of the evidence, leading to a more accurate portrayal of the case. I did dozens of cable news segments on the Peterson trial and recall the many days that went well for the defense. Press attention, though, centered disproportionately on the appearance and testimony of Peterson's ex-girlfriend, Amber Frey. She had no knowledge of the homicide but was Peterson's "other woman" before and during the time of Laci Peterson's disappearance. Outside the courtroom, the many good defense moments evaporated the moment that the sex theme appeared on the witness stand. Rather than be confined to the show-biz focus on what may be a sideshow, court watchers who watch the day-by-day account of the trial get a far more balanced view of the case.

Geragos also suggested that if the molestation trial of the late Michael Jackson had been televised, the public and pundits (including this one) would not have been surprised by the acquittal. "If people had seen the [alleged victims] as they appeared before the jury," Geragos concludes, they would have understood the case and there would have been little criticism of the verdict.[42]

The Gag Order

In the trial of the superstar rapper Sean "Diddy" Combs for a night-club shooting, Brafman confronted not only a phalanx of prosecution witnesses but also the public's "sinister picture of the rap music world." Media obsession with the case included newspapers pummeling Combs's lopsided accounts of the trial and exaggerated portrayals of the guns-and-bling culture. While an array of advisors continually clamored for defense ammunition to combat the bad press, the courtroom counsel were essentially muted by an unofficial gag order. Moreover, despite the temptation to come out swinging rather than to keep taking punches in the press, Brafman emphasized the need to avoid revealing key evidence and strategies to reporters so that attorneys keep "bullets in the gun belt" for the critical moments during the trial itself.[43]

And so Brafman developed a television sound bite to provide some image and voice for his client's cause without provoking judicial displeasure. He secured almost daily coverage with variations of the statement, "While there's a lot I would like to tell you, we are under orders not to, but I hope you are following closely today's testimony, and if the jury pays close attention, we believe we will be fine."[44]

Brafman won the case, and his highly effective and humanizing presentation of defendant Combs on the witness stand was a major factor. But, as Brafman acknowledged, getting more positive coverage on the outside never hurts the verdict delivered inside the courtroom.[45]

CHAPTER 8

THE CASE STUDIES
A "Human Monster," a Domestic Diva, the King of the Court, the King of Pop, and Governor Blabbermouth

SCOTT PETERSON—LEVELING THE PLAYING FIELD BY RAISING THE BAR

The Shocking Disappearance

The last time anybody other than Scott Peterson spoke to Laci Peterson was on December 23, 2002. She had a brief conversation that evening with her mother, Sharon Rocha, to accept an invitation to Christmas Eve dinner the following day. Then she vanished.

After the disappearance, a four-month-long search began for Laci, who was seven months pregnant at the time. As the police searched for the missing woman, disconcerting details developed about her seemingly grief-stricken husband. Police knew from the outset that Scott had gone to the Berkeley marina on the day that Laci apparently disappeared. They quickly learned that the boat he had taken fishing was not registered. Nobody knew about it. He had paid cash for the boat even though he was in financial trouble. Scott Peterson had recently made anchors—ostensibly for the boat—but most of the cement he bought seemed to be missing. Also gone was a fifty-gallon drum he had recently purchased. Yet another oddity was the fact that Peterson had driven rental cars to the Berkeley marina three times in the days after Laci's disappearance. Especially intriguing was the two-hundred-fifty-thousand-dollar life insurance policy that Scott Peterson had recently taken out on his now-missing wife.

Clouds of suspicion grew. They became a downpour when Amber Frey stepped forward to disclose her affair with Peterson.

From Husband to "Monster"

Barely a month after Laci Peterson disappeared, Frey held a press conference during which she announced that she and Scott had an extramarital affair.[1] A massage therapist, Frey repeatedly emphasized that when she was introduced to Peterson, he told her he was not married.[2]

> **SPINNING LESSON**
>
> When sex takes center stage, most everything else goes backstage.

Before going public, Frey had gone to the police. After seeing some of the flurry of news articles about Scott and the missing Laci, she got in touch with Modesto police and offered her complete cooperation. By early January, the police had their suspect in the crosshairs and were wiretapping Scott Peterson's telephone. They also installed a video camera outside the house to monitor his movements. Some of the recordings would create serious trouble for Peterson. A few created problems for the police. Sixty-nine calls were intercepted between Peterson and Kirk McAllister, a Modesto defense attorney.[3] Police monitored and recorded two of the calls, as well as a call between Peterson and a private investigator.[4] No substantive information was obtained as a result of these calls, but the defense would later make an issue of the interception of the privileged conversations.[5] During the next two months, even as the police stated publicly that Peterson was not a suspect, they kept a very close eye on him.

Although Scott Peterson was, in fact, suspected by many, he had been arrested by no one and was still at liberty. Peterson used this time to try to sell Laci's car and then their house. He also left Modesto to live with his parents in San Diego. During his time in San Diego, Peterson traveled to Mexico at least once, ostensibly to attend a trade conference.

One day, the bodies of Laci and Conner Peterson washed up on the shores of the bay where Peterson had gone fishing. When police found him, Peterson had bleached his hair blonde. His car was full of camping equipment, and he had with him nearly fifteen thousand dollars in cash and a map of California and Mexico. Police placed him under arrest for murder.

When Peterson was taken to the jail in Modesto, a crowd was waiting to denounce him as a "monster." Evidently the district attorney's view was not very different. On Friday, April 25, 2003, the Stanislaus County DA decided to seek the death penalty against Peterson.[6] A desperate mother—Peterson's—placed urgent calls to attorney Mark Geragos in May 2003. At the time, Geragos, one of the nation's top lawyers and a frequent television commentator, had already suggested to national audiences that the prosecution had a viable case against Peterson. Geragos told Peterson's mother about his earlier commentary on the case. But since his comments were neither admissible against Scott Peterson nor all that damaging, and since Mrs. Peterson badly needed him, she prevailed upon Geragos to try to help her son.

The Geragos Factor

From the moment Geragos signed on, the media looked up. First, Geragos got Peterson to wear business suits rather than prison jumpsuits for court appearances.

> **SPINNING LESSON**
>
> Television is visual, so avoid visions of guilt.

Then he announced publicly that the defense was going to "raise the bar." Not only would it prove Peterson's innocence, it would prove that someone else killed Laci and Conner. In that way Scott Peterson would vindicate himself by finding the killer.[7] Scott is "looking forward to proving his innocence," said Geragos. "And Scott looks forward to finding out who did this to Laci and his unborn child."[8] Geragos's boldness earned quick dividends. The press and public began to open their minds about the possibility that Peterson could be innocent. As one respectful observer wrote, the case went from "'Why Did He?' to 'Did He?' in Twenty-eight Days."[9]

> **SPINNING LESSON**
>
> Be upbeat even when it's uphill.

Soon the defense began to generate theories explaining the murders of Laci and Conner, theories that, of course, pointed to a killer other than Scott Peterson. Some incidents near Scott and Laci's home suggested alternative theories for the crime. As early as January 2003, only two weeks after Laci Peterson disappeared, there was some speculation that a home burglary across the street was part of the explanation for how and why Laci disappeared.[10] Scott Peterson's relatives had hypothesized that she was abducted after witnessing the burglary.[11] The burglars stole two handguns, power tools, a Gucci watch, a safe containing three thousand dollars in cash, and at least fifty thousand dollars in jewelry; two suspects were quickly arrested in the case.[12] The police, having identified Peterson as the murderer, cleared them of involvement in Laci's disappearance.[13]

Two weeks later, the Peterson home itself was burglarized,[14] and three or four items were stolen. Detectives said "nothing significant" was taken. As with the other neighborhood crimes, police insisted that there was no relation to Laci Peterson's disappearance.[15] Even as the police dismissed any connection between these events and Laci's disappearance, the defense, always hunting for theories to explain the murders, tried to connect the dots.

Or perhaps Laci had been abducted and murdered by a satanic cult. This was, after all, California. The defense would later be accused of leaking details of an autopsy to support the cult theory. But even if the sensational mention of a satanic cult was mostly an attention-getting device, it was drawing attention to something other than Peterson's guilt.

> **SPINNING LESSON**
>
> Mothers may complain about attention-getting devices, but reviled defendants need any AGDs they can get.

While trying to push helpful media messages out to the public, Geragos tried to keep some bad news quiet. He immediately moved to keep investigative records sealed. Taking some shots at the police, Geragos said that the records were "rife with inadmissible evidence, with a voodoo-type of investigation, with psychics, voice-stress analyzers, people who study facial expressions—all of which is inadmissible in court."[16]

Geragos's spring counteroffensive continued. On May 9, 2003, Geragos said that he had "made headway in finding Laci Peterson's killer and clearing her husband's name."[17] Adding further intrigue to incite media interest, Geragos said that he was looking for one particular woman who could shed light on the case. Although he would not disclose her identity, she knew who she was.[18] Geragos asked her to contact him. He emphasized, "We have so far developed three areas that we think are significant. … We have incredible information we're following up on."[19]

SPINNING LESSON

You need evidence in a courtroom, but delicious speculation is a great tidbit for hungry media.

Although Geragos's own press-savvy quotes led the way early on, the Peterson themes at times were spun only by "defense sources." By June 1, 2003, the defense had told MSNBC's Dan Abrams that they had four or possibly five people who could be the *real killers.*[20] The satanic cult theory continued to get media play premised on the grisly fact that Laci Peterson's remains were missing her head and parts of her limbs when they washed ashore.[21] An alleged leak from the autopsy reports added some legitimacy to the claim that Laci had been abducted and killed days later. If the time of death could be fixed at a time when Peterson was under surveillance, his guilt would be hard to prove. MSNBC reported that plastic tape, later found to be twine, was found around the neck of the Petersons' baby.[22] To some, this suggested the child was born alive. To the Stanislaus district attorney, it suggested defense leaks.[23]

The DA did not explicitly accuse Peterson's attorneys of leaking details of the autopsy. But the sensational details seemed to support the defense claim that Laci was first abducted and later killed by a satanic gang or some other deranged killers.[24] "The information being leaked has clearly been skewed in favor of the defense," said the DA. "By releasing the autopsy reports, the court will allow the media to see what the actual facts are, and then accurate information may be reported."[25]

> **SPINNING LESSON**
>
> Leaking information is playing with fire, but leaks are hard to prove even when the results are easy to see.

Retired Judge Alfred A. Delucchi, who handled twenty-two death-penalty cases, including the trial involving the killing of Huey Newton, had taken over the case.[26] Despite his evident concern about the apparent leakage, he concluded that one good (or bad) leak does not deserve another. Rather than add to the rampaging publicity, he ruled that the autopsy results would remain sealed, and he simultaneously issued an order preventing lawyers from talking publicly about the autopsy.[27]

As the defense continued on a spin roll, Peterson's attorneys reported on June 3, 2003, that the defense had made "great progress" toward finding Laci's killers.[28] Peterson's defense team insinuated that this progress was related to a van that the police had located. Prosecutors naturally disagreed, insisting that the van had nothing to do with Laci's death.[29] Peterson's attorneys, on the other hand, publicly trumpeted their ongoing efforts to find the van. This search was not entirely fanciful. A van had indeed been seen in the Petersons' neighborhood on the day Laci Peterson disappeared.[30] And the defense continued to hint that Laci Peterson may have been killed by members of a satanic cult.[31]

> **SPINNING LESSON**
>
> When defense attorneys need to keep hitting the news, they need to reload with new ammunition.

Along with proposing alternative hypotheses of Laci's murder, the defense also fired back at the police. In November 2003, one of Peterson's attorneys suggested that the police might have framed Peterson by planting evidence in his house.[32] The defense also blasted the earlier wiretapping. Geragos stated in court filings that it had "been orchestrated by prosecutors and constituted improper monitoring and intrusion into the defense camp."[33] "This illegal eavesdropping is in and of itself disturbing and clearly constitutes grave prosecutorial misconduct," he wrote in pleadings.[34] Arguing that because police improperly recorded several privileged conversations involving Peterson's prior counsel and investigator, the defense tried to get the many other tapes excluded because of the improper few. To no one's surprise, the judge rejected the defense motion and ruled that the scores of nonprivileged recordings were admissible.[35]

> **SPINNING LESSON**
>
> Challenges in court that a judge doesn't buy might still get the public to wonder why.

The defense counterattacks continued. Another message point was that the police were not as forthcoming as they should have been. In January, when the Petersons' house was broken into, Detective Ridenour of the Modesto Police Department had said that the Peterson's house was not under police surveillance because there was no reason to surveil it.[36] Almost eleven months later, though, the police admitted to withholding videotapes from a surveillance camera mounted on a pole across the street from the Petersons' home. Back on January 3, 2003, the DEA had installed the pole camera, and police had used it to trail Peterson.[37]

Along with attacks on the prosecutor's theories and the police tactics were challenges to their evidence. In October 2003, the defense moved to exclude the results of a mitochondrial DNA analysis of a single hair found on a pair of pliers in Peterson's boat because it failed to meet the standards for acceptable scientific evidence.[38] Mitochondrial DNA is matrilineal genetic material and can be used to connect to a subject's mother but not the father.[39] It cannot be used to identify a single person, as nuclear DNA can; rather, the mitochondrial DNA that was presented as evidence that the hair belonged to Laci Peterson could be found in approximately one in every 112 white people.[40]

As happens with most defense motions to exclude evidence, this one was denied. The judge not only ruled that the evidence was relevant, any prejudicial effect did not substantially outweigh its persuasive force. In another setback for the defense, the judge excluded the evidence that the mitochondrial DNA signature found in the hair was also present in one in every 159 Hispanics.[41]

As of the beginning of May 2003, both the defense and the prosecution asked the judge to seal the arrest warrant affidavit and a search warrant affidavit, saying that disclosure of the papers would jeopardize Peterson's right to a fair trial.[42] Shortly afterward, the judge decided to issue a gag order.[43] "Besides extensive local television and radio coverage, the national television media has embraced this case with a passion, providing frequent commentaries from notables like Larry King, Geraldo Rivera, and Katie Couric," wrote Judge Girolami.[44] Girolami also said that "a change of venue and extensive voir dire [challenge by lawyers to potential jurors] are not especially helpful in this case because of the exceptional amount of publicity which has been broadcast throughout this state and county."[45]

SPINNING LESSON

Once the judge gags the attorneys, the only press comes from the court filings and the courthouse, so the attorney should finish his press campaign during campaign season.

The preliminary hearing was pushed out all the way until mid-October 2003. Predictably, the defense lost most of its motions to suppress, and the judge found probable cause to bind Scott Peterson over for trial.

Searching for Open Minds When Notoriety Is National

In January 2004, the defense moved to change the venue of the trial. The defense argued that a change in venue was warranted because the widespread news coverage of the trial in Modesto had so influenced the potential pool of jurors that between 39 percent and 59 percent of them had already decided that Peterson was guilty.[46] Although the judge had earlier rejected a change of venue, he had, nevertheless, recognized the intense media attention the case was receiving when he wrote that "the national television media has embraced this case with a passion."[47]

This time, though, with opinion surveys confirming the toxicity in Modesto, Judge Girolami ruled that Peterson should be tried elsewhere because so many likely jurors in the city were apparently prejudiced against him.[48]

In a remarkable feat of self-promotion, Bay Area communities competed to have their county selected as the new venue for the trial. San Mateo County went so far as to send the judge a packet of information promoting the county. Having the trial in San Mateo would present "all kinds of opportunity for us to showcase [the] county to a national audience and put it on the map," said Anne LeClair, president and chief executive of the San Mateo County Convention and Visitors Bureau.[49] Apparently the tourism strategies succeeded. When San Mateo County was selected as the site of the trial, LeClair predicted that the trial would inject at least $8 million into the county's economy.[50]

SPINNING LESSON

Because it is hard to outrun bad publicity by changing cities, the key is to run up as many message points as possible before trial.

But for the defense, San Mateo was too close for comfort. In early May 2004, after two months of still incomplete jury selection, Geragos moved again to have the venue changed, this time requesting a transfer to Los Angeles County. Geragos argued that the coverage had not been as intense in Southern California and it was impossible to seat an unbiased jury in Northern California.[51] LA was too much for the judge, though, and he denied the motion, saying he was confident Peterson could get a fair trial in Redwood City.[52]

The Trial Begins

At last, in the beginning of June 2004, the supersized trial began. It took nine weeks for the two sides to pick a jury, finally seating a jury of six men and six women. Among the jurors were a school coach, a social worker, a firefighter, a former police officer, an adoption worker, and a former security guard. Also included were a teamster and a woman whose fiancée was convicted of murdering a stranger twenty years prior. Six alternate jurors, three women and three men, were also chosen.[53] The clamoring public was insatiable. Veteran AP reporter Brian Skoloff recalls how hundreds of people showed up each morning to participate in a lottery, hoping to win one of the seats reserved for members of the general public.[54]

Problems with the jury surfaced almost immediately. One of the jurors spoke briefly to Laci Peterson's brother,[55] Brent Rocha, as the two picked up their belongings while walking through the metal detectors at the courthouse entrance.[56] Although the details of their brief exchange were unclear, the *New York Times* reported that television cameras recorded the juror saying, we "could lose today."[57] After reviewing the subpoenaed tape, Judge Delucchi ruled that the exchange did not constitute misconduct and that the juror had not in fact made the reported statement.[58] Even so, two days later, the judge dismissed the juror without publicly stating a reason.[59] Replacing the dismissed juror was a corporate lawyer who also had a medical degree.[60]

Once the trial began, the prosecution got off to a stumbling start with some fumbling witnesses. Some felt that the police witnesses were neutralized and even vaporized by Geragos's cross-examinations.[61] In fact, most pundits thought the prosecution was losing during the early round—losing, that is, until Amber Frey testified. With great expectations the press and the public awaited the testimony of the "other woman." They were not to be disappointed. Her own words, alongside the wiretapped recordings that featured the voice of Scott Peterson himself, combined for a seismic change.

The presentation of sex, lies, and audiotapes was devastating to Scott Peterson. As the tape recordings were played, the cold-blooded duplicity of Peterson took center stage, and the points scored earlier in the defense examination of prosecution witnesses were seemingly taken off the scoreboard. Frey described how he "romanced her with champagne, flowers," and surprise gifts after they met in late October 2002.[62] By itself, that might have been standard-issue misbehavior by a cheating husband. But then the temperature dropped to chilling. She recounted how three weeks after they met, Peterson told her that he had recently lost his wife and would be spending his first Christmas alone.[63] As every juror and millions of Americans knew, at the time Peterson told this to Frey, Laci Peterson was still living. She would not, however, be alive by Christmas Day.[64] Meanwhile, on December 14, 2002—ten days before Laci disappeared—Frey was introducing Peterson as her boyfriend.[65] Although Frey and Peterson spent several nights together, Peterson never mentioned that he lived in Modesto.[66] In fact, on December 25, when Peterson was, by his own account, involved in trying to find his missing wife, he told Frey that he was in Maine on a family vacation.[67] The tapes found him trying to romance Frey while half of Modesto was out frantically searching to find his missing wife and unborn son.[68] The timeline of the affair was ugly enough, but it created a liar's diary that seemed to provide chronology for Peterson's plotting to free himself from his wife and child by killing them.

During Geragos's cross-examination, Frey remained calm and was not caught in any untruths or exaggerations.[69] Rather than run the risk of an all-out assault on Frey, an attempt that could badly backfire, the defense tried to use her examination to develop defense themes. Some questions suggested that Peterson might have been framed by murderous thugs trying to extort money from him.[70] Geragos also asked her about her cooperation with the police, pointing out that, at their request, she had tried to entice Peterson into confessing,[71] but he had denied involvement in his wife's disappearance.

A few defense points were scored, but not enough. Prior to Frey's testimony, many observers felt Peterson "not only had a fighting chance of being acquitted, but [also] ... wondered if Peterson had committed the crime at all."[72] Frey's testimony shifted the tide.[73] She remained calm and credible on the stand. And just as important, she provided the perfect opportunity to play the conversations she had with Peterson during the weeks after Laci Peterson disappeared.[74] Peterson emerged as a cold-blooded and heartless liar. Still, there is a difference between a serial liar and a homicidal husband, and that difference became the remaining hope for Scott Peterson.

On October 30, 2004, Judge Delucchi ruled that the jury would be allowed to consider a second-degree murder charge that would have spared Peterson the death sentence.[75] At the time, legal experts saw this as a victory for the prosecution because "allowing the lesser charges might make it easier for jurors to convict if they were unsure whether the killing was premeditated."[76]

The defense rested its case after about a week of presenting evidence, after the jury had heard the prosecution for nineteen weeks. Some commentators decried the disparity as a sign of weakness, a message with more media appeal than recognition of courtroom realities. This sort of differential is commonplace in criminal trials—many times there are no defense witnesses at all. And the few who are initially enrolled for the defense might drop out along the way because a judge excludes them as irrelevant or because the witnesses exclude themselves by changing their accounts from the version of facts they initially presented to defense counsel.

The case went to the jury in November 2004, and the jury problems were many. Early on in the trial, two jurors were dismissed—one who spoke to Laci's brother and another who was dismissed without any public explanation. This second-juror controversy would not be the last. Soon after the jury went into deliberations, Judge Delucchi dismissed yet another juror for purportedly doing her own research on the Internet.[77] The dismissed juror was replaced by an alternate juror, a woman in her thirties with tattoos and hair that changed color throughout the trial.[78] Although she was initially perceived to be pro-defense, her emotion and reaction to the autopsy photos made it far from certain which way she would lean.[79]

The foreman, Gregory Jackson, was the corporate lawyer with a medical degree. He apparently wanted to take a slow and methodical look through the evidence. This frustrated many of the jurors. Days of conflict ensued, and the foreman asked several times to be excused. Finally, Judge Delucchi dismissed foreman Jackson over the defense's strenuous objections.[80] Jackson was replaced by an in-law of the man

Ancient spin: was Socrates a martyr for truth
and philosophy—or a subversive opponent of
Athenian democracy? Jacques-Louis David's
The Death of Socrates depicts the noble inter-
pretation first spun by Plato. *Jacques-Louis
David:* The Death of Socrates, *1787.*

By the time the English burned
Joan of Arc at the stake, it was too
late. In only two years, she changed
the course of the Hundred Years'
War in favor of the French. *Courtesy
of the Library of Congress.*

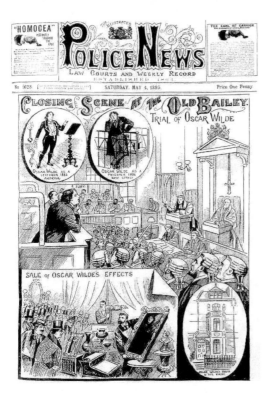

A newspaper dated May 4, 1895, depicts the closing scene of Oscar Wilde's final trial at the Old Bailey. These final stages must have brought to mind the writer's own words: "Arguments are to be avoided; they are always vulgar and often convincing." Illustrated Police News, Law Courts and Weekly Record, *May 4, 1895. London.*

A cartoon portrays Oscar Wilde's 1882 visit to San Francisco, back when all was fine and dandy. *Keller cartoon from the* Wasp *of San Francisco depicting Wilde on the occasion of his visit there in 1882.*

Convicted of the kidnapping and murder of Charles Lindbergh's infant son, Bruno Hauptmann is transferred to a prison in Trenton, New Jersey, where he was later executed on April 3, 1936. *Reprinted by permission of Getty Images.*

Dream team member Alan M. Dershowitz argues modifications to the standards for juror dismissals, while prosecutors Marcia Clark and Scott Gordon look on. *Reprinted by permission of Getty Images.*

Trying them on for size: this may have been the turning point in this "trial of the century." O. J. checks out the gloves presented by the prosecution. *Reprinted by permission of Getty Images.*

Over the course of the hotly debated O. J. murder trial, America was sharply divided, mostly along racial lines. *Reprinted by permission of Getty Images.*

October 3, 1995: the day many believe O. J. Simpson got away with murder. The defendant sits in stunned relief, joined by legal team members Robert Kardashian, Johnnie Cochran, and Robert Shapiro. *Reprinted by permission of Getty Images.*

As tensions build, the author speaks at a press conference in March 2000 in front of the Little Havana home of Lazaro, Marisleysis, and Elian Gonzalez, where a crowd of people converged daily with scores of reporters. *Reprinted by permission of Getty Images.*

The indelible image of a terrified Elian's capture by the federal government: INS agents hold the six-year-old at gunpoint at 5:14 a.m. on the Saturday before Easter. Public opinion briefly swung in favor of Elian's US family. *Reprinted by permission of Getty Images.*

The Justice Department countered with images of a happy Elian reunited with his father, Juan Miguel, who took him home to Cuba and to life under a Communist dictator. *Reprinted by permission of Getty Images.*

The two presidential candidates, then Governor George W. Bush and Vice President Gore, became two of history's most important litigants. *Reprinted by permission of Getty Images.*

Two days after the election, the author appears before the media, explaining the Democratic Party's concerns about the counting of votes, as former secretary of state Warren Christopher looks on. Miami Business Leader, *January 2001. Reprinted by permission of Business Media Leader.*

The author huddles with Gore team members during the recount proceedings in Miami-Dade County. *Copyright the* Miami Herald *2000. Reprinted with permission.*

An election official and workers inspect one of the many contested ballots from the 2000 election. *Reprinted by permission of Getty Images.*

Scooting through crowds of waiting reporters, I. Lewis Libby exits the courthouse after being convicted of four out of five counts on March 6, 2007. *Reprinted by permission of Getty Images.*

While out on bail in April 2009, the ever-classy Rod Blagojevich requested permission to travel to Costa Rica for the filming of the reality television show *I'm a Celebrity . . . Get Me out of Here!* US District Court judge James Zagel ruled against this excursion, agreeing with prosecutors that the former governor was probably thinking more along the lines of "I'm a Celebrity Potentially Facing up to Twenty Years in Prison . . . Get Me out of the Country!" *Reprinted by permission of Getty Images.*

Scott Peterson examines paperwork with defense attorney Mark Geragos on January 23, 2004, just after the trial was moved out of Modesto, California. *Reprinted by permission of Getty Images.*

Americans could not tear their eyes away from the news on November 12, 2004: Peterson was declared guilty of the horrific murders of his wife and unborn child. *Reprinted by permission of Getty Images.*

After years of positive press and friendly reporters, Martha Stewart is hounded by the media in March 2005. *Reprinted by permission of Getty Images.*

A chef proudly supports Martha, as prosecutors grill her in the courtroom. *Reprinted by permission of Getty Images.*

Allegations of sexual misconduct can bring down even the biggest names. Six-foot-six basketball star Kobe Bryant leans in for a chat with attorney Pamela Mackey. *Reprinted by permission of Getty Images.*

Lead Michael Vick attorney Billy Martin addresses a crowd outside the courthouse in Richmond, Virginia, in December 2007. Despite Martin's efforts, outraged protestors wanted to see the quarterback taken off the playing field and sent to federal prison. *Reprinted by permission of Getty Images.*

Soft-spoken King of Pop Michael Jackson turns to acknowledge his adoring fans. Throughout the case, the defense remained focused on the courtroom while using media strategies that were selective yet effective. *Reprinted by permission of Getty Images.*

who had owned the restaurant that Scott and Laci Peterson opened in their first years together (The Shack).[81] Some opined that the replacement was a plus for the defense.

They were wrong.[82] Later interviews with jurors revealed that Jackson had in fact been the sticking point for the jury.[83] After he was elected foreman, his plan was to "comb through a mound of evidence and testimony. Not only did he need detailed notes, Jackson wanted a detailed analysis."[84] Other members of the jury felt that his process made them "ineffective as a group."[85] The tension that built up eventually proved too much for Jackson,[86] who was relieved when the judge finally excused him.[87]

Once Jackson was excused, the jury returned a verdict within hours. An emotional courtroom and an enthralled nation awaited their verdict.[88] The verdict flashed across television and computer screens faster than one could say "guilty of murder."[89] In the end, the jury convicted Scott Peterson of first-degree murder in the death of his wife and second-degree murder in the death of his unborn son.[90]

The judge denied a defense motion to have a new jury decide Peterson's fate. The same jury would decide whether Peterson should die for his crimes.[91] In the death-penalty phase of a capital case, prosecutors can present "victim impact" evidence: the testimony of family members who describe the devastating impact of the loss of their loved ones. Few courtroom moments are more dramatic and painful than when close members contrast the wonderful memories of the victim's life with the shattering anguish of their loss. After the heartbreaking impact-testimony of Laci's mother, Sharon Rocha, swept across the courtroom, Peterson's fate was sealed. A unanimous jury ordered death for Scott Peterson.

In the aftermath of the mega trial, there was supersized second-guessing. Some argued that the defense pursued too many alternative theories. Rich Matthews, a jury consultant, noted that though defense counsel had floated a host of theories about what happened to Laci, they never brought forward evidence to support those theories.[92] "I'm not sure all of the alternative theories made logical sense," said Matthews. "Sometimes less is more, and maybe he should have stuck to less."[93] Others suggested that the defense lawyers erred by failing to deliver what the opening statement promised—evidence that the Petersons' baby's age proved that he had lived well past the date on which the prosecution said he must have died.[94] "All his defense did was strengthen the prosecution case," said Robert Talbot, a law professor at the University of San Francisco.[95] "Every theory suggesting when the baby died all became so unbelievable…he accomplished absolutely nothing."[96]

> **SPINNING LESSON**
>
> Second-guessing is America's favorite pastime.

But what the pundits never know is what the defense knows. Usually, when defendants present no evidence to support an alternative theory of the crime, it is because they have none. And no matter how brilliantly defense lawyers may attack prosecution evidence, they often have no evidence of their own because it does not exist.

AP reporter Brian Skoloff covered the trial on a daily basis, and his insightful stories became a major source of news for knowledgeable observers. Skoloff saw little more that the defense could have done with such an "uphill battle." He continued, "The public almost immediately embraced Laci, a pretty, pregnant woman whose picture was plastered everywhere during the Christmas season, as community vigils and volunteer searches became a mainstay for weeks." Skoloff added, "Even though he never took the stand at trial, Peterson became his own worst witness through lies and missteps that were portrayed to jurors in other testimony."[97] As to the defense strategy of raising unsubstantiated theories ranging from a satanic cult to a mysterious white man, Skoloff concluded that Peterson's lawyer had "little to lose and had to try everything he could."[98]

Peterson remains on death row, hoping that post-trial appeals will win him a new trial based on legal mistakes by the judge as well as the many problems with jurors. Appeals do not happen quickly, and even if they fail, the condemned in California dwell on death row for an average of seventeen years before they pay for their crimes. Although his lawyers did an extraordinary job of leveling the playing field, some craters are simply too deep.

MARTHA STEWART

Martha Stewart is one of the most successful businesswomen in the world. With no help from any inherited wealth, she created a billion-dollar empire, including homemaking products and television programs, through years of hard work as well as her own relentless focus and abilities. Perhaps she was not especially loveable. But hers was a career that was entirely admirable prior to the time she was convicted and sentenced on federal obstruction charges in 2004. Before and after her trial, a controversy burned over whether she was being prosecuted for what she did or for who she was. Embers from those fires smolder even today. The truth is, however, that she was prosecuted for both things. What she did—lying to the FBI during questioning—is a transgression that commonly results in federal felonies. Who she was, on the other hand, is plainly what brought her under the federal microscope in the first instance. Once in their net, being a big fish made it that much harder to wiggle through the strands.

The all-out investigation for insider trading would not have been launched by the FBI and SEC against a Martha Jones. And yet just as critically, a Martha Jones might have either stepped back, refusing to speak to investigators, or stepped up, telling them the truth about her use of inside information. This Martha focused upon her public image and refused to either hide out or fess up. So the world's most famous Martha became the most famous of the post-Enron defendants. Yet while the homemaking diva cooked her own goose, recipes for damage control ensured that even if a trial was lost, her career was not.

Radioactivity in the Post-Enron Era

After years of financial happy news during the roaring 1990s, America shuddered from waves of corporate scandals that broke in late 2001. Confidence in Wall Street sank to the lowest levels since the Great Depression (until more recently), as corporate giants such as Enron and WorldCom became symbols of corporate sleaze. Headlines blazed with news of fraudulent accounting schemes employed to inflate the value of the company's stock. When the truth about companies like Enron set free a series of disastrous financial collapses, outrage erupted.

With the court of public opinion returning a guilty verdict against Wall Street, America needed only the names of individual defendants to insert in the verdict form. In a study of jury attitudes performed by LA jury consultant Decision Quest, more than 80 percent agreed that "the events of Enron and WorldCom are just the tip of the iceberg."[99] The wheeler-dealers were seen as stealers. Decision Quest's study further found that an angry public viewed CEOs as guilty until proven innocent.[100] Congressional investigations quickly joined the parade of angry demands for *accountability*, a businesslike term for perp walks and prison. Legislation, including the Sarbanes-Oxley Act, was soon passed to impose reforms (that some would say were more like getting cosmetic surgery than like getting tumors removed). When executives such as Enron's CEO, Ken Lay, appeared before Congress but refused to explain themselves and instead invoked the Fifth Amendment, government leaders were infuriated. Demands intensified for the Department of Justice to investigate the fraudsters and replace their Rolex watches with handcuffs.

SPINNING LESSON

"Guilt by association" may not equate to conviction in a courtroom, but it is often hard to overcome in the court of public opinion.

None of the voices denouncing fraudulent accounting and phony profits initially mentioned the name of Martha Stewart. In fact, as the CEO of Martha Stewart Living Omnimedia, Inc., neither she nor her company was ever linked to the fraudulent Enron-type scams that used overly creative accounting to create overly positive portraits of company finances. Rather than cook the books, Stewart was still baking soufflés. Ironically enough, Stewart's guest appearance in the Enron era was occasioned by developments that were far afield from the accounting scandals—impending news from the field of medical science. In addition to majority ownership of her own company, Stewart's stock portfolio included almost four thousand shares of stock in ImClone, a pharmaceutical company headed by her longtime friend

Sam Waksal. On December 27, 2001, Waksal, as the chairman of ImClone, learned that the US Food and Drug Administration had declined to process the application for approval of the ImClone drug Erbitux, formulated to combat colorectal cancer. Recognizing that the bad news could be very bad for ImClone's stock price, he called his Merrill Lynch broker, Peter Bacanovic, and directed him to sell large portions of the Waksal family stock holdings in ImClone. Exploiting his position as a company insider, Waksal's action was plainly illegal. For insiders like Waksal to buy or sell stocks based on knowledge that is unavailable to the general public is a form of securities fraud commonly referred to as *insider trading*. Waksal would eventually plead guilty to crimes that included insider trading and would be sentenced to more than seven years in federal prison.

We digress no further with Waksal because he was not Bacanovic's only high-flying client. Bacanovic was also Stewart's broker. The news about a CEO's sudden dumping of his stock told Bacanovic that things were moving from green to red for ImClone. Although not in the office that day, Bacanovic directed Douglas Faneuil, his ever-faithful assistant, to notify Stewart about Waksal's sudden stock sales. As Bacanovic would later learn to his sorrow, when illicit information is being passed along, better to do it yourself—two's company, but three, including Faneuil, is a crowd. Plainly, for Stewart to use a tip not known to the general public to get the jump on Waksal's dumping would be a form of insider trading. Stewart was traveling in Mexico at the time and spoke to Faneuil between flights. A close friend standing near Stewart believed she heard her say, "Isn't it nice to have a broker who tells you these things."[101] Stewart's stock in ImClone was sold that same afternoon. On the next day, when the public learned for the first time of the FDA's rejection of Erbitux, ImClone's stock price plummeted.

For the true insider, like Sam Waksal, it is not easy to escape detection because the CEO of a publicly traded company, like other officers and directors, is required to record his or her transactions in that company's stock. Although the SEC has become notorious for missing many things, it would be difficult to miss the fact that Waksal sold large numbers of family stock the day before bad news dropped the stock price. The SEC did not miss this time. Waksal was investigated, and in the course of the review of his Merrill Lynch accounts, the authorities got wind of Stewart's own remarkable good fortune in selling ImClone stock immediately before its price fell sharply.

For all the concerns generated by insider trading on Wall Street, it is less frequently done by executives on the inside, like Waksal, who leave a paper trail of guilt. Many believe that it occurs more commonly when insiders simply tell outsider friends about a "tip," so that the friends can exploit the information about an imminent sale or purchase opportunity. Many times, outsiders who receive such tips, known as the "tippees," are not criminally prosecuted unless the circumstances are egregious. Civil lawsuits and administrative fines, though, are common against tippees when their use of inside insights can be proven. Traditionally, the far harsher consequences of a criminal prosecution are reserved for the true insiders, such as Sam Waksal.

SPINNING LESSON

Only in football is there a penalty for piling on.

But these were not traditional times for corporate investigations, and Stewart was not a traditional suspect. The US Attorney's Office in Manhattan, as well as the SEC, went into high gear with their investigations of insider trading for the ImClone stock. Starting in February 2002 there would be little domestic tranquility for the domestic diva. Spurred on by the general Enron fervor and with the added feature of a household name, a storm of headlines swirled around the investigation of Martha Stewart. Soon Congress joined the act, issuing its own subpoenas to Stewart, which further fed the voracious news cycles.

A boater surrounded by sharks should not leave the boat for a swim, and, with a voracious federal appetite for corporate heads, 2002 was a good year for CEOs to try to keep a low profile. Rather than jump overboard, a low-profile subject of federal curiosity would wisely choose to remain silent in the face of obvious peril. Such choices are not always easy, however, for high-profile targets. Stewart was the CEO of a publicly traded corporation. Because the success of the company was tied closely to her own personal image, the cloud of Stewart's investigation reached from her living room to the board room of Martha Stewart Living Omnimedia. As the investigation heated up, the stock price moved down, and, unless the air could be cleared, the downward spiral of bad news would see no bottom.

SPINNING LESSON

Keep your head down when the feds are around.

To combat the negative press, Stewart's camp needed an explanation, and it offered one. A preexisting stop-loss order, the explanation went, had already been put in place prior to any tip directing Bacanovic to sell ImClone. According to Stewart's spin, her stock was to be sold whenever the stock reached the price of sixty dollars per share, and so the sale was prompted by the stop-loss order, not by any secret sharing about Waksal's own stock sales.

SPINNING LESSON

When others claim conspiracy theory, coincidence theory is not enough—better to have an explanation (better still if it is truthful).

Putting a message through the press that is false is bad enough. Unfortunately for Stewart, she also told the same story to the FBI during the course of several interviews by federal investigators. At the time Stewart gave her explanations to the FBI, the story seemed to be safe enough. Her broker, Bacanovic, was on board and told largely the same tale. Just as critically, the go-between, Faneuil, who relayed Bacanovic's messages to Stewart on December 27, was also sticking to their story.

SPINNING LESSON

The more people needed to stick to a story, the easier it is to become unglued.

For a time, it appeared that she might tough it out with denials of wrongdoing and reliance on the stop-loss explanation. Cracks in that foundation, though, soon appeared. Rumors buzzed with reports that Faneuil might be "flipping" and cooperating with the authorities. When first questioned by the feds, Faneuil told them the version of the facts that conformed to Stewart and Bacanovic's explanation featuring the sixty-dollar stop-loss order. For him to cooperate would mean reversing fields and admitting that he was really complicit in an insider-trading scheme. Prosecutors obviously prefer cooperating witnesses who get it right when they give their first account of the key events. Cooperators who later provide new, improved, and completely different versions of the truth could also be described as liars. For Faneuil to tell two completely different stories would concede that he was lying on at least one of the two occasions. But when prosecutors really need a cooperator, late is better than never. They needed Faneuil, and the negotiations for his cooperation continued. Apparently there was a snag in the negotiations because Faneuil did not want to agree to a felony conviction even though he admitted to committing a felony. Faneuil's first version of the facts constituted the crime of false statements, a felony. When prosecutors propose a plea deal to felonious cooperators, they will consider lots of leniency at a sentencing down the road but still want a guilty plea to a felony if such is indeed the crime that the flipper committed. To let Faneuil off with a mere misdemeanor charge might make a sweetheart deal too sugary.

SPINNING LESSON

Never throw secret-keepers overboard—publicly or privately—unless they are already growing shark fins.

As these negotiations played out, others watched closely. For targets wearing bull's eyes like Bacanovic and Stewart, one of the greatest fears is a turncoat who might turn state's evidence against them. Due to the constant fear that a tattletale might tell all to the feds, targets usually refrain from dumping on potential cooperators. As long as targets still carry hope that the possible cooperator will hold out, they avoid doing anything that might push a fence-straddler over to the DOJ's greener pastures.

Hopes that Faneuil would hold out soon faded, though, amid signs that he was cooperating with the government. As the negotiations with Faneuil progressed behind the scenes, his former friends began to take aim at him in front of the public. On August 13, 2002, reports from the *Financial Times* cited sources "familiar with...Bacanovic's version of events" who blamed Faneuil for taking the initiative to tip off Stewart with "inappropriate information." Bacanovic's lawyer was reported as declining to comment on the assertion. As it became increasingly clear that Faneuil was slipping over to the prosecution's side, more potshots came from his former business partners. As the *Daily News* flashed a headline, "Martha Blames Rookie," the lines were being drawn, and the rookie was moving to the other side.

Kitchen Getting Hotter

The summer of 2002 also saw further decreases of the stock price for Stewart's company. Even more urgent information, though, was found in a series of news stories—certainly not leaking from Stewart's camp[102]—that Faneuil was near a plea deal. As the heat turned up in Martha's kitchen, the *Wall Street Journal* not only described possible civil charges by the SEC but reported that, "Merrill Aide Will Plead Guilty, Cooperate on Martha Stewart." Adding to the complications of the SEC and FBI was the investigation by the US House committee that issued subpoenas and made the rounds on network talk shows to repeat their concerns about insider trading.

> **SPINNING LESSON**
>
> When a celebrity is in hot water, there are plenty of cooks to help turn up the heat.

Even as late as 2002, Martha found her business, including the product lines with K-Mart, financially viable. Even so, leaking news in a February 2003 headline signaled that "Feds [Are] Close to Charging Martha." Later that month, anonymous sources reported that her attorneys met with the federal authorities, in a story titled "Martha in Mercy Deal to the Feds." Evidently, in this meeting strenuous arguments were made that the insider-trading issues should be treated administratively and civilly by SEC enforcement actions rather than criminally by the Department of Justice with arrest and possible jail time.

The Indictment

Not Insider Trading but Outsider Lying

Apparently those entreaties fell on deaf ears. On June 4, 2003, the US Attorney's Office in New York announced that the grand jury had returned a nine-count indictment against Martha Stewart and Peter Bacanovic. Ironically, in the immediate aftermath of the indictment, the stock in Martha Stewart Living Omnimedia rose 6 percent, perhaps reflecting a sense that things were at least bottoming out, and that her own company's operations were not implicated by the accusations.

Stewart was charged in the indictment mostly with lying to the FBI, and she was not directly charged with insider trading. Although surprising to some observers, this decision reflected the reality that criminal charges for insider trading against noninsiders are often difficult cases for prosecutors to win. Unfortunately for Martha, her lying and cover-up provided a much more traditional scenario—she was largely getting nailed not for what she did, but for lying to the feds.

An Indictment with a Twist

Federal charges unleash personal and professional devastation. Even with bombs bursting in the air around Martha, though, the Stewart camp was able to put on the media's radar the unusual character of the securities fraud charge that the government had added to the case. One news outlet described the securities fraud theory as a "twist," while others called it "novel" because it was based on Stewart's proclamations of her innocence. According to the government's theory, because Stewart made public statements defending herself, she was thereby manipulating the price of stock of her own company by creating more positive expectations about the outcome of the investigation. A scary exercise of creativity from Stewart's standpoint, her lawyers correctly diagnosed this charge as the eight-hundred-pound gorilla that would menace Martha.

Defense lawyers know that the vast majority of arrests result in convictions. For that reason, even as they battle passionately for acquittal on all counts, they never lose sight of which charges carry the most prison time. In Stewart's case, a conviction for obstruction charges would likely require jail time, but under the federal rules, the sentence could be as low as five months of incarceration and five months of house arrest. In contrast to the sentencing scheme for liars, fraudsters face much greater risk. The novel but frightening fraud charge exposed Stewart to as many as ten years in federal prison. In November, her lawyers moved to dismiss the securities fraud charge, declaring in their papers, it "is so far beyond our constitutional tradition that the government failed to find any case in the history of this country in which a person was prosecuted for asserting, explaining, or expressing her own innocence." Although the judge refused to throw it out before trial, press reports continued to question the government's unprecedented theory of securities fraud. Inside and outside the courtroom, the securities fraud count would continue to be questioned.

Martha Targeted

From the moment news broke about the investigation, a debate had ensued over whether Martha Stewart was targeted because of who she was. While this remarkably successful woman was seemingly being keelhauled by aggressive prosecutors, no charges were being fired at the captains of a pirate fleet that included Enron and WorldCom. Even conservative television hosts like Joe Scarborough expressed misgivings on the day of her indictment: "[you have] somebody buying stock as an individual stockholder [Martha] and then you have people on Wall Street defrauding billions and billions of dollars from Americans in their retirement accounts [the boys from Enron and WorldCom]." Even though it had no legal traction, this dismay over the disparity in punishment remained a strong theme in the venue of public opinion. As her trial began, columnists complained of the "Double Standard Hurting Martha." A pro-Martha site, SaveMartha.com, pointed out the difference: "How much have the top execs at companies like Enron, WorldCom, Global Crossing, Adelphia, and Tyco recently cost investors? Over 200 billion."

SPINNING LESSON

Selective prosecution seems troubling to the outside world, but it is usually trouble-free inside the courtroom.

When jury selection began in January 2004, Judge Cedarbaum made extensive efforts to downsize the damage from pretrial publicity. A strongly worded order insisted that the jurors and their families were off-limits to the press. Additionally, Judge Cedarbaum authorized a detailed jury questionnaire that included inquiries about the potential juror's exposure to news about the case. In cases of this media magnitude, judges may also consider questioning each juror privately, outside the presence of other jurors, so that more honest answers are given about the actual attitudes of each juror. An additional benefit of questioning jurors one by one is that the answers from some jurors with strong feelings ("hang 'em from the highest tree") will not be heard by other potential jurors. Because of the press intensity in Stewart's case, Cedarbaum went one step further and conducted the questioning of individual juror prospects in her own offices without allowing reporters to be present. To assure media access to the proceedings, she ordered that they receive a transcript of that questioning on the following day.

Reporters were not enthused. Day-old transcripts are not today's breaking news. Seventeen media organizations appealed Judge Cedarbaum's order on First Amendment grounds, complaining about the closed-door questioning. The federal appeals court ultimately ruled that Judge Cedarbaum should not have evicted reporters. By then, though, the trial had begun, the jury was selected, and the safeguard had accomplished its objective.

Opening statements in the trial were heard in late January. The prosecution led off, detailing the accusations that Stewart had been lying and obstructing a federal investigation. In response, the defense blasted the prosecution's "guesswork" and lack of direct evidence while portraying the star witness Faneuil as a "liar out to save himself."[103] Much of the press coverage centered on two subjects: the buildup to the testimony of Faneuil and the speculation about whether Stewart herself would appear on the witness stand. Faneuil's testimony was effective, and although he was aggressively cross-examined and his cooperation deal was underscored, he withstood the onslaught and remained believable. After all, jurors might understand his original effort to lie to save his job. For many in the workplace, the reality is either save the boss or start packing your bags.

While these topics took center stage for the press and the pundits, inside the courtroom some of the most damaging testimony came from Stewart's own assistant, Ann Armstrong. Armstrong testified that Stewart instructed her to tamper with the phone log by deleting the specific mention that ImClone's price was going down on the day she sold her ImClone shares. Stewart soon corrected the log entry, but the testimony from Stewart's friend about the attempted cover-up was entirely believable and entirely damaging.

In fact, almost all the witness testimony favored the prosecution's case. The defense, though, scored a number of key rulings from the trial judge throughout the case, persuading the court to limit some of the prosecution's damaging evidence. The media headlines included "Setback for Martha Prosecution"[104] as well as "Judge Sniffs at the Case vs. Martha."[105] Meanwhile, some of Stewart's many famous friends, including Rosie O'Donnell, Bill Cosby, Brian Dennehy,[106] Barbara Walters, and Tina Brown,[107] showed up in court to display their support.

After the Stewart prosecution rested, the defense won its biggest victory with the dismissal of the securities fraud count. This result would drastically reduce the amount of prison time Martha Stewart could face if convicted. As the trial's end drew near, the press and pundits accelerated the speculation about whether Stewart would take the stand. Defense masters like Morvillo almost invariably avoid shedding any light early in a trial so that the prosecution remains in the dark about this key issue until the last possible moment. Realistically, though, despite the usual public perception that defendants should testify, it was generally acknowledged that it "would be an enormous gamble."[108]

Stewart did not take the stand. The prosecutors argued the force of witnesses such as Faneuil and Armstrong and derided the defense contention that Stewart and Bacanovic were too shrewd to have perpetrated such a clumsy cover-up scheme. The defense lawyers argued forcefully about the weaknesses in the prosecution's evidence, but to no avail. Evidently, the jury concluded that even people who are really smart can do some dumb things. Stewart was found guilty on all counts of false statements and obstruction. Bacanovic was also convicted, and the jury's only not guilty verdict came with the count against Bacanovic for document tampering. A huge win for the Department of Justice, Stewart's conviction was its first major trial victory post-Enron and netted the DOJ its most famous defendant.

Dramatic chapters, though, still remained. The public's attention quickly turned to the sentencing. The press reported a flood of supportive letters about Stewart, ranging from testimonials about her good deeds to concerns about the survivability of her business and the loss of jobs if she were to be incarcerated. Creative forms of community service were also advanced. There were missing parts, though, from all these scripts. Martha Stewart would never say she was sorry for lying. So the Four Horsemen of sentencing leniency—acknowledgment, apology, remorse, and reform—never rode with Martha Stewart.

Sentencing Martha

Interest remained sky-high as the sentencing drew near. Alexis Stewart appeared on CNN's *Larry King Live* to say that prison for her mother would be "incredibly wrong." She also mentioned that when she heard the guilty verdict, she fainted because it was so "horrifying and incomprehensible." Alternatives for community service were also advanced, with the Women's Venture Fund advocating for a Martha Stewart curriculum through which more low-income and minority women could became entrepreneurs. At the same time, Stewart's lawyers argued that legal precedent supported keeping Martha out of jail to keep her company alive and well. When corporate figures are crucial to a company's existence, prison could be fatal to its future and to the jobs of its employees. In extraordinary cases, courts consider the impact of such layoffs upon innocent employees in determining whether to reduce jail time.[109]

Her defense team also asked for a new trial, and the request was far from routine. It developed after the trial that one of the prosecution's expert witnesses, Larry Stewart, a member of the US Secret Service, had testified falsely about the foundation for his testimony concerning Bacanovic's alleged tampering with records. The witness for the prosecution quickly became another prosecution target, and soon this other Stewart was indicted by his federal colleagues. No doubt their tough stance toward Martha's falsities ensured zero tolerance toward their own witness's fabrications. Cedarbaum focused on the evidence concerning Martha rather than Larry Stewart, though, and ultimately denied a new trial, noting that there was an acquittal on the Bacanovic document tampering charge and there was enough evidence to support Martha's convictions on the other counts.

One of the few downsides when defendants win favorable rulings along the way through a trial is the landscape for an appeal after a conviction. With the favorable rulings that Stewart's defense team had won, there were few trial mistakes that her lawyers could complain about on appeal. And Judge Cedarbaum's extraordinary efforts to ensure a fair trial despite the media blizzard assured that pretrial publicity issues would not lead to a new trial. Perhaps recognizing this reality, Stewart defied conventional wisdom by deciding to serve her jail time even before the appeal was completed. The decision for a business superstar to become a prompt and cheerful inmate proved to be a public-relations masterpiece. It accelerated not only the end of her federal ordeal but also the beginning of her public rehabilitation.

SPINNING LESSON

Usually crime means you forever have to say you're sorry—sometimes even without fessing up, though, the completely humbled can become the most forgiven.

Today she is back on television and in the living rooms of America. She continues to serve as the guiding force of Martha Stewart Living Omnimedia, even if she is not, technically speaking, its CEO. Having been a victim of her own fame as well as of her own mistakes, she survived an ordeal that would crush almost anyone else. Great lawyering kept a defeat from becoming a disaster. In fact, by beating the maximum charge and securing a minimum sentence—even for an unapologetic defendant—her team won much more than they lost. Also effective was the media campaign that paralleled the courtroom battles. It may not have created lovability, but it developed her gutsy, sympathetic qualities and played skillfully to her base. Although she never spoke to the jury during her trial and never apologized afterward, she continued to speak to her public. This was a triumph that combined lawyering, public relations, and the spirit and determination of Martha Stewart.

SPINNING LESSON

Rather than cry over spilled milk, pour the next glass.

KOBE BRYANT—AND PUTTING THE VICTIM ON TRIAL

Kobe Bryant was only the best basketball player in the world. And in a sport where athletes have legendary sexual escapades, he stood out with a squeaky-clean image. In June 2003, however, his impeccable image shattered, and his career and even his freedom were imperiled by the events surrounding one night at a hotel in Eagle County, Colorado. This incident would quickly become a sensational court case. A hotel employee claimed rape, Bryant said it was consensual, and the phrase *he said–she said* would soon be heard from the voices of virtually every television reporter in America.

The Night in Question

On that night, Kobe Bryant, the then four-time NBA champion guard for the Los Angeles Lakers, flew to the small Colorado town to have arthroscopic surgery on the cartilage of his knee.[110] The clerk learned that Bryant was going to be a guest, and, excited about meeting him, stayed well past her usual shift at the hotel.[111] Bryant arrived at the hotel at around 10:00 p.m. and checked into his room with her help, after which she showed him around the facilities.[112] She took him to see the pool and spa area and then accompanied him back to his room.[113] Once in his room, they sat down and discussed his upcoming surgery and the tattoo on her ankle.[114] Soon they began kissing, and from there, their statements diverge dramatically.[115]

The clerk told the police that Bryant began to "grope her in the breast and buttock area."[116] In response, she told him that she needed to leave and attempted to get to the door, but he blocked her way.[117] Next, Bryant allegedly grabbed her by the neck with both hands. She said that she could still breathe but was scared he was going to choke her.[118] Next, he allegedly forced her back into the room, turned her around—his hands still on her neck[119]—and forced her to bend over a chair. According to her, Bryant proceeded to have sex with her despite her saying no twice.[120]

But Bryant told the police a different story.[121] According to him, she not only displayed the tattoo on her ankle, she also offered to show him the tattoo on her back.[122] Then, Bryant said she gave him a "little kiss," which he reciprocated.[123] Bryant confirmed that she had indeed leaned over the chair and did not deny perhaps having his hand on her neck. But the sex, according to Bryant, was consensual.[124] "I treat everybody with the utmost respect," he said. After they had sex for about five minutes, she asked him, according to Bryant, to autograph some pages that she had brought to his room.[125] Promising her the autographs on the following day, Bryant said he kissed her goodnight and walked her to the door.[126]

According to the night auditor, when the clerk returned to the front desk, she did not "look or sound as if there had been any problem."[127] News about the "problem," though, would soon be echoing across the nation.

Arrest and Prosecution

The following morning, the clerk went to a rape treatment center and submitted to the intrusive and embarrassing but necessary testing required for such incidents. Based upon her sworn statements and the initial investigation, the Eagle County sheriff decided to arrest Kobe Bryant.

When law enforcement officers arrest a suspect, it usually means that prosecutors will later file formal charges, but not always. Local police, county sheriffs, and federal agents are sworn officers whose badges and guns authorize them to arrest suspects. Such arrests are based upon the decision by the officer that there is probable cause to believe a crime has been committed and that the suspect committed that crime. Although there is often consultation with prosecutors, there is no such legal requirement before the initial arrest is made. Especially if there is any prospect that a suspect will flee, officers often arrest first and later ask questions of prosecutors about possible charges. After an arrest by the police, the arrest form and other information is delivered to the prosecutors, who can conduct additional investigation to determine what, if any, formal charges should be brought.

Federal authorities and state law enforcement generally employ two different procedures in initiating formal charges. Under the US Constitution, federal prosecutors rely upon the indictment from the grand jury in felony cases. This constitutional requirement has not been applied to state criminal systems, which are governed by the state's own procedures. State laws generally do not require a grand jury's indictment, except in capital cases, where the death penalty is sought for the crime of murder. For the vast majority of state crimes, the prosecutors file an "information," which, like a federal indictment, constitutes the formal prosecution charges. For an information, no grand jury is required. It is prepared and signed by the prosecutor. A seemingly less dramatic event than a grand jury's return of an indictment, a prosecutor's signing of an information nevertheless embodies the same functions of issuing criminal charges, authorizing the arrest, and subjecting the defendant to trial and possible punishment. Like an indictment, this document sets forth the specific charges to be determined at trial and will include the basic facts of the case, the names of the defendants, a separate count for each crime being charged, plus the criminal statutes that have allegedly been violated.

After Bryant was arrested, his attorneys swung into action in an effort to persuade the local prosecutor to drop the case and not pursue formal charges for the alleged rape. Such entreaties are not futile, but they often face steep odds. Prosecutors are the chief law enforcement officials for their jurisdictions, and, in theory, they make their decision to file formal charges based upon their own evaluation of the merits of the case. In the real world, prosecutors face constant pressure to support the decision of their partners in crime fighting, the local police and sheriffs. Especially with a high-profile arrest, for a prosecutor to fail to support his local sheriff by dropping a sensational case would be an embarrassment, even a betrayal of a comrade in the face of massive public scrutiny. Failing to be a "stand-up" member of the law enforcement family could even be catastrophic for the future of the working relationship with police that is so essential for prosecutors. No such catastrophe was to occur in the case of Kobe Bryant.

SPINNING LESSON

Police and prosecutors need each other—sometimes it is better to lose a case than to lose face with your teammates.

The Press Wars Begin

On a Friday afternoon, the youthful District Attorney Mark Hurlbert, seeming even younger than usual under the glare of national media, announced that he had filed an information charging the hugely popular superstar with the crime of rape. Surely understanding the momentous battleground he had stepped upon, he looked down before the cameras and seemed to brace himself as he pronounced the prosecutorial judgment that would launch the career-defining case.

Minutes later, the defense presented its own unusual press conference with a brief but determined announcement that Kobe Bryant was innocent and would fight the charges. The visual featured Kobe Bryant flanked by lawyers on one side and his wife on the other. Bryant said nothing. Even under the most controlled circumstances, responsible defense lawyers almost never allow their clients to speak publicly about criminal charges. But Bryant did not need to say anything. The presence of his beautiful wife said that, of course, he would never take another woman by force. And the imposing presence of his counsel signaled the beginning of a ferocious battle in which there would be plenty of sharp elbows and no holds barred until the last second sounded from the time clock.

> ### SPINNING LESSON
>
> A stand-up spouse to stand by the accused is a tried-but-still-true strategy and is better than a stand alone.

A Shield for Victims?

While defense lawyers almost invariably promise vindication, prosecutors rarely brag about their case or predict a conviction. Prosecutors can afford brevity. It is easier to maintain a poker face when holding the best cards. True to tradition, Eagle County's DA properly avoided discussing the details of the evidence, instead providing only the executive summary. No boast was made about the outcome of the trial, but the DA did announce that the privacy of the alleged victim would be effectively protected by Colorado's shield law. In a high-profile case, such promises may be easier to make than to keep.

Rape shield laws have been enacted in virtually every state and are badly needed.[128] In times past, rape victims endured a violation from the legal system that reprised some of the emotional devastation of the original assault. Defense attorneys were once allowed to attack the character of the victims and could even ask questions about their prior sexual conduct.[129] Such a cross-examination would typically be calculated to suggest that the victim was a loose woman who was really "asking for it" from the defendant. This brutal gauntlet deterred most rape victims from coming forward to the police. And unless evidence of physical injury or other witnesses at trial strongly corroborated the victim's account, the rapist might win.[130]

Today, rape remains one of the most underreported crimes. The rape shield laws, though, provide at least two crucial safeguards to lessen the victim's legal ordeal. First, as a rule of evidence, rape shield laws ordinarily prevent defense attorneys from cross-examining or presenting evidence about the accusing witness's sexual past. A history of alleged promiscuity is obviously irrelevant to whether a victim was raped by the defendant on trial.[131] In fact, prostitutes can be raped, and their rapists are as accountable for their crimes as any other criminals. By preventing defense lawyers from attacking the victim during trial, the shield laws protect the witness from humiliation and the jury from senseless but nonetheless damaging distraction. Like most rules, however, rape shields have exceptions, as the clerk in this case would learn.

Shield laws have been passed also to protect prosecution witnesses from pretrial publicity. Laws that prohibit the press from publishing the name of a rape victim, however, encounter the same free-press concerns about "prior restraint" that the First Amendment imposes elsewhere.[132] As a result, the courts have found that rape shield laws cannot, under the Constitution, prevent the press from publishing the name of an adult who alleges that he or she has been raped. Because courts see the protection of minors as a more powerful concern, shield laws can be enforced to prevent media from identifying rape victims who are children.[133]

In the Kobe Bryant case, the accuser was entitled to be protected inside the court of law but, as an adult, enjoyed no safeguards in the venues of national media. In general, responsible networks and newspapers follow a self-imposed honor code and refuse to publish the names of adult rape victims and continue to respect their privacy as long as those names have not already been reported publicly. The clerk's identity soon became one of the worst-kept secrets in America. Even so, for months the mainstream media avoided using her name even as the publicity game became increasingly brutal.

SPINNING LESSON

When the accusation is sexual assault of an adult, the victim's identity is protected not by the legal system but by only the honor system.

Only a He Said–She Said

The press campaign went relatively well for Bryant—merely bad rather than horrible—almost from the start. In contrast to the menacing and controversial image of boxing champion Mike Tyson, who was convicted of rape, Bryant confronted similar allegations but presented a good-guy image that made the theoretical presumption of innocence more real. The early days of news coverage also benefited from the shrewd tactics that minimized the case as only a he said–she said. Accusations of rape are not always corroborated by clear evidence of force or other witnesses, a common scenario in a so-called date rape. The common wisdom is that the word of one witness against another is not enough for guilt because the supposed equality of evidence does not eliminate reasonable doubt, so the resulting tie goes to the defendant.

The popular thinking, though, that a he said–she said places accuser and accused on an equal footing is a popular myth. In most cases, gross inequality is the reality. Because the accuser has no apparent self-interest in being subjected to the humiliating ordeal of a rape trial while the accused has every incentive to lie and deny, the credibility contest is usually no contest at all. While date rape is a severely underreported crime, when it is prosecuted, defendants are frequently convicted unless some plausible explanation is given as to why the alleged victim is making up such extreme allegations.

SPINNING LESSON

Although prosecutors know that a he said–she said can well mean that he gets convicted, the message plays better in the court of public opinion, where real law and pop law often diverge.

For rich and famous defendants, the accusers have plenty of financial incentive because of the immensely profitable civil lawsuit that can be brought against the accused. Prosecutors recognize that a witness with a financial upside creates a credibility downside.[134] For that reason, prosecutors prefer scenarios where no civil lawsuit is brought until the criminal trial is resolved. Accusers have few legal impediments to adhering to this preferred schedule. Almost always, the statute of limitations will allow accusers to avoid filing the civil lawsuit for years,[135] opting to be better witnesses at a criminal trial by delaying the day when they may be money seekers in a civil case. Additionally, for legal reasons, a criminal conviction increases the likelihood that the same defendant will be accountable to the same victim for monetary compensation in a later civil case. As a result, the accuser not only is a more effective witness in a criminal case but also, following a criminal conviction, will be an inevitably successful plaintiff in a later civil action. For that reason, as much as an accuser's self-profiteering might help the defense argue that the rape allegations are a financially inspired invention, there may be no evidence of a money scheme. Unless a civil lawsuit is pending or at least being considered, defense counsel is left with implying that the accuser, though not presently suing for money, is still scheming for future rewards.

Another line of attack upon the accuser's credibility is the motive for revenge.[136] Although attempted occasionally in theories ranging from jilted girlfriends to prostitutes who are not paid for their services, a defense theorizing a vengeful accuser is rarely a successful one. Everyday experience teaches that the harsh ordeal of going to the police with these accusations, subjecting oneself to intrusive physical testing, and enduring months of a punishing legal gauntlet, is usually too great a price to pay for revenge. Without a strong financial motive or extreme incentive for retribution, common sense says a person would have to be crazy to make up rape allegations. Speaking of which, since mental instability could solve the defense dilemma by explaining why the "she said" is not true, defense counsel pursue opportunities to raise psychological issues, suggesting that an accusing witness is delusional. Most of the time, however, this information is more likely to reach listeners at home than jurors sitting in a courtroom.

SPINNING LESSON

In defending what "he said," defense lawyers launch a credibility offensive against what "she said"; and revenge, money, and delusion are the usual suspects.

The Kobe Prelim

Preliminary Hearing—Such a Bad Move?

In the lead-up to October, most legal commentators seemed sure that Bryant would waive his right to a preliminary hearing.[137] They thought that the judge's decision to keep the hearing open, combined with his decision not to compel Bryant's accuser to testify, would create a disastrous news cycle for Bryant that would poison the potential jury pool beyond repair.[138]

"Just taking part in a preliminary hearing was a bad move," said John Gallagher, a former federal prosecutor, in the *New York Times*.[139]

"I can't see any way there is going to be a preliminary hearing," said Jeralyn Meritt, a Denver lawyer and legal commentator.[140] "I see no benefit to Kobe Bryant where the accuser is not going to testify and the information is going to come in through the hearsay of a police officer."[141]

The district attorney's office was obviously pleased by the judge's rulings to allow the accuser to stay away from the hearing.[142] "We hope this will minimize the victim's trauma regarding this process," said a spokeswoman for the office.[143]

In light of the judge's view that the accuser's presence was unnecessary, most observers assumed that the outcome of the preliminary hearing was a foregone conclusion.[144] "It's manifestly clear that the outcome to this preliminary hearing has been predetermined. This district attorney is going to win," said former Denver prosecutor Craig Silverman.[145] "How do we know this? The judge has reviewed the prosecution evidence and has concluded that the accuser need not appear because there is probable cause without her video coming in, without Kobe Bryant's audio tape coming in."[146]

The Questionable Question

On Thursday, October 9, 2003, the judge held the first day of the preliminary hearing.[147] The Eagle County sheriff, Detective Doug Winters, testified about the accuser's version of events, including that the clerk twice told Bryant no before bursting into tears during the attack.[148] Winters also testified that a nurse with experience treating victims of sexual assault had told him that the clerk had injuries that were consistent with "penetrating genital trauma."[149]

On cross-examination, Mackey asked a stunning question of Winters: "You didn't ask her if it was consistent with a person who had sex with three different men in three days?"[150]

The court's reaction was immediate. Judge Frederick Gannett promptly ordered the lawyers and Bryant into a private room adjoining the courtroom. When they emerged an hour later, the judge declared the proceedings over for the day and confirmed that Mackey's question was responsible for the abrupt end to the day. "Things did not progress as we expected," the judge told the courtroom.[151]

Although Mackey's "three different men" scored a three-point basket in terms of inciting public speculation, it won no praise from the prosecutors or victims advocates.

Denver District Attorney Norm Early, who was following the case, commented immediately on Mackey's question. "It was contemptible, despicable, and sleazy," he said. "The only reason they had the preliminary hearing was to smear the victim."[152]

In the following days, most of the discussion focused on Mackey's use of the clerk's name and the implications of the question that brought the hearing to an end.

Silverman opined that the implication of Mackey's question—that the clerk had indeed had sex with three men in three days—could prove "compelling evidence" to a jury that the liaison was consensual.[153] "It's obvious why they [the defense] wanted the preliminary hearing now. There was some dirt out there [on Bryant] and they needed to shoot it down," he said.[154] "Last week we heard about [the prosecution's] strangulation expert. This week, we read a *Newsweek* cover story that we now know is full of baloney—it had her being attacked as soon as she entered the room, which not even the prosecution is saying—and the case was getting away from them in the court of public opinion."

> ### SPINNING LESSON
> Questions with shock value have news value.

What's in a Name?

Mackey created yet another sizzling controversy by referring to the victim by name six times in about twenty minutes. "This is very hard for me," Mackey said, apologizing to the court, "I don't think of her as 'K. F.'" "I could just go get the muzzle," replied Judge Gannett.[155]

Onlookers were incredulous that Mackey's claim of her repeated use of the clerk's name was an accident. "I think it was inexcusable," said Steve Siegel, chairman of the Denver Sex Assault Interagency Council, "And I think her minimizing her behavior was inappropriate."[156]

This was a "flagrant violation of the spirit of Colorado's rape shield law," said Jill McFadden, executive director of the Colorado Coalition Against Sexual Assault. "We find it hard to believe that an experienced litigator such as Mackey would make such a 'mistake,'" she said. "We feel that this was a calculated attempt to further intimidate this victim by circumventing the laws that our state has established in order to protect a victim of sexual assault."[157]

However, some local lawyers came to Mackey's defense. "I think that the criticism of the defense team for raising the issue of her sleeping with three men is totally unwarranted," said Dan Recht, a past president of the Colorado Criminal Defense Bar. "If the injuries came from someone other than Kobe Bryant, they certainly have the right to raise that as an issue and a potential defense."[158]

Even Cynthia Stone, spokeswoman for the Colorado Coalition Against Sexual Assault, agreed that Mackey hadn't broken any laws.[159] "When you look at what she did, she actually violated no real laws," Stone said. "She was very clever with the way she did it."[160]

Although various motives were ascribed to Mackey's use of the clerk's name, all agreed that the prohibition against using her name was in this case because of the media attention.[161] That Saturday, Tina Fey took aim at Mackey on *Saturday Night Live.*

The preliminary hearing in Kobe Bryant's rape trial turned ugly on Thursday when Pamela Mackey, Bryant's lawyer, accidentally said his accuser's name in court, violating Colorado privacy laws. And after being admonished by the judge, Mackey went on to repeat the woman's name five times. Which is really bad because what lawyer Pamela Mackey did by mentioning the woman's name is to put her at risk of further harassment. A lawyer, like Pamela Mackey of the Colorado firm Haddon, Morgan, Mueller, Jordan, Mackey, and Foreman—which is probably in the 303 area code—should know that people can look up a name, like Joe Smith or Pamela Mackey, on the Internet and learn everything about them.[162]

By early Monday, a receptionist said the firm had received numerous calls and requests to be put through to Mackey's voicemail, requests that were explicitly denied.[163]

> ### SPINNING LESSON
> Defense attorneys will ruffle feathers to keep their clients from becoming a cooked goose.

The Tide Changes

As news reports swirled around the preliminary hearing, many sensed that the defense had gained some ground. "Did a detective's graphic testimony at Kobe Bryant's preliminary hearing prove devastating to the basketball star facing a rape charge? Or did it instead buoy his case?" ran the lead in the *Denver Post.*[164]

Nathan Chambers, a Denver lawyer and commentator, said that he didn't think that the detective's testimony hurt Bryant. Chambers cited several "glaring" issues in the prosecution's case, such as the victim's failure to contact police immediately after the alleged assault and the fact that she didn't tell detectives that Bryant forced her to kiss his genitalia during her first interview.[165]

Silverman agreed the testimony supported Bryant's claim that the sex was consensual. The clerk's story "is weaker than expected," said Silverman. "She said she wanted to leave but then kissed him on the face and neck, and she agreed to it."[166]

Denver lawyer Larry Pozner had another take. "The evidence shows that this woman's credibility is low and declining," he said. "The preliminary hearing is tilted to favor the prosecution, but the defense can show a lot of problems with the woman and her story" by proceeding with the hearing.[167]

"The credibility of the complaining witness is critical to the case," Pozner went on. "She has an alleged suicide attempt, and she has law enforcement agents taking her into custody for her own safety. This could potentially be the string that unravels the whole case," said Pozner.[168]

Some saw no damage to the prosecution. The rape victim "is in shock," said advocate Steve Siegel. "And the time it takes to gather yourself varies from individual to individual." CBS's Andrew Cohen, another Denver-based legal commentator, agreed: "The whole scenario is unflattering to Kobe Bryant. It shows intent, a plan, and a scheme." The fact that the clerk made out with Bryant for five minutes didn't mean anything, Cohen argued: "[consenting] to kissing doesn't mean you consent to sex."[169]

SPINNING LESSON

Although they serve a client's interests, hard-nosed strategies create hard feelings.

Judge Gannett had issued a decorum order on July 29 preventing the lawyers in the case from using the clerk's name. However, Gannett later modified the order to say that parties were "encouraged not to broadcast, publish, or otherwise disseminate her name."[170] The revision also eliminated the threat of sanctions against any who used her name.[171]

The following Wednesday, the preliminary hearing resumed with fireworks. "Every time Pam Mackey opened a new area of inquiry through her questions, she dropped a bomb on the prosecution, and they all hit. Her aim was perfect," said Larry Pozner.[172]

On cross-examination, Mackey elicited several damaging details from Detective Winters. Under cross-examination, Winters revealed that the clerk had worked hard to figure out whether Bryant was coming to the resort, that she stayed late to meet him, and that she separated Bryant from his bodyguards—presumably to make it easier for her to get into his room. Winters also revealed that the clerk expected Bryant to come onto her, and that the night auditor working at the desk after the alleged assault who watched her close out her register said she seemed completely calm.[173]

Detective Winters also testified that when he first interviewed her, she didn't claim that she had said no to Bryant, and that he had asked her why she didn't say no.

Finally, the detective revealed that the victim acknowledged having sex with another partner around the same time that she had sex with Bryant—a story supported by the fact that when she went to the hospital to be examined the next day, the underwear she wore the night of the alleged incident with Bryant contained semen from two different men—neither of whom were Bryant.[174]

From Second-Guessing the Defense to Praising It

The question following the second day of the hearing "became not which side was winning or whether Mackey had crossed any ethical or legal lines, but why the prosecution had ever filed the case."[175]

"I can't understand why they would bring such a fatally defective case," said Craig Silverman. "It's not fair to Kobe. It's not fair to the accuser."[176] He added, "All those people who criticized Pam Mackey as sleazy and unethical owe her an apology."[177] Mike Littwin of the *Rocky Mountain News* wrote, "maybe you saw Mackey lampooned on *Saturday Night Live* for repeatedly using the alleged victim's name—a so-called slip that sounded more like an attempt to intimidate. But there were no slips this time. Mackey just calmly and relentlessly made her case for reasonable doubt."[178]

The prosecutor, however, was undeterred. Mark Hurlbert, the Eagle County district attorney, reminded reporters that all the judge needed to do was find probable cause. In Colorado and most states, this would not require enough proof for a conviction but only evidence sufficient for a neutral person to have "a reasonable belief that the defendant committed the crime."[179] Hurlbert said that he had provided a "sanitized" version of the evidence.[180] "It is not my intent to try this case in the media but to a jury of twelve in Eagle County," he said. "I will say I'm confident the judge will find probable cause and bind this case over."[181]

Hurlbert was right, but only barely. In a written opinion announcing his decision to bind Bryant over for trial, Judge Gannett found that the prosecution presented "what can only be described as a minimal amount of evidence, relying substantially on the use of hearsay evidence, particularly on those elements of submission against will or application of force."[182] Gannett also wrote: "Almost all of the evidence introduced at the preliminary hearing permits multiple inferences which, when viewed either independently or collectively, and upon reasonable inference, do not support a finding of probable cause. Simply put, this court could not make a finding of probable cause in the instant matter absent reliance upon those inferences supportive of the People's case."[183]

> **SPINNING LESSON**
>
> The difference between zealous advocacy and dirty pool is not always clear, and sometimes the waters get muddy.

The editorial page of the *Denver Post* acknowledged the aggressiveness as well as the success of defense tactics: "Some may question the tactics of the legal team representing the Los Angeles Lakers basketball star and whether defense attorney Pamela Mackey crossed the line between vigorous advocacy and dirty pool."[184] "On October 9, during the first part of the hearing, Mackey used the former concierge's name at least six times in open court, despite [Judge] Gannett having forbade it. After the first two times, Gannett should have used the power of the contempt citation to ensure no repetitions."[185] It continued, "Mackey shrewdly introduced an element of doubt that could taint all potential jurors if the case reaches district court: an assertion that is the young woman had sex with three different men in the days before the encounter with Bryant. Will any potential juror who heard the allegations be able to keep from thinking it establishes reasonable doubt even if it's never presented to the jury?"[186]

Mental and Emotional Issues

The Law v. Public Opinion

In a court of law a jury may never know that the witness has experienced psychological issues. Whatever those problems may be, such issues are not considered relevant unless they reflect on the witness's ability to testify truthfully or capacity to recall events accurately. Many psychological adversities are irrelevant to truthfulness and memory. A witness suffering from depression is not more likely to lie or forget any more than one gushing joyously. Nor would a witness's treatment for alcohol or drug abuse necessarily bear on his or her ability to recall events unless those conditions are severe.[187]

And yet in everyday life, speculation about "mental problems" depletes credibility faster than air leaves a bursting balloon. To determine whether something as explosive and damaging as a witness's past mental history should be presented to the jury, courts require proof of a demonstrated connection between the witness's condition and the ability of the witness to testify credibly. For example, do extreme mood swings result in truth swings? While in the public's eye no connector may be needed, in a courtroom the connection is typically made through the testimony of an expert or psychology witness to establish that the witness's medical condition equates to a condition of less reliability.[188] When the witness's psychology is an issue at trial, both sides are allowed to present competing experts for a duel over the impact on reliability that would be held outside the presence of the jury and decided by the trial judge.

The defense onslaught against Kobe Bryant's accuser included an aggressive attempt to target her with ammunition about past hospitalizations for depression. Some of it was live ammunition, including alleged reports of several suicide attempts and her prescription for an antipsychotic drug to treat schizophrenia.[189] Presumably, this issue was known to the prosecutors from the beginning, and they may even have assured her that such medical incidents would not become courtroom events. The issue of her psychological condition was never addressed by the trial judge. And the indications were that any evidence about depression would never have reached a jury. Even so, the defense made enough public hay with the accuser's past emotional issues.

SPINNING LESSON

While witnesses' psychological issues have little traction inside the courtroom, they have plenty of reaction outside.

In addition to attacking the accuser's mind, the defense landed body blows that questioned whether she had other sexual experiences within hours of the encounter with Bryant. This was sensational stuff for public consumption. While the information about a victim's sexual conduct would ordinarily be blocked by the shield laws, the defense argued that this evidence was relevant to issues other than one's social life.

While Bryant's DNA confirmed that he had intercourse with the clerk, the lab reports also detected the presence of DNA from at least one other man.[190] To make matters worse for the prosecution, the second man's DNA showed up on her body, in the underwear she was wearing when she was with Bryant, and in the underwear she wore the following day when she underwent the sexual-assault examination.[191] Although prosecutors argued that these semen samples came from old, dry semen on the yellow underwear, the defense, not surprisingly, had a DNA expert who disputed that explanation.[192] The judge found the controverted issue to be substantial enough for the jury to consider. Even though an accuser's alleged promiscuity is irrelevant, prior sex that created present contradictions for the accuser could be relevant. The primary line of attack the defense team argued was that if Bryant had assaulted the clerk, she would not have had sex with another man immediately after.[193] The defense team also advanced the theory that the clerk's accusations were an attempt to get the attention of her ex-boyfriend, and that the DNA found in her underwear and on her person belonged to the same ex-boyfriend.[194] Needless to say, along with their legal success, these arguments had plenty of traction in the court of public opinion.

Karen Steinhauser, a former sex crimes prosecutor and law professor at the University of Denver, told the *New York Times*, "No matter how the judge will instruct the jury, it's going to be in people's minds." She continued, "They're going to learn that she has slept with other men, and that feeds into all the stereotypes."[195] Linda Fairstein, who led the Manhattan district attorney's sex crimes unit, commented even more bluntly. "If you find the seminal fluid of two men, the train comes to a screeching halt, and it's the prosecutor who pulls the brake because there's reasonable doubt right there—a question for every juror right there," said Fairstein.[196] The pundits agreed, having sex with someone shortly after being sexually assaulted is not something that most victims do.[197]

Judge Ruckriegle also agreed. Ruling on the defense team's motion to admit evidence of the clerk's sexual activity, the judge found relevant "all evidence, whether direct or circumstantial, of the alleged victim's sexual conduct within approximately seventy-two hours preceding her physical examination."[198]

SPINNING LESSON

Rape shield laws should wall off the accuser's sexual past, but if the walls start to crumble, so might the case.

Despite the unceasing volleys against the accuser, the prosecution strove mightily to protect her. And attorneys refrained from press commentary throughout the case. The trial judge, in the meantime, did his best to protect both the accused and the accuser from the media maelstrom. More than 30 percent of the close to eight hundred pleadings in the Kobe Bryant trial were sealed by Judge Ruckriegle.[199]

But this was a case in which everything seemed to go wrong for Colorado's shield law. Along with huge cracks blasted by aggressive reporters and the hammering defense, the Colorado rape shield law suffered accidental mishaps as well. As in many high-profile cases, courts routinely post pleadings on their Web sites. In this fashion, the press has immediate access to the public records, and the judge's office is not overwhelmed with requests for paper copies of documents. While the public filings were posted electronically, the sealed pleadings, including documents protected by the shield law as well as court orders for confidentiality, were to remain behind closed doors. Unfortunately, the Eagle County clerk's office accidentally opened those doors by posting transcripts of proceedings that provided excruciating details about the accuser. Although the mistake was corrected within hours, reporters were monitoring the court Web site every minute of the day. As a result, the confidential materials were immediately splashed across the country, creating heartburn for the courthouse personnel, heartache for the alleged victim, and a new round of legal controversies.

In an effort to enforce the shield law and protect the woman who was allegedly raped, Judge Ruckriegle stepped onto the exceedingly thin ice of prior restraint by ordering the media not to publish or broadcast the accidental revelations. In an unusual decision, the Colorado Supreme Court voted narrowly to affirm Judge Ruckriegle's order. But then the US Supreme Court signaled its concern with the Colorado court decisions due to the strong traditions against press censorship. Thereafter, Judge Ruckriegle, like the federal judge in the Noriega trial, reflected further and withdrew the order that prohibited the press from publishing its news.

SPINNING LESSON

Even if the gags placed on attorneys and court records slip off, gags cannot be put on the press.

This round of publicity pummeling the alleged victim's privacy yet again may have been the last straw. As the trial drew near, the trial judge continued to try to minimize the harm of pretrial publicity and issued an extensive written questionnaire for prospective jurors to explore such exposure. But applying that ancient Latin legalism for "enough is enough," the alleged victim abandoned the criminal prosecution, the prosecutor dropped the case, and one of the highest-profile trials of the era came to a publicity-shattering close.

To no one's surprise, the alleged victim became a plaintiff in a civil claim for damages against Bryant. The burden of proving a rape in a civil case is significantly less than in a criminal trial. Rather than the need to provide enough convincing evidence to dispel any reasonable doubt, a civil plaintiff wins if there is even a slight edge in the evidence favoring the plaintiff over the defendant. The civil case was soon settled. The settlement terms were sequestered by the usual confidentiality agreement that permits neither side to say anything but allows both sides to hint smugly that theirs is the side that likes the outcome.

A civil claim is both more rewarding and less difficult for the accuser. And yet, unless the allegations are first presented to the police, there is a tall wall of skepticism about the truth behind the accusations.

> **SPINNING LESSON**
>
> Abuse victims are well-advised to prosecute now, sue later.

At least Bryant's accuser stepped forward almost immediately. Despite all the months of public bruising, the effort to pursue Bryant's criminal prosecution may have been a necessary prelude to a civil case against Bryant.

MICHAEL JACKSON—THE POP STAR PUTS THE STAR WITNESSES ON TRIAL

On November 20, 2003, an arrest warrant was issued for superstar Michael Jackson. The prosecutors and defense lawyers would not begin choosing a jury until more than a year later, in January 2005. During the intervening year, Jackson's attorneys, first Mark Geragos and later Thomas Mesereau, waged simultaneous wars in the media and in the courthouse for Jackson's acquittal.

The challenge for Jackson's defense team was daunting. They risked being overwhelmed by the "unproven accusations of inappropriate behavior with children" that had plagued Jackson for years. None of the accusations against the King of Pop had been proven in court. Still, his defense team had to contend with a multimillion-dollar settlement that Jackson had reached with his 1993 accuser. For all the rationales offered to explain hefty settlement payments, the public usually sees them as close cousins to a guilty plea. Nor was Jackson's cause helped by his comments in a BBC documentary that had aired on ABC in February of 2003.[200] In the interview, Jackson freely admitted his enthusiasm for sharing his bed with children who were not his own.[201] "Why can't you share your bed?" said Jackson, "The most loving thing to do is to share your bed with someone. It's a beautiful thing."[202] Perhaps to Jackson, underage bedmates seemed loving, but to most it seemed creepy and disturbing.

"A case could be made," opined the *New York Times*, "that Jackson's prolonged innocence—if the better word isn't infantilism—is for him a refuge from a career that both deprived him of his childhood and gave him the means to try to reclaim it."[203] But although the *Times* offered this up as a potential explanation for Jackson's fascination with children, the editors ultimately found the explanation unsatisfying. "Cruel or not," they concluded, "the world reserves a special kind of contempt for adults who choose to see themselves mainly through the eyes of children. Jackson has earned that contempt as surely as he has earned our respect for his musical talents."[204] Jackson's eccentricities, long a part of gossip and speculation, now invoked scorn from one of America's leading newspapers.

The serious accusations against Jackson were underscored by a blistering press that proclaimed "a perilous new chapter in a life of global fame, untold riches, and increasingly bizarre behavior."[205] For many, his strange ways had overtaken his stature as an international superstar. Indeed, although Jackson was one of the bestselling recording artists of all time, his recent albums had sold poorly, even as questions about his actions with children continued to cloud his reputation.[206]

The *New York Times* was not Jackson's biggest problem. Ten years earlier, Santa Barbara District Attorney Tom Sneddon had tried to bring another case against the King of Pop.[207] That one was washed away when Jackson's lawyers cleared things up with an expensive settlement paid to the alleged victim. Even if frustrated, Sneddon insisted that he had not spent the intervening years scheming to bring another case against Jackson.[208] He also denied that the timing of Jackson's arrest in 2003 was deliberate, even though it fell on the same day that

Jackson released a new album.[209] Even so, the press questions raised the specter of a prosecutorial vendetta that would cast a lingering shadow over news coverage of the case.

The real strategy for public opinion, though, paralleled the ultimate focus for the trial itself. As in the Kobe Bryant trial, the success of the prosecution's case hinged on the credibility of the accuser.[210] And, as in Bryant's trial, the Jackson team pushed the accuser's credibility immediately to center stage to try to keep the spotlight on the child and his family.

SPINNING LESSON

Believing the accuser means convicting the abuser. Credibility is everything.

The attacks on the accuser and his family began immediately. A lawyer who had advised Jackson in the past said that the child's family was simply seeking money and that the case would ultimately fall apart.[211] This message would never stop. In December 2003, the defense assault on the boy's believability made a major breakthrough, and the media widely reported the contents of a memorandum from the Department of Children and Family Services (DCFS).[212] The memo detailed a DCFS investigation of whether Jackson had molested the boy who was his accuser in the criminal case. The report included statements by the child, his mother, his sister, and his brother that all explicitly stated that Michael Jackson had never molested him. A few dents in the credibility of key witnesses are sometimes manageable, but these were craters.

SPINNING LESSON

Many a battle between Accuser Said—Accused Said has been decided because the accuser said something before that contradicts what is said now.

In September 2004, Jackson's defense team faced a *Dateline NBC* broadcast that reported that Jackson had paid $2 million to the son of an employee in 1990 to avoid molestation charges. The news of another expensive settlement of a molestation claim would certainly be very bad news for Jackson. To launch a preemptive strike on the eve of the broadcast, Jackson made a public statement.[213] "These people wanted to exploit my concern for children by threatening to destroy what I believe in and what I do. I have been a vulnerable target for those who want money."[214] Jackson's message reinforced the defense theme that the family was out for money rather than for justice.

Still, Jackson could not erase the past. The media continually reminded the public that Jackson had "been trailed by unproven accusations of inappropriate behavior with children for years."[215] While the past issues would not disappear, in the present it could appear that the family was all about greed.

Even as Jackson struggled to mute the sounds of years of rumors and the high-decimal noise of big-dollar settlements, Sneddon was never a media favorite. He was lambasted for his attempts at levity in an early press conference. When Jackson voluntarily gave a DNA sample to sheriff's deputies in late 2004,[216] commentators questioned how the prosecution was going to use the DNA and why the district attorney had not requested the samples earlier.[217] "We don't know whether this means they are scrambling or tying up loose ends, or it's just Sneddon going over the top," said Laurie L. Levenson, a former federal prosecutor.[218] Not only was Sneddon's competence questioned, but the "over the top" comment energized Jackson's theme that the case was driven by a prosecutorial vendetta. The prosecution fared better inside the courthouse. On December 10, 2004, Sneddon filed a sixty-four-page motion with the court, asking that many of these unproven prior accusations be admitted at trial.[219] The People's motion argued that it should be allowed to put forth evidence that Jackson molested at least seven other adolescent boys between 1990 and 1993.[220] The motion was graphic:

> Most of the boys were fondled in similar ways. Jackson would touch or fondle their genitals either through their clothing or under their clothing by reaching up through the open leg of a pair of shorts, or reaching down inside the waistband of the boy's pants, shorts, or underpants. Defendant showered nude with two of the boys. He per-

formed oral sex on another of the boys. He often kissed the boys, hugged and touched them in ways that many of the witnesses described as the fondling and caressing of a lover.[221]

Although Sneddon alleged that there were seven victims, only one of them was to eventually testify.[222] Other alleged incidents were to be proven by calling former Jackson employees who would testify that they witnessed the events in question.

Prior molestation allegations are live ammunition in the press and, if allowed in a trial, would usually have the same firepower.

In times past, much of this dynamite was considered too explosive for juries. For centuries, courts had often found that evidence of prior bad acts by a defendant were inadmissible at trial for two main reasons. First, judges feared that prior bad acts would swing the balance of evidence too heavily toward guilt by making it seem that the defendant also committed the crime being determined at trial. Second, judges feared that evidence of prior bad acts would make the jury want to punish the defendant for yesterday's misdeeds irrespective of whether the prosecution proved today's case beyond a reasonable doubt.[223]

During the 1990s, though, evidence of prior misdeeds in criminal trials concerning sexual wrongdoing became a point of controversy for legislatures as well as courts. In the wake of several high-profile sex crimes and child kidnappings, the legislature began enacting laws that strongly encouraged judges to allow excluded evidence of prior sexual misconduct in sex crimes cases.[224] In the late 1990s, the California Supreme Court summarized the purpose of the new laws that focus on the "'critical' need for such evidence in light of the serious and secretive nature of sex crimes and the frequent difficulty in resolving the resulting credibility contests at trial."[225]

Jackson's attorney tried to cool down the heat wave ignited by the graphic molestation allegations that continued to haunt Jackson. The defense court papers reprised anew its theme that Jackson had long been preyed upon by a litany of scam artists who saw his unorthodox relationships as an easy way to extort money from him. In rebutting the latest round of radioactivity, Mesereau's response, which was widely quoted in the press, used language that was more quotable than legal to denounce the proposed witnesses as "a collection of disgruntled former employees, paid tabloid informants, and other disreputable characters," who had lied about and stolen from Jackson in the past.[226] Mesereau had real fuel for his counterfire. A former security guard and a former domestic had unsuccessfully sued Jackson in the past, and not only had they lost and been assessed over sixty thousand dollars for lying to the court, but also they had been ordered to pay Jackson $1.4 million in court costs.[227] A former maid to Jackson, who was to provide evidence of five of the alleged seven prior bad acts, had already sold her story to *Hard Copy* for twenty thousand dollars. Her son who was also to testify had received a $2 million settlement from Jackson in 1994.[228] Mesereau argued that the ulterior motives of these witnesses in tandem with their history of contradictory statements made them so unreliable that admitting their testimony would result in a fundamentally unfair trial.[229]

Mesereau lost this pretrial battle with the judge, who ruled that the testimony of the People's witnesses concerning prior bad acts was admissible. Still, Mesereau used the occasion to trumpet once more his basic themes.[230] And he set the stage for what would be the subsequent cross-examinations at trial that would put some of the witnesses through a human shredding machine.

During the month of January 2005, just before the trial was scheduled to start, Judge Melville made other evidentiary rulings that were also damaging to the defense.[231] In particular, Judge Melville ruled that dozens of sexually explicit books, magazines, and DVDs seized from Jackson's Neverland Ranch could be offered as evidence against Jackson.[232] Prosecutors had successfully argued that these materials, some of which depicted adolescent-appearing models (like *Hustler's Barely Legal Hardcore*),[233] were evidence of Jackson's sexual interest in children. It was also reported that Jackson's fingerprints, along with his accuser's, had been found on at least one magazine.[234]

With so much publicity about past abuse and sexually graphic materials, one might think that the defense would be scurrying to find a less media-exposed venue for the trial. But none existed. Jackson's trial was an international media event. Moving the venue away from Santa Barbara to a different community would have been pointless. The defense did not even request a change of venue. Instead, shrewdly crafting a message to the community that expressed confidence to the future jurors, Mesereau publicly proclaimed his client's confidence in the fairness of the people of Santa Barbara.

The trial began amid extraordinary fanfare, from the media as well as from fans. To address the problem, Judge Rodney Melville instructed the jury as follows: "You must not read or listen to any accounts or discussion of the case reported by the newspapers or other news media, including radio, television, the Internet, or any other source."[235] At that point, the jurors had been exposed to over a year's worth of intense coverage of the Jackson case. But the admonitions are still appropriate—better late than never.

Analysts point out that juries are not particularly good at disregarding this kind of data.[236] Especially toxic were the many reports of prior molestation cases. Phoebe Ellsworth, of the University of Michigan, has shown that evidence of prior convictions, even if ruled inadmissible, predisposes a jury to find a defendant guilty.[237] However much Jackson and his past were on trial, though, the victim and his family seemingly got every bit as much scrutiny. Mesereau did not confine his arguments to the courtroom. Appearing on *Larry King Live*, Mesereau said the complaining witness had concocted the sexual abuse story with the help of his money-hungry family. Mesereau also contended that the prosecution, led by District Attorney Sneddon, had tried to "create the impression" that other people had also been molested.[238]

Inside the courtroom, Thomas Sneddon Jr. used his opening statement in late February 2005 to paint a graphic and disturbing picture of Michael Jackson's alleged molestation of the thirteen-year-old.

What the brother saw at that particular point in time was on the nightstand directly to the right of the bed which he said he had seen on numerous other occasions, were empty glasses and bottles of wine and Skyy Vodka that the three of them had shared on many occasions and were there that night.

[Michael] Jackson on the left, [the boy] on the right. What he saw was Jackson's hand. He saw his left hand, wrapped into the inside of Jackson's private parts, into his underwear. And he saw Jackson's left hand over the top of his brother and inside his brother's pants. And

what he saw was the motion of Jackson's hand inside of his underpants rhythmically moving up and down and his body moving up and
down while he masturbated with his hand under the underpants of
the motionless boy.[239]

Jackson's lawyer Mesereau countered strongly and declared that the
lurid allegations in Sneddon's opening statement were not true.[240]
Mesereau also tried to minimize the impact of the pornographic materials, while refocusing the jury and the media on the key issue—the
credibility of the family.[241] Mesereau told the jury that Jackson "will
feely admit that he does read girlie magazines from time to time,"[242]
and then he changed the subject.

The defense went after the mother to discredit her for supposedly
manipulating the child. Mesereau argued that she "saw Jackson as a
benefactor who would buy her a house, pay for college for her children,
and support her for the rest of her life."[243] Mesereau portrayed the
accuser's mother as "a serial liar who has tried to extort money from
celebrities by using her son's cancer as a hook."[244] The *New York Times*'s
coverage of Mesereau's opening statements situated Mesereau's thesis
in its lead.[245]

Increasingly, the spotlight moved from Jackson's strange ways to the
credibility of the family. When the brothers and their mother testified for
the prosecution, the tension inside and outside the courtroom was
intense. The *New York Times* reported that the testimony of the brother
was "crucial" for the prosecution, but that it was "halting, and occasionally confused."[246] The testimony from the two other siblings went as
badly, or perhaps even worse. The *New York Times* reported that the testimony was "confused," noting that Jackson's accuser "changed his testimony" and "contradicted his own grand jury testimony and the trial testimony of his younger brother" and sister.[247] One observer noted that the
alleged victim was "obviously very coached," and that he was "obviously
very eager to say what he had been trained or coached to say."[248]

The execution of the game plan for the defense was virtually flawless. Other prosecution witnesses were also chock-full of credibility gaps.

Another boy, who had received $2 million from Jackson to settle an
alleged molestation claim, was not a million-dollar man for the prosecution. Mesereau reminded him that the first time he was interviewed

by detectives in 1993, he told them Jackson had never done anything untoward.[249] The boy admitted to lying to the police.[250] Similarly, Mesereau used a deposition that his mother gave in 1994 to get her to admit on the stand that she had told lawyers she never saw Jackson molest a child.[251] Under cross-examination, another prosecution witness, a former security guard, admitted that he had been ordered to pay twenty-five thousand dollars for stealing Jackson's property. Yet another ex-domestic admitted that she had previously testified under oath that she hadn't seen Jackson molest anyone.[252]

> ### SPINNING LESSON
> Even when there's more bad news, an attorney should try to use it to keep pushing his news.

Mesereau's cross-examinations were plainly "damaging to the prosecution," and in the words of one commentator, they were the best she'd ever seen.[253] News reports noted that the prosecution witnesses "appeared to be of more help to the defense" than they were to an embattled prosecution.[254] "This week...ended much the way it began," wrote the *New York Times*, "with an onslaught of figures from [Jackson's] past saying they had seen him in compromising and scandalous positions with the boys."[255] "But the parade of former employees included some who admitted that they had stolen from their boss, sold their accounts of events to tabloid journalists for thousands of dollars, changed their testimony...and lied to investigators," the story continued.[256] As the prosecution's case kept getting pummeled in and out of the courtroom, Mesereau's strategy of portraying Jackson as a victim being exploited by a series of cheats and grifters kept gaining momentum.

> ### SPINNING LESSON
> Attorneys should keep the theme simple and, if it is scoring points, stay on point.

Many on the outside, including this author, predicted a conviction on at least some of the lesser counts. The extensive evidence of past molestation claims seemed hard to overcome. The Jackson jury, though, had seen all it needed to see of the family's credibility gaps. The Jackson jurors returned a verdict of not guilty on June 13, 2005. In the wake of one of the biggest "trials of the century" acquittals, reporters returned to Sneddon, asking whether he brought the failed case to satisfy a personal vendetta.[257] This question had never made it into the trial itself. Nor did Mesereau use the word "vendetta" in his opening or closing statements. And of course, Sneddon repeatedly denied having any vendettas. But the issue had media traction and never ceased to raise questions about the prosecution.

Many, like Marcia Clark, the prosecutor in the O. J. Simpson trial, have argued that having a celebrity as a defendant makes securing a defendant's conviction more difficult. According to that view, fame effectively raises the burden of proof from guilt beyond a reasonable doubt, to guilt beyond all possible doubt.[258] Clearly, however, many disagree. The jurors, who spoke to the media after the verdict, said that Jackson's celebrity status had not factored into their decision.[259] "We looked at all the evidence and we looked at Michael Jackson, and one of the first things we decided was we had to look at him just as another person and not [as] a celebrity," said the jury foreman, Paul Rodriguez.[260]

Indeed, it appears that the jurors, like jurors in everyday trials, took their duty seriously. And the Jackson jurors tried to look past the massive media presence. "In a case like this, you're hoping that maybe you can find a smoking gun or something that you can grab onto that says absolutely one way or another. In this case, we had difficulty in finding that," said a juror.[261] Another juror put it even more bluntly. He said that even though he thought that Jackson is or was a pedophile, the prosecution didn't prove the case.[262] It seemed that the jurors did indeed focus on the evidence inside the courtroom, despite the unprecedented commotion on the outside.

Many were astonished by the verdict. But those seated at home watching pundits on television never sat with the jurors, who saw it all. What the jurors saw were gaping holes in a prosecution that had been blasted by glaringly inconsistent versions of the truth. When there are too many inconsistencies to be reasonable, they add up to reasonable doubt.

GOVERNOR BLABBERMOUTH

Crazy or Crazy Like a Fox?

Illinois Governor Milorad R. "Rod" Blagojevich was busted on December 9, 2008, before he received any payoffs from would-be senators or other alleged victims of a purported crime spree in December 2008.[263] And yet as the federal charges detailed, his voice was captured on numerous wiretap recordings filled with scintillating pay-to-play schemes.[264] As with the excruciating narrative of animal cruelty detailed in the indictment of NFL quarterback Michael Vick, the written charges chronicled Blagojevich's corruption to a level of specificity that left few reasonable doubters about his guilt. Both Blagojevich and his counsel made, of course, the usual accusation of "witch hunt" along with predications of vindication when their side of the story would be told. Defense platitudes aside, the reality remained that by arresting Blagojevich before his wheeling and dealing reached actual stealing, prosecutors left some room for him to claim he may have neared the line of crime but never crossed it.

The arrests of Blagojevich and his chief of staff for allegedly trying to sell the gubernatorial appointment to the US Senate seat vacated by President-elect Obama seemed sudden and startling. It was an instant sensation that mesmerized politicians, the press, and much of the public. US Attorney Patrick Fitzgerald announced the arrest with high-octane commentary, calling it a "staggering" level of corruption, a "truly new low" that would have made "Lincoln roll over in his grave."[265] But it followed five years of a slow but steady investigation that hit high gear once the wiretaps commenced in October 2008. In textbook fashion, the FBI and the US Attorney's Office spent years collecting evidence as well as the convictions of smaller-fish defendants. Building from convictions at the bottom of the ladder, and getting the newly convicted to cooperate with information against higher-ups, the authorities kept moving up until in May 2008 they won the bigger-fish conviction of Tony Rezko, a Chicago political kingpin whose fundraiser's tentacles slithered throughout the state. With other fish netted, and ever-increasing evidence to implicate Blagojevich as the Great White Shark of Illinois corruption, by October the feds could meet the demanding tests to secure a federal judge's approval of gubernatorial wiretapping.

Wiretaps are less pervasive than is commonly believed because they require a strong foundation of probable cause. Electronic eavesdropping is also resource-intensive—a single ongoing interception may require twelve agents to staff the wiretap. When they are successful, prosecutors sometimes prefer to continue the wiretaps as long as guilty voices keep talking. And, at times, wiretaps lead to scenes of actual payoffs, the gold standard for slam-dunk corruption convictions. As Blagojevich moved toward appointing Obama's replacement in December, though, the feds wisely decided to arrest him before he could complete his year-end clearance sale of government goodies. Due to the perceived urgency, these arrests were effected before a grand jury returned any indictments, which are the formal charges required in federal cases by the US Constitution. As Fitzgerald explained, "we were in the middle of a corruption crime scene and we wanted to stop it."[266] When immediacy is needed because a serious crime is well on its way to perpetration, arrests can be made by law enforcement officers. They use a criminal complaint setting forth the officer's sworn statement of probable cause. In Blagojevich's case, two crimes were charged in the criminal complaint executed by the FBI: theft of government property and theft of honest services, a law violated when public officials are corrupted by private gain. But the FBI set forth seventy-six pages to detail and substantiate those charges. Under federal rules, the criminal complaint later used for the arrests could be followed by formal charges set forth in a grand jury indictment.[267] Later, after several court-ordered extensions for securing the indictment, the formal document was issued in early April 2009, relying on many of the same facts detailed in the complaint but also raising the ante to sixteen criminal charges against Blagojevich—including conspiracy and racketeering—as well as charging more defendants.[268]

The road map for the prosecution's evidence is set forth in remarkable detail about meetings, conversations between named and unnamed witnesses, and most vividly, excerpts from gubernatorial wiretaps. The tape recordings were the crown jewels of the prosecution's case, joined by a lineup of witnesses that included guilty cooperators as well as innocent victims. The alleged demands for pay-to-play by Blagojevich and his staff centered on campaign fundraisers, where there is plenty of sleaze, though it is not easy proving explicit schemes. Understandably, corruption cases became stronger when the corrupt official has extracted cash, goods, or services for personal use in exchange for doing public favors, a prominent factor in the recent convictions of former Congressmen Randall "Duke" Cunningham and Robert Ney.[269] Illustrating a dream scenario for a corruption prosecutor, Louisiana Congressman William Jefferson was caught on tape receiving one hundred thousand dollars from an undercover FBI agent, and, when his home was later searched, ninety thousand dollars of those funds were found in his freezer. Without cold, hard cash to show to a jury, Blagojevich prosecutors were still able to pursue convictions by emphasizing criminal attempts and conspiracies to perpetuate corruption, rather than relying exclusively on completed crimes.[270]

Blagojevich was arrested when he was still empty-handed, not red-handed with a bag of cash. Since reasonable doubt is all defendants need, this could leave some room for a defense to try to portray the scheme as nothing more than trash-talking inside the camp of a frustrated politician's locker room, where ill-advised comments never produced ill-gotten gain.[271] The many hours of tape recordings could also reveal some minutes professing innocence by self-conscious talkers. It is common for defendants who suspect that criminal investigations are ongoing and that wire tapping is a possibility to insert various comments into conversations to create a phony posture of innocence. Occasional phrases may appear on tape, even in the middle of unmitigated skullduggery, insisting that nothing illegal is being done or disclaimers to suggest that they are just kidding or venting. Blagojevich was already aware of the FBI investigation, and so his tapes might include interludes of professed innocence that defense counsel could use to try to downsize the passages of incrimination.

Although no defendant can be forced to the witness stand, Blagojevich had many moments to grandstand during his final weeks as governor. Impeachment proceedings were quickly launched by the state
legislature. Some had hoped the supreme court of Illinois would
impose a fast exit strategy by finding that the criminal charges against
Blagojevich constituted a "disability," authorizing his removal from
office, but the Illinois Supreme Court refused to intervene.[272] Blagojevich's counsel raised every conceivable procedural objection to the
impeachment process before the state legislature, insisting that the
mere fact of an arrest does not equate to guilt and effectively
demanding all the safeguards of a full-blown criminal trial.[273] Along
the same line, Blagojevich's lawyers demanded the right to confront
prosecution witnesses so that cross-examinations in legislative halls
might be used later to help Blagojevich in a courtroom.

SPINNING LESSON

Even negative news makes one newsworthy, and being
heavily indicted can mean being heavily televised.

Adding another wild card to an already wild story was Blagojevich's
television grandstanding. Charged with serious crimes and facing certain removal from office and severe exposure to years in federal prison,
defendant Blagojevich could not keep his mouth shut. One former
friend surmised, "I'm not sure he's playing with a full deck anymore."[274]

On the eve of his impeachment trial, Blagojevich ran from one television station to another, starting with CNN's *Larry King Live*, and then
affording equal opportunity to practically the whole industry, including
Good Morning America with Diane Sawyer, ABC's *The View*,[275] NBC's
Today Show, Fox News, and CBS's *Early Show*.[276] Mostly, it was predictable stuff—he claimed that the impeachment process amounted to a
"kangaroo court" and that, of course, he was completely innocent.[277] On
ABC's *Nightline*, he included the implausible comparison to icons like
Jimmy Stewart and Gary Cooper, but Blagojevich also interjected a
theme to explain away at a future trial his seemingly suspicious deal-

ings—captured on tape—as an unorthodox method for solving problems that other government agencies would never address. "It's my position that when the full story comes out and all of those conversations are put in proper context, it's going to show a governor who's working to try to get things done for people."[278] This built on his comments to *Good Morning America*'s Diane Sawyer that the "whole story" would show he had been "trying to position and maneuver to create jobs and expand healthcare."[279] When Blagojevich was impeached by the lower legislation body and bound over for trial before the Illinois Senate, his unusual press conference focused even more on his creative ways to find solutions for the people's problems that government as usual would not fix. In front of cameras, he was accompanied by individuals whose problems had purportedly been resolved through admittedly unconventional problem solving. These were everyday people who joined Blagojevich, perhaps the kind who would be on his jury some day. For any who missed the press conference, Blagojevich has posted dozens of television clips on his Web site, ranging from his appearances with Jon Stewart and *The Daily Show* to Fox's *Geraldo Rivera* show. Also advertised was his autobiography, *The Governor*.[280] Some experts attributed his nonstop tour of television studios to an oversized ego taking a few last bows before the final curtain drops,[281] while others suggested that the ex-governor's campaign was aimed at future jurors.[282]

Perhaps future jurors could be the intended audience for one of Blagojevich's often heavily publicized strategies. He confounded legislatures in Illinois as well as Washington by naming African American Roland Burris to the vacant US Senate post. The Senate Democrats in Washington had vowed to never seat anyone whom the disgraced governor might name. But their bluff was called when Burris went to Washington to claim his seat and soon became the junior senator from Illinois.[283] At a minimum, Blagojevich's decision to exercise his appointment authority at no cost to the winner was a counterpoint, though a tardy one, to the charges that he was bent on selling it to the highest bidder. Along the way, Blagojevich emphasized his commitment to name an African American to join what would otherwise have been an all-white Senate. No one can know whether this professed dedication to minority causes was intended by Blagojevich to create a little more sympathy from African American jurors at a trial some day. But since this defendant seemingly expected a return on every public action he ever took, it seems unlikely that his final exercise of authority was entirely altruistic.

In the summer of 2010, Blagojevich's case went to trial. His media message about helping the people through unorthodox strategies for creating jobs and expanding healthcare became a jury theme.[284] Rather than "extortion" for personal gain, Blagojevich's tactics were a "negotiation" for the good of Illinois. Supposedly, by dangling various names as possibilities to be named to the vacant Senate seat, the ex-governor had sought help from other politicians in advancing his agenda for jobs and healthcare.[285] "That man wasn't selling any Senate seat...he was trying to get three hundred thousand people healthcare," Blagojevich's lawyer claimed.[286] Even the seeming flakiness generated by Blagojevich's media stunts coincided with a defense theme. According to Blagojevich's own lawyer, he was not "the sharpest knife in the drawer."[287] So loose were his lips, the defense lawyer argued that Blagojevich could out-talk "Joan and Melissa Rivers in a room."[288]

After deliberating for fourteen days, the jury hung on twenty-three counts and convicted Blago of only one charge—lying to the FBI.[289] One juror thought "he was just talking," perhaps giving birth to a new "blabbermouth" defense.[290] While seen as a defense victory, the result might be short-lived because prosecutors vowed to try him a second time.[291]

SPINNING LESSON

Unless a "smoking gun" shows stealing, it's harder to convict for wheeling and dealing.

CHAPTER 9

PROSECUTORS AND THE PRESS

The [prosecuting] [a]ttorney is the representative not of an ordinary party to a controversy, but of a sovereignty whose obligation to govern impartially is as compelling as its obligation to govern at all, and whose interest, therefore, in a criminal prosecution is not that it shall win a case, but that justice shall be done.
—*Berger v. United States*, 295 U.S. 78, 88 (1935)

It is a rare prosecutor who isn't influenced by the press.
—LA defense attorney Mark Geragos

More than a century ago, the nation's first official code of legal ethics, the Alabama Code of 1887, warned attorneys to "avoid newspaper discussion of legal matters," and stated that "newspaper publications by an attorney as to the merits of pending or anticipated litigation . . . tend to prevent a fair trial in the courts, and otherwise prejudice the due administration of justice."[1]

In modern times, the American Bar Association has promulgated "Model Rules of Professional Conduct,"[2] which include special criteria for prosecutors, providing that they shall

> except for statements that are necessary to inform the public of the nature and extent of the prosecutor's action and that serve a legitimate law enforcement purpose, refrain from making extrajudicial comments that have a substantial likelihood of heightening public

241

condemnation of the accused and exercise reasonable care to prevent investigators, law enforcement personnel, employees, or other persons assisting or associated with the prosecutor in a criminal case from making an extrajudicial statement that the prosecutor would be prohibited from making under rule 3.6 or this rule.[3]

For federal prosecutors, regulations issued in the 1970s provided more specific directions concerning the release of information about pending criminal matters that ordinarily prohibit comments on matters such as a defendant's character, any opinion as to the accused's guilt, and the credibility of prospective witnesses, confessions, and other damaging subjects.[4]

Traditionally, prosecutors required no such admonitions because most scorned contact with the press. With all the powers of the government on their side of the courtroom, they needed media support like an eight-hundred-pound gorilla needs a parakeet. As Robert H. Jackson, US attorney general, said sixty years ago, "The prosecutors have more control over life, liberty, and reputation than any other person in America." Their power permeates their dealings with the press, which ordinarily treats prosecutors well—after all, they represent not only our government but also a never-ending news source that no one wants to alienate. Professor Alan M. Dershowitz underscores this reality by quoting former Manhattan District Attorney Robert Morgenthau, who held office for thirty-six years and would say to other attorneys, "I can make mistakes with the press and they still have to be nice to me. They don't have to be nice to you."[5] For practical reasons, as well as ethical considerations, old-school prosecutors eschewed aggressive press strategy, and many maintained strict no-comment policies. My, how times have changed.

Professor Laurie L. Levenson of Loyola Law School in Los Angeles, a former federal prosecutor herself, attributes the "press-friendly" prosecutive dynamic to a "full generation of prosecutors raised in cases in the media. They want to be part of it."[6] While judges in media-intensive cases are familiar with the challenge of trying to muzzle defense lawyers, Levenson observes that they face increasing challenges in dealing with prosecutor press strategies. Because prosecutors command so much personal and institutional respect, Levenson explains, "judges don't know how to deal with it."[7] In a recent article, Professor Levenson summarizes the growing dilemma, saying, "When even the most respected prosecutors appear to be crossing ethical lines governing pretrial publicity, it is time to reevaluate whether we have correctly set forth the standards prescribing prosecutorial behavior."[8]

The press-friendlier ways of many of today's prosecutors often focus on press conferences, which in times past were a hype-free, even colorless presentation naming the defendants and listing the charges. Frequently, efforts are made to maximize press coverage, and sound bites are no longer just for defense lawyers. Consider the highly respected former US Attorney in Chicago, Patrick Fitzgerald. In 2005, when Fitzgerald announced the arraignment of I. Lewis "Scooter" Libby, the vice president's chief of staff, he reflected the traditional dignity of such events. Three years later, when he announced criminal charges against Illinois Governor Rod Blagojevich, he hyped the allegations, saying that Blagojevich's "conduct would make Lincoln roll over in his grave."[9] Several leading commentators believed the sound bites went too far, and Professor Dershowitz described them as "unseemly," and not helpful to the government's credibility.[10]

To be sure, many prosecutors still approach the press with more reluctance than enthusiasm. Veteran Associated Press reporter Brian Skoloff, who has covered cases such as the media-intensive murder trial of Scott Peterson, believes that the prosecutors assigned to actually try the case usually do not aggressively play the press.[11] Defense superstar Roy Black believes that, apart from the initial press conference, prosecution officers have very limited dealings with the press, but he cautions that police departments as well as some federal agencies are less circumspect and may work the press by leaking information and even evidence.[12]

In addition to generating sound bites at prosecutorial press conferences, another modern development is the fact-filled indictment, a document once noteworthy for its blandness that has now become as readable as many adventure novels. New York superlawyer Charles Stillman recalls the days when an indictment—the actual document approved by a federal grand jury—presented the facts very generally, omitting the spicy stuff, in part because prior to trial prosecutors preferred to show as few of the cards as possible to the defense.[13] US Attorneys in New York would remind the prosecutors that nothing could be said publicly beyond the contents of the indictment.

In the 1980s, when Rudy Giuliani served as the US Attorney in Manhattan, the so-called "singing indictment" became a press favorite, according to Professor Dershowitz.[14] As members of the press scoured the available evidence to collect the most eye-catching allegations, they found that indictments were no longer a dull recitation of statutes and generic facts but instead often became sizzling, detailed accounts of a trial's dramatic opening statement.[15] Since singing indictments could make it in New York, they could make it anywhere, and many prosecutors' offices around the country now follow similar practices.[16]

To be sure, getting the spotlight on their cases allows prosecutors to highlight a message of deterrence to other wrongdoers. Because maximizing deterrence is clearly a laudable goal, it is often difficult to determine—except in the most extreme cases—whether attention-getting prosecutors cross the line.

JOSE PADILLA

The "Dirty Bomber" That Wasn't

When one is denounced as a "dirty bomber" by the attorney general, could any jury take a clean look at the actual evidence? The career of Jose Padilla as al Qaeda's so-called dirty bomber had unremarkable beginnings. Padilla grew up in the Logan Square neighborhood of Chicago,[17] where he joined the Latin Disciples, a Puerto Rican gang, and was in trouble with the law from age fourteen on.[18] His rap sheet grew over the years to include aggravated battery, armed robbery, assault, and resisting arrest.[19] After he was released from one of his stints in jail, Padilla gravitated to South Florida and Islam, settling on two mosques in Broward County.[20] By 1998, Padilla left for Egypt on a trip funded by "friends" interested in his education.[21] From Egypt, he moved to Pakistan, where he married the widow of a jihadist.[22] He also met with senior al Qaeda official Abu Zubaydah.[23]

When Abu Zubaydah was captured in Pakistan, he revealed to his FBI and CIA interrogators that he had talked to people about a so-called dirty bomb. With a little research, his interrogators identified Padilla as one of those people.[24] After the CIA located Padilla in Cairo, FBI agents trailed him as he flew back to Chicago.[25] When Padilla got off the plane, the FBI arrested him in June 2003.[26]

The hype that followed was spectacular. Although traveling in Moscow at the time, US Attorney General John Ashcroft hurriedly scheduled a press conference. "We have captured a known terrorist who was exploring a plan to build and explode a radiological dispersion device, or dirty bomb, in the United States," he proclaimed.[27] Ashcroft described Padilla, whose jihadist endeavors had thus far not actually harmed a flea, as, "pos[ing] a serious and continuing threat to the American people and [to] our national security."[28]

Ashcroft so oversold Padilla as a dirty bomber that within two days even the White House was backing off, saying the matter "could have been handled better."[29] To be sure, Padilla wanted to be a terrorist. Yet he was clearly more of a wannabe than a going-to-be. The meeting with Zubaydah consisted of Padilla presenting "laughably inaccurate" plans for building a nuclear bomb that he had found on the Internet.[30] Privately, some senior US officials described Padilla's presentation as "more parody than plan."[31]

The following week, the *New York Times* noted that Ashcroft's announcement of Padilla's arrest coincided with a congressional investigation into intelligence lapses by the FBI and the CIA and likened the search for "enemies within" to the McCarthy hearings of the 1950s.[32]

What's more, the *New York Times* noted, Ashcroft's announcement of Padilla's arrest contradicted the administration's previous position of not disclosing information about the plots it disrupted.[33] Many on the left echoed the suggestion that Ashcroft's press conference was "part of a pattern in which the administration orchestrated its announcements to help it politically."[34] Some critics asserted that the timing of the announcement and the decision to hold Padilla as an enemy combatant meant that the government didn't have enough to indict him[35] and sought to amp up the appearance of guilt. "The key problem," wrote Scott Horton in *Harper's Magazine*, "with prosecutors who sell their case to the public through press conferences—as was done in this case with an almost unparalleled vengeance—is that they prejudice the jurors."[36]

For more than four years, Padilla languished in detention as an "enemy combatant," without being charged with a crime or being given a chance to defend himself. After the Supreme Court signaled its concerns about designating a US citizen an enemy combatant and holding him indefinitely, he was finally indicted and arraigned for trial in Miami federal court. The dirty bomb charges were quietly discarded and were never part of the case. In 2007, Padilla was convicted and sentenced to seventeen years in prison for conspiracy to participate in terrorism.

US District Judge Marcia Cooke rejected the prosecutors' request for a life sentence, citing the defendant's years of prior detention as "conditions [that] were so harsh for Mr. Padilla...[that] they warrant consideration in the sentencing in this case." Judge Cooke, while noting the seriousness of Padilla's conspiracy, said, "There is no evidence that these defendants personally maimed, kidnapped, or killed anyone in the United States or elsewhere."[37] The government disagreed with the sentence and has asked the appeals court to order more time for Padilla, an appeal that remains pending as of this publication.[38]

THE AMERICAN TALIBAN

John Walker Lindh Becomes an American Press Campaign

Between the ages of sixteen and eighteen, John Phillip Walker Lindh transformed himself from a shy, Catholic teenager in Northern California to a devout Muslim on his way to study the Koran in Yemen.[39] When his studies weren't sufficiently orthodox in Yemen, he moved on to a madrassa in Pakistan. He would later tell reporters that it was during his time in Pakistan that he became acquainted with the Taliban, met Osama bin Laden, and received training on how to shoot an AK-47 assault rifle.[40]

By June 2001, Lindh had traveled from Pakistan into Afghanistan "to fight with the Taliban." At al Farooq, an al Qaeda camp, he received intensive training that included the use of "shoulder weapons, pistols, and rocket-propelled grenades...and [the construction of] Molotov cocktails."[41]

When Lindh completed his training in July or August 2001, he returned to Kabul, where he was issued an AKM rifle "with a barrel suitable for long-range shooting." He remained with his fighting group following the September 11, 2001, terrorist attacks. He stayed even "after learning that United States military forces and United States nationals had become directly engaged in support of the Northern Alliance in its military conflict with Taliban and al Qaeda forces."[42]

In November 2001, Lindh and his fighting group retreated from Takhar to the area of Kunduz, where they ultimately surrendered to Northern Alliance troops and were eventually transferred to Qala-i-Janghi (QIJ) Prison on November 24, 2001. The following day, the CIA's Johnny Michael Spann and another government employee interviewed Lindh. Later that day, Spann was shot and killed in an uprising of Taliban detainees. Lindh, after being wounded, retreated with other prisoners to a basement area of the compound. On December 1, 2001, Northern Alliance and American forces suppressed the prison rebellion, taking Lindh and other Taliban and al Qaeda fighters into custody.[43]

When Attorney General John Ashcroft announced that the DOJ had filed a complaint against Lindh, he did not linger on the legal issues. "We may never know why he turned his back on our country and our values," Ashcroft intoned, "but we cannot ignore that he did." He added, "Youth is not absolution for treachery, and personal self-discovery is not an excuse to take up arms against one's country. Misdirected Americans cannot seek direction in murderous ideologies and expect to avoid the consequences."[44]

Skeptics blasted Ashcroft's statements as having "no serious prosecutorial or law enforcement purpose," serving instead "as part of a public-relations campaign" to increase public support for the administration and to silence critics. More troubling than Ashcroft's stump speech, however, were his repeated statements that Lindh had voluntarily confessed to the alleged crime. Courts have often criticized prosecutors who pump up news coverage with alleged confessions or other evidence that may be held inadmissible at trial.[45]

Lindh's lawyers later moved to dismiss the indictment, arguing that the media coverage had been so prejudicial as to deprive Lindh of his Sixth Amendment right to a fair trial.[46] As an alternative, the defense requested the judge grant a change of venue to the federal courthouse in San Francisco, where the media coverage was less toxic.[47] Although acknowledging that "pervasive and inflammatory pretrial publicity" could sometimes compromise the right to a fair trial, the judge ruled that "considerable nationwide media attention" does not compel the conclusion that either dismissal or transfer is warranted.[48]

The defense motions were denied. Ashcroft was never held accountable for his loose and inflammatory public statements. Speech making gave way to deal making, and both sides agreed to a twenty-year sentence for the American Taliban.

THE LIBERTY CITY SEVEN

How the Sears Tower Joined the Landscape for a Miami Terrorism Trial

The "Liberty City Seven" were a ragtag group of men, mostly from the Caribbean, indicted in 2006 on charges of terrorism. No terrorism indictment met greater skepticism than this one.[49] Jenny Martinez, a Stanford law professor involved in the Padilla case, noted that in both cases "the government has really oversold what it's got."[50]

The charges against the Liberty City Seven came about thanks to Abbas al-Saidi, a Yemeni clerk who had been a police informant even before the FBI helped him avoid charges for assaulting his girlfriend.[51] When he reported that he had met Narseal Batiste, an unemployed construction worker who boasted of wanting to create an Islamic State in America, Abbas al-Saidi went from local arrestee to federal asset. The FBI hired al-Saidi and another informant (also originally charged with domestic abuse) to cozy up to Batiste.[52] Al-Saidi posed as an al Qaeda financier, and he and the other informant earned about one hundred twenty thousand dollars from federal authorities for their efforts in leading the Liberty City Seven deeper and deeper into trouble.[53]

At the behest of the FBI informants, Batiste provided a list of desired equipment, including "boots knee high. Automatic hand pistols.

Black security uniforms. Squad cars. SUV truck—black color."[54] Batiste never requested explosives, and though he did request fifty thousand dollars, he explained to the informants (while being taped), "I'm exhausted financially. We have nothing."[55]

Batiste's group called themselves "the Seas of David" and practiced an eclectic mix of Christianity, Islam, and Judaism. At the request of the informants, several members took pictures of the FBI field office in Miami, using a van and camera provided by the informants and the FBI.[56]

When the FBI informants failed to deliver the fifty thousand dollars, Batiste and the other six men grew suspicious.[57] To calm their doubts, the FBI rented a warehouse, wired it for video, and had Elie Assad (the other informant) lead the men in an oath to al Qaeda.[58]

The group oath taking, which was solicited and taped undercover, ignited a new wave of headlines. On June 23, 2006, Attorney General Alberto Gonzales and FBI Deputy Director John Pistole held a joint press conference to announce the indictment of the seven members of the Seas of David, accusing them of a deadly conspiracy of terrorism.[59]

"As [has] been reported, seven men were arrested yesterday in Miami on charges of conspiring to support the al Qaeda terrorist organization by planning attacks on numerous targets, including bombing the Sears Tower in Chicago, the FBI building in North Miami Beach, Florida, and other government buildings in Miami-Dade County," said Gonzales.[60]

Pistole echoed Gonzales's theme. "They conducted surveillance. They conspired to murder countless Americans through attacks that would be, in their words, 'just as good or greater than 9/11,' as the attorney general has mentioned. But we preempted their plot."[61]

Skeptical reporters immediately put Gonzales on the defensive, asking whether any of the men had actual contact with al Qaeda. "The answer to that is no," Gonzales said. Were these conspirators simply naïve and incompetent? "I think it's dangerous for us to try to make an evaluation case by case as we look at potential terrorist plots and making a decision, well, this is a really dangerous group, this is not a really dangerous group." Was there any real threat to the Sears Tower? Pistole took this one: "One of the individuals was familiar with the Sears Tower, had worked in Chicago and had been there, so was familiar with the tower. But in terms of the plans, it was more aspirational than operational."[62]

It started to look like a gang of trash-talkers rather than of bomb makers. As a reporter said quizzically, "These guys couldn't buy boots on their own?"[63]

Despite Pistole's admission that the Chicago connection was "more aspirational than operational," the Sears Tower appeared in the third paragraph of the indictment. Like a moth to a flame, the press could not resist the Sears Tower allegation—it became a kind of brand for the Liberty City Seven and soon dominated media reports of the indictment.[64]

NPR's *Day-to-Day* opened with the lead, "Seven men face charges they plotted [to] wage war against this country by attacking the Sears Tower and other buildings."[65] Even a generally critical article in *Time* magazine began: "The federal government has indicted seven men arrested in Miami on charges of conspiring with al Qaeda to conduct terror attacks inside the United States. Among the ostensible targets named in the indictment was Chicago's Sears Tower."[66] Presumably recognizing that readers are more interested in dangerous terrorists than wannabes, the *New York Times* continued to use the brand: "Trial Starts for Men in Plot to Destroy Sears Tower."[67]

After the second mistrial in the case, analysts once again criticized the government for using a criminal case for political gain.[68] The *New York Times* noted that the arrest announcement came a few months before the 2006 election, and Bruce Winick, a law professor at the University of Miami, said "politics played too important a role in this prosecution." The *Miami Herald* editorialized against any further pursuit of the prosecution.[69]

On the government's third try, five of the defendants were finally convicted. At sentencing, the prosecutors insisted on thirty- to fifty-year prison sentences for the convicted defendants. The federal judge, never reluctant to impose long sentences when justified, sentenced the ringleader Batiste to thirteen years and the others to prison terms between six and ten years.[70]

MICHAEL VICK

A Smoking-Gun Indictment with Excruciating Details Leaves
No Defenders on the Quarterback's Team

On July 17, 2007, Michael Vick, along with three others, was indicted on a federal conspiracy charge for dog fighting. Ordinarily, animal cruelty is a state crime. Indeed, state prosecutors had already been investigating Vick before the feds stepped in. Since there was little federal law targeting animal cruelty, federal prosecutors got creative, using an old law concerning conspiracy to cross state lines to commit crimes. Their use of these theories to prosecute animal cruelty was unprecedented.

William C. Rhoden, sports columnist for the *New York Times*, wrote, "My original position on the Vick investigation is that, for all its validity, it had the earmarks of overzealous federal prosecutors taking on a high-profile athlete."[71]

By answering any doubters before any questions could be asked, prosecutors made brilliant PR use of the indictment, which ran eighteen pages.[72] In times past, prosecutors summarized charges with general statutory language, in part to make it harder for defense counsel to pin down the government's specific facts. In Vick's case, though, there was plenty of devil to be put in the details. For example, "at the end of the fight, the losing dog was sometimes put to death by drowning, hanging, gunshot, electrocution, or another method."[73] According to the federal papers, construction on Vick's property was intended to better serve the "dog fighting venture."[74] The indictment described how the accused would "roll" or "test" the dogs by placing them in a short match to determine how well they fought.[75] Animals that did not "test" well were shot or electrocuted.[76] One of the electrocutions was described in especially painful and painstaking detail. As to the "approximately eight dogs that did not perform well in 'testing,' the accused executed them by various methods, including hanging, drowning, and slamming at least one dog's body to the ground."[77]

These gory facts were enough to sicken any reader—animal lover or not. And yet prosecutors presumably had evidence to back up every brutal act detailed in the indictment. The defendants were convicted in the court of public opinion as soon as the indictment's extraordinary chronicle of animal cruelty was made public. No voices were heard questioning why the feds took control of what was traditionally a matter for the local authorities. And the impact of the indictment was also felt inside the courthouse.

Shortly after the indictment, Tony Taylor, one of Vick's codefendants, agreed to plead guilty.[78] By August 14, two more of Vick's codefendants had agreed to plead guilty. This increased pressure on Vick to plead "because if this [were to go] to trial," said Carl Tobias, professor of law at University of Richmond Law School, "it [would] be more difficult to defend because there now could be three key witnesses."[79]

For a while, Vick held out legally but was missing in action publicly. The media fallout from the gruesome indictment made it hazardous to leave a bunkered silence for any attempt at public self-defense. The feds turned up the already scorching heat even further by preparing a new set of indictments that would include charges that Vick financed gambling on dog fights.[80] The NFL prohibits any association with gambling, and such involvement could result in a lifetime suspension from the league.[81] Meanwhile, the NFL appointed future US Attorney General Eric Holder to investigate the situation and make a recommendation as to Vick's future.[82]

Vick eventually pled guilty to both state and federal charges, avoiding the possible gambling indictments that would have ended his career. He never attempted to defend or minimize his crimes of animal cruelty and reported to prison to begin serving his time even before his sentence was imposed. In 2009, after serving eighteen months in prison, Vick returned to the NFL.

ON STAGE WITH JACKSON'S PROSECUTOR

Did DA Sneddon Go over the Top Trying to Nail the King of Pop?

On Thursday, November 20, 2003, a handcuffed Michael Jackson was led into the county jail and booked on child molestation charges.[83] Ten years earlier, the King of Pop avoided prosecution on similar allegations by reaching a $15.3-million settlement with the family of a teenage boy.[84]

Tom Sneddon, the district attorney in Santa Barbara County, denied that he harbored personal animus toward Jackson and insisted that he wasn't "obsessed with bringing Jackson to justice."[85] Yet, when asked whether Jackson had bought his way out of prosecution ten years earlier, Sneddon said publicly, "I think there's a sense in the public that he did that."[86]

Sneddon was criticized for the lighthearted press briefing in which he announced the warrant for Jackson's arrest. The flip comments included asking reporters to stay and spend lots of money because the county needed it.[87] He also said that his advice to any parents thinking about letting their children spend the night at Neverland Ranch was "don't do it."[88] When he formally charged Jackson with seven counts of child molestation, his press conference attracted more than one hundred journalists.[89]

As mentioned in chapter 8, Mark Geragos, Jackson's lawyer at the time, fought back, saying, "these charges are not only categorically untrue, but they're driven, driven by two things: money and revenge."[90]

Later the defense would ask the judge to remove Sneddon from the case, citing his joke-cracking press conference and saying he was "too emotionally invested in getting a case against the celebrity." The judge denied the request,[91] but Sneddon continued to be on the defense when it came to the press. "This is publicity as an extreme sport," said Howard Rubenstein, a public-relations executive in New York who represented Jackson in the past. "Nobody is adhering to any rule. This will be the PR battle for the ages."[92]

Early on, Sneddon brought in Tellem Worldwide, a public-relations agency. He denied this proved he was playing to the media. "Tellem Worldwide is simply coordinating press relations and working as a liaison with the media. The media requests were overwhelming my office. It was impossible to respond to them all and very hard to get other important work done."[93]

Brian Oxman, a Jackson family spokesman said that Sneddon's hiring of Tellem was improper because "a district attorney is supposed to try the case in court, not in the press." Oxman continued, "First we had a press conference where the DA told jokes and now we have a PR firm the DA has hired that also represents the Cartoon Network."[94]

Susan Tellem, president of Tellem Worldwide, defended Sneddon's decision. "We believe that involving a public-relations agency in such a high-profile case is setting the standard for the future," Tellum said.[95] "We went into action when we saw the first press conference get extremely negative media coverage. Since the county had no budget to speak of for any public-relations plan, we felt that in the spirit of volunteerism we would offer our services *pro bono*, which they immediately accepted."[96]

Despite professional PR help, Sneddon never connected with a public that was mesmerized by the case. His own stumbles at the beginning created an opening for the defense message that this was a personal obsession rather than a prosecutorial mission. Sneddon also failed to win a conviction. On June 13, 2005, at the end of a prolonged, media-saturated trial, a jury found Jackson not guilty on all ten counts.

MICHAEL NIFONG AND THE DUKE LACROSSE PLAYERS

A Prosecutor Gone Press-Wild

On Tuesday, March 14, 2006, at 1:22 a.m., a security guard at a Kroger grocery store in Durham, North Carolina, called 911 to report that a woman outside appeared to be drunk and wouldn't get out of her car.[97] When the police arrived, she said that she was an exotic dancer and had been performing for a group of Duke students. She proceeded to accuse three Duke lacrosse players, identified by first names, of forcing her into a bathroom and assaulting her for thirty minutes.[98]

Michael B. Nifong, the Durham County district attorney, immediately seized the national spotlight to launch a press offensive against the Duke students.[99] "The thing that most of us found so abhorrent, and the reason I decided to take [the case] over myself, was the combination ganglike rape activity accompanied by the racial slurs and general racial hostility," Nifong told the *New York Times* in a telephone interview.[100]

Nifong also took his condemnations to the cameras—on one television show he even demonstrated how he imagined the alleged victim was grabbed and held by her attackers.[101] On top of harsh incrimination, he added pure speculation when he suggested that the woman might have been given a date-rape drug. Nifong even maligned the students for their decision to hire attorneys.[102] "One would wonder why one needs an attorney if one was not charged and had not done anything wrong," he said.[103] Adding insult to legal injury, he referred to the athletes as "a bunch of hooligans," and played upon presumed resentment of the local Durhamites toward the elite university, which some still called "the Plantation."[104] "There's been a feeling in the past that Duke students are treated differently by the court system," Nifong said.[105] "There was a feeling that Duke students' daddies could buy them expensive lawyers and that they knew the right people."[106]

Although the players and their lawyers adamantly disputed Nifong's account of the events in question, Nifong said that the case was based on more than DNA evidence.[107] Defense lawyers insisted, however, that they possessed time-stamped photographs from the party that supported their clients' stories and contradicted Nifong's version of events.[108] Their evidence seemed to be ignored by a DA who had gone prime-time.

Nifong was, in his own words, someone who "most [people] didn't know before a few weeks ago,"[109] but who had become the "most recognizable face in a case that...captured national attention."[110] His meteoric rise just happened to coincide with an election in which he faced two democratic opponents.[111]

Nifong's press campaign continued, indifferent to the facts. The day after, defense lawyers announced that the DNA tests failed to link the players to the accuser, and they called on Nifong to drop the case. Instead, Nifong appeared on a panel of student and community leaders at North Carolina Central, the traditionally black college where the accuser was an honors student, and said, "My presence here means this case is not going away."[112]

Most observers were incredulous. The DA's grandstanding came under fire. Nifong "seems to want to proceed as far as he can, whether the evidence is there or not," said Arnold Loewy, a criminal law professor at the University of North Carolina's School of Law. The most charitable critics attributed Nifong's pressing forward to inexperience.

Freda Black, a former Durham assistant district attorney, explained that while Nifong had handled more than three hundred felony jury trials, he never had a chance to get used to the spotlight.[113]

Rather than drop the fatally wounded prosecution, Nifong attempted to soften the blow of the negative DNA tests by insisting that additional, higher-level DNA tests from another lab were expected back soon.[114]

On April 18, a state grand jury issued sealed indictments against two of the Duke University players.[115] The next day, two Duke lacrosse players, Reade Seligmann and Collin Finnerty, were charged with first-degree forcible rape, first-degree sexual offense, and kidnapping.[116]

The day after the charges were announced, Seligmann's lawyer presented cell phone records, a taxi driver's account, an ATM record, and a time-coded dormitory entry card that indicated Seligmann wasn't present at the house when the alleged rape occurred.[117] In light of the overwhelming alibi evidence, Seligmann's lawyer said he hoped the prosecutor would drop the charges. Nifong refused to see him.[118]

Even a weak prosecution proved strong enough for Nifong's political campaign. On May 2, he won a narrow victory over his two opponents.[119] Nifong said that his victory would have no impact on the case.[120] Nonetheless, in an extraordinary step, defense lawyers filed a motion requesting that Nifong be removed from the case because his actions showed he was trying to "bolster his election chances while prejudicing the case against the defendant."[121]

Increasingly, the prosecutor was on the defensive. On July 28, 2006, Nifong acknowledged that he had erred by openly discussing the case. "My handling of the media coverage of this case has occasioned substantial criticism, some of which is undoubtedly justified," he said. "I both underestimated the level of media attention this case would draw and misjudged the effect that my words would have."[122]

By early November 2006, though, Nifong still refused to drop the prosecution against the Duke players and blasted his growing number of critics. "They've come out really strong with the idea they would either scare me or the victim away," he said. "That's never worked for me, which they should know by now, and it didn't work for her, either. And so here we are."[123]

The end for the case came at a pretrial hearing in early December 2006. Brian Meehan, director of a private laboratory that performed extensive DNA testing on rape-kit swabs and underwear collected from the victim, found DNA from the sperm of several men, none of whom were Duke lacrosse players.[124]

Nifong dropped the rape charges but said he would proceed with kidnapping and sexual assault charges.[125] He asserted the defense attack on the DNA report revealed a ruthless strategy to vilify him and intimidate a victim of a brutal assault.[126] Nifong did acknowledge he erred in not promptly providing Meehan's test results to defense lawyers.[127] "Obviously anything that is not DNA from the people who are charged is potentially exculpatory information," he said.[128]

Finally, Nifong was removed from the case by the state attorney general, and the charges were dropped. A rare investigation of prosecutorial ethics ensued.

North Carolina, like most states, has traditionally granted district attorneys broad leeway in making public comments that "serve a legitimate law enforcement purpose." Legitimate purposes include sending messages of deterrence or reaching out to the public for leads to solve a crime. Not included are using media for self-promotion and winning elections. The state bar ultimately concluded that many of Nifong's comments were unethical because they included "improper commentary" about the defendants and the evidence.[129]

The North Carolina State Bar stripped Nifong of his license to practice law, concluding: "You can't do justice in the media, you can't do justice on [*sic*] sound bites. The way to arrive at a determination of the facts is to hear in a fair and open proceeding all of the evidence, and then for the trier of fact to determine what the facts are.... That did not happen and was not going to happen, apparently, in the Duke lacrosse case."[130]

NIFONG'S DAYS OF RECKONING

An Example to Others or a High-Profile Aberration?

Later, a contempt conviction against Nifong added a day's jail time. But while justice was served, a larger reality may have been obscured. The fact that North Carolina's aggressive prosecution of this prosecutor was a high-profile exception left broader questions about prosecutorial misconduct largely unanswered.

Historically, state bar associations have earned poor marks for their oversight of the nation's more than twenty-eight thousand state and local prosecutors. According to a 2003 study by the Center for Public Integrity, out of two thousand cases in which courts found prosecutorial misconduct, professional discipline was imposed in less than 6 percent. A 1999 study of 326 Illinois court rulings that threw out convictions due to prosecutorial misconduct found only two in which prosecutors were disciplined by state bar authorities. The consequences of such misconduct can be drastic. Although not addressing general trends, a *Texas Law Review* article in 2000 provided a snapshot of the problem, concluding that more than 12 percent of death sentences over a seventeen-year period were set aside due to prosecutorial misconduct.

Despite the profound importance of the state and local prosecutors' ethical responsibilities, the limits in existing safeguards suggest that only the rare, high-profile cases, like Nifong's, receive serious attention from state bar associations.

For the nation's five thousand federal prosecutors, on the other hand, allegations of misconduct are reviewed by an office within the Justice Department. Although no one claims the federal system is perfect, in recent years the Office of Professional Responsibility has found prosecutorial mistakes in some 40 percent of the cases it has formally investigated. In contrast to the feds or even local police, who have Internal Affairs to address any misconduct, almost no specifically assigned personnel keep tabs on state and local prosecutors.

While federal prosecutions center on many of the most visible, high-impact cases, more than 95 percent of the crimes in the country are prosecuted by state and local prosecutors. Nifong may have been an extreme example, but it is hard to believe that the only victims of prosecutorial misconduct are lacrosse players.

CHAPTER 10

POP LAW
Legal Myths and the Media

The court of public opinion is sometimes driven by popular beliefs that come more from legal thrillers, movies, and television shows than from what really happens in a courtroom.

Since the news media rarely challenges these myths, they have become favorite tools for lawyers spinning dubious positions to a willing public. With so much legal programming on television, ranging from reality court shows like *Judge Judy* to television dramas like *CSI: Crime Scene Investigation*, *Without a Trace*, and *Law & Order*, the masses have more information—but also more misinformation—about the law than ever before. When the pop law is compared to the real law, there can be some astonishing differences.

THE SO-CALLED DIFFICULTY OF WINNING WITH CIRCUMSTANTIAL EVIDENCE

> In the Scott Peterson murder trial, defense lawyers and the press got a lot of mileage out of the idea that circumstantial evidence is weaker than direct or physical evidence. That didn't stop the jury from sending Peterson to death row.

In aiming for a conviction, every prosecutor wants the best ammunition possible. Prosecutors would love to catch a defendant red-handed on video, and, of course, DAs love confessions. Impeccable eyewitnesses are also appreciated. Often, though, prosecutors must go to trial with less—sometimes much less.

In 1998, Sante and Kenneth Kimes, a mother-and-son team of grifters, were indicted for the murder of Irene Silverman, an eighty-two-year-old Manhattan socialite. Almost immediately, the pundits began to discuss an ever-popular thesis: you can't secure a conviction based only on circumstantial evidence.[1] The skepticism initially seemed warranted. Investigators in the Kimes case were unable to find any physical evidence to prove the missing Silverman had even been harmed.[2] Although several dozen cases across the nation had been successfully prosecuted without a body, most relied on self-incriminating statements by the perpetrators.[3] The case against the Kimeses featured neither a body nor self-incriminations.

Defense lawyers seized on the lack of physical evidence. "There is no body, no witnesses," said the Kimeses' lawyer, "there is no proof of any murder at all."[4] A law professor in New York emphasized the prosecution's exclusive reliance on circumstantial evidence, saying, "I think the Kimes case is going to push this to the limit."[5] Reporters for the *New York Times* were even more blunt, calling successful prosecution "seemingly impossible."[6]

Prosecutors, though, amassed some intriguing circumstances. They simply connected the dots generally between the victim and the defendants. A New Jersey insurance salesman surfaced who had first told the Kimeses about Silverman. The Kimeses used the name of Silverman's butcher and friend as a reference in renting a room in Silverman's Upper East Side townhouse. A Massachusetts doctor testified that the Kimeses used his stolen Social Security number to set up the dummy corporation through which they took possession of Silverman's mansion. The prosecution also presented the Kimeses' notebook, with entries such as "get social," and "get her signature in some way."[7]

Still, no direct or physical evidence tied the Kimeses to the actual murder—and yet jurors returned a guilty verdict. One juror, Michael Alvarez, told reporters, "to me, it seemed obvious."[8] An appellate court was equally persuaded.[9] In fact, even the Kimeses' lawyers conceded that "homicide could be proven solely by circumstantial evidence."[10]

Contrary to the popular conception, state and federal law treats circumstantial evidence as equal to direct or physical evidence. For that reason, judges issue instructions to ensure that jurors understand that the law makes no distinction between direct and circumstantial evidence in terms of their potential importance in deciding a case.

Sometimes, even circumstances from long ago can convict. When Michael Skakel, a cousin in the Kennedy family tree, was arrested in 2000 for the 1975 murder of Martha Moxley, there was little physical evidence. The prosecution did have testimony from Skakel's classmates, some saying that many years earlier he had confessed to the crime while at a drug treatment center. The witnesses, however, were chronically unreliable, and some had plenty of their own drug-abuse issues.

The prosecution showed that the bloody six-iron used to bludgeon Moxley belonged to a set of Skakel's golf clubs. There was nothing to prove that Skakel had used it, but the circumstances—he owned the club used to kill her—spoke powerfully to jurors who were also reminded to use their common sense when pronouncing their verdicts. Still, court watchers, including leading analysts, continued to debate whether Skakel could be found guilty. "It seems to fall short of a precise pinpointing of who did it and how it was done," said Harvard Professor Alan M. Dershowitz.[11]

Prosecutors had no proof that Skakel had wielded the murder weapon, but the circumstances persuaded jurors. The case, like so many others, came down to the weight of circumstantial evidence.[12]

ALTERNATIVE HYPOTHESES

Reasonable or Unreasonable?

A key defense tactic, especially in circumstantial evidence cases, is to present an alternative hypothesis that accounts for evidence in a way that exonerates the client. Courts often refer to this as a "reasonable alternative hypothesis of innocence." The simplest alternative hypothesis of all is pointing a finger at another suspect. Even suspects who cannot be specifically identified are better than no alternative suspect at all. *The Fugitive*'s Dr. Richard Kimball tried to blame a one-armed man in his trial. But until he escaped and exposed the real killer, neither the deputy marshal nor anyone else was buying the one-armed-man story.

Skakel's defense tried to present several reasonable alternative hypotheses to the jurors. For example, Skakel told a family driver that he had done something so bad that he had to either kill himself or leave the country. According to the defense hypotheses, Skakel was referring not to murdering Moxley but rather to having slept with his dead mother's dress.[13]

At the end of the case, Judge John Kavanewsky Jr. made it clear to prospective jurors that the law permits a guilty verdict based on circumstantial evidence.[14] The jury apparently found the defense's arguments for reasonable alternative hypotheses to be more hypothetical than reasonable. Of the defense suggestion that a transient had committed the murder, juror Charles Coletta said, "I just never considered that a very reasonable hypothesis. Wandering around Belle Haven, a gated community? How quickly would somebody stand out in a neighborhood like this? This isn't the kind of neighborhood where you have people pushing shopping carts up and down the street."[15]

Following his conviction, Skakel was sentenced to prison for twenty years to life. While Skakel's trial included some direct testimony, Scott Peterson's is a classic circumstantial case. Certainly some initially saw the circumstances as enough to predict a conviction. On the day Peterson was arrested, California Attorney General Bill Lockyer announced that the case against Peterson was "compellingly strong," and that it was a "slam dunk that he is going to be convicted."[16] Although less explicit, Mark Geragos, who appeared on television to discuss the case before becoming Peterson's lawyer, called the case against Peterson "damning."[17]

By the time jury selection was completed, however, the media had begun to report doubts about the case. "Prosecutors have no direct link between Mr. Peterson and the crime and instead are basing their case around circumstantial evidence and a theory that he wanted to start a new life with his mistress," wrote the *New York Times*.[18]

By mid-July, about a month and a half after the trial had started, the media's outlook on the Peterson prosecution was getting bleaker. A former prosecutor appearing on *Larry King Live* said that the trial was "all but lost."[19] "The case was built almost solely on circumstantial evidence," wrote the *New York Times*.[20] A defense lawyer and former prosecutor said that he didn't think the death penalty was "even on the table," because the case had relied so heavily on circumstantial evidence.

Upon the close of testimony, though, Judge Delucchi explained that the law does not consign circumstantial evidence to a second-class status. Its weight can be equal to or greater than direct evidence and is ultimately for the jury to decide. He also included an instruction on the reasonable alternative hypothesis rule.

Such jury instructions regarding circumstantial evidence are widely given but are not required by the US Constitution. The Supreme Court and several federal appellate courts have ruled that in federal cases as long as the jury is given an instruction that correctly explains reasonable doubt, no further instruction about the reasonable alternative hypothesis is necessary.[21] In Peterson's case, the trial judge applied California state law and decided to give the instruction on the reasonable alternative hypothesis rule to the jury.

"A finding of guilt as to any crime may not be based on circumstantial evidence unless the proved circumstances are not only (1) consistent with the theory that the defendant is guilty of the crime, but [also] (2) cannot be reconciled with any other rational conclusion," the judge told the jury. "Also, if the circumstantial evidence as to any particular count permits two reasonable interpretations, one of which points to the defendant's guilt and the other to his innocence, you must adopt that interpretation that points to the defendant's innocence and reject that interpretation that points to his guilt."[22]

Reasonable alternative hypothesis instruction can be a defendant's new best friend. Defense lawyer Mark Geragos tried from before the beginning of the Peterson case to explain how the incriminating circumstantial evidence could actually be seen as incriminating someone else. The defense, at various times, theorized that Laci Peterson was abducted while walking her dog,[23] that a vagrant or sex offender could have committed the crime,[24] that three unidentified men a neighbor saw in the front yard the day Laci disappeared had kidnapped her,[25] or that Laci had been kidnapped and murdered by a satanic cult.[26]

Despite the reasonable alternative hypothesis instruction, the Peterson jury rejected the alternative scenarios presented by the defense attorneys. Peterson remains on California's death row, one of many defendants for whom a circumstantial case resulted in a conviction.

DO CELEBRITIES GET SPECIAL TREATMENT?

> Do celebrities get kid gloves and a "get out of jail free" card, or do those who investigate celebrities take the gloves off and pursue them relentlessly to create an attention-getting case?

The public usually assumes that celebrities receive preferential treatment at every turn in criminal cases, as well as in civil proceedings. Their lawyers tell a different story. The one point of agreement is that celebrities, like other people with lots of money, can hire the best legal representation. Additionally, a Martha Stewart can afford public-relations consultants and even public-opinion surveys, while ordinary defendants may be getting advice from only their family members and drinking pals.

Except for the issue of financial resources, celebrities are otherwise less favored by the system than one might think. Certainly, when it comes to being investigated, no one receives more scrutiny than a celebrity. Prosecutors and investigators look under every rock and behind every blade of grass. After all, if proceedings are brought, famous people become famous cases, and high-profile trials define the careers of prosecutors and sometimes of police and of criminalists.

Ben Brafman, who won acquittals for such high-profile defendants as Sean "Diddy" Combs and nightclub impresario Peter Gatien, believes special treatment for celebrities is one of the biggest myths. Brafman notes that a person less famous than NFL star Plaxico Burress might not have even been arrested following his self-inflicted gunshot wound. A football star with a bullet hole in his leg attracts more attention than a football fan in the same unfortunate predicament. And once the police arrested the celebrity, the city's mayor and its newspapers made an issue about maximum punishment that likely would not have been made had an anonymous mortal broken the law. The authorities like to use high-profile cases to carry a message about obeying the law, and low-profile cases do not carry such messages very far.

Charles Stillman also believes any idea that high-profile defendants get a better break is a misconception. "They get top-flight representation," he notes, but, "apart from that, it's tougher." When high-flying people are seen as going down, "they get no good press," Stillman adds.[27]

Robert Morvillo emphasizes the inflexibility of the process as a major liability when notable figures fall into legal trouble. "Everybody changes," he notes, "people are frozen, and they become much more rigid with respect to the issues of the trial." Of course, well-regarded celebrities may fare better than the more notorious. O.J. Simpson, at the time of the initial questioning in the double homicide case, was then a popular figure who was treated respectfully, even deferentially, by police. Correspondingly, several defendants who had played for the Miami Dolphins, though tried for federal drugs or laundering charges that usually led to convictions, won acquittals from Florida juries.[28] Conversely, heavyweight champion Mike Tyson was convicted of rape in a he said–she said case that might have created reasonable doubt for a figure with a less sinister image.[29]

Additionally, celebrities may have more difficulty getting favorable plea deals. Few prosecutors want to face public outrage and press rancor for supposedly letting a celebrity off the hook. As to prison time for guilty celebs, judges usually try to sentence the rich and famous as if they were neither. When cameras are hovering nearby, judges know they will not be rewarded for leniency.

Roy Black summarizes his experience representing celebrities with two categories of reactions. "Prosecutors and judges tend to hold them to a higher standard." On the other hand, Black believes that "jurors are impressed with people who are famous." As a result, Black's conclusion is that "celebrities are more likely to get charged and more likely to get acquitted" than the rest of us.[30]

Fraudster Bernie Madoff received a one-hundred-fifty-year prison sentence, five times his likely life expectancy. At the other end of the criminal spectrum, Paris Hilton was sentenced to forty-five days in jail for violating probation by driving without a license. Her sentence was certainly not lenient to begin with, but her modest legal problems were about to become a ratings gangbuster that attracted extensive coverage from cable news. When she was released early due to medical issues, a national uproar ensued. Within hours, the judge ordered her back into court and then on her way back to Los Angeles County jail. Professor and legal analyst Laurie L. Levenson attributed Hilton's above-par punishment for traffic violations to the reality that "people are fed up with celebrity justice."[31] Being tough on Paris Hilton may have seemed harsh to her family and her fans, but for most of the public, the judge seemingly stood tall when Paris Hilton went down.

DEFENSE OF INSANITY

Overly Successful or Overrated?

> Even for defendants who are mentally ill, the legal defense of insanity is rarely successful—especially since the laws changed in the wake of the insanity-based acquittal of John Hinckley Jr., President Reagan's attempted assassin.

Insanity might seem like a really good idea, at least for a defendant caught red-handed in criminal activity. In everyday conversation, people are quick to suggest that an otherwise guilty person can get off by claiming insanity or even temporary insanity. Such defendants are crazy, the public speculates, but crazy like a fox.

The legal reality is galaxies apart from this popular wisdom. In criminal prosecutions, a plea of not guilty by reason of insanity is presented in 0.85 percent of cases, less than one in a hundred. Such strategies succeed no more than a fourth of the time. So the odds of an accused criminal beating the rap by wrapping himself in a straitjacket are roughly one in four hundred.

Ironically, even individuals who are clearly mentally ill are not necessarily considered insane for legal purposes. Unless the affliction fits an extremely narrow definition of what constitutes insanity for legal purposes, mental disease is no defense. Just consider the number of prison inmates who have serious mental disorders. This poses increasing problems for corrections officials who lack the resources to provide them with proper care.

In the past, an insanity defense was more readily available. Things changed in 1981 with the attempted assassination of President Ronald Reagan and the subsequent trial of assailant John Hinckley Jr. By any standard, Hinckley was mentally ill. Obsessed with movie star Jodie Foster, he thought killing President Reagan was a great way to get her attention. But public uproar greeted his acquittal in 1982 by reason of insanity. Some 83 percent of Americans believed that justice was not done.[32]

The angry public mood resulted in legislation to make it harder for defendants to use an insanity defense. Even more states passed the so-called M'Naghten Rule, which was created in the nineteenth century in England when a paranoid schizophrenic killed a public official and was acquitted. The M'Naghten Rule required not only the presence of a substantial mental disease or defect but also that the accused be unable to distinguish between right and wrong. Other new laws changed trial rules so that prosecutors were no longer required to disprove insanity. Defendants now had to prove they were legally insane.

Neither the public nor the jury usually knows that an acquittal by reason of insanity is not much of a victory. Insane defendants, especially violent ones, spend many years in mental hospitals that are the equivalent of prisons. In fact, Hinkley would spend close to twenty-eight years in a mental facility before being allowed limited visits to his mother's house.

Some states do not even permit an insanity defense. The US Supreme Court determined in 2006 that Arizona did not violate the Constitution by preventing a defendant from presenting the defense of legal insanity.[33] In that case, a young man, who believed that aliens were out to get him, killed a police officer in Phoenix. No one accused the defendant of faking. His mental illness was undeniable. The Supreme Court found that the state could hold him accountable nonetheless, and it allowed the conviction and life sentence to stand.

Texas mother Andrea Yates was likewise impaired when she was tried for the drowning murders of her five children. Not even the prosecutors denied that she was mentally ill. Evidence showed that she believed she had been hearing voices commanding her to save the children from eternal damnation by dispatching them to a better place. Despite abundant evidence of mental illness, in her first trial in 2002 she was found sane and was convicted of the murders.

On appeal, it developed that the state's expert presented what appeared to be fabricated testimony to the jury. He suggested that Yates had fictionalized the defense of insanity after watching an episode of *CSI* that gave her the idea she would later use to justify the murders. It turned out, though, that no such episode existed. After an appeals court ordered a new trial, Yates was found not guilty by reason of insanity in 2006. She was not, of course, let loose on the streets. Instead, she was sent to the North Texas State Hospital, a high-security mental-health facility where she is expected to remain for many years.

Therefore, while the public believes that it is too easy to escape guilt by faking insanity, it is instead a very difficult defense to establish even for those who are undeniably mentally ill. Perhaps because there is so much misunderstanding in general about mental illness, the defense of insanity is one of the most misperceived of all legal issues in the court of public opinion.

THE PROSECUTOR'S ALLEGED VENDETTA

> While a defendant's claim of a prosecutorial vendetta may raise occasional interest as a media strategy, it is not an admissible argument before a jury determining guilt or innocence.

A prosecutor's vendetta is a popular explanation for why a perfectly wonderful and innocent person is being relentlessly investigated and is later charged with serious crimes. Indeed, unless prosecutors are simply mistaken—which happens, but is not a theme with blockbuster sex appeal— the vendetta may be one of the few eye-catching explanations available for insisting that the completely innocent is being treated as guilty.

The political vendetta is an especially popular claim whenever a high-profile member of one political party is brought to trial by a prosecutor with an opposing affiliation. When congressional powerhouse Tom DeLay was charged with campaign-finance violations in Texas, the spin machine attacked the prosecution as politically driven by the Austin district attorney, a Democrat.

In Michael Jackson's case, the alleged vendetta of District Attorney Tom Sneddon was supposedly derived from his failure to be able to prosecute Jackson on sexual molestation charges back in the 1990s. Sneddon's extensive earlier effort foundered when the complaining witness settled a civil lawsuit with Jackson and dropped the criminal case.

Whether it is political or personal, the prosecutorial vendetta theory is more likely to impress the media than the jury. This is not to say that juries won't consider other alleged vendettas. For example, a vendetta against the intended victim or vindictive intentions based on the relationship between the gangs (the famous case of Sharks v. Jets) are examples of vendettas that can be perfectly relevant to explain the dynamics behind a perpetrator's acts of violence.

Another scenario for a vendetta that might be relevant if it is claimed is that police fabricated evidence against the defendant. O.J. Simpson's dream team won acquittal in part by accusing the police of framing their client. Though little real proof of a frame-up was offered, the charge succeeded in inflaming the racial sensitivities of jurors toward the Los Angeles Police Department. Mark Geragos tried a similar ploy in the Scott Peterson murder trial, but with no grudges or sympathies to exploit, he failed to sway the jury.

Unlike investigators whose testimony could theoretically be tainted by vendettas, the prosecutor is not a witness but instead an embodiment of the executive branch of government. This is basic civics: courts respect the separation of powers between the different branches, a principle based on the US Constitution and most state constitutions. The executive branch (the prosecutor) has the discretion to bring criminal charges. The constitutional function of the judicial branch (the judge) is not to second-guess who gets arrested or why but to provide a fair forum for properly adjudicating issues of evidence and culpability.

Because their functions are separate, the judicial branch is reluctant to question the motives of the executive branch.

Aside from such lofty concepts as separation of powers, a prosecutor's motivation is generally irrelevant to the question of guilt. As one court explained, "Whatever the prosecutor's motives may have been is mere conjecture by the defense and has nothing to do with the defendant's guilt or innocence."[34] The jury hears evidence of guilt or innocence. The prosecutor's motive, even if unfair or self-serving, is evidence of neither guilt nor innocence.

Still, a judge might consider whether a prosecutor's motives have violated the defendant's rights. Courts have ruled that the Fifth Amendment right to due process may prohibit the government "from prosecuting a defendant because of some specific animus or ill will on the prosecutor's part." In this sense, courts describe *vendetta* as a "vindictive prosecution claim" and consider it a form of selective prosecution. But to get a judge to consider the issue, defense attorneys must present evidence to "raise a reasonable doubt" that prosecutors acted improperly.[35]

Colorable—that is, valid or genuine—claims of a vendetta or vindictiveness are rare. Judges tend to view claims of vendetta or vindictiveness as "unsupported and irrelevant,"[36] "too incredible to warrant any serious treatment,"[37] or even "utterly nonsensical."[38]

It doesn't help the vendetta cause that most defendants who cry vindictive prosecution turn out to be guilty. In one case, the court observed, "It could hardly be said to have constituted a vendetta when the defendant admitted that he had committed all the crimes for which he had been prosecuted."[39]

Occasionally vendettas stumble into jury trials even though they are usually off-limits. While on the witness stand, under cross-examination, one defendant foolishly demanded to know why the prosecutor was out to get him. "Because I don't like people who kill women," replied the prosecutor. "How's that? You want to know why? Because I don't like people preying on women."[40]

The best strategy for defendants who think they are victims of prosecutorial vindictiveness is to win an acquittal and go shouting and chest thumping from every street corner. To the disappointment of some acquitted defendants, prosecutors cannot be sued over vindictive prosecution. In 1976, the US Supreme Court decided that prosecutors would have "absolute immunity" from civil lawsuits in connection with any criminal prosecutions they might initiate, "even when the prosecutor acts 'maliciously unreasonable, without probable cause, or even on the basis of false testimony of evidence.'"[41]

Defendants can always try to defeat a supposedly vindictive prosecutor at the election polls, and there is the theoretically possible but practically impossible remedy of impeachment. There is also the payback pursued by the late Michael Jackson. After the first investigation failed to produce criminal charges, he included a song in one of his albums about a heartless prosecutor.

SWEETHEART DEALS WITH COOPERATING WITNESSES

Too Sweet for Juries?

> Defense attorneys often suggest that they can demolish key prosecution witnesses who receive sweetheart deals by turning state's evidence against the defendant.

Defense lawyers can indeed score points by attacking the credibility of cooperating witnesses. And yet the conviction rate still remains high. Today's prosecutors have mastered the art of presenting cooperators, acknowledging their baggage up front and emphasizing for juries that plea agreements require that the witness present only truthful testimony. Results vary, of course, and much depends on the believability and likeability of the cooperating witness. But most sweetheart deals with cooperators, no matter how unsavory, are not found to be too sweet for a conviction.

When police alleged that O.J. Simpson, along with gun-toting accomplices, stormed into a Las Vegas hotel room to confiscate allegedly stolen sports memorabilia, they brought serious charges against all the defendants, including robbery and kidnapping counts with possible sentences of life in prison. Apparently, though, police were more interested in nailing O. J. than his less notorious codefendants. Three of the alleged accomplices received "deal-of-the-century" plea bargains to get them to testify. O. J.'s codefendants, even those who say they had guns, bargained their way to probation and community service.

In describing O. J.'s codefendants who turned state's evidence against him, legal expert Professor Laurie L. Levenson said, "it is a defense lawyer's dream to cross-examine these witnesses."[42] O. J.'s own lawyer said he had never been in a case where "every witness is made out to be a liar."[43] Despite his best efforts, the jury returned a guilty verdict followed by a prison sentence of up to thirty-three years for the badly bungled souvenir hunt.

Likewise, attorneys for Martha Stewart and Peter Bacanovic attacked cooperator Douglas Faneuil as a liar out to save himself. But while Faneuil got a great deal from the government, he also gave them a great result. The jury liked and believed him and convicted both defendants. Faneuil walked away from the insider-trading scandal without a felony conviction or jail time, while his former client and former boss stepped into prison.

Nonetheless, ample reasons do exist to mistrust cooperating witnesses. They are criminals themselves, sometimes worse than the defendants they testify against. They are swapping assistance to prosecutors in exchange for less time on their own sentences. In much of Europe, the concept of bargaining over criminal charges to reduce a sentence is "repulsive to their sense of justice."[44] It also bothers some people in this country.

In 1998, three federal appeals court judges were sufficiently troubled by plea-bargained testimony to find it a violation of witness bribery laws.[45] After all, "Section 201(c)(2) could not be more clear" in making it illegal when one "offers or promises anything of value" because of a witness's testimony.[46] The judges also noted that bar rules governing the conduct of lawyers make it improper to pay a witness a fee for testifying about the facts. While recognizing that reliance on deal making with witnesses was a longstanding practice, the judges disparaged it as "an ingrained practice of buying testimony."[47] Concerned that, if followed, this remarkable decision could have severely reduced the ability to use plea bargains to obtain cooperating witnesses, a majority of other judges quickly interceded to cancel that ruling. Banning plea-bargained testimony would wipe out the many convictions that depend on it and would create huge judicial backlogs for a system that, as presently structured, does not have enough courtrooms and judges to provide a full-fledged trial for every defendant charged with a crime.[48] If procuring accomplice testimony through plea bargaining is a form of witness bribery, it has been legalized by long practice.

Although the use of cooperators is "ingrained" as well as legal, popular culture has little enthusiasm for it, referring to flippers as "snitches," "tattletales," and most especially "rats." The media rarely warm to them and have characterized informants and cooperators as "disloyal, deceitful, greedy, selfish, and weak," according to one authority.[49]

And yet the cooperation system endures because it works. In fact, there are many more would-be cooperators than there are cooperation deals, mostly because they lack the combination of credibility and knowledge needed to make them useable witnesses.

The harvest of willing cooperators was heavily seeded in the late 1980s. The enactment of the Federal Sentencing Guidelines along with other tough sentencing laws limited the discretion of judges to depart from severe punishment in many cases. As a result, unless a defendant could beat the long odds that otherwise pointed to a conviction, long sentences for many crimes—especially ones involving violence, weapons, or narcotics—were virtually automatic. The only strategy for an earlier exit from many years in prison required cooperation. If prosecutors determined that a cooperator provided substantial assistance, they could file papers asking for a sentence reduction. The judge could then determine whether to reduce prison time and, if so, by how much. But only the prosecutors, in their unchallengeable discretion, could open the prison doors by deciding whether "substantial assistance" had been provided by a cooperator. No one else—not even the judge—could hold that key.

Because the system chronically tied the hands of judges and entrusted the jail-door key to prosecutors, cooperation became essentially the only strategy for leniency. "To many defendants, cooperation has become synonymous with hope."[50]

Recent Supreme Court decisions have made the sentencing guidelines for state and federal systems advisory rather than mandatory, returning some sentencing flexibility to judges. Even so, significant sentence reductions will usually not be made unless substantial assistance is given to prosecutors. Desperate defendants must still turn on their accomplices if they want less prison time. And turn they do—against associates, best friends, even family members. Whether it is a former BFF or even a relative, it is usually every defendant for him- or herself when it comes to making plea deals.

Wary prosecutors and police scrutinize offers of cooperation, testing the would-be flipper's answers against facts already known and looking for independent corroboration whenever possible. Some phonies con their way past skeptical examination, but usually prosecutors and police screen out the fakers. Once the prosecutors believe in a cooperator, getting jurors to believe him or her is no small challenge.

Experienced prosecutors have a standard explanation as to why their witness lineup may look like something off a post-office wall. After all, they tell the jury, it is the defendants, not the police, who selected their skanky accomplices. Everyone knows that you need thieves to catch a thief. As to why it is fair for one criminal to get a break by pointing a finger at another, prosecutors explain that the cooperating witness for the prosecution has remorse and has accepted responsibility for past crimes by agreeing to plead guilty, usually to a significant crime. The once-darkened souls have now seen the light.

And then there is the plea agreement itself. You might think that the written contract that documents a leniency deal would be a smoking gun for the defense. Not so. Over the years, prosecutors have developed formulaic plea agreements that say almost nothing that helps the defense. The criminal charges for the guilty plea are listed, but the amount of leniency is usually left open.

On the other hand, plea agreements generally have a truthfulness provision that invalidates any benefits if the cooperator testifies falsely. These provisions have been criticized by some courts as providing a self-created means of vouching for the witness's credibility. In fact, some courts will not allow prosecutors to read aloud the truthfulness provision to the jury unless the cooperator's credibility is attacked.[51]

But defense attacks on a cooperating witness's credibility are as inevitable as beer at football games. For that reason, jurors almost always learn about the truthfulness provisions. For example, in a particular drugs-and-guns conspiracy case, the court approved the prosecution's presentation of a truth-telling provision because, "The attack on these witnesses' credibility began from almost the first words of the defendant's opening statements."[52]

Just as prosecutors employ state-of-the-art strategies for turning criminal accomplices into cleaned-up, remorseful, and suddenly truthful witnesses, defense lawyers have their own formidable tools. The defense is entitled to discover every piece of the cooperator's baggage known to prosecutors.[53] Because many cooperators have traveled a lot of miles on very bad roads, there are often extensive court battles over whether the authorities have turned over everything that might be used to impeach a flipper. Sources of impeachment can be many—from a police or prosecutor's interview notes involving third parties to a witness's prior criminal history or any inconsistent statements by the cooperator. Once armed with all the available impeachment evidence, top defense lawyers are at their best when they attack cooperating witnesses. Because witnesses whose testimony is skewered are obviously less believable witnesses, sometimes acquittals result.

Usually, though, well-presented accomplices bring guilty verdicts, especially when there is independent information to corroborate key points of the cooperator's testimony. Despite its unsavory flavor, "cooperation has never been more prevalent than it is today."[54]

It is so prevalent because, while using "rats" and "snitches" may create questions in the world of public opinion, more often than not, it creates convictions in a court of law.

VICTIMS WOULD RATHER SUE THAN PROSECUTE A RICH DEFENDANT

Usually victims do both, but timing is everything. Suing before the criminal trial can jeopardize a conviction by creating a financial motive for the alleged victim's accusations. Besides, when a criminal conviction comes first, it makes a large damages award easier later.

Physically harming innocent people or stealing their money are crimes that usually afford the victims a basis for a civil lawsuit. Theft victims can sue for the value of stolen property, the defrauded can sue fraudsters, rape victims can sue for assault and battery, and families of murder victims can sue for wrongful death. Often no one bothers to bring suit if the perpetrator is penniless. Whenever civil lawsuits make sense in financial terms, though, they serve an important purpose in helping to compensate crime victims for their losses. Occasionally, the criminal defendant is wealthy. At times, there is a handsomely insured third party whose negligence allowed the crime to happen.

But a victim with a money motive is more suspect than the purehearted and has an obvious incentive "to perpetuate a version of the facts that maximize[s] his own injuries and the fault of the defendant."[55] For that reason, defense lawyers can cross-examine an accuser about a pending civil lawsuit, and "even a contemplated suit by a complaining witness may be shown."[56] That's why it's most often best to wait until after the conclusion of a criminal trial before filing a civil suit for damages.

In a few instances, such questioning is limited to simply whether the accuser has a lawsuit pending. Some courts have disallowed further inquiries into matters such as the amount of damages being sought.[57] Most courts, though, encourage "the airing of evidence" because juries might decide that "the willingness of a witness to lie or shade testimony would be affected not only by whether the result may benefit him but also by how much."[58] Defense attorneys are then permitted to grill the victim about the type of damages, whether the accuser has met with a lawyer, and whether a criminal conviction will aid the civil suit.

Other types of financial interest also come into play. To be exposed to scrutiny in open court, the financial interest at issue must benefit the witnesses directly. For example, even though a sheriff's office might be eagerly anticipating the seizure of the defendant's funds or assets, none of it trickles down to the testifying officers. On the other hand, when a confidential informant in one case, hoping to personally collect four hundred fifty thousand dollars in reward money, took the stand, the court found the information "of the most help to the jury in arriving at the truth."[59]

Shrewd plaintiffs not only postpone lawsuits but also avoid meeting with civil lawyers until the criminal case is resolved. The statute of limitations—the period of time during which the lawsuit must be brought—usually allows several years to sue for money damages. If a defendant is convicted of physical abuse, violence, fraud, or thievery, the victim can often present that fact to the jury in a later civil trial. In some jurisdictions, the criminal conviction automatically establishes the defendant's responsibility to pay damages.

Wise accusers focus on their present status as crime victims instead of any future role as civil plaintiffs. This is the well-traveled path to maximizing financial recovery. Desiree Washington filed suit against boxing champion Mike Tyson in June 1992, four months *after* he was convicted of raping her. Tyson's attorney claimed the lawsuit proved she was nothing but a gold digger after all.[60] By then, however, Tyson was already a guest of the Indiana taxpayers. The suit was settled for an undisclosed amount after Tyson's release from prison, three years later.

Even if never convicted, a defendant can still be sued. Acquitted of killing their wives, ex–football star O. J. Simpson and former television actor Robert Blake were both hammered by civil juries that ordered them to pay millions to the victims' families. The rape case against Kobe Bryant was dropped, but a civil lawsuit immediately followed, resulting in a settlement with undisclosed terms.

The virtue of patience is therefore a strategic virtue for crime victims who are lawsuit hopefuls. Avoiding the appearance of financial incentive amounts to more believability, and so, believable or not, well-advised victims are advised to prosecute now, sue later.

ONLY A HE SAID–SHE SAID

The popular assumption is that a case hinging on one person's word against another's will be too weak to overcome reasonable doubt. But juries can and do convict simply by choosing to believe the alleged victim.

At times the law is a one-on-one swearing contest. Two contestants, each with opposite versions of the truth, tell their side of the story. King Solomon was able to learn the truth between two alleged mothers by threatening to split a baby. That trick worked once but is not available today when judges and jurors want to know what really happened.

The scenarios can range from an arrested suspect who claims mistreatment by a police officer to feuding spouses or embittered business partners. It especially includes the issue of sexual assault in date-rape cases: she said she was raped, he said it was consensual. To most people, the swearing contest might have to be scored as a tie. The legal reality, though, is different, beginning with the arrest.

Arrests are not based on guilt beyond a reasonable doubt. Instead, they are based upon the determination, usually by a police officer or a federal agent, of probable cause. For legal purposes, an alleged victim's sworn statement accusing someone of a crime is enough to justify an arrest. As one court explained, "[the alleged victim] told the police she had been raped...and provided the police with a sworn statement to that effect.... This alone is sufficient to show probable cause."[61] Another court explained, "It is difficult to imagine how a police officer could obtain better evidence of probable cause than identification by name of assailants provided by the victim."[62]

On the other hand, a defendant's denial, by itself, is not sufficient to avoid arrest. The accuser has no apparent motive to falsely name a perpetrator, but the accused has an overwhelming incentive to deny—early and often. Circumstances beyond a mere denial are often needed to eliminate probable cause and a probable arrest. Minor discrepancies in the accuser's account or a lack of forensic evidence may not defeat probable cause, either.

After an arrest is made and a he said–she said goes to trial, the she-said can still be enough, even to overcome reasonable doubt, if she is the one who is believed. However, courts recognize that cases without third-party witnesses or forensic evidence can be a close call. Trial judges often allow greater latitude in considering other evidence in the quest for a valid tiebreaker. Appeals courts likewise may look more closely at the incriminating evidence allowed in the original trial, as well as any defense evidence that was disallowed, to assure that a conviction was fair.[63] Trial mistakes not ordinarily considered significant can result in a new trial.[64]

In civil cases, the he said–she said dynamic almost always guarantees that the plaintiff will have the right to get to trial. After a producer for the *Montel Williams* show claimed that she had been terminated due to a brain aneurysm, she sued CBS for violating the Americans with Disabilities Act. CBS tried to get the case thrown out due to the lack of evidence. But the federal court found, "at its core, this case represents the classic he said–she said scenario, which involves an assessment of credibility and the resolution of competing inferences from the disputed facts."[65]

As many defendants can attest, prosecutors can win these essentially single-witness cases. Still, there are certainly acquittals, such as that of William Kennedy Smith, a nephew of the late Senator Ted Kennedy. Plenty of defendants become prison inmates like Mike Tyson. Since the accuser's own statements are legally sufficient for an arrest, without an effective attack on the accuser's credibility, conviction may be an inevitability.

THE SILENT DEFENDANTS

Don't the Innocent Want to Testify?

> Defendants usually do not testify—often because they are guilty. Even for the innocent, putting the defendant on the stand risks turning the trial into a one-witness case. All other testimony and evidence becomes much less important than the believability of the defendant's own words.

Whether a defendant will take the stand generates as much public speculation as any factor in a criminal case. What is less commonly considered is that it really helps if the defendant is in fact innocent. Usually he or she is not. Taking the stand to lie is a really bad idea—even skilled criminals are often readily exposed through cross-examination. Jurors ignore previous defense gains once they have seen the defendant lie before their very eyes.

Additionally, a defendant who takes the stand but is then convicted often faces stiffer jail time. The Federal Sentencing Guidelines, like those of many states, provide that punishment should be more severe if a "defendant willfully impeded or obstructed, or attempted to impede or obstruct the administrators of justice during...the prosecution of the instant offense."[66] As the Supreme Court applies this rule, if the trial court finds "that the defendant was untruthful with respect to material matter, the sentence is to be increased."[67] The court may conclude that by convicting the defendant, a jury necessarily found that the defendant's sworn testimony was false. Conviction after a defendant's own testimony can be legal proof of false testimony.

Additionally, once a defendant takes the stand, it becomes all the more difficult to win a reversal on appeal. "[A] statement by the defendant, if disbelieved by the jury, may be considered as substantive evidence of the defendant's guilt."[68] As courts explain this seeming paradox, "when a defendant chooses to testify, he runs the risk that, if disbelieved, the jury might conclude that the opposite is true,"[69] and so the jury can consider "the perjured testimony as affirmative evidence of guilt."[70] The already-difficult task of convincing an appeals court that there was not enough evidence for conviction becomes infinitely harder.

On the other hand, when a defendant chooses not to take the witness stand, jurors naturally wonder what he or she has to hide. Because the Fifth Amendment protects the defendant's right to remain silent, judges remind jurors that "every defendant is presumed innocent" and that "the law does not require a defendant to prove innocence or to produce any evidence at all." And the judge will instruct jurors—even though there is no guarantee that they listen—that if a defendant elects not to testify "you cannot consider that in any way in your deliberations."[71]

What's more, prosecutors are forbidden to comment about the defendant's failure to take the witness stand.[72] One prosecutor got away with telling the jury that "this case would have been a lot more complete if we had one more witness...."[73] While the appeals court found that the statement was too ambiguous to constitute an improper comment about a defendant's silence, most prosecutors try to win without walking so close to the edge. If they go too far, the resultant constitutional violation—commenting about a defendant invoking the Fifth Amendment right not to testify—could require a new trial.

Although the right to remain silent is honored in a criminal case, it does not get much respect in a civil court. A polar opposite of the scenario in a criminal case, the law says that based on such silence, judges and juries can infer that the truth is being withheld. This is deemed a negative inference against the person taking the Fifth, and it usually results in a negative outcome in a civil case.

The other cost when accusation is answered by silence may be a shattered reputation. St. Louis Cardinal Mark McGwire was a favorite of fans and a nemesis to baseball pitchers. Home runs rocketed off his bat. His then-unprecedented seventy home runs in the single season of 1998 followed months of dueling to set a new record against Chicago Cubs slugger Sammy Sosa. A banner year for baseball, it made McGwire a national celebrity with virtually a guaranteed place in the Baseball Hall of Fame. But in 2005, when McGwire refused to answer questions about steroid use at a congressional hearing, he went from hall of fame shoo-in to being shooed out because only 25 percent of the hall's voters supported his induction—a minimum of 75 percent is needed.

At the congressional hearing, McGwire repeatedly told inquisitors he would not talk about the past. When one ducks accusations by refusing to discuss the past, the risk to reputation is that there may not be much of a future.[74]

Poised to rejoin the Cardinals as a hitting coach, McGwire finally came clean on January 11, 2009, admitting for the first time he used steroids off and on for a decade—including the record-setting 1998 season. He tried to repair the enormous damage his silence inflicted upon his once-stellar image by fessing up to steroid use and following the usual principles of acknowledgment, apology, remorse, and reform. Local fans seemed appreciative, but only time will tell whether he will reach his once-assured place in the Baseball Hall of Fame.[75]

SELECTIVE PROSECUTION

Illegal or Just Unfair?

> So-called selective prosecution is only illegal if a defendant is singled out for a purpose that itself is wrongful, such as discrimination based on race, gender, or political or religious affiliation. Like claims of a prosecutor's vendetta, allegations of selective prosecution may get some press play but are almost never heard by juries.

Actually, there is nothing illegal about prosecutors being selective. Law enforcement has every right to allocate limited human and financial resources and pursue some but not all perpetrators. No matter how many people are traveling 72 mph in a 55-mph zone, the two who are pulled over have no right to complain of the hundreds who continued to speed on down the highway.[76]

Nor is there anything illegal about targeting high-profile wrong-doers. In fact, in the federal system, where only a small fraction of potential crimes are actually the subject of federal indictments, prioritizing high-impact cases is the name of the game. From the prosecutor's standpoint, a defendant loaded with publicity value creates plenty of free advertising for the message of law enforcement about crime and punishment. Prosecuting Winona Ryder for shoplifting at Saks Fifth Avenue made a more potent warning to prospective thieves than the conviction of an unknown. Similarly, bringing a tax evasion case against actor Wesley Snipes or businesswoman Leona Helmsley was a powerful message to potential tax cheats.

What makes selective prosecution illegal is an improper purpose. A prosecution mainly motivated by vindictiveness, if provable, would qualify. So would targeting particular political leaders or members of a racial or ethnic minority. But the last time the Supreme Court validated a selective prosecution defense was during the nineteenth century. In the famous case of *Yick Wo v. Hopkins*,[77] the court found that a San Francisco ordinance imposing stricter requirements on laundries was only enforced if the operators happened to be Chinese. Unless a discriminatory effect as well as a discriminatory purpose can be proven, no claim will be sustained.[78] Such selectivity could also be a constitutional violation if, say, a prosecutor targeted only defendants of a particular faith or political affiliation. In such instances, it is not the mere fact of selecting some defendants rather than others. It is instead selecting them on grounds that violate their First Amendment or equal-protection rights.

Much of what is claimed to be discrimination results from efforts to target prominent people. Perhaps celebrities and politicians are indeed discriminated against in this sense, but such extra scrutiny is an occupational hazard. As long as neither political ideology nor demographics are the motivation, it is not illegal discrimination. It is the price of fame.

HOMICIDE

Who Needs a Body?

> In the case of disappearing American teenager Natalee Holloway, the father of the lead suspect supposedly said, "No body, no case." Although a common understanding—and certainly a fact that weakens a homicide prosecution—the law is much more complicated.

Murder cases, like other crimes, have a rule called *corpus delicti*, which includes the Latin word for "body." But it refers to the "body" or essence of the crime (*delicti*), not the body of the victim. As a result, corpus delicti does not require evidence that a victim's body ever be found. Instead, the need for the body or essence of the crime means there must be independent evidence, apart from a defendant's own out-of-court statements, that the alleged crime actually occurred. With respect to the crime of murder, there must be evidence that a human being is dead, and that the death was caused by criminal conduct, not accident. Therefore, corpus delicti is simply a limited test to assure that there is a foundation for the prosecution and trial. As with most other issues, circumstantial evidence can provide this foundation, and it does not have to be compelling.

The "no body required" rule is not a recent innovation: "Historically, the production of the body of a missing person was generally not required under the common law in order to establish the corpus delicti for homicide."[79] Otherwise, as the Supreme Court once explained, killers would be rewarded for their ingenuity in concealing the remains.[80]

In a Delaware case, Thomas Capano, once a powerful Washington lawyer, was tried for shooting his mistress and dumping her body in the Atlantic Ocean.[81] When apparent victims vanish without a trace, the unexplained and complete disappearance itself contributes to the inference of homicide. Additionally, the case included suspicious purchases—like a gun and a large cooler—as well as testimony from the accused's brother who took Capano on the boat ride and saw him toss the cooler overboard. Capano was convicted of first-degree murder and sentenced to death. In his appeal to the supreme court of Delaware, his counsel raised sixteen issues, but none contested whether there was enough evidence to support a finding of guilt. Nor did he argue "no body, no case." The state supreme court rejected all the objections, approving the conviction and death sentence.

In a California case that legal enthusiasts often study, the victim's body was never found, and the corpus delicti—the foundation for the existence of a homicide—consisted essentially of the unexplained disappearance of the defendant's wife.[82] After being sent home from work for want of a proper uniform, she was never seen again. The court also based inferences of foul play upon the fact that she left behind the wallet containing her driver's license and other information at her home. Nor did family or friends ever hear from her again. Because such circumstances established, even if barely, the corpus delicti, the court then allowed the jury to consider the defendant's own incriminating statements, which led to his conviction for murder. Highly suspicious disappearances are often enough to show that someone was likely a murder victim:

- One victim left behind a house, his wealth, and even his dentures and eyeglasses and never again contacted any friends.[83]
- Another missing man, known to pick up hitchhikers, disappeared without cashing a pay voucher.[84]

- A week after his wife disappeared, the defendant began to dispose of her clothing. Incidentally, he had also been seen carrying a large, body-sized box out of his bedroom and taking it away in his car.[85]
- A woman with physical impairments abruptly disappeared without contacting friends, relatives, or her pastor and abruptly stopped using any Social Security benefits.[86]

Of course, testimony linking the defendant to the disappearance can further establish the corpus delicti, especially when a defendant was the last one seen with the victim.

As with other circumstantial cases—body or no body—a conviction can be obtained if every other reasonable hypothesis is excluded except the one that condemns the defendant. Still, a murder case without a body leaves a giant hole in the evidence. When remains are found, the case for the prosecution is revised upward.

Despite the mounting evidence Modesto police had been compiling against Scott Peterson, his arrest followed immediately once the remains of his wife, Laci, and unborn son, Conner, washed ashore. In 2008, police in Orlando charged Casey Anthony for the murder of her daughter, Caylee, before the child's body was discovered. When the remains were found, the prosecution added the death penalty to the case.

For the family of Natalee Holloway, though, the American teenager who disappeared in 2005 while vacationing in Aruba, the lack of remains has left a gap in the case that immobilized the prosecution, which was governed by homicide laws similar to our own.[87] Despite the assertion made by a suspect's father to his son and several alleged accomplices, "no body" does not automatically equate to "no case."[88] Still, there are times when it sadly means no justice.

ENTRAPMENT

Stuck in the Trap or Beating the Rap?

> When the police place the bait and defendants take the cheese, can they get out of the trap?

The term *entrapment* is a favorite of the television law shows. It is frequently understood to mean that when a defendant takes the bait dangled by police, the entrapped defendant can count on an acquittal. The scenarios for setting up defendants are known as "stings" and are a common tool of law enforcement in cases ranging from public corruption to drug deals. Thus, the Department of Justice has long recognized that undercover operations have been "especially effective in public corruption investigations."[89]

In one of the most famous of sting operations, the FBI during the late 1970s provided a fake Arab sheik who approached various members of Congress to lure them into accepting a bribe on videotape. By 1981, the "ABSCAM" investigation had netted convictions of six members of the House of Representatives and one US senator. Unsurprisingly, there was little applause from Congress, which criticized the FBI's tactics, finding that the "use of undercover techniques creates serious risks to citizens' property, privacy, and civil liberties."[90] Responding to such concerns, the attorney general imposed a broad array of preconditions limiting future attempts to use a sting operation to "set up" a public official.

These were, of course, completely fictitious bribery shams, and there was neither a real sheik nor a real transaction to be purchased with bribe money. Even though a sting operation does not present a real-life deal and rests entirely upon a fiction, courts nevertheless hold that the conduct of the defendant is as criminal as if the participants were real.

The cry of entrapment is frequently heard outside the courtroom when defendants are stung. In the actual trial, though, entrapment is a difficult defense to win. As the US Supreme Court explained, rather than the government's conduct, "the entrapment defense focuses upon the intent or predisposition of the defendant to commit the crime."[91] The absence of a defendant's preexisting criminal tendency must be clear.[92] Most basically, a defendant has to show that he was actually turned into a criminal by the enticements of the police. If the defendant was simply repeating an already-existing practice of similar misconduct, he was not entrapped—he was just finally caught.

An entrapment defense is a high-risk strategy. Presenting entrapment requires acknowledging that the defendant perpetrated the acts alleged by the prosecution. Instead of rolling the dice and taking this huge gamble, defendants may prefer to argue that their words and actions had meanings that were innocent rather than criminal. Because sting operations are planned in advance, they typically have audio and video recordings to capture every memorable moment. After the arrest, the defense listens carefully to such tapes to decide whether to argue that the defendant's conduct was arguably innocent (deny, deny) or inarguably guilty (set up, conned, and, of course, entrapped).

When the defendant's own voice includes guilty-sounding words, almost no amount of explanation will suffice. If, on the other hand, the meaning of the defendant's recorded words is unclear, he or she may choose to profess innocence. (Arguing, for example, that "more pay" on a barely audible tape was really "no way.") In instances of cryptic or ambiguous statements, or when the tape's sound quality is poor, some lawyers argue that the defendant was simply playing along rather than engaging in foul play.

On occasion, the entrapment defense will overcome all odds and spring the defendant from the trap. When John DeLorean, the former head of Chrysler Motors, was busted, the tape captured his voice negotiating an illegal narcotics transaction. Remarkably, he was nonetheless acquitted on an entrapment theory: jurors were deeply troubled by the aggressiveness with which the government went after him.

For the most part, though, defendants who get set up by sting operations remain stung. The best way to escape the trap is to avoid the bait in the first place.

CHAPTER 11

A MEDIA PRIMER FOR SPINNERS

PART ONE

For all the fascination with trials in the court of public opinion, no one really knows how much media campaigns actually affect the verdict. Ultimately, what matters is winning the courtroom battle for life and liberty rather than the contest over the next news cycle. No matter how important publicity may be to clients, the best press releases are written about winning, just as woefully bad news follows defeat. The legendary Johnnie Cochran had the memorable sound bite, "If it doesn't fit, you must acquit," but without the jury's own words of "not guilty," his phrase would have been pointless rather than timeless.

That said, even if the benefits of spin are difficult to quantify, there are many reasons to believe they are not illusory. Studies conducted of mock jurors—simulated jurors in simulated trials—suggest that negative news contributes to negative verdicts.[1] And even though real jurors routinely deny that they are media influenced, it is undeniable that cases are decided by jurors who are media exposed. It is neither necessary nor realistic, however, to disqualify jurors simply because they were previously subjected to onslaughts of publicity about a case—the law does not require an empty mind, only one that is open. Although media-drenched jurors must assure the court that they will be fair and will consider only the evidence and law presented inside the courtroom, those assurances are more comforting when the groundwork for fairness has been laid by balanced news coverage.

Once selected, jurors are instructed repeatedly to avoid media coverage of the case they are deciding. The law assumes that they honor their oath, but common sense says some may not. And even jurors who read nothing about a case live among others who may be reading everything. When a community is buzzing about a trial, no one wants to be remembered as one of the jurors fooled by clever defense lawyers into acquitting a notoriously guilty defendant.

The ears of judges often have chronic buzzing, particularly because they are not prohibited from following the news coverage of their cases. The law presumes that judges will ignore the media monsoons drenching the courthouse and decide every legal issue as if nary a drop had fallen. If we assume, though, that judges are real people who live in the real world—sometimes a world of judicial elections—it follows that they are acutely aware of community feelings about media-intensive cases. And judges live in more than one community. Most care deeply about maintaining respect from their peers in the courthouse and from the attorneys who practice in the same locale. Because the legal community reads newspapers much more than most, the articles that judges and lawyers will be reading should be balanced as much as possible if the playing field is to be level.

Legal icon Dershowitz recently recalled some advice he received from a local lawyer when he was handling the appeal for convicted wife-killer Claus von Bülow: "The only way you can win this appeal is if these three judges (all male back then) can explain to their wives why they let off a wife-killer." Absorbing the daunting reality, Dershowitz focused not only on the legal brief but also on facts about the medical evidence that would raise questions in the minds of reasonable readers.[2]

Good press is also a recruitment poster for lawyers, experts, and even fact witnesses. Winnability magnetizes cases. Lawyers and experts may be mercenaries, but even hired guns prefer to be retained by winners. For the top professionals who can pick and choose their cases, many prefer a cause that is acclaimed to one that is being defamed. Even fact witnesses, the main determinant of most cases, can be more effective if they believe their testimony will be featured in a success story. Just as many prefer to join the team with all the cheerleaders, horrible publicity can impair recruitment efforts. (Note: large, up-front payments to attorneys and experts can make even beastly cases seem beautiful.)

Occasionally, the fear of negative publicity can inspire the parties to negotiate a solution before the judicial process reaches its own conclusion. Several years ago I represented a woman who shipped herself to the United States by plane, arriving inside a DHL box. This elegant but—no surprise here—petite client might have had an uphill battle seeking asylum to remain here. In theory, a so-called stowaway is among the least favored of all newcomers for purposes of immigration law. Her case began to attract attention, however, because while gift DHL packages are common, a gift immigrant understandably created a news stir. As press interest intensified over her battle for asylum, we held our fire and postponed the ever-present temptation to trash-talk the immigration service for trying to deport a young woman who was obviously courageous, even if too ingenious for safety's sake. The government's press anxieties actually helped us make a deal providing that if the authorities agreed not to send her away, we would keep the television cameras at bay. Along with downsizing our press strategies, we assured the government that our client would travel with passengers rather than inside packages in the future.

Effective Press Strategies in the Age of Spin

Use Helpful Hooks to Formulate Your Message

The late Kurt Cobain, founder of the 1990s rock phenomenon Nirvana, once attributed his success to writing songs with "hooks," melodic phrases or lyrical segments that would catch on and stay with a listener as soon as they were heard. Like music, the best media strategies rely on themes that can be reduced to a single thought that will play to the game plan in court. Many experts believe that the most effective litigation messages should take ten seconds or less to deliver.[3]

Unless it targets human feelings, though, the message will not hook human beings. In litigating the battle to keep Elian Gonzalez in this country, we saw the case as centering upon his best interests and having those interests determined by a family court—the usual judicial forum for a child's needs—rather than by the chronically insensitive immigration bureaucracy. Those legal issues drowned, however, under waves of emotional reactions to the so-called battle between the rights of the natural father and the anti-Castro sentiments of the Cuban American community. No amount of information about legal issues could overcome the lifetime of feelings people have about age-old issues such as parental rights. In the end, winning themes for media—and law—need to be as human and simple as possible. One father reclaiming his son overwhelms other issues, just as a single dead voter can symbolize an entire election case.

Although some favorite themes are recent innovations (the client is now in rehab), most media messaging relies on the retreaded ghosts of trials past: the accusers are lying scoundrels (sometimes true); it's a political vendetta (even if true, rarely provable or relevant); the accusers are just going after the defendant because he or she is rich and famous (sometimes true, but riches and fame rarely score sympathy points); the witness is psychotic (occasionally true, but not always relevant); the defendant is psychotic (often true, but almost never suffices as legal insanity); someone else did it (preferably with at least threads of supporting evidence); and, the defendant was somewhere else at the time of the crime (better have video or at least documents to prove it).

Avoid Inconsistency, the Hobgoblin of Legal Minds

Lawyers are trained to present alternative theories in court, even when those theories are completely incompatible positions. But in the court of public opinion, there is zero tolerance for contradictory positions. In the 2000 presidential recount litigation, the Democratic lawyers' message for the public was reported early and often: "count all the votes." In fact, legal maneuvers at odds with counting every vote—such as trying to invalidate absentee ballots in Republican counties—were avoided. With media-intensive cases, speaking to the press means speaking out of only one side of your mouth—if you want to have it your way, do not try to have it both ways.

Show Your Adversary's Deficiencies and Inconsistencies

High-profile cases attack an accuser's credibility by putting the alleged victim on trial before the court of public opinion as well as before the jurors. This venerable strategy has countless antecedents, such as the case of Captain Bligh, who was initially the heroic victim of the famous mutiny on the *Bounty* but was later portrayed as a tyrant when the accused mutineers were brought to a well-publicized trial in eighteenth-century London. These tactics can be risky—one of the mutineers against Bligh skated with a royal pardon, but three were hanged. Still, whenever believing the accuser means convicting the alleged abuser, the battle plan becomes an all-out attack on that witness's credibility.

Prior inconsistent statements of accusers are the gold standard for negating accusations in any venue. Michael Jackson's defense team struck a gold mine that included documented instances of the allegedly abused boy previously denying Jackson's wrongdoing. Even when the public may have empathy for an alleged double-talker, the fact of the inconsistency is almost always more powerful than the excuses.

Court-Weak Messages Can Still Be Media-Strong

Some messages may never reach the court of law but still register big time with public opinion. For example, a jury will not hear evidence about a witness's psychological problems unless the conditions are severe enough to impair his or her ability to recall events and to tell the truth. But even if legally harmless, a wide variety of mental issues can send the witness's credibility crashing with the public. Kobe Bryant's team repeatedly scored points with the public by disclosing his accuser's past hospitalizations for depression, which a judge almost assuredly would not have allowed to reach a jury.

Other facts that may be press-worthy but not court-worthy may include some of the more appalling allegations about a witness's past. With the latest O.J. Simpson case prosecution—for the dumb-and-dumber souvenir hunt in a Las Vegas hotel room—his past arrest for murder would officially be excluded from jurors (which could have indeed mattered to the three adults in Nevada who did not already know). To counteract the nuclear fallout from O.J.'s past, his attorney proclaimed publicly that the sketchy prosecution witnesses had enough baggage to assure decimating cross-examinations. To be sure, when codefendants make sweetheart deals to turn state's evidence, defense counsel can indeed pummel the past of the cooperator to portray him as a rat lying to save his own hide. Apart from cooperating witnesses, though, a lot of baggage gets checked outside the courtroom. Most misdeeds and even misdemeanor convictions of witnesses are not discussed in court. Felony convictions are usually revealed but not described in detail.

Although some of the spiciest menu items may never be served to a jury, they can be fed routinely to the press because some themes that never appear in trial transcripts will splash hugely in newsprint transcript.

Ineffective PR Strategies That Spin You in Circles

For many legal teams, a professional spokesperson is the mainstay of messaging as well as the hub for media relations. When hiring outside consultants, however, elaborate tactics meant to manipulate the media should not become an overt operation.

Be Careful about Overt Operations

Calls from obvious media handlers are resented, especially when reporters feel they are being walled off from the real sources. That being said, the high-profile case is no place for amateurs. Attorneys with minimal media experience should not handle media relations without true professional help. As a compromise, outside press consultants should strategize regularly, but a client's regular spokesperson or a media-savvy member of the legal team should handle the communication. Commitment to this process is critical because lawyers often mistake a reporter's seeming friendliness for a guarantee that stories will be friendly. Bear in mind, though, that communications with a press specialist may not be privileged from subpoenas, and care should be exercised, particularly when exchanging correspondence and e-mail.

Silence Is Golden, Especially When Required

With legal news, as with diets, some of the most delicious tidbits are off-limits. In fact, some laws make it a federal crime to disclose confidential information about especially sensitive subjects. In cases with national security implications governed by the Classified Information Procedures Act (CIPA), a leakster could potentially face criminal prosecution. Grand jury proceedings are also confidential, and prosecutors and government agents could be prosecuted themselves for disclosing those secrets. Significantly, witnesses are under no such restraints, and some are surprisingly talkative.

In ordinary circumstances, the rules prohibit attorneys from creating publicity that they know or should know will have a "substantial likelihood of materially prejudicing" the judicial proceedings.[4] Publicity hounding early in a case is more tolerable, but as the trial draws near, the risk skyrockets that publicity reaching future jurors will influence their later decisions. Judges understandably perceive that the likelihood of prejudice is greater with publicity that is near the time of trial as opposed to negative stories much earlier that are mostly forgotten by the average juror.[5] Moreover, for prosecutors at least, extensive chest-thumping about their case is rarely a good idea. Especially if defense attorneys are seeking to move the case to a different city, they will pounce upon press-happy prosecutors as purveyors of excessive pretrial publicity that prejudices potential jurors.

An even greater restriction on press communication is, of course, the gag order. Although the term *gag order* is often used loosely to describe an assortment of limitations, in its extreme form, a true gag order prohibits virtually any communication about a pending case by the litigation team or courthouse personnel. Ordinarily disfavored due to concerns for rights of the press and the public, gag orders were imposed in the Scott Peterson and Michael Jackson trials because nothing else could adequately protect the defendants from barrages of relentless news coverage.

Some confidentiality orders are less drastic, even routine. For example, in cases about business trade secrets, courts frequently prohibit the disclosure of confidential processes, patents, or formulas. Perhaps because these restrict access to technical tedium rather than to courtroom dramas, they are often agreed upon by all parties and raise fewer objections from the media.

The Arsenal for Effective Spin Doctors

Dwight D. Eisenhower, former president and mega general, once famously explained that planning is everything, but often plans become useless due to the onrush of unexpected surprises. Despite the frequent uselessness of making plans, media planning can help create some certainty in an uncertain process, and it should rely on a toolbox that includes public relations as well as legal devices.

Pitching the Press

Calls to reporters, the seemingly friendly as well as the patently hostile, are critical except in circumstances of the Invisible Client who is hoping to have no profile in a high-profile controversy that is ensnaring others. Before making calls that could wind up on the front page, careful planning is needed to craft the public message points as well as to ascertain the private lobbying tactics that rely on "background" comments, which remain off the record. Often, the most important function of background discussions is simply to clarify the client's position and to assure that the main issues are understood. Even when bad stories are unavoidable, a confusion-infected disaster may be preventable by providing legitimate clarifications to reporters before the damage is done.

Finding the right person to pitch to can be easy in frenzied cases because the reporters are calling the lead lawyers anyway. Veteran AP reporter Brian Skoloff recommends that lawyers "know [their] reporter and learn about their previous work to gauge their style, history of accuracy, and any perceived bias or slant."[6] In lower-profile matters, attorneys, the client, or an outside PR agent may have existing relationships with the media. If not, simply identify the newspaper and television reporters assigned to the courthouse and make a cold call.

Although reporters usually do not mind the sales pitches, the pitcher should establish any ground rules concerning what is background at the front end. Without an explicit agreement, all comments are fair game, and the consequences can be an unfair story. Local reporters generally honor such agreements, especially if they plan on continuing to work effectively in the same community. Skoloff points out that just as attorneys are trying to identify reporters to speak to about their cases, journalists are trying to develop a network of sources. "Each can use the other as an important tool in their respective tasks." Even if reporters take what lawyers say with the proverbial grain of salt, Skoloff advocates a collegial relationship and believes that mutual trust is a legitimate goal. "Defense attorneys who don't view and use reporters as an additional tool to try their cases are missing out, in many instances, on a key component aimed at the court of public opinion, which can sometimes bleed into the jury box."[7] Caution should nonetheless be exercised, though, when dealing with unknown, out-of-town reporters who may not care about a future relationship with the local legal team. Dershowitz points out that a common mistake for the would-be legal spinmeister is to assume that because a reporter seems friendly to counsel, the news will be kind to the client.[8] In all events, even background comments should be judicious, all the more so when they are about a judge.

File Press-Friendly Pleadings

Courthouse files largely immunize their contents from the laws of defamation, so reporters rely overwhelmingly upon court papers and hearings. As a result, press-savvy lawyers craft court papers that not only nourish procedural requirements but also feed the press.

The graphically detailed indictment of Atlanta Falcons star quarterback Michael Vick in 2007 is a striking example of prosecutorial sophistication in stating a case to the public. Even though the rules for federal indictments do not require all the details of a crime, the Vick indictment included devastating specifics, stating that codefendants and "Vick, and two others known and unknown to the grand jury 'rolled' or 'tested' additional 'Bad Newz Kennels' dogs by putting the dogs through fighting sessions at 1915 Moonlight Road to determine which animals were good fighters." Reading more like the opening statement of a trial than the bland boilerplate of most indictments, the charges by themselves were enough to appall readers who returned an immediate guilty verdict in the court of public opinion.

Since a litigant's best facts can be launched aggressively and with legal immunity in court papers, the party who files first has a huge advantage over an adversary with no papers in the courthouse. Even litigation weaklings can appear muscle-bound when they are juiced by a "court document" with "facts" that go unanswered. Although defending parties will file detailed written responses down the road, they may become media's road kill while they wait. With few exceptions, reporters demand same-day service in responding to the day's breaking news. In the highest-profile cases, the defense's response, even weeks later, may generate a story by itself. But the later story about the defendant's denial gets much less ink and often no air time.

Some legal strategists anticipate the initiator's huge advantage by preparing their own legal document with their key facts. While the defense will rarely have enough time to fully respond in writing to the just-filed accusatory document, first responders should consider something as basic as a motion for a status conference—a request to discuss general issues about court scheduling—loaded with the defendant's best facts. Given the critical nature of securing balanced coverage on day one, legal papers readied for almost immediate filing may help to balance the news cycle that will otherwise be owned by the other side. As maestros such as Alan M. Dershowitz and Roy Black note, being late for the news cycle means being too late to have an impact on the public's initial reactions—the first impressions that often become lasting ones.[9]

On a cautionary note, as former Durham, North Carolina, District Attorney Michael Nifong learned in the Duke lacrosse team case, when public statements go beyond the public record, misinformation can result in suits for defamation. Had Nifong stuck to the script of the court papers containing the false rape allegations, he likely would have escaped being sued because even the most unjust prosecutions do not, in general, allow victims to sue for damages.

Speak Loudly in Hearings When Reporters Are Listening

Court hearings, traditionally the centers for legal advocacy, have increasingly become the center stage for press strategies. While preliminary hearings are typically limited in scope, they can become minitrials, as the Scott Peterson case, the Kobe Bryant case, and the O.J. souvenir case demonstrated.

Media-friendly prosecutors are also part of the prosecution business. In the Liberty City Seven case of alleged terrorists, rather than the usual executive summary, the prosecution provided hours of specific evidence including excerpts from the defendants' intercepted telephone conversations. Those details may not have been necessary for purposes of the bond hearing, but they were certainly impressive. The evidence also demonstrated to a skeptical press corps that the alleged terrorists were indeed far more lethal than laughable.

Press Conferences Offer Benefits and Burdens

Press conferences are perilous whenever they are interesting enough to be newsworthy, but they can be tremendously powerful. In criminal cases, prosecutors enjoy all the advantages because, as the voices of our government, the mere fact that they have decided to bring a significant prosecution equates to major news. When prosecutors, dauntingly flanked by law enforcement officers, read their indictments, their words resound like the hammer of judgment rather than as one side of a case to be disputed and even refuted. Defense press conferences in criminal cases are less common and usually less effective. In the Kobe Bryant case, his exceptional celebrity status kept the cameras rolling throughout his attorney's presentation and even during Bryant's reading of a prepared statement, accompanied, of course, by his beautiful wife. In general, though, even when the defense secures press attendance, counsel's commentary usually generates only a few sentences of coverage rather than a major story. Moreover, to attract any interest at all, most defense press conferences require something more engrossing than the standard denial of the defense lawyer because while the announcement of a major indictment is news, the fact of denial is not.

Since defense lawyers avoid tipping their hands about their best evidence, the effort to generate good press coverage may lead to press themes that are more eye-catching than relevant. For example, a strong showing of community leaders to condemn a police investigation or prosecution can generate news without involving the participation of the defense camp. This can be the optimal setting for grievances about a political agenda and a prosecutor's vendetta, popular favorites even though they are legally irrelevant.

In the summer of 2001, Congressman Gary Condit was never charged with a crime but was nonetheless being convicted by the public for having some undefined but nefarious connection to the disappearance of government intern Chandra Levy. While Condit did not, and apparently could not, deny the allegations of an affair with Ms. Levy, the even darker clouds of her inexplicable disappearance were surrounding him. In responding to the devastating insinuations swirling across Washington, attorney Abbe Lowell shrewdly opted to avoid the affair and focused entirely on the speculation about Condit's connection to Levy's disappearance. He held a press conference to reveal the results of a lie-detector test administered by a respected polygrapher. Although Condit would not be reelected and Levy's tragic death would remain a mystery for years, Lowell largely erased the sinister speculations about his client.

Unless the client is a sports superstar or other press magnet, a news conference does not guarantee news coverage. An outside PR professional can give a blunt assessment of whether you have enough news to draw the media (clients, and even their lawyers, invariably overrate the enthusiasm of busy reporters for being summoned to hear all about the Great Injustice). A PR professional is also invaluable in organizing a press conference. If one such professional is not available or affordable for the client, simply invite every newspaper, television, radio, and Internet media outlet with any conceivable interest in the case. Whether using e-mail, faxes, phone calls, or some combination thereof to pitch the new conference, the target list at each news organization should include the news director, the courthouse reporter, the political or business reporter when applicable, or all of the above. One-page releases are best, hitting the press with the most fascinating facts and pegging those facts to any larger stories that are obsessing the media that week. E-mails and faxes are enough for stories that sizzle, but for stories that generate no more than room-temperature reactions from the press, releases will need follow-up phone calls.

Be Careful, Leaks Are the Perilous Catnip of Press Relations

Ever since J. Edgar Hoover mastered the art of rewarding favored reporters, providing inside information has opened an inside track with media. Leaks that are forbidden by statutes, ethics rules, or court orders are to be avoided for many obvious reasons—as former vice-presidential aide and felon "Scooter" Libby learned—investigations about illegal leaks can be hazardous to your legal health.

Some leaks, though, violate no laws and instead constitute an early release of information to the chosen few that other media will receive only after the story is broken. The lucky reporter with a news leak and, therefore, a scoop will be the hero at the newsroom, sometimes for as much as an hour, and, theoretically, the reporter will therefore love your client—at least for a day or two.

Defense leaks may create a brief benefit if a favorable article results, but they can also provoke leaks from prosecutors, who usually have far more leakable ammunition at their disposal. Leaks also contribute to unhappy moments before judges, most of whom resent leaky lawyers. In the Scott Peterson case, the defense gained some ground with the media following the leak of a portion of an autopsy report that seemed to support a defense theory. The judge was not amused, though, and imposed a sweeping gag order that criticized "leaks of information that could be considered favorable for one side or the other."[10]

Often the biggest backfire comes from the other reporters, the ones who got scooped and got called out on the carpet because the leakster sent press nuggets to their competitors. While many simply try harder to get the next leak, sometimes slighted reporters, still feeling those carpet burns, may play to the other side to get their own scoops from the adversary.

That's What Friends Are For

Clients with bad facts need good quotes to achieve balanced press coverage. Reporters will occasionally accept suggestions about other sources to contact for quotes, and when they ask for names to call, lawyers should have a list ready. The best choices are people whose opinions are client-reliable and publicly credible, as reporters dislike overt manipulation. Some strategists send talking points to their allies, especially recognized experts who are regularly quoted by the media. Other methods include getting friends to write op-ed pieces as well as letters to the editor. Today's spinners will also most assuredly hit the blogging circuit.

While pitching to allies is risk-free, care should be exercised in dealing with opposing viewpoints. During the Michael Jackson case, a press handler for DA Tom Sneddon contacted Professor Laurie L. Levenson following her critical legal commentary to try to get her to "go easy" on Sneddon. She was decidedly unimpressed.[11] Contrastingly, when I was providing commentary on the Rush Limbaugh case and received a memorandum with legal points concerning the controversy, the materials were helpful and appreciated.

Spinning the Unspinnable

The Shocking Allegation

As the ultimate news vampire, the Shocking Allegation (often involving sex, molestation, and—recently—animal cruelty) sucks up all of the attention devoted to a subject, making it virtually impossible to tell the rest of the story since many people care about only the headline. As a result, the defense spin is often of little help in such cases. The only defense worth promoting is complete denial, and the only distraction may be Another Shocking Allegation, preferably involving someone else's client. As at least one former governor experienced, it becomes very difficult to use a litany of past good deeds to humanize a client who is being demonized by sensational allegations, for example, frequent sex with prostitutes.

Insisting that the Shocking Allegation about a sex scandal is overstated (it was twice, not three times) or that the media is exaggerating about the embezzlement from a children's charity (it wasn't nearly that much) confesses to infinitely more than it denies. If the proof is undeniable—video recordings are especially bothersome—it may be a convenient time to revise one's philosophy about a media campaign and minimize press interaction, insisting, for example, that your client does not believe in trying his case in the press. Sometimes, the only exit from an unrelenting press onslaught is the miraculous arrival of someone else's disaster to replace your client's disaster with new headlines above the fold.

Even so, at times, the Shocking Allegation can be met with another Also Sensational Allegation. After ex-Congressman Mark Foley abruptly resigned from office, he was being battered by horrific publicity due to overly friendly e-mails to underaged congressional pages. His attorney, David Roth, shrewdly softened the blistering coverage by convening a press conference to announce that Foley had been abused as a boy by a Catholic priest. Although irrelevant in legal terms, it was interesting enough to generate significant press coverage because the Also Sensational Allegation was apparently true.

Scott Peterson was accused of an Even More Shocking Allegation—murdering his wife and unborn son—and so attorney Mark Geragos captured some badly needed attention for the defense by suggesting that a satanic cult might have committed the murder. Taking the offensive in a seemingly indefensible case, Geragos also proclaimed that the defense had evidence to "totally exonerate" Peterson. Within weeks, commentators were suggesting that reasonable doubt about Peterson's guilt might not be as unreasonable, with such articles as "From 'Why Did He?' to 'Did He?' in Twenty-eight Days." Although the press coverage became more balanced, winning some battles in the media does not mean it is possible to win the war in the courtroom—as Peterson now sits on California's death row.

Speak Softly or Not at All

When the truth is too ugly for cosmetics and too obvious for denials, there may be nothing useful to say. Specific denials that are demonstrably false accomplish little and can sacrifice any remaining scraps of credibility that should be saved for the remorse and repentance that should come later. Moreover, bogus denials can fuel more counterpoints that give more life to a story that might otherwise spin itself off the front pages. Fortunately, even the most lamentable culprits are allowed to make general denials with the obligatory, "We look forward to the opportunity to develop the real facts at the proper time in a court of law." For the client who is ambushed walking out of home, office, or rehab clinic, the only possible words may be, "It is a legal matter and my attorneys have directed me not to discuss it." Less may not be more, but it may be all there is.

No tried-and-true formula was available for Michael Vick. Lying low and silent, pleading guilty, and entering prison even before prison was ordered may prove to be the only long-shot hope for eventual rehabilitation. After his release from prison, he was signed by the Philadelphia Eagles, a return accepted by the National Football League. Public acceptance may prove more elusive. Sometimes a symbolic return to the scene of the crime is needed. Perhaps charitable support for abused animals or working at or contributing to shelters could help convince skeptics that Vick is sincere in his remorse rather than just glad to be out of prison. In that event, perhaps, now that he has left prison, he will appear in front of cameras with happy, healthy canines at his side.

Rocket Man or Invisible Man

Meanwhile, as the baseball steroid scandal unraveled, one wonders whether Roger "the Rocket" Clemens, the greatest baseball pitcher of his generation, should have hunkered down quietly, taken some short-term press hits, and reappeared after the worst of the storm subsided. Instead, Clemens launched an astonishing publicity offensive. In a strident attack against the ex-trainer who accused him of using steroids, Clemens sued for defamation and even tape-recorded an ambiguous telephone conversation between them that Clemens then proclaimed to be clear proof of his innocence. After rocketing himself to the center of the steroids controversy, Clemens's adamant congressional testimony was contradicted not only by his former trainer but also by statements of Clemens's longtime friend, pitcher Andy Pettitte. Clemens's samurai strategies not only stole all the negative attention but also won him a congressional referral to the Justice Department that led to federal charges of perjury (*United States v. William R. Clemens*, case no. CR-10-223).

Like others, I had advised another baseball player about the joys of invisibility. When high-profile legal problems are casting about for potential actors, the best role for a client may be the Invisible Man. Scores of other baseball players hoping to vanish from the press radar must have silently thanked Clemens's show-stopping tactics that stole the thunder and acid rain of a media downpour. Whatever may be the truth of the Clemens controversy, the results include, at least in the short term, a battered reputation and the painful ordeal of a federal trial that could land him in prison's Hall of Shame.

Avoid the Press with E-Ducking

Sometimes, there is no helpful answer to inevitable questions, and even saying "no comment" could seem incriminating. When asked specific questions about appalling allegations (why so much greed and child abuse?), rather than leave a client completely mute and unprotected, you can avoid phone discussions by e-mailing or faxing a brief statement to the press. While ducking behind an e-mailed statement invariably leads to a punishing story, it usually assures that some portion of your response will appear among all the painful paragraphs.

Hideouts and Stakeouts

In most strategies for invisibility, communication is carefully minimized. Sometimes, the only strategy can be "no comment," or even no phone calls taken from reporters. Although rare, these circumstances arise when distressing rumors are being floated and even the words "no comment" could signal a sinking client. If the reporter's question is going to be whether your client is under criminal investigation, and an investigation is indeed under way, there is rarely a good answer: declining comment does not help, and a false denial could eventually hurt. When the subjects of the inquiry are political figures, some are reluctant even to acknowledge the fact of legal representation since others may assume that hiring a criminal defense lawyer equates to involvement in a criminal matter. Politicians are sitting ducks for press confrontations, so it can be risky for counsel to speak at all to the media during early investigative stages. Although hiding is a least favorite press strategy, in extreme situations, it may be the only one.

Taking the Offensive

Saber Rattling with a Double-Edged Sword

For most clients, the worst media nightmare is an imminent, extremely damaging story fraught with inaccuracies. Understandably, when the client's war cry demands ballistic counterattacks, canceling one's subscription to the offending newspaper hardly seems sufficient. Many, including the guiltiest, demand that counsel write every misbehaving media and threaten every manner of lawsuit against reporters, editors, producers, and even the maintenance crew. Despite the obvious therapeutic value, such threats may not have much legal force.

If publicly filed court records are fueling the news engines, the media are versed enough in their craft to know that those documents can be used for devastating news reports that avoid legal exposure. When bad news is arriving before judicial proceedings are commenced, the immunity shield surrounding the story may be more fragile, but it is still imposing. With celebrities and politicians, even cub reporters know that the law has declared open season on public figures except in the most extreme cases of blatant falsehoods. To be effective, counterpunchers should concentrate on the media's most reckless allegations, those that are contradicted by clear evidence or based on sources with giant credibility gaps.

Threatening lawsuits and even making good on those threats can be legitimate weapons to protect reputations. Few clients, though, will endure the years of tribulations required to pursue even a strong defamation lawsuit all the way to trial. One prominent leader who was falsely called a "mobster" eventually settled a suit against a national magazine for a charitable contribution after enduring days of depositions that were anything but charitable.

Since such suits become a costly ordeal for the defamation victim, they are occasionally filed not for litigation recoveries but for message deliveries. The event of suing for defamation is by itself a proclamation of innocence to the public. It is also a warning to other reporters. Using lawsuits as a publicity stunt may stand on a dubious footing ethically. Still, such filings occasionally have a deterrence effect—even the most zealous reporters do not relish the prospect of being sued and having to explain the lawsuit to every future employer. As a result, lawsuits, as well as the threats of litigation against reckless media, can be necessary tools for lawyers who recognize that reputation can be as important as a client's legal rights.

Speak to the Reporter's Boss

If reporters persist in unjustified attacks on a client, there may be a limited opportunity for an informal appeal to their editors or news directors, as long as there is enough time before a news deadline. Requests for such meetings should be highly selective and not a generalized gripe session, so that they will be seen as rare indignation rather than chronic complaining. Usually, only provable mistakes in the facts or clear failures to consider contrary information are worth raising. Most stories cannot be killed in their entirety, and the best hope is usually for a more balanced story that avoids glaring falsities. When getting stonewalled by the newsroom, grievances concerning over-the-top stories can also be directed to senior management, the ownership, and even the news organization's counsel.

Taking Your Marbles away and Quitting the Game

Perhaps the least effective strategy in damage control is to threaten to stop speaking to an organization's reporters if they persist with brutal coverage. The desire to never speak again to a news abuser is understandable, but it rarely helps. A reporter may surface on the phone someday concerning a different news story for a different client. Only clients with exceptional importance to the media—police agencies and professional sports teams seem to have juice—create real problems for reporters. For instance, if a courthouse reporter faces retaliation from the district attorney for embarrassing prosecutors, the cutoff in access to a key news source could even require the reassignment of the reporter to a different news desk. In general, threats are neither advisable nor necessary. Of course, reporters already know that positive stories promote cooperation, just as they know that negative stories can leave some news sources frozen like the tundra.

Clients who spend major advertising dollars could threaten to punish newspapers and television stations by refusing to buy ads from those media when they publish or broadcast offending stories; however, while this is a potentially serious and occasionally effective defense tactic, it too is uncool and could pose problems. As with the joys of being sued, no rational news director enjoys the prospect of angering one of the Sales Department's biggest customers. When aggressive business-people menace the media where it really counts, harmful media coverage is occasionally reduced. Plainly, though, attorneys should not go near these heavy-handed tactics. Threatening to pull ads from a television station or newspaper is hardly a proper or ethical function of lawyers, and apart from serious professionalism concerns, any lawyer who issues such threats can expect reporters to retaliate some day.

Bad News Bears

Bad press can become a self-fulfilling prophecy. In the early stages of an investigation before the targets of an investigation are fully defined, it is crucial to keep hot water from boiling over into scathing publicity. When possible, defense lawyers should steer the media toward a more tantalizing subject, and occasionally their focus may veer away from the client. A case based on the law of nature illustrates the strategy. A bear abruptly appeared in a meadow and began to charge at two hunters. The first hunter began running. Standing flatfooted, the second hunter told the first that trying to outrun the faster and more powerful bear was a complete exercise in futility. The first hunter yelled back to the second that it was not necessary to outrun the bear—the only need was to outrun the second hunter.

Be careful, though, about going to a seemingly friendly reporter to plant a news story about an adversary. Surprises may grow from such plantings since news sources (especially self-serving lawyers) do not control the direction of news. Once a case kicks into high gear, reporters doing their job will hear the adversary's version of the facts—a version detailing all the reasons why your own client is the real culprit. More than a few investigations (by police as well as by media) were initially launched in one direction but then boomeranged back to the original complainant.

Life beyond Trial

While winning at trial is paramount, defendants care deeply about the attitudes of their professional and personal constituency. When there is a happy ending to a case, good press along the way contributes to a more complete vindication of the falsely accused than does a perception of a lucky defendant who beat the rap.

No matter how well the media messages are spun, though, the vast majority of criminal cases result in guilty verdicts. In federal prosecutions, 97 percent or more of indictments ultimately lead to either a guilty plea or a jury conviction on at least one of the charges. With state cases, the conviction rates vary but still range from 80 to 90 percent. As far as the press is concerned, once found guilty, continued denials compound the original crime with a succession of lies that would "insult the intelligence" of a Michael Corleone and most everyone else.

In recent years, the formula for cushioning the enormous disaster of guilt focuses on remorse, repair, and attempted rehabilitation. To be effective, remorse generally requires an unqualified acceptance of guilt for the crimes that have been proven. Also to be included are deep expressions of shame, apology to all the injured parties, and a stated willingness to take personal responsibility for all the consequences.

Although remorse often follows a largely predictable script when guilty pleas are entered, it becomes difficult, almost impossible, for a defendant to seek forgiveness for crimes in cases that are going to be appealed. Inevitably, defendants who seek to appeal their convictions will fail to exhibit remorse, much less acceptance of responsibility. They are, after all, continuing to maintain their innocence. This complicates the scenario at sentencing, often the final chapter for the court of public opinion, which counts on tearful apologies to begin the road back to redemption. Since nothing can be admitted when appealing the verdict, the sentencing strategy is limited to words about the defendant's past good deeds as well as sympathy for the victims with words that sidestep any complicity. At Martha Stewart's sentencing, neither apologies nor tears were offered, and instead, she pursued an appeal. By choosing to serve her prison sentence while the appeal was being taken, however, she accepted the court's punishment even if she never accepted her own guilt.

Martha Stewart is the most spectacular example of losing at trial but winning enough public support to keep a career alive and thriving. Even for the less rich and famous, getting convicted against a backdrop of positive press allows the remaining supporters (sometimes only a spouse and family dog) to argue that the conviction was the product of the flaws in the legal system ("political motivation," a "setup," or "sweetheart deals with the lying witnesses") rather than the flawed character of the defendant ("he was actually guilty as sin").

Apart from the human importance of promoting more favorable reactions within one's personal universe of family and friends are the economic consequences with respect to future livelihood. News coverage that is sympathetic can create attitudes that are empathetic and see a conviction as an isolated, even overblown, mistake in an otherwise honorable life. There is usually life after trial for convicted defendants, and once the prison sentence is completed, a difficult but critical chapter of that life is still to be written.

PART TWO

SPINNING LESSONS FOR THE INTERNET

Forget about Newspapers and Television—It's the Internet, Stupid

Robert Morvillo and Charles Stillman began their legal careers in the 1960s, when it was decidedly uncool for lawyers to consort with reporters. Back then, lawyers "were raised to believe that's not the way we do things," as Stillman notes. But he adds, "It's not the world we live in today."[12] Morvillo and other veterans similarly acknowledge that attitudes toward pretrial publicity have markedly changed.[13] So too have the power sources that energize publicity.

Alongside Morvillo's courtroom defense of Martha Stewart was a pioneering use of a Web site for her public defense. Morvillo gives credit for the innovation to her media strategists, and he viewed the Web site as a great asset. In addition to posting defense pleadings, press statements, and fan mail, the Web site included "the few positive pieces" written in newspapers about the most famous defendant in the post-Enron prosecution wave.

MarthaTalks.com

It may not have been the first defendant's Web site. Others, such as the late Michael Jackson, made modest use of a defense Web site to present a personal letter to the public and some press releases. But Stewart's pioneering site launched a full-fledged media campaign. By the time of her trial, more than 6 million visitors had seen its tasteful green-and-light-blue color scheme.[14] Loaded with supportive letters and selected e-mails from the over eighty thousand sent to the site, it also included photos of the defendant for Martha fans.[15]

As Stewart described it, the Internet was her means to "stay in direct touch with her public." Launched immediately after her indictment, Stewart fired back with an electronic appeal to the public through an open letter saying, "I want you to know that I am innocent—and I will fight to clear my name."[16] In its first day, the site received a million hits. Best of all were friendly e-mails soon posted to the site, such as "somebody's grandstanding and using you to get their name with the press."[17] The site occasionally included statements from her lawyers, who criticized "frequent errors" in media coverage.[18] They answered the indictment with a statement saying, "Even though insider trading was the subject of the criminal investigation she supposedly obstructed, the insider-trading charge is included only in the civil complaint."[19] It also included Stewart's court pleadings.

Most experts praised the strategy, including LA's mega strategist Elliot Mintz. Some even suggested it should have been used sooner.[20] Lawyers know, however, that prior to an indictment, it is never wise to tug on Superman's cape or otherwise annoy prosecutors with press strategies—at least as long as there is any hope for a nonindictment.

Throughout the proceedings, press reports about the site were almost universally positive, some describing it as "brilliant," even as some diagnosed its none-too-subtle ulterior motives. On the eve of the trial, the *Wall Street Journal* described it as "stylish" (would one expect anything less?) and reported that experts deemed it "remarkably thorough." The *Wall Street Journal* further explained, "Image consultants say the site is an attempt to hold on to supporters believing she was being targeted as a woman."[21]

It also provided a way to initiate a media offensive without being too offensive. One strategist described the analysis as searching for a "middle ground" between hiding in the background and being too upfront and visible. As another expert for the *Wall Street Journal* noted, "The Internet gives you the freedom to talk right to your audience without filtered interpretation."

YouTube: Going Public with No Questions Asked

With state and federal investigators searching his offices and home, Dr. Conrad Murray's role as the doctor for the late Michael Jackson brought him vastly more blame than acclaim. Numerous reports identified him as a target of criminal inquiries into whether his treatment of Jackson with high-powered sedations caused the death of the King of Pop. Although Dr. Murray generated vast amounts of media interest, he was much too endangered legally to be answering a reporter's questions. As a result, he appeared publicly—with no questions asked—by posting a video statement on YouTube. The statement said little, but a testimonial that cannot be cross-examined assures that there is little risk of making things worse than they already are. In addition to thanking friends for their support, he assured them that, "I have done all I could do, I have told the truth, and I have faith the truth will prevail."[22] Such a statement is better than no comment at all, according to LA media guru Mintz, and is the best strategy available under obviously difficult circumstances.

Naturally, some skeptics posted several rebuttals on YouTube. One posting featured a spoof by a speaker posing as Dr. Murray who essentially fessed up and whined about going to prison. Still, by last count, the real doctor's own video had five times more traffic than all the imposters combined. For a target wearing a bull's eye on his back, those numbers may be better news than a spike in the Dow Jones Industrial Average. Most assuredly, his innovative use of YouTube to provide a presence and a voice to an otherwise faceless and notorious target of a criminal investigation will not be the last.

Making the News—Having It Your Way

In California, some people who are in the news are creating their own news. Relying on their own Web sites to communicate to the public, they are hiring ex-reporters to write the articles. The Los Angeles Kings as well as the Consumer Attorneys of California, a trial lawyers association, say the articles they post on Web sites will offer journalistic merit rather than self-serving press releases.[23] Although the Web site writers insist that they are not doing public relations, some skeptics may conclude that you don't have to have a six-shooter to become a hired gun.

E-Contamination

Like Robert Morvillo, fellow New Yorker Charles Stillman embraces the need for change, recognizing the pervasive role of the Internet, but he worries about its reach, as Google and Wikipedia penetrate jury deliberations: "The opportunity for taint is so great compared to what it was with television and newspapers."[24]

Even prior to trial, legal blogs chat about ongoing cases, sometimes never aiming at the truth. In fact, some strategists hire bloggers to bombard a small but focused audience with e-shilling for one side of a controversy. The few, the anonymous, and the bloggers represent only a fraction of the reaction but a majority of Internet content. Internet messages do not die, and, unlike old soldiers, they do not even fade away. Years after a case is closed, the ill tidings can remain in the ocean of news to be found by a Google search.

When opposing bloggers invade a case, the client often feels besieged. Even when the legal proceedings are going well, "clients can get the impression they're losing," Stillman cautions.[25] Like the general public, the legal profession, especially twenty- and thirty-something lawyers, are increasingly reliant on electronically induced information. Unverified information is all too commonplace because, as Mark Geragos notes, "no sources are needed for the blogosphere."[26]

Some shudder at the thought. I do. When my daughter, Meredith, attended the University of Pennsylvania, she and several classmates were delighted to learn that rock star Elvis Costello was a Penn alum. Problem is, he is not. Another one of their classmates had mischievously created a Wikipedia entry for Costello indicating that Penn was his alma mater. The misinformation was quickly corrected by that student. And Wikipedia has since moved toward quality-control measures to improve the accuracy of its articles. But while the Internet may be fair game for low-stakes humor, it can also generate unfair games in high-stakes cases.

There are much worse things than bothersome buzz on the legal grapevine or college pranks. The fact of jury contamination is one of them. Although research studies have not fully analyzed the issue, the anecdotes are troubling and substantiate Stillman's concerns. In the supersized trial of Scott Peterson, the judge dismissed a juror, Frances Gorman, because she had done her own research.[27] In fact, Gorman had gone fishing on the Internet to explore a perceived discrepancy in the testimony regarding a Web site that Peterson had visited.[28] The defense had argued he had visited a fishing Web site to determine currents in the San Francisco Bay *before* Amber Frey's best friend confronted him about being married. The prosecution asserted he had checked it afterward—suggesting evidence of premeditation.[29] Although Gorman was dismissed, it is increasingly clear that others are conducting their own surreptitious e-research using many unsubstantiated and irrelevant sources.

In a complex federal conspiracy case involving the allegedly illegal sale of prescription drugs, after eight weeks of trial a juror admitted to the federal judge that he had undertaken his own investigation of the case using Internet tools such Google and Wikipedia. When the judge questioned other jurors, it turned out that eight more admitted to doing cyber research on the case. The judge properly declared a mistrial.[30] What the judge could not declare, though, is a guarantee that nosy jurors in the next trial would not be nosing around the Internet.

Other reports about this form of juror misconduct show that the virus is becoming highly contagious. Typically, the problem is juror research:

- Gallingly, a Philadelphia juror sent a note to the judge to complain that he was learning more about the case from the Internet than from counsel for the parties.[31]
- A juror in Florida looked up the definition of *prudent* on his iPhone, a clear violation of the law providing that only judges may define legal terms for juries.[32]
- A Tulsa juror investigated the information from a party's expert witness in a civil case and found contrary reports.[33]
- A juror in South Dakota Googled the defendant and passed along that the defendant had never been sued before to five other jurors.[34]
- In Bartow, Florida, a juror investigated the defendant online, pulled up his "rap sheet," and informed the other jurors in the case.[35]
- In a Riverside, California, murder trial, two jurors were dismissed after searching the Internet for information on the death penalty and bringing the research into the deliberations.[36]
- In a Maryland trial of a homeless man's murder, a mistrial was declared after a juror looked up the word *lividity* on Wikipedia.[37]
- In the trial of the taser-induced death of a Kentucky man, the jury foreman researched the case on the taser manufacturer's Web site and used that information to convince other jurors that tasers are "nonlethal" and cannot cause fatal injuries.[38]

At other times, jurors are engaged in e-chatter about the ongoing trial:

- In a Philadelphia public-corruption case, jurors were posting trial updates on Twitter and Facebook.[39]
- In San Diego, jurors admitted they were reading about their fraud trial on a local legal blog.[40]
- A juror in New York City sent a friend request to a witness during deliberations.[41]
- In a Maryland trial involving the alleged corruption of Baltimore's first female mayor, jurors friended each other on Facebook despite the judge's instructions not to communicate with each other outside the jury room.[42]

- In an Arkansas case, a juror in a $12.6 million judgment sent Twitter messages during the trial such as, "Oh and nobody buy Stoam [company]. It's bad mojo and they'll probably cease to exist, now that their wallet is 12m lighter," and, "So Johnathan, what did you do today? Oh nothing really, I just gave away TWELVE MILLION DOLLARS of somebody else's money."[43]

Some episodes result in new trials while others do not. In confronting this perplexing new retrofit of an age-old problem, the courts are still struggling to find consistent responses to the e-taint that creeps into jury deliberations.

The Web of Lawyers

If wayward jurors are the Curious Georges of Internet contamination, the Look Who's Talking characters spouting one-sided e-propaganda are sometimes the lawyers themselves. Increasingly, attorneys use Web sites to tout their ongoing accounts of ongoing cases. At least lawyers hawking their positions on their own Web sites are not hiding anything. A California defense lawyer, without disclosing who hired him, blogged about the trial concerning the financial collapse of San Diego's Peregrine Systems.[44] And he, at least, was not an unidentified blogging missile. Others prefer to fire from the shadows by using anonymous bloggers to attack the adversary. Needless to say, secret cyber snipers are resented, but recourse is limited. To date, bar associations have not written rules that specifically address Internet-bashing of a client. The existing rules amount to general prohibitions concerning public dissemination of statements where there is a "substantial likelihood" that they will interfere with a fair trial or otherwise prejudice the due administration of justice.[45] Although a useful guidance for scrupulous lawyers, this is not a sharp sword against misbehavior.

Whatever may be the prohibitions, the overriding concern is that, like the rest of us, most jurors are Internet junkies who will be unable to resist Google and Wikipedia during a trial. The irresistible Internet creates grave concerns that the right to a fair trial based only on the evidence inside the courtroom will suffer serious but invisible damage.

The usual measures to control traditional forms of publicity—careful questions from lawyers during jury selection and strong warnings from judges throughout the trial—will help some in treating this increasingly usual problem. But for cases that demand more, some will consider combating jury poisoning with some cyber medicine of their own.

Cyber Strategies for Search Engines

Most of us are addicted to Internet search engines, and most addicts traffic in Google. Currently, Google has captured between 65 percent and 70 percent of Internet users, compared to the 17 percent who use Yahoo! and the 9 percent who use Bing.[46] Often turning to Google, Internet-savvy jurors with inquiring minds may want to know more. Unless they are sequestered without computers or handheld devices, they enjoy instant access to research about a defendant, a lawyer, a judge, or almost any issue that could arise in a trial.

Defendants and other litigants can do little to affect the newspaper story, much less the headline or the placement of the article. The Internet, though, has given birth to a cottage industry of tech companies that specialize in Search Engine Optimization (SEO). Normally, SEO companies provide a marketing function by utilizing tactics to elevate a client's Web site to a higher ranking. If, for example, a local company wants to be seen by Internet searchers, they want to appear, if possible, on the first page of Google and other search engines, as close to the top as possible. In promoting a business, appearing way at the end of a search is an e-bummer. Many millions of dollars are spent by companies who strategize with SEO marketers to brainstorm their way up the ladder of a search engine's ranking so that a distant, essentially invisible, position on page ten is replaced by a listing on page one. For defendants in ugly lawsuits or defendants facing never-pretty criminal charges, however, an elevated ranking is the last thing they desire. In fact, if publicity-battered litigants could get Google and Yahoo! to banish their names from the Internet entirely, they would, no doubt, be thrilled to do so.

No such erasure, though, is possible. Instead, what SEO companies can provide is a strategy and a campaign for improving the first few pages of search engine results by trying to boost favorable or neutral items ahead of the unkind ones. The naysayers will never go away, but hopefully they can be pushed from the front door to the back of the room.

Visible Technologies, based in Seattle, Washington, is one such company. It was founded a few years ago when a hugely successful entrepreneur, Don Gatno, delivered a speech in the Philippines and was surprised to learn that the introductory remarks cobbled from his Google searches omitted many of his career highlights. Apparently other content had risen ahead of the many favorable pieces about him in Google's ranking. As he inquired further into the marketing and technology dynamics behind those rankings, he became intrigued with the possibility for improving a client's search engine results. Such strategies not only could provide a marketing edge—the conventional role of SEO strategies—but also could do damage control concerning adverse publicity. Since reputation is everything for most successful people, and since today's reputation is increasingly defined by the Internet, SEO strategies can be as vital to repairing a tattered image as they are to boosting a new product.

Rebecca Bilbao, a seasoned SEO consultant and former Visible Technologies team leader, explains that the first step in improving Internet health is doing a thorough check-up.[47] Upon examining the existing search results, an assessment is made of positive content so that these pieces can be pushed up to higher positions in order to effectively push down the ranking of the unfriendly pieces. Once the basic diagnosis is completed, a strategy is developed to use links to other sites to move up as many neutral or favorable pieces as possible. In some instances, SEO companies like Visible Technologies help build Web sites to create items that will rank higher in a client's search engine results. Moreover, a client's existing or additional Web sites can be linked to other Internet sources.

By all accounts, Google, Yahoo!, and other search engines prioritize articles that are heavily linked to other legitimate Internet pieces. While links are emphasized by search engine optimizers, the actual algorithms used by the major search engines are not disclosed publicly. The formulas for rankings are a secret because so many Internet subjects are inevitably trying to improve their good news and push down the bad stuff. (By the way, do not bother having friends click on the favorable sites because hits do not determine placement.) While some trade secrets are a single set of unchanging ingredients, the search engines change their algorithms regularly in order to stay ahead of the experts who are constantly studying the systems in order to manipulate them for better rankings. Coca-Cola's recipe would be easier to find.

In the middle of September 2009, the first five pages of Martha Stewart's Google search contained no articles about her arrest, conviction, and prison sentence. This was a remarkable achievement, considering the thousands of negative pieces that accumulated from 2002 through 2004. No doubt her own marketing strategies contributed to the rise of the trouble-free pages. When other bad news arrived about her company's stock price, though, by the beginning of October, Stewart's first page suddenly included one of the old stories about the lying and obstruction charges. Bilbao notes that, "The court of public opinion is never completely out of session online."[48]

Search engine optimizers may or may not be an optimal use of a client's finite resources for litigation. Superstar lawyers like Richard Sprague recognize the jury problems created by bloggers and Google searches but are not inclined to develop strategies for Google placement or counterblogging to neutralize Internet hostility. For Sprague, a lawyer's job is winning inside the courtroom.[49] While there are disquieting concerns about the Internet, and some thoughtful advocates believe in aggressive Internet strategies, all agree that the surest way to winning in the court of public opinion is winning in the court of law.

AFTERWORD

In virtually every court case that appears on the media's radar, lawyers are attempting to spin reporters, control the message, and win the verdict of public opinion. With today's vast universe of cable television stations, Internet broadcasts, Web sites, and blogs, an ever-increasing number of cases receive media attention in one form or another. No one knows exactly to what extent a victory outside the courthouse translates to a favorable verdict inside the courtroom, but as I have described, it is too important to be left to chance.

By examining celebrated trials from antiquity through colonial times to the early twentieth century and right up to the sensational tabloid-and-Internet-driven trials of present times, we have seen that the impulse to spin the law and influence the court of public opinion is nothing new. It helped convict Socrates, acquit Aaron Burr, and condemn Richard Hauptmann. It may have enabled O.J. Simpson to get away with murder, but it also helped convict Scott Peterson of the same charge. It sent Elian Gonzalez back to his father in communist Cuba, and it played a vital role in determining that George W. Bush, not Albert Gore Jr., won the 2000 US presidential election. All that has changed since ancient times is the magnitude of the thing, the size of the bullhorn.

The present legal framework juxtaposes two constitutional rights in frequent conflict, rights held equally dear by the American people: the right to a fair and speedy trial, and the freedom of the press. The Founding Fathers could not foresee the Internet or the twenty-four-hour cable television news cycle, two of the most powerful forces driving the spin in today's celebrated legal cases. But they did live in an era of vigorous, often viciously partisan journalism. Newspapers and pamphleteers reported not only news but also rumors and gossip and known falsehoods, with the intention of arousing the public and influencing the course of everything from government policy and patronage to the outcomes of legal cases. In their astonishing foresight and wisdom, the Founding Fathers comprehended the balance needed between the competing demands of justice and free speech, and they wrote that balance into the fundamental document of the American nation—the Constitution.

As we saw, the Supreme Court has consistently ruled in favor of open trials and the freedom of the press to cover them. One of the sometimes-forgotten principles of the framers of the Constitution is the imperfectability of institutions run by fallible human beings. But the Founding Fathers also believed that institutions can be improved, if not perfected, and that openness is a crucial tool in the pursuit of that improvement. Openness, the Supreme Court has said, "guards against the miscarriage of justice by subjecting the police, prosecutors, and judicial proceedings to extensive public scrutiny and criticism."[1] Such openness also helps educate the public about the legal system—a function of great importance. As Justice William Brennan emphasized, access will "contribute to public understanding of the rule of law and to comprehension of the function of the entire criminal justice system."[2]

That is the spirit in which I have written this book. Like most lawyers, I have taken the world as I find it and have tried to practice my profession within the limits of its rules and realities, both written and unwritten. In this book I have tried to present this world accurately as it pertains to the interplay between lawyers and the legal system on the one hand, and reporters, the media, and the public on the other. That interplay was examined through treatment of high-profile cases from Socrates and the Lindbergh kidnapping trial to modern marvels of spin such as the cases of O.J. Simpson, Martha Stewart, Scott Peterson, Michael Jackson, and Kobe Bryant. The examination also included politically charged cases ranging from the international custody fight over Elian Gonzalez and the 2000 presidential recount to the indictment of ex–Illinois Governor Rod Blagojevich.

I have sought not to criticize our institutions but to describe them as working as best as they can. Since graduating from law school in 1978, I have pursued a career that has given me a privileged view of many sides of the legal system, from law clerk to private law practice, to US Attorney, to private lawyer again. I have served as counsel in cases of intense public interest and media scrutiny, and I have sat in television studios, both as an interview subject and as an independent commentator, on hundreds of occasions. These experiences have helped me better understand the interlocked dance between the legal system and the media.

Perhaps in a perfect world defense attorneys would restrict themselves to presenting evidence exonerating their clients in a courtroom, while prosecutors, with the enormous power of the state behind them, would refrain altogether from speaking to the press and to the public. The media would report the facts only as they emerged in testimony or could be discovered by the most upright standards of investigative reporting, with careful fact-checking and double sourcing of every tidbit of testimony. Spin would not exist in the legal system. Lawyers would have no need to resort to public-relations consultants, publicity stunts, or press conferences.

We do not live in a perfect world. Instead, we live in the world I have attempted to describe in the preceding chapters. It is a world in which lawyers, litigants, and media alike relentlessly pursue their own interests, and where the public hungers for the details of the famous and their trials. In large part, it is the job of lawyers to seek every advantage, which sometimes drives them to the often shifting borders of permissible conduct. Still, our system is based on an adversarial principle, and it is the defense lawyer's obligation to present his client's case as compellingly as possible.

For journalists, every high-profile case creates a potential for more viewers and readers, and greater market share and profits, all of which pushes some (certainly not all!) reporters and commentators to relax the standards of objective journalism. Dramatically compounding the already-daunting issues of mainstream media are the dizzying new challenges of Internet-driven coverage that can be created by anyone who can type on a keyboard.

In a free society, extending access and understanding to the public about constitutionally protected processes is the way to deal with these issues. The best course is for everyone on all sides to understand as fully as possible not only the way things are supposed to work but also the way they really work—while vigorously upholding the strictures and the values of the Constitution.

NOTES

INTRODUCTION

1. Complaint, Case no. 09-059301 (Broward Cir. Ct. November 2, 2009).

2. Jon Burstein, "Lawyer Returns as Uproar Grows," *Sun Sentinel*, November 4, 2009, http://articles.sun-sentinel.com/2009-11-04/news/0911030436 _1_law-firm-s-partners-law-office-fort-lauderdale-executive-airport (accessed January 11, 2010).

3. *Miami Herald*, "Surprise from Rothstein's Scheme Unlikely," November 4, 2009.

4. *Miami Herald*, "Office Showcase of a High Roller," November 6, 2009.

5. Ibid.

6. *Sun Sentinel*, "Life in the Fast and Secret Lane," November 6, 2009.

7. *Daily Business Review*, "Inner Sanctum a Display of Power, Secrecy," November 6, 2009.

8. *Miami Herald*, "Rothstein Partner Denies Carrying $6M," December 8, 2009.

9. *Miami Herald*, "Rothstein Changing His Plea to Guilty," January 6, 2010.

CHAPTER 1: DEAD MAN VOTING AND THE ABC'S OF LAW SPIN

1. Mark Sell, "Inside Miami: A Letter," *New England Review* 18, no. 1 (1997): 23.

2. *New York Times*, "National News Briefs: Two Arrested in Inquiry into Miami Election," November 13, 1997, http://www.nytimes.com/1997/11/13/us/national-news-briefs-2-arrested-in-inquiry-into-miami-election.html (accessed January 11, 2010).

3. Karen Branch and Manny Garcia, "Absentee Ballots Favor Suarez, Not Carollo," *Miami Herald*, November 6, 1997.

4. *State ex rel. Whitley v. Rinchart*, 140 Fla. 645m 192 So. 819, 823 (1939).

5. *St. Petersburg Times*, "Former Hialeah Mayor Defeats Bitter Rival," December 7, 1994.

6. David Lyons, "Passionate Pleas End Vote Trial: Carollo, Suarez Lawyers Present Final Arguments," *Miami Herald*, February 26, 1998.

7. Joseph Tanfani and Andres Viglucci, "Dozens of Votes Questionable in City Absentee Ballots Cast from Homes Linked to Commissioner's Aides," *Miami Herald*, December 9, 1997.

8. Andres Viglucci and John Lantigua, "Cashing in on Helping the Elderly Retired Caseworker Got Clients' Votes," *Miami Herald*, January 4, 1998.

9. *Miami Herald*, "Dubious Tactics Secured Votes for Suarez, Hernandez," February 8, 1998.

10. David Lyons and Gail Epstein, "Sergeant, Wife Refuse to Testify in Vote Case. Pair Tells Lawyer: We'll Take the Fifth," *Miami Herald*, February 11, 1998.

11. *Miami Herald*, "It's a Crime, but Felons Vote, Too," February 15, 1998.

12. *Miami Herald*, "One Hundred Convicted Felons in Miami Election," February 15, 1998.

13. Joseph Tanfani, Karen Branch, and Manny Garcia, "Coach, 34, Charged in Vote Scheme: Ballots Bought in Miami Mayor's Race," *Miami Herald*, February 21, 1998.

14. David Lyons, "Mayor's Attorney Faces Daunting Task as Case Resumes Today," *Miami Herald*, February 17, 1998.

15. Lyons, "Passionate Pleas End Vote Trial."

16. In re the Matter of the Protest of Election Returns and Absentee Ballots in the November 4, 1997, Election of the City of Miami, Florida, 707 So. 2d 1170 (Fla. 3rd DCA 1998).

17. Mireya Navarro, "Fraud Ruling Invalidates Miami Mayoral Election," *New York Times*, March 5, 1998, http://www.nytimes.com/1998/03/05/us/fraud-ruling-invalidates-miami-mayoral-election.html (accessed October 26, 2009).

18. David Lyons and Maria Morales, "Carollo Back as Miami Mayor, Saurez Says He'll Keep on Fighting," *Miami Herald*, March 12, 1998.

19. *Miami Herald*, "Citing Massive Fraud, Judge Voids Vote, Orders New City Election in Sixty Days," March 5, 1998.

20. *Miami Herald*, "Who's the Mayor of Miami?" March 5, 1998.

21. *Tallahassee Democrat*, "Mayor of Miami Is Anybody's Guess," March 5, 1998.

22. *Miami Herald*, "Investors Skittish on Miami," March 8, 1998.

23. *Miami Herald*, "City's Political Crisis Could Upset Economy," March 8, 1998.

24. Lyons and Morales, "Carollo Back as Miami Mayor."

25. Elaine de Valle and Ana Acle, "Carollo's Return as Mayor Stuns Miami," *Miami Herald*, March 12, 1998.

CHAPTER 2: SPINNING CASES THROUGH THE AGES

1. Xenophon, "Memoribilia," in *The Works of Xenophon*, 4 vols., trans. H. G. Dakyins (London: Macmillan, 1897), 3:1.

2. Ibid.

3. Douglas O. Linder, "The Trial of Socrates," University of Missouri at Kansas City School of Law, 2002, http:www.law.umkc.edu/faculty/projects/ftrials/Socrates/Socrates.htm (accessed October 12, 2009).

4. Ibid.

5. William Stearns Davis, *A Day in Old Athens: A Picture of Athenian Life* (New York: Allyn and Bacon, 1914), p. 139.

6. Linder, "Trial of Socrates."

7. Ibid.

8. I. F. Stone, *The Trial of Socrates* (New York: Anchor Books, 1989).

9. I. F. Stone, "I. F. Stone Breaks the Socrates Story: An Old Muckraker Sheds Fresh Light on the 2,500-Year-Old Mystery and Reveals Some Athenian Political Realities That Plato Did His Best to Hide," *New York Times Magazine*, April 8, 1979, http://www.law.umkc.edu/faculty/projects/ftrials/socrates/ifstoneInterviewed.html (accessed January 11, 2010), p. 23.

10. Ibid., p. 34.

11. Stone, "I. F. Stone Breaks the Socrates Story," p. SM6.

12. Stone, "I. F. Stone Breaks the Socrates Story," p. 26.

13. Kelly DeVries, *Joan of Arc: A Military Leader* (Gloucestershire: Sutton Publishing, 1999), pp. 27–28.

14. Ibid., pp. 15–19.

15. Stephen W. Richey, *Joan of Arc: The Warrior Saint* (Westport, CT: Praeger-Greenwood, 2003), pp. 2–3.

16. Stephen W. Richey, "Joan of Arc: A Military Appreciation," St. Joan of Arc Center, 2000, http://www.stjoan-center.com/ (accessed September 29, 2009).

17. M. G. A. Vale, *Charles VII* (Berkeley: University of California Press, 1974), p. 55.

18. Richey, *Joan of Arc: A Military Appreciation.*

19. Ibid.

20. Regine Pernoud and Marie-Veronique Clin, *Joan of Arc: Her Story*, trans. Jeremy Duquesnay Adams (New York: St. Martin's Griffin, 1999), p. 108.

21. Ibid., pp. 100–101.

22. Ibid.

23. Mark Twain, *Personal Recollections of Joan of Arc* (San Francisco: Ignatius, 1989), p. 23.

24. Pernoud and Clin, *Joan of Arc: Her Story*, p. 112.

25. Ibid.

26. Deborah A. Fraioli, *Joan of Arc: The Early Debate* (Suffolk: Boydell, 2000), p. 131.

27. DeVries, *Joan of Arc: A Military Leader*, pp. 179–80.

28. Jrank.org, "Levi Weeks Trial 1800—The Two-Day Trial," http://law.jrank.org/pages/2400/Levi-Weeks-Trial-1800-Two-Day-Trial .html (accessed November 2, 2009).

29. Doris Lane, "The Original 'Dream Team,'" *Crime Magazine: An Encyclopedia of Crime*, http://www.crimemagazine.com/wellmurd.htm (accessed November 2, 2009).

30. John D. Lawson, *American State Trials: Sixteen Fifty-Nine to Nineteen-Twenty* (Lanham: Rowman and Littlefield, 1972), 1:1.

31. Ibid.

32. Lane, "Original 'Dream Team.'"

33. Lawson, *American State Trials*, 1:2

34. Ibid.

35. Ibid.

36. Ibid., 1:2–3.

37. Ibid.

38. Jrank.org, "Levi Weeks Trial 1800."

39. Lane, "Original 'Dream Team.'"

40. Ibid.

41. PBS, "Alexander Hamilton and Aaron Burr's Duel," People & Events, http://www.pbs.org/wgbh/amex/duel/peopleevents/pande17.html (accessed October 29, 2009).

42. Douglas O. Linder, "The Treason Trial of Aaron Burr," University of Missouri at Kansas City School of Law, 2007, http://www.law.umkc.edu/ faculty/projects/ftrials/burr/burraccount.html (accessed October 28, 2009).

43. Ibid.

44. Matthew Gottlieb, "Aaron Burr's Conspiracy," History Channel Club, http://www.thehistorychannelclub.com/Projects/Project.aspx?id=1192 (accessed October 28, 2009).

45. Gordon S. Wood, *Empire of Liberty: A History of the Early Republic, 1789–1815* (New York: Oxford University Press, 2009), p. 384.

46. Linder, "Treason Trial of Aaron Burr."

47. Profiles of US Presidents, "Thomas Jefferson—Conflict with Britain and the Burr Trial," http://www.presidentprofiles.com/Washington-Johnson/Thomas-Jefferson-Conflict-with-britain-and-the-burr-trial.html (accessed November 1, 2009).

48. Linder, "Treason Trial of Aaron Burr."

49. Ibid.

50. Ibid.

51. John Marshall, "*United States vs. Burr.* 25 Fed. Cas. 30, no. 14,692d C.C.D.Va. 1807," in *The Founders Constitution*, ed. Philip B. Kurland and Ralph Lerner (Chicago: University of Chicago Press), http://press-pubs.uchicago.edu/founders/documents/a2_1_1s19.html (accessed November 2, 2009).

52. Ibid.

53. Linder, "Treason Trial of Aaron Burr."

54. PBS, "Alexander Hamilton and Aaron Burr's Duel."

55. Federal Judicial Center, "Virginia Argus," December 4, 1807, http://www.fjc.gov/history/burr.nsf/autoframe?openForm&header=/history/burr.nsf/page/header&nav=/history/burr.nsf/page/nav_mediaandcontent=/history/burr.nsf/page/media_main (accessed November 2, 2009).

56. PBS, "Alexander Hamilton and Aaron Burr's Duel."

57. Linder, "Treason Trial of Aaron Burr."

58. Douglas O. Linder, "An Account of the Three Trials of Oscar Wilde," University of Missouri at Kansas City School of Law, http://www.law.umkc.edu/faculty/projects/ftrials/wilde/wildeaccount.html (accessed January 26, 2010).

59. Ibid.

60. Ibid.

61. Ibid.

62. Oscar Wilde, *De Profundis* (New York: Dover Publications, 1996), p. 26.

63. Linder, "Account of the Three Trials of Oscar Wilde."

64. Oscar Wilde, *The Complete Works of Oscar Wilde* (New York: Oxford University Press, 2005), p. 67.

65. "Testimony of Oscar Wilde in His Libel Trial," University of Mis-

souri at Kansas City School of Law, http://www.law.umkc.edu/faculty/projects/ftrials/wilde/Wildelibelowfact.html (accessed January 26, 2010).

66. Ibid.

67. Linder, "Account of the Three Trials of Oscar Wilde."

68. Ibid.

69. Ibid.

70. Wilde, *Complete Works*, p. 88.

71. "Sentencing Statement of Justice Wills," University of Missouri at Kansas City School of Law, http://www.law.umkc.edu/faculty/projects/ftrials/wilde/sentence.html (accessed January 26, 2010).

72. Douglas O. Linder, "The Trial of Richard 'Bruno' Hauptmann: An Account," University of Missouri at Kansas City School of Law, 2005, http://www.law.umkc.edu/faculty/projects/ftrials/Hauptmann/AccountHauptmann.html (accessed November 2, 2009).

73. Lloyd C. Gardner, *The Case That Never Dies: The Lindbergh Kidnapping* (Piscataway, NJ: Rutgers University Press, 2004), p. 26.

74. Ibid., p. 25.

75. AllExperts, "Lindbergh Kidnapping," http://en.allexperts.com/e/l/li/lindbergh_kidnapping.htm (accessed November 3, 2009).

76. US History Encyclopedia, "Lindbergh Kidnapping," http://www.answers.com/topic/lindbergh-kidnapping (accessed November 2, 2009).

77. Thomas French, ed., *FBI Files on the Lindbergh Baby Kidnapping* (The Woodlands, TX: New Century Books, 2001), p. 76.

78. Gardner, *Case That Never Dies*, p. 1.

79. Russell Aiuto, "The Lindbergh Kidnapping," TruTV Crime Library, http://www.trutv.com/library/crime/notorious_murders/famous/lindbergh/2b.html (accessed November 2, 2009).

80. All Academic Research, "Kidnap and Ransom Insurance: Micropractices of Security through Risk Embracing," http://www.allacademic.com/meta/p_mla_apa_research_citation/0/9/8/1/4/pages98146/p98146-6.php (accessed November 3, 2009).

81. Gardner, *Case That Never Dies*, p. 10.

82. US History Encyclopedia, "Lindbergh Kidnapping."

83. Jim Fisher, *The Lindbergh Case* (New Brunswick, NJ: Rutgers University Press, 1994), p. 27.

84. US History Encyclopedia, "Lindbergh Kidnapping."

85. *Time Magazine*, "Books: The Liar," review of *Spectacular Rogue: Gaston B. Means*, by Edwin P. Hoyt, July 19, 1963, http://www.time.com/time/magazine/article/0,9171,896919,00.html (accessed November 1, 2009).

86. US History Encyclopedia, "Lindbergh Kidnapping."

87. *Time Magazine*, "Crime: Never-To-Be-Forgotten," May 23, 1932, http://www.time.com/time/magazine/article/0,9171,743741,00.html (accessed November 1, 2009).

88. Ibid.

89. Federal Bureau of Investigation, "Famous Cases: The Lindbergh Kidnapping," www.fbi.gov/libref/historic/famcases/lindber/lindbernew.htm.

90. US History Encyclopedia, "Lindbergh Kidnapping."

91. Tony Russell, *Country Music Records: A Discography* (New York: Oxford University Press, 2004), p. 621.

92. Ibid.

93. Gregory Alghren and Stephen R. Monier, *Crime of the Century: The Lindbergh Kidnapping Hoax* (Boston: Branden Books, 1993), p. 120.

94. Linder, "Trial of Richard 'Bruno' Hauptmann."

95. *Hunterdon County Democrat*, "The Trial of the Century," http://www.nj.com/lindbergh/hunterdon/index.ssf?/lindbergh/stories/trial.html (accessed January 11, 2010).

96. Ibid.

97. Alfried Delahaye, "The Case of Bruno Hauptmann," in *The Press on Trial: Crimes and Trials as Media Events* (Westport, CT: Greenwood, 1997), p. 128.

98. Ronald P. Lovell, *Reporting Public Affairs: Problems and Solutions* (Prospect Heights, IL: Waveland, 1992), p. 224.

99. Delahaye, "Case of Bruno Hauptmann," p. 128.

100. Lovell, *Reporting Public Affairs*, p. 225.

101. Gardner, *Case That Never Dies*, p. 101.

102. Delahaye, "Case of Bruno Hauptmann," p. 127.

103. Ibid.

104. Lovell, *Reporting Public Affairs*, p. 226.

105. Ibid.

106. David T. Wilentz, "*State v. Hauptmann*: Summation of Mr. Wilentz for the Prosecution," University of Missouri at Kansas City School of Law, http://www.law.umkc.edu/faculty/projects/ftrials/Hauptmann/wilentzsumm.htm (accessed November 4, 2009).

107. Delahaye, "Case of Bruno Hauptmann," p. 124.

108. Leonard Mosley, *Lindbergh: A Biography* (New York: Doubleday, 1976), p. 192.

109. Gardner, *Case That Never Dies*, p. 401.

CHAPTER 3: THE O. J. REVOLUTION

1. *Entertainment Weekly*, "Encore: O. J. Simpson Runs," June 12, 1999.

2. Jeffrey Toobin, *The Run of His Life: The People v. O. J. Simpson* (New York: Random House, 1996), p. 106.

3. Douglas O. Linder, "The Trial of Orenthal James Simpson," University of Missouri at Kansas City School of Law, 2000, www.law.umkc.edu/faculty/projects/ftrials/ftrials.htm.

4. Thomas L. Jones, "The O. J. Simpson Murder Trial: Prologue," TruTV Crime Library: Notorious Murders, www.trutv.com/library/crime/notorious_murders/famous/simpson/index_1.html.

5. Linda Deutsch, "Famous Trials Force Society to Face Its Ills," *Daily Herald* (Chicago), December 28, 1999.

6. Jones, "O. J. Simpson Murder Trial: Prologue."

7. Gilbert Geis and Leigh B. Bienen, *Crimes of the Century: From Leopold and Loeb to O. J. Simpson* (Boston: Northeastern University Press, 1998), p. 186.

8. Jerrianne Hayslett, *Anatomy of a Trial: Public Loss, Lessons Learned from The People vs. O. J. Simpson* (St. Louis: University of Missouri Press, 2008), p. 25.

9. Toobin, *Run of His Life*, p. 229.

10. Geis and Bienen, *Crimes of the Century*, p. 182.

11. Vincent Bugliosi, *Outrage: The Five Reasons Why O. J. Simpson Got Away with Murder* (New York: Norton, 1996), p. 67.

12. Thomas L. Jones, "The O. J. Simpson Murder Trial: Bloody Sunday in Brentwood," TruTV Crime Library: Notorious Murders, http://www.trutv.com/library/crime/notorious_murders/famous/simpson/brentwood_2.html.

13. Toobin, *Run of His Life*, p. 31.

14. Bugliosi, *Outrage*, p. 31.

15. Toobin, *Run of His Life*, p. 49.

16. Ibid., p. 51.

17. Jones, "O. J. Simpson Murder Trial: Bloody Sunday in Brentwood."

18. Toobin, *Run of His Life*, p. 35.

19. Ibid., p. 52.

20. Geis and Bienen, *Crimes of the Century*, p. 172.

21. Bugliosi, *Outrage*, p. 328.

22. Jones, "O. J. Simpson Murder Trial: Bloody Sunday in Brentwood."

23. Toobin, *Run of His Life*, p. 21.

24. Geis and Bienen, *Crimes of the Century*, p. 177.

25. Toobin, *Run of His Life*, p. 35.

26. Bugliosi, *Outrage*, p. 354.

27. Alan M. Dershowitz, *Reasonable Doubts: The Criminal Justice System and the O. J. Simpson Case* (New York: Touchstone, 1997), p. 49.

28. Toobin, *Run of His Life*, p. 38.

29. Ibid., p. 59.

30. Geis and Bienen, *Crimes of the Century*, p. 174.

31. Bugliosi, *Outrage*, pp. 20–21.

32. Linder, "Trial of Orenthal James Simpson."

33. Geis and Bienen, *Crimes of the Century*, p. 174.

34. Bugliosi, *Outrage*, pp. 97–98.

35. Dershowitz, *Reasonable Doubts*, p. 27.

36. Toobin, *Run of His Life*, p. 172.

37. Geis and Bienen, *Crimes of the Century*, p. 188.

38. Toobin, *Run of His Life*, p. 181.

39. Ibid., p. 7.

40. Ibid., pp. 146–47.

41. Ibid., pp. 148–50.

42. Ibid.

43. Ibid., pp. 153–54.

44. Dershowitz, *Reasonable Doubts*, p. 21.

45. Ibid., p. 27.

46. *Jet Magazine*, "O. J. Simpson's Bizarre Saga in Ex-Wife's Murder Ends in Not Guilty Plea," July 4, 1994, p. 7.

47. Ibid.

48. Dershowitz, *Reasonable Doubts*, p. 27.

49. Ibid.

50. Toobin, *Run of His Life*, p. 113.

51. James Wolcott, "Murder, He Wrote (Sort Of)," *Vanity Fair*, January 22, 2007.

52. Toobin, *Run of His Life*, p. 115.

53. Jrank.org, "Marcia Rachel Clark," http://www.jrank.org/pages/5265/Clark-Marcia-Rachel.html.

54. Geis and Bienen, *Crimes of the Century*, p. 174.

55. Bugliosi, *Outrage*, p. 60.

56. Alan M. Dershowitz, interview with author, January 20, 2010.

57. Bugliosi, *Outrage*, p. 64.

58. Geis and Bienen, *Crimes of the Century*, p. 175.

59. Toobin, *Run of His Life*, pp. 118–19.

60. Bugliosi, *Outrage*, p. 64.

61. Dershowitz, *Reasonable Doubts*, p. 30.

62. Toobin, *Run of His Life*, p. 117.

63. Ibid., p. 141.

64. Ibid., p. 186.

65. Ibid., pp. 186–87.

66. Ibid., p. 213.

67. David Margolick, "Uneasy Quiet after Turmoil on the Team for Simpson," *New York Times*, January 17, 1995.

68. Toobin, *Run of His Life*, pp. 223–24.

69. Pat Morrison, "Jerrianne Hayslett: Trials and Errors," *Los Angeles Times*, October 3, 2009.

70. Charles Montaldo, "*Free Press vs. Free Trials*: Book Challenges Influence on Trial Verdicts," review of *Free Press vs. Fair Trials: Examining Publicity's Role in Trial Outcomes*, by Jon Bruschke, About.com: Crime/Punishment, http://crime.about.com/od/issues/a/blosu041226_2.htm.

71. Donna Petrozzello, "O.J. Doubles Ratings for News/Talk Stations," *Broadcast & Cable Magazine*, May 1, 1995, p. 33.

72. Toobin, *Run of His Life*, pp. 126–27.

73. Ibid., pp. 138–40.

74. Ibid., p. 201.

75. Ibid., p. 202.

76. Morrison, "Jerrianne Hayslett."

77. Jones, "O.J. Simpson Murder Trial: Prologue."

78. Geis and Biennen, *Crimes of the Century*, p. 180.

79. Toobin, *Run of His Life*, pp. 398–400.

80. Ibid., p. 400.

81. David Margolick, "Racial Epithets by Detective Fill Simpson Courtroom," *New York Times*, August 30, 1995, A14.

82. Toobin, *Run of His Life*, p. 407.

83. Bugliosi, *Outrage*, p. 43.

84. Ibid., p. 47.

85. Dershowitz, interview.

86. Geis and Bienen, *Crimes of the Century*, pp. 187–88.

87. Toobin, *Run of His Life*, p. 436.

88. Ibid., p. 431.

89. Hayslett, *Anatomy of a Trial*, p. 3.

CHAPTER 4: ELIAN GONZALEZ—THE BATTLE FOR THE CHILD AND FOR PUBLIC OPINION

1. Sue Plemming, "Cuban Boy Draws Picture of Shipwreck Drama," Fox News, March 27, 2000, http://www.cubanet.org/CNews/y00/mar00/27e4.htm (accessed October 26, 2009).

2. Diana Ray, "A Love Supreme," *Insight on the News*, February 14, 2000, http://findarticles.com/p/articles/mi_m1571/is_6_16/ai_59585370/ (accessed October 24, 2009).

3. *Guardian*, "Who's Who in the Elian Saga?" June 28, 2000, http://www.guardian.co.uk/world/2000/jun/28/usa.cuba1 (accessed October 28, 2009).

4. Brief of Appellant, *Gonzalez v. Reno*, 215 f.3d 1243 (11th Cir. 2000).

5. Ibid.

6. Ibid.

7. Ibid.

8. Plemming, "Cuban Boy Draws Picture."

9. Reuters, "Castro Vows Cuba Will Keep Up Pro-Elian Protests," *Guardian*, January 29, 2000, http://www.guardian.co.uk/world/2000/jun/28/usa.cuba1 (accessed October 27, 2009).

10. *Miami Herald*, "Rafters Helped Open Entry Door," August 22, 2004, http://www.latinamericanstudies.org/exile/entry-door.htm (accessed October 26, 2009).

11. Luve Clotilde, "New Cuban Exodus Stirs Up Old Tensions," July 27, 1999, *Christian Science Monitor*, http://www.cubanet.org/CNews/y99/jul99/27e6.htm (accessed October 25, 2009).

12. Ibid.

13. CNN.com, "What Should Be Done with Elian Gonzalez," January 8, 2000, http://transcripts.cnn.com/TRANSCRIPTS/0001/08/smn.05.html (accessed October 25, 2009); CNN.com, "Clinton Addresses Elian Gonzalez Situation," http://transcripts.cnn.com/TRANSCRIPTS/0004/22/bn.07.html (accessed October 25, 2009).

14. *Johns v. Department of Justice*, 635 F.2d 884 (5th Cir. 1981), appeal after remand, 635 F.2d 884 (5th Cir. 1981).

15. 8 U.S.C. § 1158(a).

16. CNN.com, "Federal Judge Rules Attorney General Should Decide Elian Gonzalez Asylum Matter," March 21, 2000.

17. David Bauder, "Elian Tells ABC He Wants to Stay," Associated Press, March 29, 2000, http://www.cubanet.org/CNews/y00/mar00/29e1.htm (accessed October 26, 2009).

18. Ibid.

19. *USA Today*, "Gore Split with Boss over Elian," March 31, 2000.

20. Associated Press, "Elian's Best Interest Reunion with His Dad while Awaiting Appeals," *Miami Herald*, April 7, 2000, http://nl.newsbank.com/nl-search/we/Archives?p_action=doc&p_docid=0EB72D8F36170D8A (accessed October 28, 2009).

21. *Washington Times*, "Elian, Relatives in Miami under Federal Deadline," April 3, 2000, http://www.highbeam.com/doc/1G1-61193771.html (April 3, 2000).

22. Corky Siesmaszko, "Elian's Dad Called Unfit W. House: No Basis to Charges," *New York Daily News*, April 3, 2000, http://www.nydailynews.com/archives/news/2000/04/03/2000-04-03_elian_s_dad_called_unfit_w__.html (accessed October 27, 2009).

23. *New York Times*, "Stand over Cuban Highlights a Virtual Secession of Miami," April 1, 2000, http://www.nytimes.com/2000/04/01/us/stand-over-cuban-highlights-a-virtual-secession-of-miami.html (accessed October 28, 2009).

24. Rick Bragg, "Their Fury in Check, Thousands Hold Peaceful Protest in Miami over Cuban Boy," *New York Times*, April 30, 2000, http://www.nytimes.com/2000/04/30/us/their-fury-in-check-thousands-hold-peaceful-protest-in-miami-over-cuban-boy.html?pagewanted=all (accessed October 28, 2009).

25. Laura Parker and Kevin Johnson, "Support Is Strong for Justice but Americans Frown on Tactics in Elian Raid," *USA Today*, March 2, 2000, http://www.cubanet.org/CNews/y00/may00/02e13.htm (accessed October 27, 2009).

26. *Miami Herald*, "Seized: Raid Returns Elian to Father; How It Happened, Lightning Move Took Agents Just 154 Seconds," April 23, 2000, http://nl.newsbank.com/nl-search/we/Archives?p_action=doc&p_docid=0EB72DAFC9CA8A01&p_docnum=2&s_dlid=DL0109102901363823043 (accessed October 28, 2009).

27. Stephen Hunter, "The Gun Seen Round the World," *Washington Post*, April 23, 2000, http://www.washingtonpost.com/wp-dyn/articles/A1898-2000Apr23.html (accessed October 27, 2009).

28. *Miami Herald*, "Seized."

29. Elian Saga, "Reno Says She Has 'No Regrets' over Raid," *Miami Herald*, April 24, 2000, http://www.cubanet.org/CNews/y00/apr00/24e2.htm (accessed October 26, 2009).

30. Ibid.

31. *Miami Herald*, "Elian Poll Signals Wake-up Call," April 23, 2000, http://nl.newsbank.com/nl-search/we/Archives?p_action=doc&p_docid =0EB72DAFC9CA8A01&p_docnum=2&s_dlid=DL0109102901363823043 (accessed October 28, 2009).

32. Felicity Barringer, "The Elian Gonzalez Case: The Hometown Newspaper; Newspaper in Sea of Outrage over Coverage of Elian Case," *New York Times*, April 24, 2000, http://www.nytimes.com/2000/04/24/us/elian -gonzalez-case-hometown-newspaper-newspaper-sea-outrage-over -coverage-elian.html (accessed October 27, 2009).

33. Karen Branch, "Cubans Move to Scrub Dems," *Miami Herald*, April 25, 2000.

34. Bragg, "Their Fury in Check."

35. *Gonzalez v. Reno*.

36. Ibid.

37. Brief of the lawyers' committee for human rights, the Women's Commission for Refugee Women and Children, in the Florida Immigrant Advocacy Center as *amici curiae*, in support of neither party, pp. 17, 18.

38. Ibid.

39. *Miami Herald*, "Elian's Critical Appeal—Case Affects Many Immigrant Children," May 11, 2001, 6B. Also, see note 37.

CHAPTER 5: POLITICAL LITIGATION AND CHANGING HISTORY— FROM HANGING CHADS TO MISSING E-VOTES

1. Richard Berke, "Bush Barely ahead of Gore in Florida as Recount Holds Key to Election," *New York Times*, November 9, 2000.

2. Ibid.

3. Kevin Sack, "The Forty-third President: After the Vote—A Special Report: In Desperate Florida Fight, Gore's Hard Strategic Calls," *New York Times*, December 15, 2000, 1A.

4. Ibid.

5. *Siegel v. LePore*, 120 F.Supp.2d 1041, 1045 (S.D.Fla.), aff'd, 234 F.3d 1163 (11th Cir. 2000).

6. Ibid.

7. *Siegel v. LePore*, 1049–50.

8. Ibid.

9. Ibid.

10. Ibid.

11. Berke, "Bush Barely ahead of Gore."

12. In re Matter of the Protest of Election Returns and Absentee Ballots in the November 4, 1997, Election for the City of Miami, 707 So.2d 1170 (Fla. 3d DCA 1997), rev. den., 725 So.2d 1108 (Fla. 1998).

13. Ibid.

14. CNN, "Newspaper: Butterfly Ballot Cost Gore White House," March 11, 2001, http://archives.cnn.com/2001/ALLPOLITICS/03/11/palmbeach.recount/index.html.

15. Sack, "Forty-third President: After the Vote—A Special Report: In Desperate Florida Fight, Gore's Hard Strategic Calls."

16. Jake Tapper, "Buchanan Camp: Bush Claims Are 'Nonsense,'" *Salon*, November 10, 2000, http://www.salon.com/news/politics/feature/2000/11/10/buchanan.

17. §102.168, Fla. Stat. (2000).

18. Berke, "Bush Barely ahead of Gore"; *Bush v. Palm Beach County Canvassing Board*, 531 U.S. 70 (2000).

19. *Siegel v. LePore*, 1045.

20. Ibid.

21. *Siegel v. LePore*.

22. Ibid., 1044.

23. *Siegle v. LePore*, 1051–52.

24. Ibid.

25. Berke, "Bush Barely ahead of Gore."

26. *Siegel v. LePore*, 1050.

27. *Touchton v. McDermott*, 120 F.Supp.2d 1055, aff'd, 234 F.3d 1133 (11th Cir. 2000), cert. den. 531 U.S. 1061 (2001).

28. Berke, "Bush Barely ahead of Gore."

29. Adam Nagourney and David Barstow, "Resisting the Recount: GOP's Depth Outdid Gore's Team in Florida," *New York Times*, December 22, 2000.

30. Caryn James, "The Forty-third President: The TV Coverage—Critic's Notebook: An Apocalyptic Attitude Gripped the TV Commentators, Not Their Viewers," *New York Times*, December 17, 2000.

31. Ibid.

32. Abner Greene, *Understanding the 2000 Election: A Guide to the Legal Battles That Decided the Presidency* (New York: New York University Press, 2001), p. 46.

33. Ibid.

34. Berke, "Bush Barely ahead of Gore."

35. American Presidency Project, "Text: Bush Spokeswoman Karen

Hughes," Documents Related to the 2000 Election Dispute, November 13, 2000, http://www.presidency.ucsb.edu/showflorida2000.php?fileid=hughes13.

36. Don van Natta Jr. and Dana Canedy, "The 2000 Elections: The Palm Beach Ballot; Florida Democrats Say Ballot's Design Hurt Gore," *New York Times*, November 9, 2000.

37. Todd S. Purdum and David Firestone, "Counting the Vote: The Overview: A Vote Deadline in Florida Is Set for Today," *New York Times*, November 14, 2000.

38. *McDermott v. Harris*, 2000 WL 1693713 (Fla. Cir. Ct. Leon Co.), rev'd by, 772 So.2d 1220 (Fla. 2000), vacated by 531 U.S. 70, on remand, 772 So.2d 1273 (Fla. 2000).

39. Greene, *Understanding the 2000 Election*, p. 43; Sack, "The Forty-third President: After the Vote—A Special Report: In Desperate Florida Fight, Gore's Hard Strategic Calls."

40. *Bush v. Hillsborough County Canvassing Board*, 123 F.Supp. 2d 1305 (N.D. Fla. 2000).

41. Berke, "Bush Barely ahead of Gore."

42. Greene, *Understanding the 2000 Election*, p. 43.

43. Ibid.

44. *Palm Beach County Canvassing Board v. Harris*, 772 So.2d 1220 (Fla. 2000).

45. *Siegel v. LePore*, 234 F.3d 1163 (11th Cir. 2000).

46. Nagourney and Barstow, "Resisting the Recount"; Purdum and Firestone, "Counting the Vote: The Overview: A Vote Deadline in Florida Is Set for Today."

47. *New York Times*, "Political Memo: Ferocious Fight to Woo Public," November 18, 2000.

48. Richard Berke, "Counting the Vote: The Overview: Republican Rejects Offer That Two Sides Accept a Count by Hand," *New York Times*, November 16, 2000.

49. CNN.com, "Bush Spokespeople Call Florida Counties Manual Counts 'Fundamentally Flawed,'" November 18, 2000.

50. *New York Times*, "Political Memo."

51. *Miami Herald*, "In Florida's Court, Justices Delay Final Result, Set Monday Hearing, Absentees Push Bush Lead to Seven Hundred Sixty," November 18, 2000, 1A.

52. Ibid.

53. Motion for the Preservation of Evidence, *Allen v. Canvassing Board of Miami-Dade County, et al.*, Case no. 00-30338 CA 13 (Miami-Dade Cir. Ct. 2000).

54. Order Denying without Prejudice Plaintiffs' Emergency Motion for Temporary Injunction, *Allen v. Canvassing Board of Miami-Dade, et al.*

55. *Gore v. Harris*, 772 So.2d 1243, 1258 (Fla. December 8, 2000), rev'd, 531 U.S. 98 (Fla. December 12, 2000), after remand, 773 So.2d 524 (Fla. December 22, 2000).

56. *McDermott v. Harris.*

57. Ibid.

58. Ibid.

59. *Palm Beach County Canvassing Board v. Harris*, 775 So.2d 1220 (Fla. November 21, 2000), cert. granted, 531 U.S. 1004 (November 24, 2000), vacated by *Bush v. Palm Beach County Canvassing Board*, 531 U.S. 70 (December 4, 2000).

60. *Miami Herald*, "In Florida's Court, Justices Delay Final Result."

61. Al Kamen, "Miami 'Riot' Squad: Where Are They Now?" *Washington Post*, January 24, 2005, http://www.washingtonpost.com/wp-dyn/articles/A31074-2005Jan23.html; John Lantigua "Miami's Rent-a-Riot," *Salon*, November 28, 2000, http://www.salon.com/news/politics/feature/2000/11/28/miami.

62. Ibid.

63. Lantigua, "Miami's Rent-a-Riot."

64. Ibid.

65. Ibid.

66. *Gore v. Harris*, 772 So.2d 1243 (Fla. December 8, 2000), rev'd and remanded, 531 U.S. 98 (U.S. December 12, 2000), after remand, 772 So.2d 12 (Fla. December 22, 2000).

67. Dexter Filkins and Dana Canedy, "Counting the Vote: Miami-Dade County; Protest Influenced Miami-Dade's Decision to Stop Recount," *New York Times*, November 24, 2000; *Miami-Dade Democratic Party v. Miami-Dade Canvassing Board*, response to Petition, Case no. 3D00-3318 (Fla. 3rd DCA November 22, 2000).

68. *Gore v. Harris.*

69. Frank Bruni, "Counting the Vote: The Governor Bush Claims Victory, Urging Gore to Bow Out," *New York Times*, November 27, 2000.

70. David Firestone, "Counting the Vote: Contesting an Election; Democrats Claim State Certified Wrong Total in Three Counties," *New York Times*, November 27, 2000.

71. Greene, *Understanding the 2000 Election*, p. 63.

72. Firestone, "Counting the Vote: Contesting an Election; Democrats Claim State Certified Wrong Total in Three Counties"; *Gore v. Bush.*

73. *Gore v. Harris*, 772 So.2d 1243 (Fla. December 8, 2000), rev'd in part, 531 U.S. 98 (December 12, 2000), after remand, 773 So.2d 524 (Fla. December 22, 2000).

74. *Gore v. Harris*.

75. *Bush v. Gore*, 531 U.S. 1046 (December 9, 2000).

76. *Bush v. Gore*, 531 U.S. 98 (December 12, 2000).

77. Will Weissert, "Elian Gonzalez Is Not Angry at Miami Relatives," Associated Press, July 1, 2010, http://www.msnbc.msn.com/id/38035742/ns/world_news-americas/; Richard Adams, "Elian Gonzalez, Ten Years On," *Guardian*, July 1, 2010, http://www.guardian.co.uk/world/richard-adams -blog/2010/jul/01/elian-gonzalez-cuba-ten-years-florida.

78. See U.S.C. art. I, sec. 5 ("Each House shall be the Judge of the Elections, Returns and Qualifications of its own Members"); *Morgan v. United States*, 801 F.2d 445, 447–50 (D.C. Cir. 1986) (Scalia, J.).

79. *Sarasota Herald Tribune Editorial*, "Voting Paper Trail: One Victory to Celebrate," May 14, 2007.

80. Associated Press, "Sidelined Congressional Hopeful Takes on Election Reform," June 14, 2007.

81. *Charlotte Sun/Venice Gondolier*, "Sometimes One Person Can Make a Difference," May 23, 2007.

CHAPTER 6: OPEN TRIALS—PRESS FREEDOM OR PRESS FREE-FOR-ALL?

1. *Irvin v. Dowd*, 366 U.S. 717 (1961).

2. *Richmond Newspapers, Inc. v. Virginia*, 448 U.S. 555, 565–67 (1980).

3. Susan D. Ross, *Deciding Communication Law: Key Cases in Context* (Mahwah, NJ: Lawrence Erlbaum Associates, 2004), p. 181n7.

4. *Sheppard v. Maxwell*, 384 U.S. 333 (1966).

5. *Richmond Newspapers, Inc. v. Virginia*, 448 U.S. 555, 572 (1980).

6. *Nebraska Press Association v. Stuart*, 427 U.S. 539, 587 (1976).

7. Robert Morvillo, interview with author, September 15, 2009.

8. Dennis J. Devine, "Jury Decision-making, Forty-five Years of Empirical Research on Deliberating Groups," *Psychology, Public Policy, and Law* 7 (September 2001): 622, 687–88. See also Christian Studebaker and Stephen Penrod, "Pretrial Publicity: The Media, the Law and Common Sense," *Psychology, Public Policy, and Law* 3 (1977): 428, 430–35.

9. Studebaker and Penrod, "Pretrial Publicity," p. 440.

10. Ibid.

11. Devine, "Jury Decision-making," pp. 667–68.

12. Robert Hardaway and Douglas B. Tumminello, "Pretrial Publicity in Criminal Cases of National Notoriety: Constructing a Remedy for the Remediless Wrong," *American University Law Review* 46 (October 1996): 39, 62n206.

13. *Murphy v. Florida*, 421 U.S. 794, 808 (1975) (Brennan, J. dissenting).

14. *Nebraska Press Association v. Stuart*, 427 U.S. 539, 551 (1976).

15. Ibid., 539.

16. Ibid.

17. Ibid., 539, 547.

18. *Sheppard v. Maxwell*, 384 U.S. 333 (1966).

19. Ibid., 333, 357–62.

20. *Murphy v. Florida*, 421 U.S. 794 (1975).

21. Ibid., 803.

22. *Nebraska Press Association v. Stuart*, 427 U.S. 539, 555 (1976).

23. *Irwin v. Dowd*, 366 U.S. 717, 722 (1961).

24. *Rideau v. Louisiana*, 373 U.S. 723 (1963).

25. *State v. Smart*, 136 N.H. 639, 649, 622 A.2d 1197, 1204 (N.H. 1993).

26. *People v. Manson*, 132 Cal. Rptr. 265, 312 (App. Superior Ct. 1976).

27. CNN.com, Transcripts for June 17, 2002, 10:00 p.m.

28. *Stroble v. California*, 343 U.S. 181, 195 (1952).

29. *State v. Atwood*, 171 Ariz. 576, 832 P.2d 593 (1992) *en banc*, disapproved on other grounds; *State v. Nordstrom*, 200 Ariz. 229, 25 P.3d 717 (2001).

30. Order, *United States v. Martha Stewart and Peter Bacanovic*, Case no. 03 Cr. 717 (MGC) (January 2, 2004).

31. CNN.com, "Gag Order Issued in Peterson Case: Another Judge Rules Arrest Warrants Can Be Released," June 17, 2003.

32. *Gentile v. State Bar of Nevada*, 501 U.S. 1030 (1991).

33. Ibid., 89–1836.

34. *United States v. Cutler*, 58 F.3d 825 (2d Cir. 1995).

35. Ibid.

36. Ibid.

37. Ibid.

38. *People v. Michael Joseph Jackson*, 128 Cal.App. 4th 1009, 1015–16, 27 Cal.Rptr. 3d, 596, 600 (Ct. App. 2d Dist. 2005).

39. John Gilbeaut, "Celebrity Justice," *ABA Journal* (January 2005), http://www.abajournal.com/magazine/article/celebrity_justice/ (accessed January 11, 2010).

40. Associated Press, "Prosecutor Calls Martha Stewart a Liar in Opening Statement," January 27, 2004.

41. Richard Sprague, telephone interview with author, September 28, 2009.

42. Ben Brafman, interview with author, August 25, 2009.

43. Robert Morvillo, interview with author, September 15, 2009.

44. Mark Geragos, interview with author, September 29, 2009.

45. Laurie L. Levenson, telephone interview with author, January 12, 2010.

46. Brafman, interview.

47. Charles Stillman, interview with author, September 14, 2009.

48. Morvillo, interview.

49. Ibid.

50. Ibid.

51. Roy Black, telephone interview with author, January 21, 2010.

52. Ibid.

53. Alan M. Dershowitz, interview with author, January 20, 2010. In making this suggestion, Professor Dershowitz notes that such criteria would be largely aspirational and may not be legally enforceable due to First Amendment concerns.

54. Morvillo, interview.

CHAPTER 7: DEFENSE LAWYERS—THE UNDERDOGS AND THEIR UPHILL STRATEGIES

1. Charles Stillman, interview with author, September 14, 2009; Robert Morvillo, interview with author, September 15, 2009.

2. Ibid.

3. Morvillo, interview.

4. Ibid.

5. Stillman, interview.

6. Morvillo, interview.

7. Roy Black, telephone interview with author, January 21, 2010.

8. Ibid.

9. Alan M. Dershowitz, interview with author, January 20, 2010.

10. Ben Brafman, interview with author, August 25, 2009.

11. Stillman, interview.

12. Black, interview.

13. Ibid.

14. Dershowitz, interview.

15. Brafman, interview.

16. *Miami Herald*, "Stallworth Tries to Move beyond Deadly Accident," July 31, 2010, p. ID.

17. *United States v. Tate*, 821 F.2d 1328 (8th Cir. 1987); *People v. Massie*, 66 Cal. 2d 899, 59 Cal. Rptr.733, 428 P.2d 869 (1967).

18. *Britt v. Embry*, 202 Fed. App. 774,782 (10th Cir. 2008) (radio interview); *Allen v. State*, 662 So.2d 323 (Fla. 1993).

19. Brafman, interview.

20. Ibid.

21. Stillman, interview.

22. Elliot Mintz, interview with author, September 29, 2009.

23. Mark Geragos, interview with author, September 29, 2009.

24. Stillman, interview.

25. Ibid.

26. Morvillo, interview.

27. Black, interview.

28. Dershowitz, interview.

29. Geragos, interview.

30. Richard Sprague, interview with author, September 28, 2009.

31. Geragos, interview.

32. John M. Broder, "Michael Jackson Is Booked on Molesting Charges That He Calls Lies," *New York Times*, November 21, 2003, 18A.

33. John M. Broder, "Jackson Is Formally Charged with Child Molesting," *New York Times*, December 19, 2003, 24A.

34. David Carr, "Persistent New Leaks Fuel Coverage of Jackson Case," *New York Times*, November 29, 2003, 9A.

35. Gary C. King, "Who Murdered Bonny Lee Bakley: Blake Arrested," Tru TV, http://www.trutv.com/library/crime/notorious_murders/family/bakley/20.html (accessed January 12, 2010).

36. CNN.com, "Blake behind Bars after Arrest in Wife's Slaying," April 20, 2002, http://archives.cnn.com/2002/US/04/19/robert.blake.case/index.html (accessed January 12, 2010).

37. *Los Angeles Times*, "Bryant, Wife and Lawyer Profess His Innocence in Statements," July 19, 2003, http://articles.latimes.com/2003/jul/19/sports/sp-excerpts19 (accessed January 12, 2010).

38. Black, interview.

39. Dershowitz, interview.

40. Ibid.

41. Geragos, interview.

42. Ibid.
43. Brafman, interview.
44. Ibid.
45. Ibid.

CHAPTER 8: THE CASE STUDIES—A "HUMAN MONSTER," A DOMESTIC DIVA, THE KING OF THE COURT, THE KING OF POP, AND GOVERNOR BLABBERMOUTH

1. Stacy Finz, "'Other Woman' Comes Forward," *San Francisco Chronicle*, January 25, 2003.
2. Ibid.
3. Henry K. Lee, "Judge Lets Peterson Team Hear Bugged Calls to Lawyer," *San Francisco Chronicle*, May 28, 2003.
4. Ibid.
5. Ibid.
6. *New York Times*, "Death Penalty Is Sought in Modesto Killings," April 27, 2003.
7. Stacy Finz, "Peterson's Lawyer Tees Off," *San Francisco Chronicle*, May 3, 2003.
8. Ibid.
9. Harriet Ryan, "'Why Did He?' to 'Did He?' in Twenty-eight Days," *Court TV News*, April 5, 2008.
10. Henry K. Lee, "Two Suspects Cleared in Modesto Case," *San Francisco Chronicle*, January 4, 2003.
11. Ibid.
12. Ibid.
13. Ibid.
14. Janine DeFao, "Modesto Home Burglarized as Man Hands Out Flyers to Find Wife," *San Francisco Chronicle*, January 21, 2003.
15. Ibid.
16. Stacy Finz and Kevin Fagan, "Peterson Investigation Likened to Voodoo," *San Francisco Chronicle*, May 6, 2003.
17. Stacy Finz, "Peterson Lawyer's Mystery Woman," *San Francisco Chronicle*, May 10, 2003.
18. Ibid.
19. Ibid.
20. Debra J. Saunders, "Now the Search for Laci's 'Real Killers,'" *San Francisco Chronicle*, June 1, 2003.

21. Ibid.

22. Ibid.

23. Suzanne Herel, "Peterson DA Wants Autopsies Released," *San Francisco Chronicle*, May 30, 2003.

24. Ibid.

25. Ibid.

26. *New York Times*, "National Briefing: West: California: New Judge for Peterson Trial," January 28, 2004.

27. Ibid.

28. Henry K. Lee, "Peterson Team Cites Progress," *San Francisco Chronicle*, June 4, 2003.

29. Ibid.

30. Ibid.

31. Ibid.

32. Ibid.

33. Ibid.

34. Ibid.

35. *People v. Peterson*, Case no. 1056770, Notice of Motion and Motion for New Trial, March 16, 2005.

36. DeFao, "Modesto Home Burglarized."

37. Henry K. Lee, "Peterson's Attorneys Accuse Prosecution of Hiding Tapes," *San Francisco Chronicle*, November 13, 2003.

38. *People v. Peterson*, Notice of Motion and Motion in Limine to Exclude Mitochondrial DNA Evidence, October 20, 2003.

39. Henry K. Lee, "Hair DNA Allowed in Peterson Case," *San Francisco Chronicle*, November 18, 2003.

40. Ibid.

41. *People v. Peterson*, Mitochondrial DNA Evidentiary Ruling, November 18, 2003.

42. Stacy Finz, "DA, Defense Both Want Peterson Evidence Sealed," *San Francisco Chronicle*, May 8, 2003.

43. Henry K. Lee, "Judge Issues Gag Order in Peterson Murder Case," *San Francisco Chronicle*, June 13, 2003.

44. Ibid.

45. Ibid.

46. *People v. Peterson*, Notice of Motion and Motion to Change Venue, January 8, 2004.

47. Lee, "Judge Issues Gag Order."

48. *New York Times*, "National Briefing: West: California: Peterson Trial Will Be Moved," January 9, 2004.

49. Dean E. Murphy, "Bay Area Communities Compete to Welcome a Murder Trial," *New York Times*, January 19, 2004.

50. Dean E. Murphy, "Judge Chooses San Mateo County as Site of Murder Trial," *New York Times*, January 21, 2004.

51. *New York Times*, "National Briefing: West: California: Bid to Move Trial," May 4, 2004.

52. *New York Times*, "National Briefing: West: California: Judge Refuses to Move Trial," May 12, 2004.

53. *New York Times*, "Six Men and Six Women to Serve as Jurors in Peterson Trial," May 28, 2004.

54. Brian Skoloff, telephone interview with author, January 20, 2010.

55. Elizabeth Ahlin, "Peterson Judge to Subpoena Videotape of Juror Remark," *New York Times*, June 20, 2004.

56. Ibid.

57. Ibid.

58. Elizabeth Ahlin, "National Briefing: West: California: Juror in Peterson Trial," *New York Times*, June 22, 2004.

59. Elizabeth Ahlin, "National Briefing: West: California: Peterson Juror Is Dismissed," *New York Times*, June 24, 2004.

60. Diana Walsh, Stacy Finz, et al., "Behind Closed Doors," *San Francisco Chronicle*, December 16, 2004.

61. Stacy Finz, "Experts Say State Botching the Case," *San Francisco Chronicle*, June 6, 2004, http://www.sfgate.com/cgi-bin/article.cgi?f=/c/a/2004/06/06/PETERSON.TMP (accessed January 18, 2010).

62. Dean E. Murphy, "Key Prosecution Witness Testifies in Peterson Trial," *New York Times*, August 11, 2004.

63. Ibid.

64. Ibid.

65. Ibid.

66. Ibid.

67. Ibid.

68. Diana Walsh, Stacy Finz, et al., "Jury Finds Peterson Murdered Wife, Unborn Son," *San Francisco Chronicle*, November 13, 2004.

69. Carolyn Marshall, "Peterson Defense Questions Prosecution's Star Witness," *New York Times*, August 24, 2004, A13.

70. Ibid.

71. Carolyn Marshall, "National Briefing: West: California: Peterson's Denial to Mistress," *New York Times*, August 25, 2004.

72. Walsh, Finz, et al., "Jury Finds Peterson Murdered Wife, Unborn Son."

73. Ibid.

74. Ibid.

75. *New York Times*, "Option for Jury in Peterson Case," October 30, 2004, http://www.nytimes.com/2004/10/30/national/30peterson.html.

76. Ibid.

77. Carolyn Marshall, "Peterson Judge Dismisses Juror for Misconduct," *New York Times*, November 10, 2004, http://www.nytimes.com/2004/11/10/national/10peterson.html.

78. Ibid.

79. Ibid.

80. Carolyn Marshall, "Judge Dismisses Foreman from Peterson Jury," *New York Times*, November 11, 2004, http://www.nytimes.com/2004/11/11/national/11peterson.html.

81. Ibid.

82. Carolyn Marhsall, "Jury Finds Scott Peterson Guilty of Wife's Murder," *New York Times*, November 13, 2004, http://www.nytimes.com/2004/11/13/national/13peterson.html.

83. Walsh, Finz, et al., "Behind Closed Doors."

84. Ibid.

85. Ibid.

86. Ibid.

87. Ibid.

88. Ibid.

89. Ibid.

90. Ibid.

91. Ibid.

92. Walsh, Finz, et al., "Jury Finds Peterson Murdered Wife, Unborn Son."

93. Ibid.

94. Ibid.

95. Ibid.

96. Ibid.

97. Skoloff, interview.

98. Ibid.

99. Tamara Loomis, "Business of Law: The Haunting," *Daily Business Review*, October 25, 2002.

100. Ibid.

101. FoxNews.com, "Prosecution Rests in Martha Stewart Trial," February 20, 2004.

102. Charles Gasparino and Jerry Markon, "Merrill Aide Will Plead Guilty, Cooperate on Martha Stewart," *Wall Street Journal*, September 26, 2002.

103. FoxNews.com, "Broker's Assistant to Provide Key Testimony against Martha Stewart," January 29, 2009, http://www.foxnews.com/story/ 0,2933,109772,00.html.

104. CNNMoney.com, "Setback for Martha Prosecutors," February 17, 2004, http://money.cnn.com/2004/02/17/news/companies/martha/?cnn =yes (accessed January 12, 2010).

105. Greg B. Smith, "Judge Sniffs at the Case vs. Martha," *New York Daily News*, October 9, 2003, http://www.nydailynews.com/archives/news/2003/ 10/09/2003-10-09_judge_sniffs_at_the_case_vs_.html (accessed January 12, 2010).

106. Associated Press, "Martha Stewart Convicted on All Four Counts," March 8, 2000.

107. *New York Magazine*, "Full-Court Press Martha Reporters Hand Over Chicken Salad—And Dish about the Outcome of the Trial," February 2004, http://www.nymag.com/.

108. Bootie Cosgrove-Mather, "Second Setback for Martha Prosecutors: Judge Says They May Not Speculate on Telephone Call Content," February 17, 2004, http://www.cbsnews.com/stories/2004/02/17/national/main 600809.shtml?tag=mncol;lst;1.

109. *United States v. Milikowsky*, 65 F.3d 4 (2d Cir. 1995).

110. Mindy Sink, "Pro Basketball; No Decision Made about Charges against Bryant," *New York Times*, July 8, 2003, http://www.nytimes.com/ 2003/07/08/sports/pro-basketball-no-decision-made-about-charges-against -bryant.html (accessed September 20, 2009).

111. *People v. Bryant*, Order re. Probable Cause Determination, 03 CR 204 (Co. Ct., Eagle Co., CO, October 20, 2003), http://www.courts.state.co.us/ Courts/County/Case_Details.cfm/Case_ID/20 (accessed September 21, 2009).

112. Ibid.

113. Ibid.

114. Ibid. See also *People v. Bryant*, Transcript of Defendant's Statement (Exhibit 81), 03 CR 204 (Co. Ct., Eagle Co., CO, April 26–28, 2003), http:// www.courts.state.co.us/Courts/County/Case_Details.cfm/Case_ID/20 (accessed September 21, 2009); *People v. Bryant*, "Transcript of Katelyn Faber's Interview with Detective Winters," http://www.thesmokinggun.com/ archive/1004041accusera2.html (accessed September 22, 2009).

115. *People v. Bryant*, Order re. Probable Cause Determination. See also

People v. Bryant, Transcript of Defendant's Statement (Exhibit 81); *People v. Bryant*, "Transcript of Katelyn Faber's Interview with Detective Winters."

116. *People v. Bryant*, Order re. Probable Cause Determination (internal quotation marks omitted).

117. Ibid.

118. Ibid.

119. Kirk Johnson, "In Kobe Bryant Case, Issues of Power, Not of Race," *New York Times*, August 27, 2004, http://www.nytimes.com/2004/08/27/us/in-kobe-bryant-case-issues-of-power-not-of-race.html (accessed September 21, 2009).

120. *People v. Bryant*, Order re. Probable Cause Determination.

121. *People v. Bryant*, Transcript of Defendant's Statement (Exhibit 81).

122. Ibid.

123. Ibid.

124. Ibid.

125. Ibid.

126. See also ibid.

127. *People v. Bryant*, Order re. Probable Cause Determination.

128. Richard I. Haddad, "Shield on Sieve? *People v. Bryant* and the Rape Shield Law in High-Profile Cases," *Columbia Journal of Law and Social Problems* 39 (2005): 185.

129. 29 Am.Jur. 2d Evidence § 511 (2010).

130. Miguel A. Mendez VII, "Relevance: Definition and Limitations—Confirming the California Evidence Code to Federal Rules of Evidence," *University of San Francisco Law Review* 42 (2007): 329; Federal Rules of Civil Procedure 412.

131. *F. Doe v. United States*, 666 F.2d 43 (4th Cir. 1981).

132. David A. Anderson, "Confidential Sources Reconsidered," *Florida Law Review* 61 (2009): 883; *Florida Star v. B.J.F*, 491 U.S. 524 (1989).

133. Daniel A. Murdock, "A Compelling State Interest: Constructing a Statutory Framework for Protecting the Identity of Rape Victims," *Alabama Law Review* 58 (2007): 1177; *Globe Newspaper Co. v. Superior Court for the County of Norfolk*, 457 U.S. 596, 102 S. Ct. 2613 (1982).

134. Tom Lininger, "Is It Wrong to Sue for Rape?" *Duke Law Journal* 57 (2008): 1557.

135. Ibid.

136. Wharton's Criminal Evidence § 9:19 (15th ed., IV. Motive); *United States v. Wilson*, 787 F.2d 375 (8th Cir. 1986); *United States v. Sanchez*, 44 M.J. 174 (U.S. Ct. of Appeals for Armed Forces, 1996); *United States v. Saipaia*, 24 M.J. 172 (U.S. Ct. of Military Appeals, 1987); McCormick on Evidence § 193 (5th ed.).

137. Howard Pankratz and Steve Lipsher, "Judge Orders Bryant Hearing Open: Accuser Need Not Appear, and Access to Her Medical Records Is Denied; Star Likely to Waive Proceeding," *Denver Post*, October 3, 2003.

138. Ibid.

139. Frank Litsky, "Outside Lawyers Question Bryant's Defense Strategy," *New York Times*, October 11, 2003.

140. Pankratz and Lipsher, "Judge Orders Bryant Hearing Open."

141. Ibid.

142. Ibid.

143. Ibid.

144. Ibid.

145. Ibid.

146. Ibid.

147. Charlie Brennan, "Drama in Courtroom: Bryant Lawyer's Line of Questioning Halts Preliminary Hearing," *Denver Rocky Mountain News*, October 10, 2003.

148. Charlie Brennan, "Officials Taped First Interview: Investigators Carried Concealed Recorder During July 1 Visit," *Denver Rocky Mountain News*, October 6, 2003.

149. Ibid.

150. Ibid.

151. Ibid.

152. Ibid.

153. Steve Lipsher and Howard Pankratz, "Judge Halts Bryant Hearing; Move Comes after NBA Star's Defense Raises Issue of Accuser's Sexual History," *Denver Post*, October 10, 2003.

154. Ibid.

155. Brennan, "Officials Taped First Interview."

156. Ibid.

157. Charlie Brennan, "Bryant Lawyer Kicks Up Ruckus; Attorneys Attack, Defend Mackey's Tactics in Hearing," *Denver Rocky Mountain News*, October 11, 2003.

158. Ibid.

159. Steve Lipsher, "Bryant's Lawyer's Tactics at Hearing Criticized," *Denver Post*, October 12, 2003.

160. Ibid.

161. Ibid.

162. Steve Lipsher, "*SNL* Mocks Attorney for Bryant," *Denver Post*, October 14, 2003, 5D.

163. Lipsher, "Bryant's Lawyer's Tactics at Hearing Criticized."

164. Howard Pankratz and Steve Lipsher, "Analysis: Who Has Advantage Isn't Clear," *Denver Post*, October 10, 2003.

165. Ibid.

166. Ibid.

167. Ibid.

168. Ibid.

169. Ibid.

170. Brennan, "Bryant Lawyer Kicks Up Ruckus."

171. Ibid.

172. Howard Pankratz, "Experts Say Bryant Defense Scores, Casting Doubt on Case Analysis: Trial Still Likely, but Bombshells Raise Questions about Decision to File," *Long Beach Press-Telegram*, October 16, 2003.

173. Karen Abbott, "Verdict Is in on Legal Teams; Experts Praise Defense but Criticize Prosecution for Apparent Gaps in Case," *Denver Rocky Mountain News*, October 16, 2003.

174. Ibid.

175. Ibid.

176. Mike Littwin, "Bryant Case May Set Back Victim's Rights," *Denver Rocky Mountain News*, October 16, 2003.

177. Peggy Lowe, "Bryant Attorney Called Bright, Personable, Zealous [...]," *Denver Rocky Mountain News*, October 17, 2003.

178. Littwin, "Bryant Case May Set Back Victim's Rights."

179. *People v. M.V.*, 742 P.2d 326, 329 (CO, 1987).

180. Howard Pankratz, "Experts: Case Riddled with Doubt; Unwinnable," *Denver Post*, October 16, 2003.

181. Ibid.

182. Charlie Brennan, "Bryant Will Go on Trial, Defense Gets Boost from Judge's Ruling Sending Case Ahead," *Denver Rocky Mountain News*, October 21, 2003.

183. Howard Pankratz and Steve Lipsher, "Judge Orders Bryant to Stand Trial; But Ruling Chides Prosecutors for Presenting This Evidence at Preliminary Hearing," *Denver Post*, October 21, 2003.

184. Editorial, "Defense Tainted Kobe Case," *Denver Post*, October 17, 2003.

185. Ibid.

186. Ibid.

187. *United States v. Richards*, 118 F.3d 622 (8th Cir. 1997); *Olesen v. Class*, 164 F.3d 1096 (8th Cir. 1999).

188. 20 A.L.R. 3D 684 (originally published 1968); *Chicago & N.W. Ry. Co. et al. v. McKenna*, 74 F.2d 155 (8th Cir. 1934); *State v. Reese*, 692 N.W. 2D 736 (S.Ct. Minn. 2005); *United States v. Falcon*, 245 F.Supp.2d 1239 (S.D. Fla. 2003); *United States v. Beasley*, 72 F.3d 1518 (11th Cir. 1996); *United States v. Partin*, 493 F.2d 750 (5th Cir. 1974).

189. *People v. Bryant*, Defendant's Motion to Admit Evidence of the Accuser's Purported Suicide Attempts and Prescribed Medication, 03 CR 204 (Co. Ct., Eagle Co., CO, October 20, 2003), http://www.courts.state.co.us/Courts/County/Case_Details.cfm/Case_ID/18 (accessed September 21, 2009).

190. Adam Liptak, "Papers Reveal New Details in Kobe Bryant Rape Case," *New York Times*, August 4, 2004, http://www.nytimes.com/2004/08/04/us/papers-reveal-new-details-in-kobe-bryant-rape-case.html (accessed September 21, 2009).

191. Ibid.

192. Ibid.

193. Kirk Johnson, "Burden in Bryant Case Rises for Judge and Accuser," *New York Times*, July 26, 2004, http://www.nytimes.com/2004/07/26/us/burden-in-bryant-case-rises-for-judge-and-accuser.html (accessed September 21, 2009).

194. *People v. Bryant*, Defendant's Motion to Admit Evidence of the Accuser's Purported Suicide Attempts and Prescribed Medication.

195. Johnson, "Burden in Bryant Case Rises."

196. Kirk Johnson, "The Bryant Trial: Anatomy of a Case That Fell Apart," *New York Times*, September 3, 2004, http://query.nytimes.com/gst/fullpage.html?res=9F0CE6D91331F930A3575AC0A9629C8B63 (accessed September 21, 2009).

197. Ibid.

198. *People v. Bryant*, Order re. Defendant's Motion to Admit Evidence Pursuant to C.R.S. § 18-3-407 and People's Motions in Limine #5 and #7, 03 CR 204 (Co.Ct., Eagle Co., CO, October 20, 2003), http://www.courts.state.co.us/Courts/County/Case_Details.cfm/Case_ID/20 (accessed September 21, 2009).

199. John Gibeaut, "Celebrity Judge: The Rich and Famous Get Star Treatment, Creating the Appearance of a Two-Tiered Court System," *ABA Journal*, January 25, 2005, http://www.abajournal.com/magazine/article/celebrity_justice/.

200. John M. Broder, "Michael Jackson Faces Arrest on Charges of Child Molesting," *New York Times*, November 20, 2003, http://www.nytimes.com/

2003/11/20/us/michael-jackson-faces-arrest-on-charges-of-child-molesting
.html (accessed September 28, 2009).

201. Ibid.

202. Ibid.

203. Ibid.

204. Editorial, "The Childhood of Michael Jackson," *New York Times*, November 22, 2003, http://www.nytimes.com/2003/11/22/opinion/the -childhood-of-michael-jackson.html (accessed September 28, 2009).

205. Ibid.

206. Broder, "Michael Jackson Faces Arrest."

207. Ibid.

208. Ibid.

209. Ibid.

210. Ibid.

211. John M. Broder, "No Charges for Jackson for a Week," *New York Times*, November 22, 2003, http://www.nytimes.com/2003/11/22/us/no -charges-for-jackson-for-a-week.html (accessed September 29, 2009).

212. Ibid.

213. Charlie LeDuff, "Official Memo on Jackson Casts Doubt on Charges," *New York Times*, December 10, 2003, http://www.nytimes.com/ 2003/12/10/us/official-memo-on-jackson-casts-doubt-on-charges.html (accessed September 27, 2009).

214. *New York Times*, "Jackson Acknowledges Settlements," September 4, 2004, http://www.nytimes.com/2004/09/04/national/04Jackson.html (accessed September 27, 2009).

215. Ibid.

216. Broder, "Michael Jackson Faces Arrest."

217. *New York Times*, "Jackson Provides DNA Sample to Deputies," December 6, 2004, http://www.nytimes.com/2004/12/06/national/06 jackson.html (accessed September 27, 2009).

218. Ibid.

219. Ibid.

220. *People v. Jackson*, California Criminal Case no. 1133603, Plaintiff's Motion for Admission of Defendant's Prior Sexual Offenses; Memorandum of Points and Authorities, December 10, 2005, http://www.sbscpublicaccess .org/ctdocs.php (accessed October 1, 2009).

221. Ibid.

222. Ibid.

223. Ibid.

224. See, for example, *People v. Acala*, 36 Cal.3d 604, 630-631 (Ca. 1984). The rule excluding evidence of criminal propensity is nearly three centuries old in the common law (1 Wigmore, Evidence [3d ed. 1940] § 194, pp. 646–47). Such evidence "is [deemed] objectionable, not because it has no appreciable probative value, but because it has too much." Inevitably, it tempts "the tribunal ... to give excessive weight to the vicious record of crime thus exhibited, and either to allow it to bear too strongly on the present charge, or to take the proof of it as justifying a condemnation irrespective of guilt of the present charge."

225. See, for example, F.R.E. 413, 414, 415; Cal. Evidence Code § 1108.

226. *People v. Falsetta*, 21 Cal.4th 903, 911 (Ca. 1999).

227. *People v. Jackson*, Opposition to District Attorney's Motion for Admission of Alleged Prior Offenses, January 4, 2005, http://www.sbscpublicaccess.org/ctdocs.php (accessed October 1, 2009); *People v. Jackson*, Supplemental Brief in Support of Opposition to District Attorney's Motion for Admission of Alleged Prior Offenses, March 25, 2005, http://www.sbscpublicaccess.org/ctdocs.php (accessed October 1, 2009).

228. Charlie LeDuff, "Son of Former Maid Testifies That Jackson Molested Him," *New York Times*, April 5, 2005, http://www.nytimes.com/2005/04/05/05jackson.html (accessed September 27, 2009).

229. Ibid.

230. *People v. Jackson*, Opposition to District Attorney's Motion for Admission of Alleged Prior Offenses, January 4, 2005, http://www.sbscpublicaccess.org/ctdocs.php (accessed October 1, 2009).

231. John M. Broder, "Judge in Jackson Trial Permits Sexually Explicit Evidence," January 29, 2005, http://www.nytimes.com/2005/1/29/national/29Jackson.html (accessed September 27, 2009).

232. Ibid.

233. Nick Madigan, "Jackson's Prints Identified on Sex Magazines," *New York Times*, March 26, 2005, http://www.nytimes.com/2005/03/26/26jackson.html (accessed September 27, 2009).

234. Broder, "Explicit Evidence."

235. *People v. Jackson*, Opening Statement of Thomas W. Sneddon Jr. (for the people), February 28, 2005, http://web.archive.org/web/20080227111416/http://www.mjj2005.com/transcripts/MJJCaseOpeningStatements1.pdf (accessed September 29, 2009).

236. Jonathan D. Glater, "Debating the Role of Celebrity in the System," *New York Times*, June 15, 2005, http://www.nytimes.com/2005/06/15/national/15celebrity.html (accessed September 30, 2009).

237. Ibid.

238. *Larry King Live,* "Michael Jackson's Attorney Speaks Out about Trial," June 14, 2005, http://transcripts.cnn.com/TRANSCRIPTS/0506/14/lkl.01.html (accessed September 28, 2009).

239. *People v. Jackson,* Opening Statement of Thomas W. Sneddon Jr.

240. *Larry King Live,* "Attorney Speaks Out."

241. John M. Broder, "Greed Drove Abuse Claims, Lawyer for Jackson Says," *New York Times,* March 2, 2005, http://www.nytimes.com/2005/02/03/national/02jackson.html (accessed September 27, 2009).

242. Ibid.

243. Ibid.

244. Ibid.

245. Nick Madigan, "Boy's Brother Links Jackson to Sex Acts," *New York Times,* March 8, 2005, http://www.nytimes.com/2005/03/08/national/08jackson.html (accessed September 27, 2009).

246. Nick Madigan and John M. Broder, "Trial Memo; Witnesses' Youth Tests Both Sides in the Jackson Case," *New York Times,* March 12, 2005, http://query.nytimes.com/gst/fullpage.html?res=9D01E7D8143CF931A25750C0A9639C8B63 (accessed September 27, 2009).

247. Ibid.

248. LeDuff, "Son of Former Maid Testifies."

249. Ibid.

250. Charlie LeDuff, "Jackson's Ex-Maid Testifies about Shared Beds and Baths," *New York Times,* April 6, 2005, http://www.nytimes.com/2005/04/06/national/06jackson.html (accessed September 27, 2009).

251. *New York Times,* "Witness Says He Watched as Jackson Molested a Boy," April 8, 2005, http://www.nytimes.com/2005/04/08/national/08jackson.html (accessed September 27, 2009).

252. John M. Broder, "Jackson's Accuser Acknowledges Denying Any Abuse," *New York Times,* March 15, 2008, http://www.nytimes.com/2005/03/15/national/15jackson.html (accessed September 27, 2009).

253. *Larry King Live,* "Attorney Speaks Out."

254. LeDuff, "Son of Former Maid Testifies."

255. Charlie LeDuff, "Duplicity, Greed and Dubious Characters Are on Parade at Jackson Trial," *New York Times,* April 9, 2005, http://www.nytimes.com/2005/04/09/national/09jackson.html (accessed September 27, 2009).

256. Ibid.

257. John M. Broder and Nick Madigan, "Michael Jackson Cleared after Fourteen-Week Child Molesting Trial," *New York Times,* June 14, 2005, http://www.nytimes.com/2005/06/14/national/14Jackson.html (accessed September 27, 2009).

258. Glater, "Debating the Role of Celebrity."

259. Broder and Madigan, "Michael Jackson Cleared."

260. Ibid.

261. Ibid.

262. *Larry King Live*, "Attorney Speaks Out."

263. Criminal Complaint, *United States v. Blagojevich and Harris*, U.S.D.C., Ill. Under Seal (December 7, 2008).

264. Ibid.

265. *Chicago Tribune*, "Illinois Governor Rod Blagojevich Arrested on Federal Charges," December 10, 2008.

266. CNN.com, "US Attorney: Blagojevich Has Taken Us to 'New Low,'" December 9, 2008.

267. Associated Press, "Extension Sought in Blagojevich Case," January 1, 2009.

268. CNN.com, "Blagojevich Indicted on Sixteen Federal Felony Charges," April 3, 2009.

269. US Department of Justice, "Press Release: Former Congressman Robert W. Ney Sentenced to Thirty Months in Prison for Corruption Crimes," January 19, 2007.

270. Ibid.

271. *New York Times*, "In Blagojevich Case, Is It a Crime, or Just Talk?" December 16, 2008.

272. *New York Times*," Blagojevich Denies Any Criminal Wrongdoing," December 20, 2008.

273. Peter Slevin and Kari Lydersen, "Blagojevich's Attorney Assails Proceedings; 'Zero' Evidence Supports Effort to Impeach Governor, He Tells Illinois House Panel," *Washington Post*, December 18, 2008, http://www.washingtonpost.com/.

274. MSNBC.com, "NYT: Portrait of Disgraced Blagojevich," December 10, 2008.

275. CNN.com, "Blagojevich Makes TV Rounds as Impeachment Trial Set to Begin," January 26, 2009.

276. KansasCity.com, "Who Skips an Impeachment Trial? TV Star Blagojevich," January 26, 2009.

277. *International Herald Tribune*, "As Trial Starts, Blagojevich Mounts Defense on TV," January 27, 2009.

278. ABC News, "Transcript Excerpts: Cynthia McFadden Interviews Governor Rod Blagojevich," January 29, 2009.

279. ABC News, "Full Transcript: Governor Rod Blagojevich Interview with Diane Sawyer," January 26, 2009.

280. Rod Blagojevich, "Rod Blagojevich," http://www.thepublicityagency.com/rod-blagojevich/rod-in-the-news.htm.

281. Laurie L. Levenson, telephone interview with author, January 12, 2010.

282. Alan M. Dershowitz, interview with author, January 20, 2010.

283. CNN.com, "Democrat: Blagojevich 'Called Our Bluff' on Senate Pick," January 7, 2009.

284. Natasha Korecki, Dave McKinney, and Sarah Ostman, "Blagojevich Defense Gives Theatrical Closing Argument," *Chicago Sun-Times*, July 28, 2010, http://www.suntimes.com/news/metro/blagojevich/2541330,CST-NWS-blago28.article.

285. Ibid.

286. *USA Today*, "Blagojevich Attorney: Government Didn't Prove Case," July 27, 2010, http://www.usatoday.com/news/nation/2010-07-27-blagojevich-trial_N.htm.

287. Korecki, McKinney, and Ostman, "Blagojevich Defense Gives Theatrical Closing Argument."

288. John Yang, Stephanie Himango, and Phil Rogers, "Bribery, Joan and Melissa Rivers, Pink Elephants in Blago Closing Arguments," NBC News: First Read, July 27, 2010, http://firstread.msnbc.msn.com/_news/2010/07/27/4762817-bribery-joan-and-melissa-rivers-pink-elephants-in-blago-closing-arguments.

289. Jeff Coen, John Chase, Bob Sector, Stacy St. Clair, and Kristen Mack, "Blagojevich on Trial: Updates from Federal Court—Guilty on One Count, Blago Vows to Fight On," *Chicago Tribune*, August 17, 2010.

290. *Today*, "Blagojevich Juror Speaks Out," MSNBC, August 18, 2010.

291. Coen et al., "Blagojevich on Trial."

CHAPTER 9: PROSECUTORS AND THE PRESS

1. Henry Sandwith Drinker, *Legal Ethics* (New York: Columbia University Press, 1953), pp. 23, 356, as quoted in *Gentile v. State Bar of Nevada*, 501 U.S. 1030, 111 S.Ct. 2720 (1991).

2. American Bar Association, "Model Rules of Professional Conduct," § 3.8(f) (2002).

3. Ibid.

4. 28 C. F. R. §50.2. Release of information by personnel of the Department of Justice relating to criminal and civil proceedings.

5. Alan M. Dershowitz, interview with author, January 20, 2010.

6. Laurie L. Levenson, telephone interview with author, January 12, 2010.

7. Ibid.

8. Laurie L. Levenson, "Prosecutorial Sound Bites: When Do They Cross the Line?" *Georgia Law Review* 44 (2010).

9. Chicago Breaking News Center, "Fitzgerald: 'New Low' in Illinois Politics," December 9, 2008, http://www.chicagobreakingnews.com/2008/12/us-attorney-fitzgerald-press-conference-blagojevich.html.

10. Dershowitz, interview; Levenson, interview.

11. Brian Skoloff, telephone interview with author, January 20, 2010.

12. Roy Black, telephone interview with author, January 21, 2010.

13. Charles Stillman, interview with author, September 14, 2009.

14. Dershowitz, interview.

15. Ibid.

16. Ibid.

17. Amanda Ripley, "The Case of the Dirty Bomber," *Time Magazine*, June 16, 2002, http://www.time.com/time/printout/0,8816,262917,00.html.

18. Ibid.

19. Ibid.

20. Ibid.

21. Ibid.

22. Ibid.

23. Ibid.

24. Ibid.

25. Ibid.

26. Ibid.

27. CNN.com, "Ashcroft Statement on Dirty Bomb Suspect," June 10, 2002, http://archives.cnn.com/2002/US/06/10/ashcroft.announcement.

28. Ibid.

29. John King, "DOJ Announcement of Padilla Arrest Criticized," CNN.com, June 12, 2002, http://archives.cnn.com/2002/ALLPOLITICS/06/12/white.house.ashcroft/index.html.

30. Ripley, "Case of the Dirty Bomber."

31. Ibid.

32. Richard Gid Powers, "The Enemy That Lurks in the Enemy Within," *New York Times*, June 16, 2002.

33. Neil A. Lewis, "Arise with New Information," *New York Times*, June 12, 2002.

34. Ibid.

35. Ibid.

36. Scott Horton, "Jose Padilla and the Unfinished Business of Justice," *Harper's Magazine*, August 19, 2007, http://www.harpers.org/archive/2007/ 08/hbc-90000925.

37. Ibid.

38. *United States v. Hassoun, et al.*, Case no. 08-10494-SS (appeal pending).

39. James Tyrangiel, "The Taliban Next Door," *Time Magazine*, December 9, 2001, http://www.time.com/time/nation/article/0,8599,187564,00 .html.

40. Mark Jackson, "Has Attorney General John Ashcroft, in Alleged Terrorism Cases, Violated Government Ethics Rules Governing Prosecutors' Comments about the Accused?" Findlaw.com, January 23, 2003, http:// writ.news.findlaw.com/commentary/20030130_jackson.html.

41. Tyrangiel, "Taliban Next Door"; *United States v. Lindh*, 212 F.Supp.2d 541, 546–47 (E.D.Va. 2002), see Affidavit in Support of a Criminal Complaint and an Arrest Warrant, January 15, 2002, http://www.justice.gov/ag/criminal compliant1.htm.

42. John Ashcroft, "John Walker Lindh Press Conference," DOJ Conference Center, January 15, 2002, http://www.usdoj.gov/archive/ag/speeches/ 2002/011502walkertranscript.htm.

43. Jackson, "Has Attorney General John Ashcroft."

44. Ashcroft, "John Walker Lindh Press Conference." See also ibid.

45. Jackson, "Has Attorney General John Ashcroft." See also *Aversa v. United States*, 99 F.3d 1200 (1996): "Although statements to the press may be an integral part of a prosecutor's job, and may serve a vital public function, that function is strictly limited by the prosecutor's overarching duty to do justice. Those who wield the power to make public statements about criminal cases must be guided solely by their sense of public responsibility for the attainment of justice. The public statements asserted to have been made in the course of Aversa's criminal case have been condemned as false, misleading, self-serving, unjust, and unprofessional by every court to look at them. We therefore refer the matter of Assistant United States Attorney Walsh's conduct to the Office of Professional Responsibility of the Department of Justice, and to the Professional Conduct Committee of the New Hampshire Supreme Court" (internal citations omitted).

46. *United States v. Lindh.*

47. Ibid.

48. Ibid.

49. Damien Cave, "Mistrial Is Declared for Six Men in Sears Tower

Terror Case," *New York Times*, April 17, 2008, http://www.nytimes .com/208/ 04/17/us/17terror.html.

50. Ibid.

51. Eric Umansky, "Department of Pre-Crime: Why Are Americans Being Locked Up for 'Un-American' Thoughts?" *Mother Jones*, February 29, 2008, http://www.motherjones.com/politics/2008/02/department-pre-crime.

52. Ibid.

53. Ibid.

54. Ibid.

55. Ibid.

56. Ibid.

57. Ibid.

58. Ibid.

59. Alberto Gonzales and John Pistole, "Transcript of Press Conference Announcing Florida Terrorism Indictments," Washington, DC, June 23, 2006, http://www.usdoj.gov/archive/ag/speeches/2006/ag_speech_0606231.html.

60. Ibid.

61. Ibid.

62. Ibid.

63. Ibid.

64. Indictment, *United States v. Batiste et al.*, Case no. 06-20373 (S.D. Fla.).

65. Alex Chadwick and Larry Abramson, "Seven Held in Miami for Domestic Terrorism Plot," NPR, June 23, 2006, http://www.npr.org/ templates/story/story.php?storyID=5506454.

66. Tony Karon, "The Miami Seven: How Serious Was the Threat?" *Time Magazine*, June 23, 2006, http://www.time.com/time/printout/0,8816 ,1207412,00.html.

67. Abby Goodnough, "Trial Starts for Men in Plot to Destroy Sears Tower," *New York Times*, October 3, 2007, http://www.nytimes.com/2007/ 10/03/us/nationalspecial3/03liberty.html.

68. Cave, "Mistrial Is Declared."

69. Ibid.

70. *Miami Herald*, "Two More Liberty City Terror Suspects Get Prison Terms," November 19, 2008.

71. William C. Rhoden, "The Elusive Vick Takes His Hardest Hit," *New York Times*, July 20, 2007, http://select.nytimes.com/2007/07/20/sports/ football/20rhoden.html.

72. *United States v. Peace et al.*, Indictment, July 17, 2007, http://assets .espn.go.com/media/pdf/070717/vick_indictment.pdf.

73. US Attorney's Office, Eastern District of Virginia, "Four Individuals Indicted in Virginia Dog Fighting Venture," July 17, 2007, http://www .justice.gov/usao/vae/Pressreleases/07-JulyPDFArchive/07/20070717peace _phillips_taylor_vicknr.html.

74. *United States v. Peace et al.*, Indictment.

75. Ibid.

76. Ibid.

77. Ibid.

78. Michael S. Schmidt, "Vick's Co-Defendant Agrees to Plea Deal," *New York Times*, July 31, 2007, http://www.nytimes.com/2007/07/31/sports/ football/31vick.html.

79. Michael S. Schmidt, "Two Co-Defendants Likely to Plead Guilty in Vick Case," *New York Times*, August 14, 2007, http://www.nytimes.com/2007/ 08/14/sports/football/14dogs.html.

80. Michael S. Schmidt, "Greatest Threat to Vick May Be Links to Gambling," *New York Times*, August 15, 2007, http://www.nytimes.com/2007/08/ 15/sports/football/15vick.html.

81. Ibid.

82. Ibid.

83. John M. Broder, "Michael Jackson Is Booked on Molesting Charges That He Calls Lies," *New York Times*, November 21, 2003.

84. Ibid.; see also KTVU.com, "Jackson Critical of Settlement Leak," June 17, 2004, http://www.ktvu.com/news/3431294/detail.html.

85. Nick Madigan, "Man Who Leads Prosecution Has Reputation for Tenacity," *New York Times*, November 21, 2003.

86. Ibid.

87. BBC News, "Tom Sneddon: Dogged Prosecutor," January 31, 2005, http://news.bbc.co.uk/2/hi/entertainment/4216779.stm (accessed January 12, 2010).

88. RedOrbit, "Jackson Urged to Surrender on Warrant," November 19, 2003, http://www.redorbit.com/news/general/24315/jackson_urged_to_surrender _on_warrant/index.html.

89. John M. Broder, "Jackson Is Formally Charged with Child Molesting," *New York Times*, December 19, 2003.

90. Ibid.

91. MSNBC.com, "Judge Rejects Request to Remove Jackson DA," November 4, 2004.

92. David Carr, "Persistent New Leaks Fuel Coverage of Jackson Case," *New York Times*, November 29, 2003.

93. Associated Press, "District Attorney Answers Most Frequently Asked Questions," *San Diego Union Tribune*, December 18, 2003.

94. Associated Press, "DA Announces Intention to File Jackson Charges," *USA Today*, December 16, 2003, http://www.usatoday.com/life/2003-12-16-jackson-charges_x.htm.

95. Public Relations Society of America, "Behind the Headlines of the Michael Jackson Case," http://media.prsa.org/article_display.cfm?article _id=87. These quotes were given to the PRSA, which was selling a fifty-dollar-per-head online seminar by Tellem about her experiences in the Jackson case.

96. Ibid.

97. *New York Times*, "911 Calls Lead the Police to Duke's Lacrosse Team," March 30, 2006, http://www.nytimes/com/2006/03/30/sports/30timeline .html.

98. Cave, "Mistrial Is Declared."

99. Viv Bernstein and Joe Drape, "Rape Allegation against Athletes Is Roiling Duke," *New York Times*, March 29, 2006, http://www.nytimes.com/2006/03/29/sports/29duke.html.

100. Ibid.

101. Peter J. Boyer, "Big Men on Campus," *New Yorker*, September 4, 2006, http://www.newyorker.com/archive/2006/09/04/060904fa_fact?printable =true.

102. Ibid.

103. Ibid.

104. Ibid.

105. Ibid.

106. Ibid.

107. Joe Drape, "Lawyers for Lacrosse Players Dispute Accusations," *New York Times*, March 31, 2006, http://www.nytimes.com/2006/03/31/sports/31 duke.html.

108. Duff Wilson, "Duke Case Could Turn on Players' DNA Tests," *New York Times*, April 10, 2006, http://www.nytimes.com/2006/04/10/spors/ 10duke.html.

109. Juliet Macur and Duff Wilson, "Duke Inquiry to Continue, and So Will a Campaign," *New York Times*, April 12, 2006, http://www.nytimes .com/2006/04/12/sports/12duke.html.

110. Ibid.

111. Ibid.

112. Ibid.

113. Ibid.

114. Juliet Macur, "Lawyers for Lacrosse Players at Duke Say They Expect Indictment in Rape Case," *New York Times*, April 13, 2006, http://www.nytimes.com/2006/04/13/sports/sportspecial1/13lacrosse.html.

115. Duff Wilson, "Lawyer Says Two Duke Lacrosse Players Are Indicted in Rape Case," *New York Times*, April 18, 2006, http://www.nytimes.com/2006/04/18/sports/18duke.html.

116. Duff Wilson and Juliet Macur, "Two Duke Athletes Charged with Rape and Kidnapping," *New York Times*, April 19, 2006, http://www.nytimes.com/2006/04/19/sports/sportsspecial/19duke.html.

117. Duff Wilson, "Duke Player Has Proof of Innocence, Lawyer Says," *New York Times*, April 20, 2006, http://www.nytimes.com/2006/04/20/sports/sportsspecial1/20duke.html.

118. Ibid.

119. William Yardley, "Prosecutor in Duke Case Wins Election," *New York Times*, May 3, 2006, http://www.nytimes.com/2006/05/03/us/03durham.html.

120. Ibid.

121. Ibid.

122. Associated Press, "Official in Duke Players' Case Admits Errors," *New York Times*, July 29, 2006, http://www.nytimes.com/2006/07/29/us/29duke.html.

123. Duff Wilson, "Duke Rape Case Shadows an Unusual Race," *New York Times*, November 1, 2006, http://query.nytimes.com/gst/fullpage.html?res=9502E2DF133FF932A35752C1A9609C8B63&sec=&spon=&&scp=1&sq=Duke%20Rape%20Case%20Shadows%20an%20Unusual%20Race%E2%80%9D,%20&st=cse.

124. David Barstow and Duff Wilson, "DNA Witness Jolted Dynamic of Duke Case," *New York Times*, December 24, 2006, http://www.nytimes.com/2006/12/24/us/24duke.html.

125. Ibid.

126. Ibid.

127. Ibid.

128. Ibid.

129. David Barstow and Duff Wilson, "Prosecutor in Duke Case Faces Ethics Complaint," *New York Times*, December 29, 2006, http://www.nytimes.com/2006/12/29/us/29nifong.html.

130. *North Carolina State Bar v. Nifong*, Findings of Fact and Conclusions of Law, June 16, 2007.

CHAPTER 10: POP LAW—LEGAL MYTHS AND THE MEDIA

1. Laura Mansnerus, "Experts Assert Case Can Be Pressed without Body," *New York Times*, December 17, 1998, http://www.nytimes.com/1998/12/17/nyregion/experts-assert-case-can-be-pressed-without-body.html (accessed September 13, 2009).

2. Ibid.

3. Ibid.

4. David Rohde and Julian E. Barnes, "Without a Body, Murder Case of Widow Relies on Circumstantial Evidence," *New York Times*, May 16, 2000, http://www.nytimes.com/2000/05/16/nyregion/without-a-body-murder-case-of-widow-relies-on-circumstantial-evidence.html (accessed September 14, 2009).

5. Mansnerus, "Experts Assert Case Can Be Pressed."

6. Rohde and Barnes, "Without a Body."

7. Ibid.

8. Julian E. Barnes, "Lack of Body Was No Barrier to Conviction, Jurors Say," *New York Times*, May 19, 2000, http://www.nytimes.com/2000/05/19/nyregion/lack-of-body-was-no-barrier-to-conviction-jurors-say.html (accessed September 14, 2009).

9. *People v. Kimes*, 37 A.D.3d 1, 831 N.Y.S.2d 1 (N.Y. App. Div. 2006).

10. Ibid.

11. Paul Zielbauer, "Moxley Murder Case Is a Circumstantial Challenge for Prosecutors," *New York Times*, February 7, 2000, http://www.nytimes.com/2000/02/07/nyregion/moxley-murder-case-is-a-circumstantial-challenge-for-prosecutors.html (accessed September 15, 2009).

12. Ibid.

13. David M. Herszenhorn, "Memo from Norwalk; The System Broke Down, but the Law Still Prevailed," *New York Times*, June 16, 2002, http://www.nytimes.com/2002/06/16/nyregion/memo-from-norwalk-the-system-broke-down-but-the-law-still-prevailed.html (accessed September 15, 2009).

14. Ibid.

15. Ibid.

16. Stephen Gillers, "The World; Upholding the Law as Pretrial Publicity Goes Global," *New York Times*, April 27, 2003, http://www.nytimes.com/2003/04/27/weekinreview/the-world-upholding-the-law-as-pretrial-publicity-goes-global.html (accessed September 16, 2009).

17. Dean E. Murphy, "For Lawyer, It's Michael Jackson on Line 1, Scott Peterson on Line 2," *New York Times*, November 23, 2003.

18. *New York Times*, "Six Men and Six Women to Serve as Jurors in Peterson Trial," May 28, 2004, http://www.nytimes.com/2004/05/28/us/6-men-and-6-women-to-serve-as-jurors-in-peterson-trial.html (accessed September 16, 2009).

19. Sharon Waxman, "The Trial Outside the Court; TV 'Experts' Have a Verdict in the Laci Peterson Case," *New York Times*, July 29, 2004, http://www.nytimes.com/2004/07/29/arts/the-trial-outside-the-court-tv-experts-have-a-verdict-in-the-laci-peterson-case.html (accessed September 15, 2009).

20. Carolyn Marshall, "Jury Finds Scott Peterson Guilty of Wife's Murder," *New York Times*, November 13, 2004, http://www.nytimes.com/2004/11/13/national/13peterson.html (accessed September 15, 2009).

21. In cases where the evidence is purely circumstantial, courts suggest that the jurors should not focus solely on the reasonable possibility of innocence. See *Holland v. United States*, 348 U.S. 121, 139–40 (1954), "The petitioners assail the refusal of the trial judge to instruct that where the government's evidence is circumstantial it must be such as to exclude every reasonable hypothesis other than that of guilt. There is some support for this type of instruction in the lower-court decisions, but the better rule is that where the jury is properly instructed on the standards for reasonable doubt, such an additional instruction on circumstantial evidence is confusing and incorrect" (citations omitted); *United States v. Russell*, 971 F.2d 1098, 1109 (4th Cir. 1992), "It is well settled that as long as a proper reasonable doubt instruction is given, a jury need not be instructed that circumstantial evidence must be so strong as to exclude every reasonable hypothesis other than guilt"; *United States v. Stone*, 748 F.2d 361, 363 (6th Cir. 1984), "It is not necessary that circumstantial evidence remove every reasonable hypothesis except that of guilt."

22. Instructions to the Jury and Swearing of the Deputies, "Transcript from Scott Peterson Trial," http://pwc-sii.com/CourtDocs/Transcripts/Jury-Nov3.htm (accessed September 14, 2009).

23. Marshall, "Jury Finds Scott Peterson Guilty of Wife's Murder."

24. Waxman, "Trial Outside the Court."

25. *New York Times*, "Six Men and Six Women."

26. *New York Times*, "National Briefing: West: California: Peterson Autopsy Sealed," June 7, 2003, http://www.nytimes.com/2003/06/07/us/national-briefing-west-california-peterson-autopsy-sealed.html (accessed September 15, 2009).

27. Charles Stillman, interview with author, September 14, 2009.

28. *New York Times*, "Pro Football; Marten Acquitted of Money Laun-

dering," August 27, 1999; *Sun-Sentinel*, "Ex-Dolphin Mark Duper Cleared of Drug Charges," March 16, 1995.

29. *New York Times*, "Tyson Gets Six-Year Prison Term for Rape Conviction in Indiana," March 27, 1992.

30. Roy Black, telephone interview with author, January 21, 2010.

31. Laurie L. Levenson, telephone interview with author, January 12, 2010.

32. *New York Times*, "Should John Hinckley Go Free?" November 16, 2003.

33. *Clark v. Arizona*, 548 U.S. 735 (2006).

34. *State v. Dixon*, 152 Ohio App.3d 760, N.E. 2d 349, 359 (Ct. App. 3d Dist. 2003).

35. *People v. Peterson*, 397 Ill. App.3d 1048, 1056, 923 N.E. 2d 890, 896–97 (Ct. App. 3 Dist. 2010).

36. *Johnson v. State*, 675 N.E. 2d 678, 683 (Ind. 1996).

37. *United States v. Antonelli*, 2006 WL 1049616, at 5 (N.D. Ill. 2006).

38. *McCloy v. Berghuis*, 2008 WL 5062895, at 18 (W.D. Mich. 2008).

39. *People v. McMillin*, 352 Ill. App. 3d 336, 344, 816 N.E. 2d 10, 18 (5th Dist. 2004).

40. *Gore v. State*, 719 So.2d 1197, 1201 (Fla. 1998).

41. *Henry v. Farmer City State Bank*, 808 F.2d 1228, 1238 (7th Cir. 1986), citing *Imbler v. Pachtman*, 424 U.S. 409, 431 (1976).

42. FoxNews.com, "O.J. Simpson Attorneys to Examine Co-Defendants' Legal Run-ins," October 16, 2007, www.foxnews.com/story/0,2933,302183,00 .html.

43. *New York Times*, "O.J. Simpson Faces Trial in Hotel Confrontation," November 14, 2007.

44. J. Spencer, *Introduction to European Criminal Procedure* (Cambridge: Cambridge University Press, 2004), 1:28.

45. *United States v. Singleton*, 144 F.3d 1343 (10th Cir. 1998).

46. Ibid., vacated en banc, 165 F.3d 1297 (10th Cir. 1997), cert. den., 527 U.S. 1024 (1999).

47. 144 F.3d, 1360.

48. *Santobello v. New York*, 404 U.S. 257, 260 (1971), recognizing the value of properly administered plea bargaining "and observing, if every criminal charge were subjected to a full-scale trial, the states and federal government would need to multiply by many times the number of judges and court facilities."

49. Michael A. Simons, "Retributions for Rats: Cooperation, Punishment and Atonement," *Vanderbilt Law Review* 56 (2003): 1, 2.

50. Cohen, "What Is True? Perspectives of a Former Prosecutor," *Cardozo Law Review* 23 (2002): 818, 819–20.

51. *United States v. Borello*, 766 F.2d 46 (2d Cir. 1985).

52. *United States v. Cruz*, 805 F.2d 1464 (11th Cir. 1986).

53. *Brady v. Maryland*, 373 U.S. 83 (1963).

54. C. Blaine Elliot, "Life's Uncertainties: How to Deal with Cooperating Witnesses and Jailhouse," *Snitches* (Fall 2003).

55. *State v. Tiernan*, 941 A.2d 129, 135 (R.I. 2008).

56. *Villaroman v. United States*, 87 U.S.App. 240, 184 F.2d 261 (D.C. Cir. 1950).

57. *Kanatser v. Chrysler Corp.*, 199 F.2d 610 (10th Cir. 1052).

58. *State v. Tierman*, 941 A.2d (R.I. 2008).

59. *United States v. Sarras*, 575 F.3d 1191, 1214 (11th Cir. 2009); *United States v. Williams*, 954 F.2d 668, 672 (11th Cir. 1992).

60. *St. Petersburg Times*, "Rape Victim Sues Tyson," June 23, 1992.

61. *Ullah v. Office of the District Attorney*, 2009 WL 2151357 (S.D.N.Y. 2009).

62. *Torchinsky v. Siwinski*, 942 F.2d 257 (4th Cir. 1991).

63. *State v. Murphy*, 2009 WL 1643442 (Tenn. Crim. App. 2009).

64. *State v. Foster*, 244 SW 3d 800 (Mo. App. S.D. 2008).

65. *Primmer v. CBS Studios, Inc.*, 667 F. Supp. 2d 248, 2009 WL 2876248 (S.D. N.Y. 2009).

66. US Sentencing Guidelines § 3C1.1 (adding two points to the calculation for sentencing purposes).

67. *United States v. Dunnigan*, 507 U.S. 87 (1993).

68. *United States v. Allison*, 908 F.2d 1531 (11th Cir. 1990).

69. *United States v. Brown*, 53 F.3d 312, 314 (11th Cir. 1995).

70. *Wright v. West*, 505 U.S. 277, 296 (1992) (plurality opinion of Thomas, J.).

71. *U.S. v. Thomas*, 172 Fed. Appx. 970, 2006 WL 826108 (11th Cir. 2006).

72. *Griffin v. California*, 380 U.S. 609 (1965).

73. *Baster v. Thomas*, 45 F.2d 1501, 1508 (11th Cir. 1995).

74. *Miami Herald*, "Cards Add McGwire to Staff," October 27, 2009.

75. *New York Times*, "Mark McGwire Admits Steroid Use," January 11, 2010; StLToday.com, "McGwire Relieved He's Back in Swing," January 14, 2010.

76. Supreme Court Justice Scalia has described successful claims of selective prosecution as a *rare avis*, that is, rare bird. *Reno v. American-Arab Anti-Discrimination Committee*, 525 U.S. 471, 489 (1999) (Scalia, J. concurring).

77. 118 U.S. 356 (1886).

78. *United States v. Armstrong*, 517 U.S. 456 (1996).

79. *Government of the Virgin Islands v. Harris*, 938 F.2d 401414 (3d Cir. 1991).

80. *St. Clair v. United States*, 154 U.S. 134 (1894).

81. *Capano v. State*, 781 A.2d 556 (Del. 2001).

82. *People v. Johnson*, 233 Cal. App. 3d 425, 284 Cal. Rptr. 579 (Ct. App. 6th Dist. 1991).

83. *People v. Scott*, 176 Cal. App. 2d 458, 1 Cal. Rptr. 600 (1959).

84. *People v. Bolinski*, 260 Cal. App. 2d 705, 67 Cal. Rptr. 347 (1968).

85. *People v. Scott*, 274 Cal. App. 2d 905, 29 Cal. Rptr. 587 (1969).

86. *People v. Ruiz*, 44 Cal. 3d 589, 244 Cal. Rptr. (1988).

87. CNN.com, "Prosecutor: 'No Doubt' Natalee Holloway Is Dead," November 30, 2007.

88. MSNBC.com, "Van Zandt: Aruba Update: Father Knows Best," December 20, 2007.

89. US Department of Justice, Office of the Inspector General, "The Attorney General's Guideline on FBI Undercover Operations," in *The Federal Bureau of Investigation, Compliance with the Attorney General's Investigation Guidelines* (September 2005), http://www.justice.gov/oig/special/0509/final.pdf.

90. Ibid., n250, citing United States Senate Select Committee to Study Undercover Activities (December 1982).

91. *Hampton v. United States*, 425 U.S. 488 (1975).

92. *Hampton v. United States*, 425 U.S. 484 (1976).

CHAPTER 11: A MEDIA PRIMER FOR SPINNERS

1. Dennis J. Devine et al., "Forty-five Years of Empirical Research on Deliberating Groups," *Psychology, Public Policy, and Law* (September 2001), http://www. westlaw.com/. An excellent treatment of the media challenges for lawyers in high-profile trials is found in an article authored by Los Angeles attorney Mark Geragos, who has handled many such cases: "The Thirteenth Juror: Media Coverage of Supersized Trials," *Loyola of Los Angeles Law Review* 39 (December 2006): 1167.

2. Alan M. Dershowitz, interview with author, January 20, 2010.

3. Laurie L. Levenson, interview with author, January 12, 2010.

4. American Bar Association, *Model Rules of Professional Conduct*, Rule 3.6: Trial Publicity.

5. *State v. Avery*, 374 S.C. 524, 649 S.E.2d 102 (Ct.App. 2007). A venue change was denied when a vast majority of potential jurors recalled nothing about the defendant and could remember only that the crime had been committed.

6. Brian Skoloff, telephone interview with author, January 20, 2010.

7. Ibid.

8. Dershowitz, interview.

9. Ibid.; Roy Black, telephone interview with author, January 21, 2010.

10. CNN.com, "Gag Order Issued in Peterson Case," June 17, 2003, http://www.cnn.com/2003/LAW/06/12/peterson.case/index.html?iref =storysearch.

11. Levenson, interview.

12. Charles Stillman, interview with author, September 14, 2009.

13. Robert Morvillo, interview with author, September 15, 2009.

14. Erin McClam, "Martha Stewart Says Six Million Have Visited Web Site She Set Up to Tell Her Side of Story," *Washington Post*, June 9, 2003, http://www.washingtonpost.com/wp-dyn/articles/A35783-2003jun9.html.

15. *Wall Street Journal*, "Martha Stewart Appeals to Supporters on Personal Web Site," January 11, 2004, http://online.wsj.com/article/0,,BT _CO_20040111_000521,00.html.

16. Constance Hays, "Martha Stewart Uses Web to Tell Her Side of Story," *New York Times*, June 6, 2003, http://www.nytimes.com/2003/06/06/ business/media/06ADCO.htmal?ex=1055897387&ei=1&en=5c7e5858db 721b6a.

17. Ibid.

18. CNN Money, "Martha's Lawyers Hint at Defense," June 10, 2003, http://money.cnn.com/2003/06/10/news/companies/martha_defense/index .htm.

19. Ibid.

20. Hays, "Martha Stewart Uses Web."

21. *Wall Street Journal*, "Martha Stewart Appeals to Supporters."

22. Conrad Murray, "Dr. Conrad Murray Thanks Supporters," YouTube, http://www.youtube.com/watch?v=x1bjDWRJx9I&feature=related.

23. James Rainey, "A New Spin on Inside Stories," *Los Angeles Times*, September 30, 2009.

24. Stillman, interview.

25. Ibid.

26. Mark Geragos, interview with author, September 29, 2009.

27. Carolyn Marshall, "Peterson Judge Dismisses Juror for Misconduct," *New York Times*, November 10, 2004, http://www.nytimes.com/2004/11/10/ national/10peterson.html.

28. Ibid.

29. Diana Walsh, Stacy Finz, et al., "Behind Closed Doors," *San Francisco Chronicle*, December 16, 2004.

30. Ibid.

31. Fred Grimm, "Juries without Web Junkies? Impossible," *Miami Herald*, May 19, 2009.

32. Teresa Baldas, "Juries Gone Wild," *Daily Business Review*, May 18, 2005, https://www.dailybusinessreview.com/archive/purchase_article.html?news_id=35061.

33. Ibid.

34. Ibid.

35. Ralph Artigliere, Jim Barton, and Bill Hahn, "Reining in Juror Misconduct: Practical Suggestions for Judges and Lawyers," *Florida Bar Journal* 84, no. 1 (2010): 9.

36. Ibid.

37. Associated Press, "Jurors Tossed for Using Web," CBSnews.com, May 5, 1998, http://www.cbsnews.com/stories/1998/05/07/tech/main8948.shtml (accessed January 30, 2010).

38. Del Quentin Wilber, "Networking of Jurors Trying Judges' Patience," *Washington Post*, January 9, 2010, http://www.washingtonpost.com/wp-dyn/content/article/2010/01/08/AR2010010803694.html (accessed January 30, 2010).

39. United Press International, "Lawyer: Juror Used Internet Info in Case," January 10, 2010, http://www.upi.com/Top_News/US/2010/01/10/Lawyer-Juror-used-Internet-info-in-case/UPI-51351263163800 (accessed January 30, 2010).

40. Baldas, "Juries Gone Wild."

41. Ibid.

42. Hilary Hylton, "Tweeting in the Jury Box: A Danger to Fair Trials?" *Time Magazine*, December 29, 2009, http://www.time.com/time/nation/article/0,8599,1948971,00.html (accessed January 30, 2010).

43. Brendan Kearny, "Despite Judge's Warning, Dixon Jurors Went on Facebook," *Daily Record*, December 2, 2009, http://mddailyrecord.com/2009/12/02/despite-judge's-warning-dixon-jurors-went-on-facebook (accessed January 30, 2009).

44. John Schwartz, "As Jurors Turn to Web, Mistrials Are Popping Up," *New York Times*, March 17, 2009, http://www.nytimes.com/2009/03/18/us/18juries.html?pagewanted=2&_r=2 (accessed January 30, 2010).

45. Teresa Baldas, "Tainted Talk," *Daily Business Review*, May 9, 2008.

46. Juan Carlos Perez, "ComScore: Google Gains More Ground Than Bing in September," *PC World*, October 14, 2009, http://www.pcworld.com/businesscenter/article/173690/comscore_googl e_gains_more_ground_than_bing_in_september.html.

47. Rebecca Bilbao, interview with author, October 1, 2009.
48. Ibid.
49. Richard Sprague, telephone interview with author, September 28, 2009.

AFTERWORD

1. *Sheppard v. Maxwell*, 384 U.S. 333, 350 (1966).
2. *Nebraska Press Association v. Stuart*, 427 U.S. 539, 587 (1976) (Brennan, J. concurring).

INDEX

Whitewater, 157, 172
Wikipedia, 315, 316, 318
Wilde, Oscar, 50–53
Wilentz, David, 59
Wilkinson, James, 47, 49
Williams, Brian, 126
Wilson, Thomas, 27, 29–30, 32
Winchell, Walter, 58
Winick, Bruce, 250
Winters, Doug, 214–15, 218–19
wiretaps, 236, 237
Without a Trace (television show), 261
witnesses, 274
  bribing, 80, 274–75
  cooperative witnesses, 197
  credibility of, 227, 229, 232–34,
    242, 273, 275, 276–77, 281,
    295
  expert witness's false testimony in
    Martha Stewart trial, 205
  failure to be interviewed, 83
  having a money motive, 278
  jury may never know witness has
    psychological issues, 221–22,
    295
  myth of sweetheart deals for,
    273–77

  myth that a defendant not testi-
    fying is proof of guilt, 281–83
  selling stories to media, 80–81, 230
  turning states evidence, 47
  who receive a payoff, 80
WorldCom, 193–94, 201, 202
World War II, 43
World Wide Web, 79
wrongful death suit against O.J.
  Simpson, 75, 84

Xenophon, 37, 38

Yablonsky, Joseph, 171
Yahoo! 319, 320
Yates, Andrea, 269–70
Yeltsin, Boris, 62
Yick Wo v. Hopkins, 284
Yip, Manuel, 25–26, 27, 33
YouTube, 314–15

Zack, Steve, 120, 124
Zamora, Ronnie, 176–77
Zubaydah, Abu, 244–45